A Path of 21 Ms

A Path of 21 Ms

PETER SHAW

First published in Great Britain in 2024

Copyright © Peter Shaw

The moral right of the author has been asserted.

All rights reserved.

No part of this publication may be reproduced, stored in a retrieval system, or transmitted, in any form or by any means, without the prior permission in writing of the publisher, nor be otherwise circulated in any form of binding or cover other than that in which it is published and without a similar condition including this condition being imposed on the subsequent purchaser.

Editing, Design, typesetting and publishing by UK Book Publishing

www.ukbookpublishing.com

ISBN: 978-1-916572-79-9

Contents

Preface	vii
Introduction	1
CHAPTER 1 M is for Manchester!	16
CHAPTER 2 M is for MGS	52
CHAPTER 3 M is for "Mere"	63
CHAPTER 4 M is for the Metazoa	69
CHAPTER 5 M is for Mycorrhizas (and Merlewood)	81
CHAPTER 6 M is for Megawatts	109
CHAPTER 7 M is for 'Made it!'	134
CHAPTER 8 M is for Marriage!	178
CHAPTER 9 M is for Mitosis	198
CHAPTER 10 M is for the Martial Arts	208
CHAPTER 11 M is for Marathons	230
CHAPTER 12 M is for Meditation and Mushrooms	238
CHAPTER 13 M is for Machete!	262
CHAPTER 14 M is for 'Mediterranean'	293
CHAPTER 15 M is for Meltdown!	316
APPENDIX 1 My publications – books, papers and other outputs	392
APPENDIX 2 Acronyms used in the text	404

Preface

(M is for Me! Also for Mathematics and for Molecules)

Call me Peter. Dr Peter Jonathan Alexander Shaw, DoB 11 July 1961, to officialdom. This is my version of my story.

The aim of this autobiography is to leave an impression of my lifetime, as a memento for family members and, just maybe, a wider legacy to convey some of the Zeitgeist of my day-to-day life, starting in Manchester in the 1960s through to retirement in Dorking and France from 2020. Inevitably this account is a wholly personal choice, with most of the key experiences being about my daily life rather than any wider historical/societal significance. Having read a few such "vanity publishing" autobiographies, the points that stick in the memory tend to be little observations of unquestioned attitudes that look dated or anachronistic with the benefit of hindsight. By way of example, back in the 1970s, Mother never seemed to query that she should stay home tidying the house and cooking dinner while Dad and I went for a long muddy afternoon walk – it is only when I try to model what modern women would say if I dared suggest this that I see how far things have moved on in terms of gender equality. I expect that some sensitive souls may be shocked by some of the grim details of life on the Wythenshawe estate in the 1970s. The biodiversity that was routine around Cheshire in my childhood looks remarkable by 21st century standards, with lapwings nesting at the bottom of the road, corn buntings, yellow wagtails and grey partridge in the local fields, tree sparrows and redpolls in the local park, curlews nesting nearby. No red legged partridges, ring necked parakeets or red kites, but these are literally garden birds for me now. A report of a red kite near Manchester in the 1970s would have been like a maroon going off near a lifeboat station – blokes would have run out of their offices, jumped into their cars and zoomed off at full pelt. Now little egrets and kites nest nearby, unthinkable 50 years ago.

A Path of 21 Ms

For ease of planning, the contents are arranged chronologically, but the length of each section bears little relationship to its actual duration – if there's little to say, I say little! There is a strong influence of my working environment, on the basis that this set the theme for all the life around it. The idea is that the 'hard copy' (a paper book) is matched by a digital archive, since things like the hypertext family tree work fine as hypertext but just don't translate into paper. You can't search books for a key word or phrase either. On the flipside, a book should remain legible in >100 years' time but digital document formats will change beyond recognition. It is easier to read Egyptian text carved into limestone 3500 years ago than it is to read computer files from the 1960s. Hopefully my descendants will inherit both versions. (This is also why I keep photos as hard copies in the loft.)

As for the title to this autobiography, 'A path of 21 Ms', it needs a little unpacking. There is nothing special about the letter M, nor yet the number 21. Nor do I make any claim to have special wisdom to be followed as a guru, except in trying to get people to apply mathematics and logic to evidence-based reality. Maybe I should have just called it 'Peter's autobiography'. Boring! The background to the whole project is given in the first half of the chapter 14 (called 'Provence'), where Catherine's father and uncle Paul gently joshed each other with titles of their self-published autobiographies. As the idea evolved, I kept noticing that some important aspects of my life happened to start with the letter M. If you take a small random sample of almost anything you will habitually find non-random-looking patterns. This tells you a lot about human perception and nothing at all about randomness. (The tendency to see meaningful patterns in random noise is called 'pareidolia' and is why we must rely on statistical analyses to interpret data – our emotions and intuition are worse than useless.) At the head of most chapters, there is a quip along the lines of "M is for . . ." (Me, molecules, Manchester, mycorrhizas, martial arts, marathons, metazoa or whatever). Count these, and you should find that I came up with 20 of these. 20 – so why talk of 21? Can't you count, Shaw? This hidden joke comes from the chapter about mushrooms, because they are the genus *Psilocybe* – the magics. A silly deciding factor for me was the realisation that I could claim twice for these – the joke being that "Magic Mushrooms count twice", a multi-level truth that brings a smile so helps stick in most minds.

Finally, a silly quip. Peter comes from the Latin root "Petros" or stone. (Eg in French, Pierre means Peter and means stone. There is a joke in the Bible about this – "On this stone I build my church"). Shaw is an old English word for a small wood (from 'sceaga'). So Peter Shaw roughly translates as "Stone of the Woods", which suits me perfectly as I like stones and I like being in woods. My wife has quipped that "Stoned of the woods" might be more apposite. Guilty as charged! When I got French citizenship I was offered the chance of a new official name, and seriously considered becoming Pierre Dubois, the literal translation. I like my name and hate officialdom querying my paperwork, so stuck with Peter Shaw, but Pierre Dubois can be a handy nom-de-plume for booking restaurants etc. This is all about who I was. Like the Ignobel prizes, the ambition is that it makes you laugh at first, then think.

Just to be pedantic, some old genealogical texts about the clan Shaw give a different interpretation (eg Shaw 1871). There were two branches of Shaws in Scotland, the lowland Shaws and the highland Shaws (formerly of Rothiemurchus). The lowland Shaws are said to be derived from the Saxon word for a small wood, while the (more fearsome) highland branch has their name derived from old Gaelic, with the exact interpretation contested but options include 'wolf', 'strong minded' and some sort of spirit of the woods. The documentation probably won't help, but my Y chromosome might. I'm haplogroup I-M253, which might be enough to identify the lineage. I got a strange feeling of homecoming in Rothiemurchus, so favour that lineage, but we need to ask the DNA!

Peter Shaw, North Holmwood, Dorking, November 2023

Introduction

To start at the beginning, I was born on 11 July 1961 in Sale, Manchester, to John Robert Shaw (dentist) and Elizabeth Nancy Shaw (primary school teacher). I gather that I was named after a university friend of my father's, one Peter Einstein. Peter Einstein was the same family as the famous Albert, and was similarly monumentally intelligent. He was one of the first computer programmers, when this became a possibility in the 1950s. He left Manchester to work on coding at Aldermaston in the 1960s and died of a brain tumour shortly afterwards, leaving me a legacy of my name, some memories of a big bowl of sweets in his house (!), and a couple of really hard puzzles that he sent me for my amusement.

My favourite Peter Einstein story concerns a coffee morning in the 1950s, when his hostess asked him how much cake he would like. Peter replied, "About 30 degrees". The lady was no mathematician, and looked puzzled. "How much is that?" she asked. "It's about half a radian," he replied, and was given the cake knife to cut it himself.

What would I most want people to know about what matters to me? Easy – that I need to be outdoors, in nature – preferably woodland. A field guide might describe me as a solitary creature of open forest. Being in woodland feels like being in a favourite old sweatshirt, just comfortable in my own skin and at ease with Planet Earth. This goes for almost all my interaction with almost all animals – and plants come to that. Maybe my trying to get close to a deep growling noise in scrub in the Masai Mara wasn't very wise, but the guide ran after me with a machete before anything interesting happened. I listen to the chattering of nature to tell me about the seasons, seasonality being predicated as much on birds as on Christian holidays. Hearing warblers in the bushes and seeing swallows overhead says "summer" to me. Redwings and bramblings in the bare trees say "winter", especially with added fieldfares.

Mushrooms mean autumn, and vernal bulbs (snowdrops, crocus etc) mean the magical phase when winter turns into spring, heralded by frogs spawning en masse.

Peter Einstein's puzzles, sent to little Peter Shaw about 1972

1. In this rebus, every letter is a different integer 0-9. Clearly D = 1, what are the others?

    C R O S S +
    R O A D S =
    D A N G E R

I worked at this for 2 years on a pocket calculator, before solving it as S = 3, O = 2, A = 5 (you solve the rest). My French nephews cracked it in one evening with computers, either by brute force (Eliot) or by searching the internet (Loic)!

This diversity of solutions reminds me of a joke story about an engineer, a physicist and a psychologist who were all given a barometer and asked to use it to find the height of a church tower. The physicist measured the difference in air pressure between top and bottom. The engineer dropped it off the side, timed its fall to oblivion and used the equation s=g/2*t*t (metres = 5 * seconds squared). The psychologist gave it as a gift to the vicar then asked him what the height was.

2. Visualise a perfect cube. It has a perfect cylinder drilled into each face, which all intersect in the middle. Let's say the cube has side = 10 and the cylinders all have radius = 1. What is the volume left?

I still have not solved this algebraically, but finally wrote R code to simulate the function with progressively smaller voxels, to iterate down to a limit. The numerical answer (942.5ish after a few million calculations) tells me that that the shape formed when the cylinders intersect is not a perfect sphere, contrary to my intuition. If it were the answer would be 1000-30π+8π/3 = 914.13. I still doubt my coding after two re-writes – the value looks too high – and would love someone to show me the analytical solution!

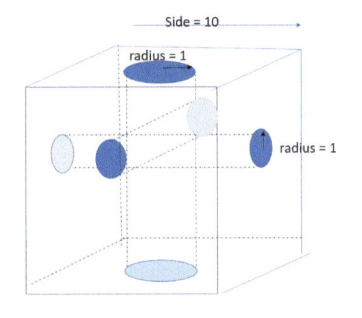

I realise that I owe a small and unusual vote of thanks to the strange libertarians who came up with the notion of "seasteading", and in particular the ill-fated SS Satoshi. https://www.theguardian.com/news/2021/sep/07/disastrous-voyage-satoshi-cryptocurrency-cruise-ship-seassteading

The idea behind this is that all land is controlled by governments who impose rules, extract taxes, and generally interfere with your ability to do exactly what you please unfettered by considerations of the well-being of other humans. Since about ⅔ of the earth is covered by open sea and is largely ungoverned, the idea of seasteading is to live in floating communities out on the seas and have no government. The SS Satoshi was an experiment to create such a "utopia", using the cryptocurrency Bitcoin for all payments. (Hence the name – Mr Satoshi is the mythical founder of Bitcoin.) They bought up an old cruise ship, and offered the rich and rebellious a chance to buy a cabin on this ship, then sail around the world, happy in the knowledge that no government existed to tell them what to do or to extract taxes. You will not be surprised to know this went catastrophically badly, notably because no-one let them drop anchor to collect food, water or fuel. What this story did was to make me think about life onboard, or in any of the other "seasteading" neocommunities on offer. You would never stand on soil, only ever feel vibrating steel underfoot. You would never dig your garden soil, never hear a wild bird sing or see winter turn into spring, never hold onto a tree, probably never touch any animal except on your dinner plate. The only other life forms would be humans – not just a random sample of the species (bad enough), but humans so egocentric and anti-social that they would tear up their family roots for ever just to be able to indulge themselves untrammelled by thoughts of other. The phrase "swivel eyed loons" may not be biologically accurate but conveys the impression – people I would want to avoid at all costs, but in fact would be stuck with for the indefinite future in a small space. The more I think about this, the more it sounds like an unmitigated nightmare. I get a rising sense of panic just thinking about how much I would feel stuck in an endless trauma. Like being stuck in hospital in 2019, but even worse and even further from home. As I live now, I can put on old running shoes and in minutes be alone in ancient woodland, feeling mud under my feet and smelling leaf mould on the wind. Birds sing telling me their species and the season, mushrooms pop up telling me about the soil. I see the land from which my family drew their atoms going back millennia. I have taken to thinking about life of the SS Satoshi each time I go running, to remind myself how deeply and profoundly grateful I am for the experience of being here. It really makes me appreciate my existence. Sod the money, if the price of NOT being on that ship for life is paying a tithe to some distant egotists in government, it's a bargain. I therefore feel a weird gratitude to the selfish delusional narcissists behind this daft scheme for helping me find a deep happiness in normal life!

It might be illustrative of my value systems to ask about which humans have been influential to me, whom I might most hope to emulate. I have asked myself this, and come up with a short list of my all-time heroes. Top of the list must be my father John Robert Shaw, who was multi-talented, and who never let me down. If there was a problem, he would see how to fix it, then actually make the fix work. He also knew first hand all about parents choosing careers against children's wishes, and always trusted me to find my own way. He had a low opinion of many of his university lecturers, so had doubts about me becoming one, but let me choose my path anyway, for which I am eternally grateful. Another real-life figure would be my Oxford tutor Dr Henry Bennet-Clark, who seemed to know and understand everything. My other icons influenced me solely through their writings – I was a very bookish youngster. For most of my animal-obsessed childhood I would have picked Gerald Durrell ("My family and Other Animals", and much more) for hero worship, along with David Attenborough (for his lifelong work promoting natural history, eg the Zoo Quest series) and Richard Dawkins (eg "Selfish Gene" – he writes with lucid clarity about the most important processes underlying evolutionary biology). Away from pure biology, my personal admiration shines on Richard Feynman ("Surely you're joking, Mr Feynman" and "What do you care what other people think?"), Alexander Shulgin ('PIHKAL'), and Kary Mullis ('Dancing Naked in the Mind Field'). Reading each of these books is a mind-expanding experience that taught me a great deal, and left me in awe of their achievements. In terms of legacies, Shulgin gave us MDMA and 2CB, Mullis gave us PCR, while Feynman gave us Hiroshima and modern quantum physics.

One more icon for me, less well known is the physicist Paul Dirac. He was a leading light in the early development of quantum physics, and is best known for discovering that half the universe is missing by scribbling equations on the back of an envelope. (Where is all the anti-matter?) My favourite Dirac anecdote was one time in an academic conference when Paul gave a talk about his work, and at the end took questions, as is normal. Someone stood up in the audience and said, "I do not understand that equation." Paul nodded and said nothing. Eventually the chairman asked, "Are you going to answer that question?" Paul looked puzzled. "That was not a question," he replied, "that was a statement."

This is an embarrassingly all-male list! I must add two high profile women that I deeply admire: Professors Hannah Fry and Alice Roberts. In both bases they are clearly brilliant researchers who have publicised mathematics and anthropology through their books and TV programmes, while equally clearly being lovely, warm people. Alice Roberts is a leading light in the humanist movement, opposing faith schools for example, while Hannah Fry takes time out from the fundamental equations of quantum reality to being a caring mother and talking about her cancer. I giggle at her description of the advocates of the "many worlds" interpretation of quantum mechanics (Rutherford & Fry 2021).

One more thing that I have come to realise is important to me: I hate losing information. When the CEGB laboratories were closed down in 1990, someone threw out the entire microfiche archive of all its research reports back to the CEGB's creation in the 1950s. I have this down as an over-looked national tragedy. It is tempting to lay into the character and personality of the corporate jobsworth who did this, but he probably had no idea – blame his managers, who then transfer blame to the politicians. My supervisor in York University gave 15 years of records from 'his' nature reserve to the Yorkshire Wildlife Trust, who promptly lost them. I think that to be awful, appalling, shocking, indefensible, and have spent much time and effort trying to ensure that after my death the records from "my" nature reserve (Inholms Clay Pit – it gets its own chapter) are kept safe. My home is where my family archives are kept – there are about a dozen family members for whom no personal records, photos or anecdotes exist anywhere except in my storage system. I have my birdwatching notes from childhood, cross-linked by a card system, and treasure them as I can often still recall the exact moment (eg) of seeing a purple gallinule or an osprey. As someone on the Mole Valley Conservation Group observed, accurately if bluntly, when meeting my illegible field notes for the first time "You should transcribe this legibly. Frances Rose made that mistake and after his death staff in the Welsh Museum had a terrible job sorting out his notebooks". I doubt any museum will give a damn about transcribing my notes, so this book is my best opportunity to tell posterity what I think should be told.

To start by explaining the quip "M is for Mathematics and Molecules" at the start of this chapter, here is my 'path': Everything you meet is composed of molecules, and is controlled by laws coded in mathematics. Understand the properties of the molecules, you understand the substance. (That's chemistry.) Understand the mathematics, you understand the behaviour. (That's physics.) Understand these together, you have evidence-based reality nailed down. Almost all of reality – just not human behaviour – the species seems incomprehensible.

In terms of my underlying models, there are just a few really general principles that make my life tick over. Easily learned, not always obvious. One comes from a story I picked up years ago, an apocryphal anecdote that defines an algorithm. (A path of three As?) This concerns a technique supposedly used by wild-west cowboys to get a big awkward bull back home to its farm when it is tens of miles away, happy where it is grazing out in the chaparral, and far too big to pull back by horse. So, the cowboy trick (allegedly) was to take out a mule on the roundup. [As an aside, this part of the story looks implausible – remember this is defining an algorithm, not giving a historiography of US ranching techniques. If I were the mule I just wouldn't go out in the first place.] When they encounter the bull they lasso it and rope it to the mule. The mule has a good sense of direction, wants to go home, but cannot pull the bull. But it can be stubborn, and just refuse to move. The next day, bull and mule are back home. The reason is that each time the bull goes in the correct direction for home, the mule goes too and probably leads the way. Each time the bull goes away from home the mule literally puts its foot down and refuses. Yes, the bull can drag it, but that is inevitably slower and harder than before, so on long-term average the animals will head home. Mathematically, the distance function will consistently decrease over time, and that is enough in itself to solve the problem. So how does this quaint rustic story link to daily life? Each object in your life should have a defined home, and often isn't in its defined home. So, the model is that each time I encounter something out of place I move it TOWARDS its home. Maybe all the way, maybe just up to a staging post. What matters is that you can see a picture in your head of where each object belongs, then apply this simple algorithm: Repeat for each object you encounter this little flowchart: Should it be there? Yes? Enjoy a brief blip of dopamine at this little success! No? Move it towards where it belongs, and reward yourself with a little blip of dopamine.

This alone will ensure that after a few iterations, the patterns in real life will approach the image on your mind of how they should be, the distance function declining exponentially with number of iterations. You may want to tweak your internal rules to avoid people complaining about things left lying around in awkward spots! The really important requirement is that (as far as possible) things only get moved towards where they belong, or stay put – not moved away from it. Just like the bull either stayed put or moved closer to the farm. As soon as things move away from target you get pseudo-random chaos (in the strict sense of the words), as long as things either stay put or move towards home, disorder will decay exponentially. I like this because it defines a low effort, low stress universal algorithm. Low stress because it is just fine for something to hang around waiting to continue its journey! Sadly, not so low stress when your partner starts muttering about things lying around waiting to be tidied away!

Another general principle I work on, and advocate, comes from playing chess. In chess you only get one move at a time, but you can often find moves that do more than one thing. Uncovering a long-distance attack by a rook or a bishop perhaps, while initiating a second attack at the same time. Likewise in life, I try to look for actions/plans that achieve more than one result at once. Obvious when stated!

One more – a bit more nerdy. I like invoking the power of exponential mathematics. One of the few positive outcomes of the 2020/22 Covid-19 pandemic is that lots of people have had to come to terms with the power of exponential functions, which will overcome any linear solutions. Covid patient demand crippled health services around the world, and when politicians saw what the mathematical modellers were predicting, they preferred to shut down entire economies than face the exponential growth in demand. Exponential functions have a doubling time, or a half-life (= a doubling time going backwards in time). They take the generalised form $N_t = N_0 \exp(K*t)$ where t is time, N_t is number at time t and N_0 is number at time 0. Exp(x) means raise 2.7182818 ... to the power x. The key parameter here is the "exponential parameter" K. When K>0 you get exponential growth, like cases of virus infections as an epidemic explodes, or like neutrons inside a fission bomb as it detonates. When K<0 you get exponential decay, like radioactive decay or like the temperature of your cup of teas as it cools down. (Typically a cup of tea will cool down with a half-life of about 10 minutes – this halving function applies to its 'distance function' which is how much hotter it is than room temperature). So the most important part of my financial planning (IMHO) has been to set up a shares ISA in which shares (chosen to pay a dividend, about 4% currently) stay protected from tax. I re-invest these dividends' tax-free cash in buying more shares within the ISA. This defines exponential growth. I see a deep parallel between this financial model, and my cultivation of snowdrops. Each April I put the ISA cash limit into my ISA and re-invest the accumulated dividends of the last year, so I have a linear input plus endogenous exponential growth. Each March I dig up as many hedgerow-flytipped snowdrops as I can carry, plant them around my garden or the estate where the previous years' snowdrops have finished flowering and are now growing. Then I split the existing clumps, doubling them. So again I have a model based on a linear annual increment plus endogenous exponential growth.

Animals have been a life-long theme, love and fascination of mine. Lecturing in zoology you'd expect that, but not everyone is lucky enough to have their life's work exploring their favourite subject. My mother described how I saw a stork in Chester Zoo at age two, and was too small to speak then but described what I had seen by standing on one leg. I am assured that my first word was "zoo"! My father grumbled about my fascination with birdwatching (to be fair he put up with a lot, as I now realise). Not just birds, I like almost all animals, but not all. I don't like swimming with dangerous cnidaria (jellyfish) as the danger is random and unpredictable. Chimpanzees are rather too like humans for my comfort. The species that really does my head in is of course *Homo sapiens*. It's not that I'm knowingly callous. I want to do what I can to make life better for everyone, I give money to my kids and to charity, and routinely go round the local nature reserve with a bin bag picking up litter to make the place nicer for visitors. Yes, there are bits in this book about meditation, mindfulness and magic mushrooms, and yes, I have often publicly proclaimed myself to be the emotionally sensitive old hippy of the family (this refers just to the family I had before marrying Anne Catherine Neubert on 12 Dec 1992), but to be honest this bar is not set very high. The family precedents are not indicators of emotional sensitivity. Grandfather Alexander (Sandy) Shaw spent months at sea in all-male company fiddling with boat engines while seeing pictures in his head. Great-grandfather Robert Kershaw might be described as the Oldham slum landlord (with an amazing ability to see images in his head) who terrified every company director in Manchester by turning up unexpectedly at shareholders' meetings and publicly, loudly pointing out errors in their balance sheets. ("Can we approve these accounts?" "NAY, lad, NAY" was the sequence that haunted many MDs after Robert Kershaw turned up.) I was the strange one who recorded data on local birds, then applied least-squares fits to estimate parameters of gaussian curves. Having spent a lot of my formative years with genuine old hippies, I have come to realise that my position on this continuum is well towards the 'hard rational' end.

A very important point to know about me is that my "primary access mode" is visual. I operate by seeing pictures in my head, and remain flatly baffled that the majority of the species do not all work the same way. How on earth do you understand mathematical functions without seeing pictures in your head? I defy anyone to explain Euclidean geometry, cartesian functions or differential calculus without invoking pictures that you must understand as pictures in your head. When teaching regression models or multivariate analysis, I was explicit that students must see the model as a picture in their head, ideally a high-dimensional picture. All the scientists I have worked with ran visual models to understand their data. When trying to help my daughter with her A level maths, what kept on happening was I said "You need to see a picture in your head of this function" and she said "I don't" then I said "then how are you going to see the function?". This didn't help her as much as I thought it should have done, though she got a well-deserved A. Perhaps linked to this, I have been diagnosed – informally – as an 'Asperger's syndrome' – on the basis of behaviour that both my mother's and father's family and ancestors would recognise well and describe as "normal male" or "sensible". It just means I am not telepathic. This is called 'Mind Blindness'. I first met the concept of 'Mind-blindness' while chairing the committee overseeing the PhDs in our Psychology department, and was baffled by it. Everyone is mind-blind surely and logically? You cannot see into other people's minds, so the concept is logically worthless. Probably because of this, I never really got on with the psychologists, especially not the counsellors whose so-called experimental designs never had control groups. (If you have an alleged treatment for an alleged psychological ailment that is based on chatting to people, you should randomly allocate the subjects into three groups. One gets treated by your special chat, one gets equal anodyne chat time off an untrained random human, the third gets left to stew in their own juices. Then test the null model that all three treatments have equal clear-up rates.) I was told this model was inappropriate, and as far as I am concerned means that you can never know whether your so-called therapy has any actual value. Probably I didn't endear myself to the counsellors by observing that counts of suicides would constitute nice clean data, ideal for a chi-squared test. You see each event as a dot in a high-dimensional dataspace, and consider how those dots should be distributed under your null model. They didn't seem keen on that analysis, and tried to get me taken away from their committee.

One of our neighbours in Pixham Lane, married to a brilliant particle physicist at Surrey University, was heard to moan "They are all Asperger's", referring to male scientists. This analysis has become fashionable, often associated with saying someone is "on the autistic spectrum". One of the better quips from a TV series 'The I.T. Crowd' was one software support engineer proudly announcing "I'm an artist you know. I've been told I'm on the artistic spectrum". What this means is that you think by seeing pictures in your head, and that you are not telepathic. It is true that in most university science departments you meet people who do not pick up body language clues very well. This can be illustrated with a few examples of lovely people I really liked. In York the next office to mine was Dr CR, a tropical entomologist who allowed me to fill his window ledge with my overflow cacti because my bedroom was full and my own supervisor would not. CR once offered in a staff meeting to pay his personal savings to help keep the university library stocked. Everyone liked him. He was a cyber nerd before his time, took his pocket calculator to pieces and inserted a new large memory chip to make it programmable with the capacity of a small computer. (I couldn't do that – could you?) But he would talk at you and talk and talk, and you could try waving bye-bye and turn round and point at your watch and he carried in talking. The solution was to walk down the corridor, and when you were out of earshot he stopped. Next time you saw him he was exactly as friendly as before, quite unruffled by what most people would see as rudeness.

In Whitelands, I published papers with a lecturer called Ron, who was fascinated by human bone data. I did his statistical analyses for him, and helped him show that one of the biggest changes in *Homo sapiens* in the last 10,000 years is that our teeth became smaller antero-distally. In simple English, stone age humans had thicker teeth than nowadays and the evolutionary selection pressure for this remains unclear. I got this into a letter to New Scientist saying that my father was taught this as a dental student. This is an interesting and important general result that will be remembered long after I am not. Ron also talked about his subject incessantly. One day when my daughter Louise was off school ill with glandular fever, she sat in my office, bored and miserable. Ron came in, and talked to me about the regression models for our next publication. The fact I had a small, ill, blonde girl in my chair simply meant that he had to stand in the doorway instead of sit down, and otherwise he paid her no attention whatsoever. I also paid her no attention whatsoever since she was irrelevant to the regression models. It was only weeks later that Louise told me how upset she was to be utterly ignored – how were we to know that? It was the dean of research Professor Ann Maclarnon who told me how to handle Ron, and it is a really simple general solution that worked every time, and with anyone who works the same way. You simply said: "Ron, please shut up and go away". Like a computer executing a line of code he then obediently shut up and went away. Next time he saw you he carried on as if nothing had happened, unbothered by what socially-sensitive people might see as rudeness. Subtle indirect routes like saying you have a meeting soon or that you needed time to think about the problem were like water off a duck's back.

The people who are really hard to deal with are thin-skinned hypersensitive 'neurotypicals' (NT), who are prone to exploding without warning over trivia that don't matter, and carrying grudges about non-existent slights that they thought (falsely) that you knowingly inflicted on them. The typical scenario is that you are interacting with an NT and the NT experiences some emotional response, probably arising from activity in their neo-chimpanzee limbic system. Maybe originating in something utterly trivial and superficial like your tone of voice, personal state of being, clothes or hair! Because they assume that you are telepathic, they assume that you DO realise that they are having this emotional response, and because they are telepathic they CAN tell that you are not changing your behaviour accordingly. They then decide that you are doing this as a calculated insult, maybe to demonstrate something about your position in some neo-chimpanzee dominance hierarchy or maybe just to stimulate a negative reaction for your own amusement. So, they intensify their display of body language, and interpret your continued lack of response as clear evidence of your utter contempt for their personal worth, and eventually they snap. In the meantime, I'm toddling on with whatever the conversation is about, then discover that (oddly) this person has started being pointedly unpleasant, as if it is their standard default communication mode. Really not my style at all, but since I am equal to you and you are equal to me, then if that is how you communicate with me that is how I communicate with you – simple logical equality. So, I reply in kind, using the same sharp manner. Unlike Asperger's, such people DO carry grudges, often for ever. One PhD student got so upset with me that they refused all permission to use anything from her PhD in any research output, and told a whole academic mailing list this, thereby damaging the university's public profile. (And didn't do her reputation any good either.) I expect I will die without ever having a clue what she was making a pointless fuss about. Give me Asperger's any day. Thin skinned NTs are like a minefield.

Just as a cautionary aside, I am very sorry to say that the benign nature and widespread occurrence of 'being Asperger' has led to it being parasitized by people who are nothing of the sort but altogether far more unpleasant. One case sticks in mind as a cautionary example. RH was an anthropology student who came in with a 'Statement' that he was Asperger's, having doubtless hoodwinked some soft-hearted and gullible psychiatrist with a sob story about being a mis-understood outcast. In fact, based on all the evidence that accumulated around his behaviour, I am sure that he COULD see people's thought processes and enjoyed watching them suffer. His game was to see how far he could get away with pushing people. Luckily, he went on the South Africa Field course not the biosciences field course, so I never had to deal with him. Luckily for both of us, I think. Once the staff and students were isolated, staying in a remote African village, where everything depended on the goodwill of the locals towards the university, RH went round pointedly insulting all the locals about their religious beliefs and skin colour. This was just after Anton Brevik had massacred kids on an island in the Baltic, and there was a general concern that RH would steal a gun off a guard and launch his own attack. (The staff requested permission off the university to send him home, but the university lawyers said that this was not legally possible due to the statementing.) RH was utterly unbothered by social feedback. I once watched him sit down next to a Professor (Stuart) in a (non-smoking) pub and started puffing on an e-cigarette (which was technically legal at the time). Stuart, a splendid chap for whom I have the deepest respect, told him that he would not talk to a total arsehole and walked off, at which point RH smiled broadly and plonked himself down next to someone else to start talking about how much better medicine could be if we abolished these stupid rules against animal cruelty. RH was not Asperger's, he was a dangerous manipulative psychopath, hiding under the cloak of invisibility that being statemented as 'Autistic Spectrum' gave him. For some reason he was allocated to me as a tutee, but only ever bothered to come see me once after being thrown out of the university. I told him I couldn't help him, and wish I'd said a lot more (like being ashamed to be the same species). He never asked me for a reference, maybe realising that I'd have warned potential employers not to let him into the building or to reply to his emails. So, I am very sad to say that when someone loudly proclaims that they are Asperger's and need special treatment, big red warning lights come on in my head. The reassuring sign is when they start talking about something obscure in immense detail with no concern that you may not be equally fascinated. Listen patiently and you will benefit from learning a great deal. They are probably a lovely person and may become a world expert in years to come.

Just to get the scene set, a key axiom that I follow and expect everyone else to follow is: "We share one evidence-based reality. Reality is right about reality. If you cannot deal with what reality says about reality that is between you and reality, your problem and no-one else's". Several times in the university, such as lectures about the philosophy of experimental design, I have said something like "No evidence, no belief", and students have stormed out with some incomprehensible emotional outburst. Typically males as it happens, but the sample size is too small to reject the null model that it was just a random sample. Twice the resulting exchange of ideas led to them leaving the university early with what looked like a nervous breakdown. Good riddance. One made a creditable effort to prove me wrong by researching the evidence, and was last heard of doing very well in an M. Res. in evolutionary zoology – good for him.

What does evidence-based reality have to say for itself? Some key points seem not to bother people: almost everything you encounter is molecules made of atoms of the 92 naturally occurring elements, at least until you get near trans-uranics like the plutonium in nuclear bombs. The atoms in your body are borrowed from planet earth, stardust from a second-generation solar system about 5 billion (=5000 million = 5E9) years old. We know it must be second-generation stardust because of the existence of heavy metals like gold and lead that – models assure us – can only be forged from hydrogen and helium in unusually big supernovas. Joni Mitchell was almost right ('Woodstock') when she said we are 'stardust, billion-year-old carbon', but about five times too young. When you ask about what DNA sequences and neurophysiology have to say, it becomes clear that your ancestors were having sex with the ancestors of chimpanzees until about 6.5 million (=6.5E6) years ago, and that all aspects of your sentience, memory, agency, actions and emotions come from patterns of electro-chemical activity in your central nervous system, mediated by sodium rushing into nerve cells and potassium rushing out. Under anaesthesia this still happens, just with less connectivity, and that is enough to wipe out your sentience. For some reason some people find this aspect of reality rather more indigestible. I was out on Wimbledon Common with a Muslim girl in her headscarf, getting soil samples for her dissertation when she started making a fuss about dogs. Apparently there is something 'haram' about dogs in Islam. I pointed out that they were on her family tree – your ancestors were having sex with dogs' ancestors as recently as 110 million years ago, showing the Old Testament to be false – if their lineage is haram, your lineage is haram. I don't think she accepted this logic.

If you can't deal with what reality says about reality, that is between you and reality (. . . but you really should not mislead kids about basic facts, just because you have decided that reality is giving the wrong answers . . .) Some aspects of reality make no sense to our simplistic models of the world, since our nervous systems evolved to cope with living as social apes on the African savannah in the Pleistocene. One of the most important papers in physics, the EPR paper (Einstein-Podolsky-Rosen, 1935), was written by Albert Einstein to show that the mathematics of quantum physics must be wrong because if it were right then two particles created in the same event must share a common wave function and would remain in communication across indefinite gaps of space and time – this is called entanglement. Einstein did this to show that since such entanglement made no sense the whole mathematical edifice must be wrong. Then people set up the experiments, and showed entanglement is indeed a standard feature of reality. It has been used to send unbreakable coded messages from satellites to earth. Albert Einstein was also convinced that the universe must be static, and when his equations all showed a static universe was impossible (implicitly requiring the Big Bang) he spent the rest of his life working on a "cosmological constant" to fix this, a search he later described as the worst mistake of his life. In other words, Albert Einstein had difficulties facing with what reality actually says about reality. Similarly, Isaac Newton could not deal with reality, at least in as much as he thought it should follow some mystical principles when it just doesn't. Not just that he apparently thought there was some God, he also imagined that there must be seven colours in the rainbow when in fact we perceive six. (Like there were seven known planets at the time. Not true now of course!) So he invented a false dichotomy between blue and indigo, to make the list up to the mystical seven. Don't believe me – look at a proper rainbow and try to see Red Orange Yellow Blue Indigo and Violet. Just blue then violet. The only reason that we talk of the seven colours of the rainbow is that the artistic/literary community picked up the mind virus – science students get told it's false for GCSE.

Sometimes reality says things that simply make no sense. When you fire a particle at two adjacent holes, it goes through both of them at the same time and interferes with itself like a wave to generate a wave-like interference pattern. Unless you install a monitor on the holes, and ask the particle which of the two holes it went through, in which case the particle only goes through one hole and gives a particle-like target distribution. This effect has been seen and repeated in many experiments and is not contentious. It matches predictions from quantum mathematics. It makes absolutely NO SENSE whatsoever. This is how reality behaves. A friend asked me, "Are you satisfied with that?" My answer is simple: "Yes, entirely. This is how reality is." I could have added, "How can I tell reality what it is meant to do?" We can check for internal mathematical consistency, but that's all.

Reality does tend to turn out to be right about reality. Reality also says that you are next cousin to a chimpanzee with no possibility of sentience after death, in a universe with no God. You are completely alone, and if you can't face looking reality in the face that is your problem and no-one else's. As a general result this shows your holy man to be deluded and your holy book to be false. (This is when believers start punching my desk and storming out. Tough – go on then, prove me wrong.)

I have heard people saying "I know I must have a purpose". Remember this – in this context your emotions are worthless. Everything that you point to in your body or mind as evidence of planning and a purpose can be explained better (=more accurately with fewer assumptions) as the accidental by-product of a tautology. The tautology in question is "The DNA sequence that gets commoner, gets commoner". After that, and given 4E9 years of Darwinian evolution, everything else falls into place. Read Richard Dawkins' collected works. Richard Dawkins gave me lectures at Oxford. I was slightly disappointed once in January 1981 seeing Richard Dawkins demonstrating algorithms by playing chess against a BBC microcomputer, as he got the 5th move wrong in the standard opening Guico Piano, 1 e4e5 Nf3Nc6, 2 Bc4Bc5 then he played 3 b3 not the usual move c3. I always wondered whether he really meant to fianchetto his queen's bishop or was just mucking around in front of undergraduates before getting on with his lecture on animal behaviour.

A deep argument about the creation of the universe is the curious point that the atomic parameters defining the carbon atom just happen to allow carbon to be created in supernovae, while quite a small deviation in values would stop carbon, hence stop us from existing. Surely proof of design? Maybe not – a powerful counter argument here is the anthropic principle, which basically points out that the only reason information can be held in our nervous systems is that we happen to exist in a universe where carbon can be formed in supernovae. If one could be sure that this is the only reality ever anywhere ever, that looks like a weird coincidence. However, as soon as one allows for multiple universes (say the big bang was just one of many spawned as two high dimensional fields interacted), the problem disappears into a statement of the blindingly obvious. There are many configurations of fundamental constants which might generate perfectly good universes (say of hydrogen-helium), but not much else. Unsurprisingly, these universes can never generate a set of macromolecules complex enough to allow a life form to develop, let alone form one that can generate a thought like "that must mean I'm really special". Hence, the fact that a set of macromolecules is able to get complex enough to form a network of cells able to hold such an idea (or indeed any other data) means that the universe it occupies must have the fine constants tuned just right for life. Just as the blackness of the night sky (Olber's paradox – worth reading up about) shows that there was a big bang and that light has a finite speed (two big deductions from one simple fact), so the coincidence of parameters fitting life can be seen as statistical evidence for a multiverse, a happy accident of random parameters rather than planned design. One of the many mind-blowing ideas from my favourite magazine "New Scientist" was that the initial universe must have existed in a state of quantum superposition, whereby all possible descendant universes co-existed. The wave function collapsed by finding the solution that gave observers, immanent in the collapse of a quantum wave function, thereby (by the anthropic principle) finding the unique combination of parameters that allow sentient life to evolve somewhere. So your self-awareness is part of the property that led this universe to be configured as it actually is. (Maybe. Or maybe just a weird untestable day dream).

While musing on this model, read on about my life experiences. As you do so, remember that these are (as far as I can manage) a mental version of a screendump. I want to record what happened and how things were. Sometimes the ensuing experiences may seem extreme or eccentric, but the underlying logic was always simple and linear, and the result generally some combination of interesting and fun. You might even learn something – I hope so!

CHAPTER 1

M is for Manchester!

39 Ferndown Road, Manchester M23 9AW: From my birth to starting university: 1961-1979

I was born on 11 July 1961, into what became a tight-knit family of four, the Shaw family, in the cohort loosely known as 'baby boomers'. Certainly our parents were shaped by their wartime experiences, and spent the 1950s enjoying themselves before settling down to have kids. We were (in age order) Father (John Robert Shaw, 24 April 1926), Mother (Elizabeth Nancy Shaw, née Kershaw, 18 Jan 1928), myself Peter Shaw, and my sister Caroline (18 August 1963). My parents were both single children, so we had no true aunts/uncles/cousins.

The dominant personality in the household was my father, John Robert Shaw, who was a dentist, by accident rather than choice. At heart he was a musician – only became a dentist because his mother said he had to. John Robert Shaw was

Fig 1.1 My father John Shaw as a young man.

certainly talented, primarily as a musician but also a linguist and an organiser. He was also proudly Scots, and quite iconoclastic – see this snippet about Dad opposing Concorde. He grew up in Aberdeen until the age of four, and was moved as his father Alexander Will Shaw sought employment as an engineer in the great depression. Whenever I hear of people grumbling at 'foreigners' who only leave their homeland to come to England as economic migrants – that describes my family too. (And my maternal grandmother, and my wife come to that.) When it comes to citizens of the USA who grumble about immigrants, I am rendered aghast by their hypocrisy. Look up the "Trail of tears", then look at Trump's ideas about immigrants changing native culture with a new contempt.

Born in Aberdeen in 1926, John Shaw grew up in a rather poor family background. He never said much about the earliest period of his life, but used to go back to Aberdeen for holidays for most of his life while living with his parents. Here he met his first cousin Helen Landery, with whom he re-established contact with in 2002 due to the internet. (One little story captures the zeitgeist of this inter-war period. On holiday in Scotland with his parents, little John was bought an ice cream. By some mischance a large hen appeared, grabbed the ice cream and ran off with it. That was the end of John's ice cream – they could not, or would not, afford to buy a replacement.)

Around John's 4th birthday his parents moved south to Manchester, presumably as his father Sandy looked for work in the depression. (It was only years later when clearing the loft we found a certificate showing that Sandy Shaw had been the head of the Masonic lodge in Aberdeen.) Many Scots families came as far south as Manchester then stopped. John Shaw was always proud of being a Scot, despite never having any trace of a Scots accent (or drinking whisky). John later played for and helped organise the Manchester Scottish Xmas festivities, and wore a kilt when he played music for Sophie Neubert's wedding.

It must have been about the time of the move to Manchester that John's interest in music appeared: by the age of five he was said always to make a beeline towards any piano, and after a while his parents relented in the face of such evident fascination, and let him start piano lessons. He carried on playing the piano until a week before his death. His parents never encouraged his musical development, and one of the deepest gripes John had about his mother was that she never came to his performances. (He never forced either myself or my sister Caroline to take music lessons, on the basis that if we wanted to we would, and if we didn't we shouldn't be forced.) He was always disappointed that we turned out quite non-musical, but with hindsight trying to get me into an orchestra would

A Path of 21 Ms

Fig 1.2 John and Elizabeth Shaw c. 2000.

have been flogging a dead horse. (I once shut down the school choir merely by joining in from the audience.) I remember lying in bed as a child trying to get to sleep and listening to Father playing the piano for hours, both for fun and practice. I did complain occasionally but generally enjoyed and felt privileged to listen to his playing. John could play anything on the piano, with his signature tune being 'Moon river' from Breakfast at Tiffany's. He could sight read anything, but usually just used a hand-written notebook giving the keys of named songs, then remember the songs note-perfect, playing for hours without once reading a note. He never actually took any formal music examinations, but earned the respect of many serious musicians. Quite late on in life (in his 50s) he took up the accordion, and acquired an electronic keyboard for public performances to avoid relying on whatever rickety old piano might be supplied on the night. He could never listen to music on a car stereo while driving as it interfered with his concentration, whereas most people find that the auditory and spatial regions of their minds can run independently. He also played the church organ, and on learning of his inoperable cancer in June 2004 one of his first actions was (characteristically) to produce a detailed written plan of his funeral service, on the grounds that he had played for several very uninspiring funerals where the deceased had failed to plan for a good send-off.

John really enjoyed entertaining the whole household/party with his music, singing along on a few pieces. A particular party piece was his rendition of "The Darkie Sunday School", a song that was described as a silly funny song in its day, but looks rather dated in its value systems to subsequent generations:

Chorus

"Bring your sticks of chewing gum and sit upon the floor
And we'll tell you Bible stories that you've never heard before

Lots of verses, including this gem of sensitivity:

Solomon and David both led naughty lives
They whiled away their afternoons with other people's wives;
Then later in the evening when their conscience gave them qualms -
One wrote the Proverbs and the other wrote the Psalms.

Remarkably, while trying to find out a bit about the background here I found a source linking this so-called joke to some lines written in German by Haydn during his visit to London c. 1790. How it ever got picked up by some Glasgow song writer will probably never be known! Anyway, this song was associated with Glasgow, so Aberdeen was not far to travel. I routinely objected to the verse about Jonah booking a passage on a transatlantic whale, "but when the fishy atmosphere got heavy on his chest, Jonah pushed a button and the whale did the rest" – "But Daddy a whale is not a fish it's a mammal".

John Shaw had many strings to his bow, many aspects of his personality. One that was very important to him in the 1960s and early 1970s was his support of "The National Council for Civil Liberties" (NCCL, later rechristened "Liberty" and associated with Shami Chakrabarti), of which he rose to be the north west chairman. He was most concerned to support freedom of speech, and saw our governments as philosophically opposed to this freedom. At the time Manchester had a "Speakers Corner", a zone of Platt Fields where anyone could stand up and make a public proclamation. Most of them were of course somewhat bonkers, to variable extents. All that the authorities needed to do was ignore them, and they would have gone home, harmless and ignored, having changed nothing. For some reason the chief constable of Manchester decided that such activity was a threat to the public well being, and sent police to arrest the speakers. My father made it his business to go along as a legal observer, and give evidence in support of the speakers when the cases came to trial. I vaguely remember the weary resignation in my mother's voice when Dad announced he was off to Speaker's Corner yet again. He was warned that his phone was tapped by HMG, to which he replied with characteristic bluntness that if someone in MI5 wanted to listen to his mother-in-law prattling on for hours they were welcome to it. After a few years, NCCL rebranded itself as "Liberty", and changed its focus from freedom of speech to equality for minority groups. John took this opportunity to resign the post, and had little contact with the charity after that.

Interestingly, the contrast between John Shaw and myself is exemplified by what we could/can do inside our heads. I was baffled for years how the same name of musical note (eg two versions of "C" an octave apart) could be given to two different noises that were clearly different. My father explained by saying that the way to prove to yourself that (eg) middle C deserves the same name as the next C up is by playing one note inside your head in one ear, and the other note on the other side of your head, and listen to them playing together in the middle of your head. If they are the same note an octave apart they do not clash, if they are different notes they do clash. Hmm – thanks, Dad but normal people don't work like that. It was a long time later that I understood octaves in terms that my nervous system can handle. I need to see the two notes as a sinusoidal function against time, and if they are the same note you see as the wave functions touch that some of the peaks will coincide precisely, so the interval of one sine wave must be some integer multiple of the other. An octave up means half the wavelength, so every second maximum must coincide exactly. This immediately explains octaves, and by a little logarithmic mathematics allows you to reconstruct the modern western music scale. My father couldn't see a non-linear mathematical function in his head to save his life, whereas by default I see mathematical functions as dancing 2D (or 3D) images. It also meant that Father could and did entertain a party with endless music all evening for fun, while for me having to make any music or sing a note in public is a nightmare to be avoided at all costs. I am, however, perfectly happy to give an hour-long lecture on visualising multivariate statistical mathematics as 3D mental images, which is perhaps more publishable but lousy for making people happy :-) Set against this, music has been a profoundly important part of my life, with specific songs reminding me of particular phases. For years my maxim was "Home is where the hi-fi is". A few of these songs I mention in the text below because they mattered deeply to me at the time, but to be honest the information means little to anyone outside my nervous system.

Given this effusive musical talent and love for music, one might have expected this to show through in his education. Not so, for which we have to blame his parents' attitudes coupled with the financial realities of the pre-war years. John went to the Manchester Grammar School for Boys, an institution he thought very highly of and supported practically and financially throughout his life. He was there 1937-1943, and read the equivalent of A levels in English, French and German. Music was presumably not seen as a serious option, and one of

John's proudest achievements was that he was the first boy at MGS to take music for school certificate, in 1941. (The school gave him no help, and he relied on an organist called Harold Kirkham for tuition.) He grumbled bitterly (and understandably) that his mother never came to hear any of his public musical performances.

More remarkably, John then went to the Manchester Dental school and graduated as a dentist in 1950. This involved a basic medical training, which in turn assumed scientific subjects at school. John had a hard time here and failed several courses, but it is a testament to his intelligence and tenacity that he completed the degree and worked the rest of his life as a dentist. It is also a testament to the stubbornness and fixity of opinion of his parents (especially his mother Flora, of Calvinist descent), since John always hated the job of a dentist and never chose the career as a vocation. The history behind this choice shows an example of contingency, the ability of small random effects to get magnified by subsequent events. His mother Flora once worked for a short while in a shop in Aberdeen, making friends with a lady called Milly Dalgarno. Milly became a lifelong friend of Flora, and expressed the opinion repeatedly that John should become a dentist like Milly's husband: easy money and no formal training. That was true in the 1920s, but by insisting on this career path Flora put John though

Fig 1.3 John and Elizabeth Shaw at their golden wedding anniversary June 2003.

Fig 1.4 John Shaw in his surgery.

Fig 1.5 I managed to combine my father's WW2 dental training with a plug for a research paper of my own in a letter to New Scientist!

Civilisation of teeth

From Peter Shaw
Your article on "Homo civicus" referred to recent evolutionary changes in *Homo sapiens* that suggest the continual refinement of our bodies (19 March, p 36). One additional line of evidence that wasn't mentioned is the reduction in human tooth size over the past 10,000 years, which, unlike bone thickness, cannot be a direct response to reduced physical activity. Samples collected by Ron Pinhasi in the Levant (*American Journal of Physical Anthropology*, vol 135, p 136) show that the buccolingual thickness of 13 different human teeth (most clearly molars) declined linearly at around 0.1 millimetre per thousand years from the end of the last ice age.

As a dental student in the 1950s, my father was taught that Stone Age people had much bigger teeth than nowadays, making this an example of once commonplace knowledge being forgotten.
London, UK

16 April 2011 | NewScientist | 31

a gruelling university medical / dental training (a requirement that came in after Mr Dalgano entered the profession). Dentistry also gave John a bad back, which tormented him for years, but which vanished after retirement. (To cap it all, pay as an NHS dentist was never marvellous.)

To return to the 1940s, John Shaw was inevitably profoundly affected by WW2. He was in the air training corps at school (getting two stripes and firing a Bren gun once or twice), and in the home guard though without seeing action. His wartime stories included the time that his father saw bombs (incendiaries or markers, I assume) being dropped in a rough circle around Manchester and said "We're in for it tonight" – Manchester was hammered that night, though Withington was undamaged. Their wartime stories were pretty tame by comparison with people who got blitzed, but included the impossibility of keeping water out of their garden shelter (which was next to a stream), so eventually they gave up and reinforced a room in the house. Father spoke little about his war, Mother slightly more, recounting how she walked out of a department store in Manchester with her mother and watched spitfires and Messerschmitts having a deadly dog fight in the sky above. At this distance this sounds like a computer game, but when you are a pre-computer schoolchild, and you know a man up there has come over here to kill you, that sticks in your mind for life.

It was only in 2021 that I saw John's name on a list of children evacuated from Manchester to Blackpool in September 1939. (This came out of a Y chromosome search.) It turned out that this was not a secret, he just hated the experience and rarely spoke about it.

John Robert Shaw lived at home with parents in 50 Brooklawn Drive, Withington, as a student, and presumably had a rather limited social life. I know that he had a brief engagement to a lady called Doreen Walker, but that this was broken off by John in 1947. Doreen came from 68 Long St, Easingwold, Yorkshire, and by a bizarre coincidence when John visited Yorkshire in 1985 (to see Peter, then doing a PhD at York University), John was taken aback to observe that 68 Long St Easingwold was occupied by a dentist called Mr Walker. Doreen out of the way, John dated Elizabeth Kershaw. The key date was their second meeting, at Belle Vue pleasure gardens in Manchester, and they married on 20 June 1953. John remained devoted to Betty for the rest of his life, and could not have lived without her.

Despite his background in languages and music, John had to take a partial medical degree to graduate as a dentist (something that had not been true a generation before). This was clearly a stiff challenge – Dad told me he failed a few exams here, but that is no shame. Lots of proper science-trained medics fail these exams first time. The syllabus had other biology on it, and I know that John (who responded to his mother's adoration of flowers by disliking all things botanical) was most miffed that he had to learn about the life cycle of mosses and ferns in order to drill holes in people's teeth! He also had to study human anatomy – this meant a term in the "DR" (dissecting room). He never said much about this side of his degree, but when we cleared out his stuff one little legacy was a microscope (that I knew all about) and some hand-made slides (that I did not). It was not till May 2022 that I finally got round to taking these slides into the university lab to have a proper look at them, and I confess to being blown away. My plan had been to leave them for the university to use, since we had biomedical students who got taught some histology. Up to this point these had been filthy-dusty glass slides in a decaying carboard box in the gloom at the back of the loft, clearly of some interest but not clear beyond that. So I cleaned them up with meths, put a few under a modern compound microscope with a proper light source (Dad's needed a desk lamp and a mirror). The slides were excellent quality, well sliced and nicely stained with no oxidation of the mountant. I have to say that history will judge that my father's microscope slides were neater than mine, like everything else that he did was neater than me. A few had his name on them – I scanned these, oddly all human teeth. See image overleaf.

Being a careful and diligent person, John had kept a list of what each slide contained. As well as the quality of the slides, this list blew my mind and – ironically – stopped the university from taking the slides. Apart from a few zoological slides, most of these were human tissue. John had dissected multiple

A Path of 21 Ms

Fig 1.6 John Shaw's dental slides.

Fig 1.7 A scan of some of the contents of John Shaw's histology collection.

nameless corpses, extracted tissue, then processed it though the long tedious sequence of mounting – dehydration – microtoming – staining – fixing. This was just after WW2 when resources must have been scarce, so the quality of the work was outstanding, showing his tutors were very good both at their trade and at teaching students how to do it. But human tissue comes with all sorts of legal issues nowadays. Bluntly, unless you know whose body it was and have next-of-kin consent, it is illegal for a public institute to own them. Father left me about 40 slides of undocumented human remains, plus an undocumented human skull. (He thought that the skull came from a "Tower of Silence" in India, after the vultures finished with the flesh. One tooth, upper L canine, has a groove on it like it was used to hold thread/cotton, so I suspect a weaver, and it appears to be female.) The university took one look at the list of slide contents and said that they could not possibly take them. Pity – some historical samples. One labelled "carbon in lung" which was nicely stained lung tissue with hundreds of black specks. This was (I assume) a coal miner from near Manchester who died of lung disease just after WW2, whose lungs Dad dissected out. Look at the scanned list! Apparently, material over 100 years old is easier to accommodate legally, but I drew the line at making up a false date and false story, so the slides came home again, to stay with the skull as undocumented human remains!

When not being a dentist or playing piano, John was very involved in helping steam-powered railways. He was especially involved with the Ffestiniog railway in Wales, where he supplied volunteer labour some weekends. In later years we had many family holidays in this part of Wales, and John maintained connections with the Ffestiniog and the Stevenson locomotive society throughout his life.

Mother was called Elizabeth Nancy Shaw, and with hindsight was something of a glamourous blonde in the 1950s. Her oldest friends did not call her Elizabeth but Bessie, because she was born Bessie Kershaw, and changed her name to Elizabeth Nancy Kershaw by deed poll on her 18th birthday. (This complicated my application for French nationality in 2019 because they spotted Mother's marriage and birth certificates were in a different name.) By then she was a student at Whitelands College, and we suspect she had been getting teased about "Bessie" since a popular book series at the time featured a very fat girl called Bessie Bunter. (Sister of Billy Bunter, "The fat owl of the remove" if you read the old Billy Bunter books. Very non-PC by modern standards. We now know that Prader-Willi syndrome children look and behave in ways reminiscent of how Billy Bunter was rather contemptuously portrayed. I found myself wondering whether some unrecognised early Prader-Willi case might have tangentially inspired the Bunter stories.) Maybe Mum just wanted to show some independence – I'd understand the sentiment, though it would have been her one rebellious act. They married in 1953, and Father worked a dentist in south Manchester. Although trained as a teacher and able to act as a dental nurse, Mother did not work from my birth in 1961 till well after Caroline left home more than 20 years later– in those days married women were expected not to work, and Father was opposed to her being anything other than a housewife while there were kids to raise. So Mother did the cooking and the clothes, being good at both. (It was only when I tried wielding needle and thread myself that I realised that her ability with a sewing machine was very impressive!) While Father was auditory, Mother was visual, liking art galleries and creating clothes. Cooking revolved heavily around potatoes, often with a pressure cooker to speed up the process. The height of exotic cuisine might be pasta, though spaghetti was almost always out of tins and covered in tomato sauce. (The first few times we had proper Italian spaghetti the younger generation complained that it wasn't proper spaghetti like we were used to.) My recollection was very much meat, two veg, gravy and pudding every dinner, though I am assured that Mother's choice of recipes were seen as fashionable in the 1970s. No curry – a pleasure I discovered in Oxford.

Caroline was two years younger than myself, and went on to be a student at Whitelands 1981-84, then married a close university friend of mine, John Shelvey. Less enthusiastic than myself about our numerous (cold, wet, muddy) ornithological outings! Her guinea pig (Snuffles 1972-79) became a central character in our daily life for a few years. Caroline had the backup master bedroom, much larger than mine, which was actually a liability more than an asset since grandparents could sleep there at Christmas whereas no one else could be expected to sleep among my piles of books, bird food, wires and toxic chemicals. She carried on my Oxford connections by living there with John. She also continued Mother's interest in art, collecting a range of paintings and becoming a talented silversmith making a variety of finely crafted ornaments.

Away from direct family we grew up with three out of four grandparents. My father's father, Alexander Will Shaw 1897-1955, died (of a brain tumour) far too young, aged 58, before I was born, so I only knew him from family stories and emptying out a whole string of wonderful but dangerous molecules from his garage. I consider that he is the ancestor I would most like to have met. He was an engineer specialising in heavy machinery. We have photographs of a big quarry near Aberdeen where he worked, before becoming a ship's engineer. He went round the world, fixing ships' boilers and enjoying places like Formosa (=Taiwan, his favourite place), India and Australia. In Peter's coin collection is a necklace made of Indian coins (1/2 anna and 1/12 anna – not worth much) soldered onto a chain, which came from Sandy's times in India. We have a picture below of a mongoose-cobra fight in Bombay in 1925. Plus a nameless pretty woman in Australia! No sign of a DNA legacy out there, but you never know your luck.

Fig 1.8 Alexander Will Shaw – the man himself, c. 1930.

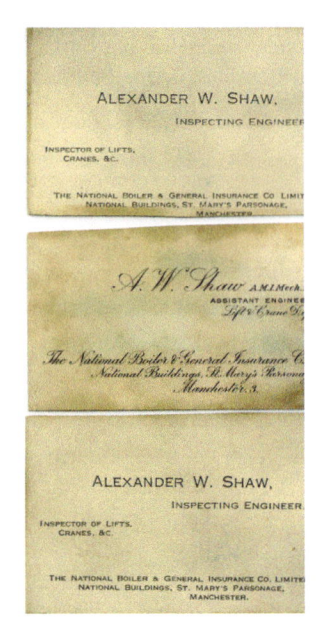

Fig 1.9 His business cards.

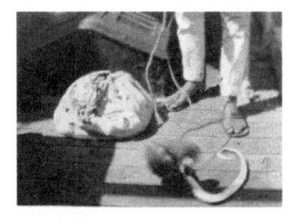

Fig 1.10 The Bombay cobra fight.

Alexander W. Shaw ("Sandy Shaw") stopped going to sea around the time of the move to Manchester in 1930, as the great depression annihilated industrial jobs. (This marine career must have posed a huge toll on family life. Sandy's son John passed on the story that when three years old he was woken up by his mother to greet his father, newly returned from the sea. Poignantly, he later asked his mother "Who was that boy I was playing with?".) In Manchester Sandy worked for the National Boiler and General Insurance company, later specialising in lifts. Sandy – knowing what he did about Manchester lifts – refused to travel in any lift in Manchester! My favourite Sandy Shaw anecdote concerns the time Flora decided she wanted a bubble bath, and Sandy saw how to make one, He reverse-wired the house vacuum cleaner so it blew instead of sucked, then immersed the nozzle in a tub of soapy bath water. Of course it then blew all the dirt and dust back out of the vacuum bag into the bath were they combined with the soap to make black sticky suds and – indeed – black bubbles. During WW2 Sandy tried to make a bomb-proof shelter at the bottom of the garden, but there was a small stream there and he never managed to keep the water out, In the end he re-enforced a room in the house. He left a legacy of a garage full of tools and chemicals, plus a few detailed notebooks that I wish I'd kept, plus slide rules (solid state calculators which I used for doing exams at school, astonishingly). Sandy Shaw was the head of the Aberdeen masonic lodge in the 1920s, a curiosity that somehow everyone except me knew and that only came to light decades later when loft clearing. I remember my father coming down from clearing the loft in 50 Brooklawn Drive saying "I must sort out my loft – I won't have you saying the things about me that I've been saying about my father". Needless to say, when the time came I had a great deal to say about the vast accumulation of junk in Dad's loft, though I can't beat the discovery that Alexander Shaw had a stash of sandbags, still full of sand. I then said to my son, "I must clear out my loft – I won't have you saying the things about me that I've been saying about my dad". Needless to say when a colony of rats moved into 4 Larkspur Way while we were out of the country, my kids had to hire a skip to empty my loft. Presumably the next generation down the line can look forward to some heavy loft clearance about the year 2050? Sandy Shaw died of a brain tumour aged 58, an event which deeply scared me when I got a brain tumour at the age of 58. With modern scanning techniques they were able to locate and remove it, but that was existentially scary.

The wonderful legacy of Sandy Shaw's garage included molecules you just can't get nowadays. Concentrated acids – Hydrochloric acid HCl ('spirit of salts') and sulphuric acid H_2SO_4 ('oil of vitriol'). Plus some highly explosive Sodium chlorate ('weedkiller'), and some rather mysterious unlabelled bottles I was probably wise to leave alone. I found a live round of ammunition one day – with hindsight it was lucky no-one got killed. My father pulled a funny face, and said, "I'll take that if that's OK?", before taking the bullet away. I never saw it again, though about 20 years later while helping my widowed mother tidy under the back-garden oil tank, I found an old, decayed bullet. I suspect it was the same one, but gave it to the police who took it away unconcerned. Alexander Will Shaw seems to have been a top notch practical engineer who saw pictures in his head, but Father grumbled that he was not emotionally supportive, that he (John) could not talk to his father about personal issues. I didn't understand what he meant, and to be honest I still don't – I aim to keep my internal self strictly to myself, and on the unlikely off-chance I uncovered some emotional angst and felt like dumping it uncensored onto some unfortunate soul, Father would have been well down towards the bottom of my list.

Alexander Will Shaw's widow, Father's mother, Flora Shaw, née Wiseman, was a diminutive demure old lady with a mild Scots accent whom we always called "Little Nan", to separate her from Mother's mother who was a good 20cm taller, so called "Big Nan". She features in photos below, one in our back garden, one on a picnic. She used to make a remarkably delicious pink lemonade from home-picked blackberries; sadly no-one thought to get the recipe, which died with her. She said almost nothing about her early years in Aberdeen. When she pulled a pullover off a child she would say "skin a rabbit", which made no sense at all until I actually did skin a rabbit! You cut the fur round the feet, slice the skin of the legs and abdomen, and it just pulls off exactly like a pullover. From this I assume that they ate locally caught bunnies as cheap meat.

Flora was always fond of flowers and flower arranging, and active in her local church (more for the social side than any religiosity). Perhaps my most treasured plant is a *Crassula ovata* (jade plant or money tree) that came from her front room, almost certainly picked up for a few pence in a church fair in the 1960s. I had it on my desk in Oxford in 1982 after we cleared her house, and it wasn't a young plant then. I also treasure a "jungle cactus" that came from Flora. It used to be

Fig 1.11 *The red flowered jungle cactus* Disocactus akkermanni. *Inherited from my grandmother Flora Shaw. A pink, sweet sugary nectar drips from each flower for a day – a plus if tasted on your fingers, a minus if it stains your white tablecloth.*

Fig 1.12 *Our two grandmothers 1976. Flora Shaw is on the left, Bessie Lershaw on the right.*

called *Epiphyllum ackermanii*, but I gather it is now *Disocactus ackermannii*. Flora had a gentle Scots accent, and it was a real shock to speak to a long-lost cousin of my father's years after Flora's death to hear exactly the same soft Aberdeen accent. In theory she retained her Scottish roots throughout life, with continued family in Aberdeen. In practice, sad to say, the Shaws seem to have been rather fissiparous, to the extent that I never met any Aberdeen family, and Flora's sister refused to come to her funeral in 1983. My father's comments about his extended family were pithy and unflattering, such as observing that the house of his Aunty Nell was "always cold but there was always plenty of whisky". One of Nell's sons shot a bank manager dead during an abortive robbery in Newcastle, then committed suicide.

We did get to know both our maternal grandparents, though her father George Kershaw was crippled by a stroke when I was about four, so I only have one dim memory of him as a fit man (kicking my football). I am afraid that for most of our childhoods he was a sad figure immobile in a wheelchair, utterly dependent on his wife Bessie. George was very medically demanding – and a heavy weight to manipulate, but died in 1974, giving his wife Bessie Kershaw a second lease of life.

After my tumour surgery I had some facial palsy (from neurological damage) and an abiding nightmare that "I do not want to end up like Grandpa Kershaw". In his younger days George was a fighter pilot and a master tailor, so must have been a good catch. He also came with a good financial background, from his father Robert Kershaw. One of the few bits of advice George gave me was "never miss a rights issue". [A rights issue is when shareholders can buy more of the same shares at a discount.] They were among the first people in the town to have a car, though it was only allowed out of the garage in dry weather! Given the climate of north Manchester, this was infrequent. At least once an honoured guest had to wait in the rain to get a bus to the station because the car could not be used because of a heavy downpour.

I only heard about great-grandfather Robert Kershaw from family stories, but he seemed to have been a very interesting and talented man. Robert Kershaw lost his sight (detached retinas) but had such good mental imagery that he could walk people round Manchester and tell them what they were seeing. He was clearly good with money, investing and re-investing wisely, at one stage owning more than 100 houses in North Manchester. He inspired fear in company directors for turning up at shareholders' meetings and publicly, loudly correcting errors in their balance sheets. By way of example his holding in Wilsons' brewery in Manchester in the 1930s gave me a splendid shareholding in Diageo in the 2010s! Robert Kershaw had a penchant for the herb Comfrey (or knitbone) *Symphytum officinale*. He paid men to collect comfrey leaves, scenting the whole house. Comfrey is well known as a healing herb, being used to treat injuries. We now know it contains allantoin, which acts as a scaffold for cells to lay down new tissue. Because of my stupidly wide feet (another Kershaw legacy), I have been plagued by abrasions and blisters on my feet from long distance running, which take weeks to heal. I have several times applied a poultice of boiled comfrey mucilage to old blisters, and each time the new skin formed perfectly almost overnight as if by magic. A bit like Robert Kershaw, I keep a bag of comfrey leaves in the freezer for this reason. We also now know that comfrey contains pyrrolizidine alkaloids that cause severe liver damage / cancer, and that you must never put comfrey on a fresh wound, still less eat it. Robert Kershaw drank comfrey tea every day. This probably explains why he went yellow then died quickly and prematurely of liver failure, though my mother refutes the idea and suggested his liver cancer was just bad luck. Take it from me – comfrey is really good, but only when used externally (boiled, as a poultice) on part-healed wounds to accelerate skin growth.

Bessie Kershaw née Holland was known to us as "Big Nan", and was indeed a head taller than Flora. Although my mother's childhood was in their tailor's shop in 33 Ratcliffe Street, Royton, by the time I knew her they lived in 41 Broadway. This was a rather cold, damp house on the edge of town by a main road. Knowing what I know now about their finances, they could have done a bit better! Bessie came from Wales. In 2021 I was sent a cassette tape by a distant relative Pat Carmichael, on which I heard Bessie Kershaw talking about living in peasant conditions in north Wales in the village of Ruabon (Flintshire). Her father Thomas Holland seems to have worked as a coal miner. We know that two of her sisters (Madge and Ginny) spoke Welsh, so I am sure that she was brought up in a Welsh-speaking society, though neither she nor her sister Edith ever appeared to admit to a word of Welsh in later life. My guess is that if she had re-met a sister they could have lapsed into childhood Welsh, but we will never be sure. She left that life behind when she stopped her education aged 14, getting a bus from Flintshire to work in service in a big house far away in north Manchester. She described leaving her childhood home for ever, seeing troops assembling to be massacred in the trenches of the Somme. She met my grandfather George Kershaw through the local church. She died in 1997, and I never thought I'd hear her voice again. Due to the tense family relations in the Scottish Shaws, it was the Holland/Kershaw side of the family that gave us some approximation to an extended family. Bessie Holland's sister Edith had a daughter Edith Barlow, whose daughter Kathleen was in friendly contact with us. She lived in Yorkshire with her three sons (twins Richard and Philip, plus younger brother Christopher) whom we played with regularly, and with whom we remain in good contact.

There were a few people who were important in day-to-day life but were not genetically family. We saw so much of them while living in 3FD in the 1960s and 1970s that they felt more like family than genuine but distant relatives like our second cousins in Yorkshire. One such turned out to be our cleaner, Sheila Gregory. Cleaners come and cleaners go, but somehow after Sheila entered our lives in the 1970s she stayed around. Latterly, after Dad died (2004), when Mum was alone and not really coping, it was Sheila who helped keep the show on the road as long as it did. You only learn who your true friends are when things start to melt down. We were still exchanging Xmas cards with Sheila in 2021, by which time I had retired. By the time 39FD was sold, Sheila was almost the only person left in Wythenshawe who knew us, and she had become a grandmother plus respected and active member of her church. We also had much help from a long-standing local handyman called Roy Potts, who helped with gardening, fixing light bulbs etc. As with Sheila, it was only later on that it became clear what a valuable support Roy Potts was to my mother. Roy Potts died about 2015.

I should mention 'Aunty Elsie', Elsie Jenkinson, who was not an aunt at all but happened to be a neighbour living on Ferndown Road, opposite 39FD with her husband John Jenkinson. John Jenkinson was a market gardener, Elsie was the housewife who went to arts classes with my mother. Everyone got on so well that it took me years to realise that they were not actually family, and owed us nothing beyond friendship. Sadly, my only memory from the Jenkinson household in Ferndown Road was when I was very little, went round with Mum, played around and somehow fell over and put my hand into the fireplace when it was alight. On the bigger scale of injuries it was pretty minor, but the event is almost literally burned into my memory and I can still clearly see the room and the fireplace as it happened, and recall the pain in the palm of my hand. (You can see why evolution equips our nervous system for this sort of deep and rapid learning.) By about 1966 the Jenkinsons had moved to a new, much bigger house near Manchester airport, but we stayed family friends for years. More than once, my mother went to some art exhibition with Elsie, bought and came home with some abstract modern art that they both liked, only to have their respective husbands saying things like "What is that mess meant to be?" and "If it is meant to be a tree why doesn't it look like one?" etc. John died aged about 70 of a heart attack, Elsie died about 2020 in her 90s.

Our family home was a good-sized four-bedroom house on the southern outskirts of Manchester, 39 Ferndown Road, Wythenshawe, M23 9AW. Henceforth 39FD. It was unusual in having a dental surgery and waiting room built in at the construction phase. I gather that it was one of several such houses in the Sale/Altringham area built by a Mr Bracewell.

My father named the house "Invercauld", a Scots place name to echo his mother's house being called "Lochnagar". It was not till 2012 that I realised that John Shaw had done something very clever here. There is a deep connection between the place name "Invercauld" and the highland clan Shaw. I only found this by chance in 2012 when teaching a course near Braemar, and on arrival passed a Braemar pub called "The Invercauld Arms", whose pub sign displayed the Shaw motto "Fide et fortitudine". A history of the clan Shaw (Shaw 1871) refers to a Farquar Shaw of Invercauld. I wish John had explained this deeply hidden gem of Shaw history while he was alive.

In practice this meant that Dad worked at home, that we usually had a dental nurse at morning and afternoon tea, and that quite a lot of the downstairs was a no-go area in the working day. Apart from some horrid noises when kids had a panic attack in the dental chair (fairly common) and the odd cache of old teeth turning up in the flower beds where Dad had buried them, this had surprisingly little influence on our day-to-day lives. The first time I played Pink Floyd's classic album 'The Dark Side of the moon' (borrowed from Wythenshawe library), Mum heard the track 'The Great Gig in the Sky' and thought it was just another person screaming in the dental chair.

Several small points emerged from this setup: the plus side was that Dad could, and did, have a lie down in his own bed after lunch for a 30 minute snooze, every working day. Very few professionals can aspire to that! It also meant that I inherited some excellent quality dental tools when we cleared out the house! (Dental pliers are the best.) Dad was also recognised and earned respect as an NHS dentist by the local parents, though not so much by their offspring! The downside was a regular dribble of dental emergencies walking to the front door each weekend, hence Dad's enthusiasm for long walks in the Pennines. No mobile phone, no possibility of contact, no clear hour of return, sorry, try the hospital A&E!

When we sold 39 Ferndown Road, I compiled a small history of it (and left a copy for the new owners). This is held in the digital archives associated with this autobiography, but is of too little interest to publsh in full. In summary, when my parents bought the house in 1955 it came with a pre-made dental surgery, and stood alone on the edge of the Cheshire countryside, with farmers' fields off into the distance. I still, just, recall a line of trees that dominated the southern skyline. They ceased to be, when the area was built up as the outer edge of the Wythenshawe estate about 1965.

You can see in the adjacent photo that there were fields and hedges where a council estate later sprouted. Behind my mother you can see the chestnut paling fence that defined the boundary, and beyond that the land which became Arden Lodge Road.

Fig 1.13 Peter in the 39FD garden about 1962. Note the 'Leave the baby balanced in a folding seat on a wobbly chair in the snow' approach to childcare, with slight overtones of ancient Sparta!

Fig 1.14 With Grandma Flora Shaw in our back garden.

This extension of the council estate to around our house was probably one of the deepest traumas in my parents' lives, and I remember walking around the new houses picking up bits of wood left by the builders while Dad shook his head sadly. The council estate certainly changed / ruined the atmosphere of the area. I am sure many people would have just sold up and moved on, but Dad didn't leave so easily and instead developed a fortress mentality, locking and barricading the Wythenshawe estate out as much as possible. They did all they could to stop us socialising with any kids off the estate, even perfectly nice ones I knew and played with at Sandilands primary school. With hindsight this looks insensitive and class-ist, though there were certainly some nasty bits of work living on the local estates and kids got robbed for cash on a daily basis.

Fig 1.15 The newly married Mrs Elizabeth Shaw in her new garden, 39FD, looking to the NE corner of the garden c. 1954.

I am sure that most of the new inhabitants of Wythenshawe were good people who knew how humans should interact. Some of the local families were lovely people. Our cleaner Sheila Gregory and her social circle, for example. A friend from primary school called John Baxter (with whom I re-established contact some 50 years later). The best known well-meaning product of Wythenshawe is the philanthropic footballer Marcus Rashford, who about 2021 actually persuaded Boris Johnson's conservatives that children going hungry was a problem that they should attempt to address. Marcus Rashford went to Button Lane primary school, where my sister and I had some classes and where my mother used to be a teacher.

Set against these good examples, it was unfortunate that those who did not match this description seemed to be able to do what they wanted untrammelled by fear of consequences. As recently as 2007 the New York Times described the Wythenshawe estate as representing an "extreme pocket of social deprivation and alienation" (Lyall, 2007). It is symptomatic that the best known name from Wythenshawe is the world-champion heavyweight boxer Tyson Fury, whom I think of as a dangerous professional psychopath (though he may be perfectly pleasant out of the ring). There was a well known TV series called Shameless, about a the family of the dysfunctional alcoholic Frank Gallagher on a violent dysfunctional neighbourhood in south Manchester. [https://en.wikipedia.org/wiki/Shameless_(British_TV_series)].

Although set on the fictional Chatsworth estate, 'Shameless' was initially set and filmed on the Wythenshawe estate. They had to transfer filming to the adjacent Gorton estate after too many episodes of theft, vandalism and violence from the real-life thugs who actually lived there. To give some idea about the calibre of some of the denizens of the Wythenshawe estate in the 1970s, consider these anecdotes: One neighbour shot birds in our back garden with his air rifle, firing from his bedroom across a public road. I habitually met (and avoided) gangs of boys armed with air rifles shooting birds in the local meadows (not in the parks – the "parkies" kept discipline there). We had stones through the windows too often, and lead flashing ripped off our roof. Kids climbed our fence most summer nights to trespass and steal apples – since they were inedible cooking apples, we regularly found ruined apples on the lawn with one bite mark. My sister made a point of getting off the school bus half a mile away to walk back unseen, rather than risk meeting locals outside Brookway comprehensive school by getting off at the bus stop near our house. There were streets within 100m of my house I never dared enter until I was a 40-year-old black belt. I still feel uncomfortable in underpasses, because that is where the muggers lurked, a group at each end of the tunnel to trap you in the middle. When crossing the A560 to get the 99 bus I felt much safer running across two lanes of traffic then using the pedestrian underpass. Everyone carried a penknife. One cheery piece of advice I recall from somewhere in the school system was "If someone threatens you, do not get your knife out. Because all that happens is that they get their knife out and theirs is bigger, so you are worse off". Where the motorway passed through the Wythenshawe estate, the local hobby was to throw stones off bridges onto passing cars. My father had to swerve one day to dodge stones, expressing horror that anyone would throw stones at a car with a parent and two young children. A musical schoolmate called Jez Hartley composed a song that he played in school assembly parodying this behaviour, whose chorus went "That's how we all get our kicks, chuckin' bricks at the M56". One day at school a boy told of a friend of his, walking around minding his own business when a car full of young males screeched to a halt by him, jumped out and beat him up badly. In hospital a surgeon said that they probably would not need to operate in this case. A long-haired street-wise supporter of Manchester City called Alan looked across, puzzled. "Why are you surprised?" he asked – "It happens all the time." One of the sons of our cleaner Sheila got attacked in similar circumstances. In "A Clockwork Orange" Anthony Burgess used the phrase 'ultra violence' for such

A Path of 21 Ms

Fig 1.16 *The drawing of myself following Dad as he mowed our lawns – by a neighbour Jean Gledhill, c. 1970.*

Fig 1.17 *Caroline Shaw plus hamster c. 1977, in the dining room of 39FD.*

Fig 1.18 *John Shaw with myself and my sister Caroline, Wythenshawe park horticultural centre 1968.*

Fig 1.19 *The bird table hanging from our apple tree c. 1975. I proudly took this to show the coal tit, but in fact it shows the back garden oil tank corner quite well. The large window visible above the oil tank is the flat across the road where Jean Gledhill lived and sketched.*

behaviour – on the Wythenshawe estate it was called 'routine'. Similar behaviour can be seen in some wild chimpanzee troops, but when my wife Catherine worked as a probation officer for 25 years with the alcoholics, opiate addicts, burglars and wife beaters of Redhill, she never encountered such gratuitous violence. The over-riding impression of being middle class in Wythenshawe in the 1970s was of a "them and us" dichotomy, and that their attitude to us was of aggressive contempt. It is not obvious who to blame or what social policy was at fault – the same species in France seems not to have such painful divisions. Things around our part of Wythenshawe gradually settled down to a passable approximation of civility by the time I finished my PhD, but this gentrification was slow and the dark shadow of fear was always in the background as we grew up.

39FD was surrounded by its garden, though the main extent was the back garden, dominated by a lawn and a Bramley apple tree planted in the 1960s (I just recall its planting). For a long time there were also two large oil storage tanks in the back garden, for the central heating (behind the swing – see picture).

I derived inordinate pleasure from my bird feeding station in front of the living room window, a bird table hanging from the apple tree (see photo). The species mix was oddly unfamiliar by my local standards – yes certainly blue and great tits, but lots of greenfinches and sparrows, neither of which ever come to my feeders nowadays. I could sit on the dining room table basking in the heat of the big new hot radiator while watching the bright yellow flashes of greenfinches squabbling over nuts. Nowadays in 4LW I like to stand in the spare bedroom leaning on a nice hot radiator and watching birds on my feeders, getting much the same pleasure. No greenfinches though.

One curious little bit of family history is that a disabled lady lived opposite us, in a council flat, who passed her time drawing. She saw my father mowing our lawn a lot, and that I always followed close behind, like a little shadow. We have a painting of this in the loft, showing little Peter following Dad mowing the lawn. I thought she was old because she was older than me, frail and unable to walk – sadly, in fact, she was young but very disabled – she died about age 30.

I recall the first night central heating was installed in 39FD, about 1970, after about 25 years of minimal heat (just small coke fires). It sounded like the house was full of burglars as all the floorboards creaked all night! The boiler had oil flow in from a narrow pipe running through the garden from the oil tanks. The first winter we got the wrong fuel oil, not the winter mix, so it stuck in the pipe across the garden, so we had no heat. Father managed to set up a bucket dripping fuel oil into the boiler, so we had heat again (and once the garage warmed up the oil flow improved), but in the process a huge pool of oil crept across the concrete garage floor. It seeped into the paper of the great big bag of potatoes that were always kept in the dark of the garage, so that every single spud became marinated in fuel oil. The WW2 spirit can be seen – obviously you keep enough potatoes in stockpile to feed you for weeks if needed, and obviously you cannot waste them. Nowadays we buy enough potatoes for a meal or two, keep then in the kitchen and if they taste funny we compost them. No such luck – we had chips tasting of fuel oil, mash tasting of fuel oil, baked potatoes tasting of fuel oil, roasties tasting of fuel oil . . . then one day Mum announced with relief that this was the last of the oily batch, the rest of our potatoes would taste of potato not oil! I suspect that our long-term cancer risk was tweaked upwards by this dietary contamination!

Before central heating, 39FD was cold in winter, heated only by a small fireplace or gas fire in each room. I think there was a gas fire in the surgery as well. One of the annual jobs was DIY double glazing – Father used drawing pins to attach thick plastic sheeting to each window. This did, slightly, improve insulation, but meant we couldn't see outside for nearly half the year. Thankfully Father graduated onto a proper DIY double glazing with nice clear glass screwed into place over the windows. After that the house really was warm. (Father disliked cold houses after some bad experiences in Aberdeen as a child. One family member he especially disliked was described as having a house that was always cold, but always had plenty of whisky.)

A typical Shaw weekend day would feature a cooked breakfast (bacon, sausage and fried bread), then a mid-morning sandwich making, for a picnic somewhere out in the countryside, followed by a brisk walk. Favourite local haunts included Tatton Park and Lyme Park, but with many, many other places visited too. High on his list would be the Goyt Valley, Kinder Scout, Winnats Pass (Derbyshire), and Macclesfield forest (Wildboarclough), but Dad knew dozens of other local (and no-so-local) walks. Often we all went out together – the other common scenario was that Dad, myself and +/- Caroline, would enjoy some long muddy walk then come home to the smell of dinner being cooked. Years later I took my kids on a walk to the 'hunting lodge' in Lyme Park, walked on a path I couldn't have walked on for 20 years, and had a Proustian-style flashback to the smell of roast meat and gravy that would have waited for us at home. I should also mention here Alderley Edge – a famous local hill full of copper ore that had been mined since pre-Roman times. We would park outside Alderley centre, walk up a hill past a carving of a wizard, to Stormy Point where you could still enter an old mine (now blocked off – H&S gone mad). I remember Caroline and I played on a huge heap of sand by some car park at Alderley Edge, being told later it was Victorian sand that should have been covered with plants but for its high arsenic and lead content.

If I was lucky (and Caroline less lucky) we'd go to a birding spot – The Wirral estuary in winter being the best. If the tides were favourable we could park by Red Rocks and walk a couple of minutes to see the sky blacken with hundreds of thousands of wading birds, mainly knot and dunlin. Other times (low tide, good weather) we walked out past 'Little Eye' to Hilbre Island, where a small cluster of huts acted as a seasonal base for some naturalists / researchers. (With hindsight I do not know who employed them or what they did – no need to manage the intertidal mud! Probably employed to count birds and seals – you often saw seals hauled out on the mid near Hilbre; not sure which of the two species they were.) Hilbre also featured a goat that stole visitors' sandwiches. Through membership of local ornithological societies, I knew that there was a single Kentish plover in among >10,000 ringed plovers – not that I ever found it. RSPB Leighton Moss was another top spot (bitterns!), but a long motorway drive up the M6 to Carnforth.

For really nerdy birdwatching the best venue was Sandbach Flashes, a series of small shallow lakes near Sandbach caused by subsidence from the salt mines there. This sounds like the Cheshire gulags, but actually involved pumping fresh water into ancient evaporite deposits, washing out the brine and evaporating it. These salt chambers run for great distances around Sandbach. Tatton Park has two lakes, the smaller being called "Melchett Mere", after Lord Melchett whose salt mine it was that caused the subsidence that formed the lake. I clearly recall seeing cormorants perching on tree branches in the middle of Melchett Mere in the 1960s, showing how young the lake was. The oak (?) involved must have been about 10m tall when it was killed by the flooding, yet its upper twigs were tough enough to support cormorants when I was a child. I gather that the subsidence was in the 1920s.

The many small shallow flashes near the Sandbach salt works were biologically fascinating (like so many ex-industrial landscapes). For a start the salt extraction meant some were salty, and far from being lifeless they contained saltmarsh plants, miles inland. (I found the same thing on fly ash deposits from power stations, again due to coastal plants tolerating salt and boron toxicity.) Because of this, or simply because they were shallow, the flashes were excellent places to see waterside birds, especially sandpipers on migration in late summer. It was there I saw my first little stint, learned what corn buntings sound like (yes, like a bunch of keys jangling just like the books say. Such a rare bird nowadays – I have not seen or heard one this millennium. Extinct in Ireland c. 2020). Saw an American vagrant, a spotted sandpiper, there (this latter with a local birder Martyn Stanyer who read zoology at Catz with me). The best bird there ever was a purple gallinule in 1972, a giant Mediterranean moorhen, which had the good grace to appear for an RSPB group (with me in). Goodness knows what it was doing there – weak flier from southern Europe, maybe an escape, but they are not commonly kept in UK zoos and no-one reported one missing. I have seen them subsequently in the Camargue, and learned that they were kept like chickens in pre-history on some Mediterranean islands, but that brief sighting of a big purple bird in a Cheshire reed bed remains one of my best ever birding experiences. It got into the Guardian country diary! See the scanned image of the cutting I displayed proudly on my bedroom wall for years.

One of my most treasured possessions, probably my MOST treasured possession, is the old card index on which I record dates and locations of noteworthy birds. This is a compilation resulting from long evenings going through my primary field notebooks, just summarising them by interesting species. The point about this is that I can usually associate some holiday, or event, or visit, with an interesting bird, which I can then cross reference on the card index.

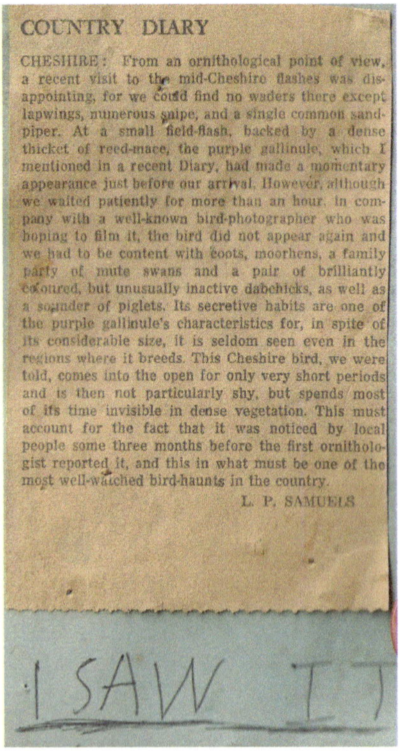

The inspiration behind this was that I was learning to write computer code – BASIC of course – and got into the habit of giving each statement a line number that incremented by 10 each time. Why? So that when you insert more code (as you will) you have space to stick extra lines in without renumbering – this is a GREAT tip for developing code in a language that requires line numbers, and I did the same with groups of birds. Not 32 Waders 33 Warblers but 320 Waders 330 warblers. The Cover card shows why this was a good idea.

My respect for my father has gone up over time as I realise how good he was at navigating – we never got lost either on roads or footpaths. I thought that was normal till I started doing it myself! We did plenty of physically challenging walking, notably in the Pennines. This range has few really steep bare cliffs, unlike Provence for example,

Fig 1.20 The purple gallinule I saw got into the Guardian country diary!

but lots of wet paths going steeply up / down heather-covered moorland. Dad was creditably sensible about checking the weather – we had it drilled into us that mountains kill people and the going out without correct boots and coats was irresponsibly dangerous. Quite true, I don't think we actually did anything genuinely dangerous.

The Pennines were always there in the background in Manchester – on any clear day on a high point, look due east and you see the line of hills glowering over the Cheshire Plain. (This also explains why so many American planes crashed fatally in the Pennines in WW2: the pilots trained in Texas, which is as flat as a pancake and has so few clouds you can see for hundreds of miles. Come to Ringway and you don't realise that the thick cloud obscures a solid line of mountains just inland.)

The apogee of such weekend Pennine walks was going up Kinder Scout, parking near Hayfield (the car park of the famous Kinder mass trespass) and going up across open moorland to the plateau, the highest point in Cheshire. Picnic at Kinder Downfall, the scariest cliff of huge loose boulders in the Pennine chain, with a waterfall that sometimes went up not down due the force of the wind. The rest of the Kinder plateau was a "moonscape" of bare eroded peat for literally miles, horrid to walk on. (Yes, I know there is no organic matter on the moon so the term is inaccurate.) Dad avoided this stuff entirely, and I felt very brave navigating there with a GPS map and compass, on my own, years later. (This was when I found that Kinder Downfall has a smaller mirror on the north face of the plateau, a waterfall running off huge slabs of millstones, with a crashed WW2 plane on the bogland north-west.) The boulders along the edge of the Kinder plateau alone make the visit worthwhile to see the shapes that have been moulded into by the wind, some like mushrooms, others more like Henry Moore's sculptures. Although bleak, there were good birds in summer. As you get into the remote boggy heights you start hearing a sad low whistle – that's a golden plover, they nest here. (In Iceland this bird was the favourite of a farmer we stayed with as its arrival heralded the return of sunlight.) I have a clear memory of a curlew song-flighting on the slopes of Kinder – a curlew's bubbling is the loveliest natural sound I know. In Celtic mythology their song helps the soul leave the body, based on naff-all evidence I am sure. (It seems hard to believe now but curlew nested by Melchett Mere in Tatton Park in the 1970s.)

The other 'standard' Pennine walk we enjoyed started in Lyme Park, the National Trust property that features in 'Pride and Prejudice'. It wasn't till I went round the Mediterranean seeing classical art that I realised that the creators of Lyme Hall were having a good go at recreating a neoclassical atmosphere in the Pennines near Macclesfield – marble sculptures and classical style paintings. Anyway, if instead of 'doing' the hall you walk up through the grounds you cross tall drystone walls and get onto open Pennine moorland. There are circular walks here, eg going past 'Bowstonegate', bleak open moorland but with some old stones there (the Bowstones), admiring the herds of red deer across the moors. Maybe red grouse, and wheatears in summer. Then back down to the formal gardens, the car park, and home for tea.

The park we visited most was Tatton Park, Cheshire. This remains one of my favourite places, due to its complexity as well as beauty. Initially family visits went to the Hall, so regularly I got quite fed up with it, and made a fuss about wanting to visit the wilder parts. This was a bit unfair – the hall had some great features, especially the display of stuffed heads in the Tenants Hall, mainly African big game shot by Lord Edgerton. These included buffalo and (amazingly) rhinoceros – at least two rhino heads whose horns are (at time of writing) worth their weight in gold. Also, some flint tools found in the main lake, Tatton Mere. In the gardens was / is a rather mossy approximation to an African hut, because Lord Edgerton loved being in Kenya (forced home to Cheshire by WW2). The same Lord features as a walk-in part on the film 'White Mischief' as 'Edgerton', who died of a fever. I don't think anything in that part of the story is historically accurate beyond him being there. (There is a plausible story that he fathered a son in Kenya – needs DNA testing but I don't think he'd get the house back whatever happens.) We went on family holiday to Kenya and – on the long tortuous drive from the Masai Mara to the coast – we went past a sign for the Edgerton Agricultural College, which I assume was a direct legacy of the Lord's interest in Kenya.

Once I became a bit more independent I really enjoyed exploring the wilder parts of Tatton Park on my own, primarily for birdwatching. The main lake is long and thin, c. 2k, by 100m wide, running north-south. The southern end is surrounded by trackless swampy woodland, leading into a wide reed bed ('Knutsford Moor'). This was my haunt – there were trees you could climb to see the lake, and get good views of the ducks that thought they were invisible. I started exploring here in 1977, which happened to coincide with the arrival of large numbers of the American Ruddy Duck, an escape from collections. The (handsome, red and black) males display by blowing bubbles from sacs in the chest, and I have happy memories of counting displaying ruddy ducks here each weekend. There was a clear dynamic, with quite a big flock (>30 birds) turning up. I even got this mentioned in the Cheshire bird report – fame! The hand-drawn graphs below show just how often I went there. As an aside you won't find ruddy ducks there any more as RSPB policy is to exterminate them, to

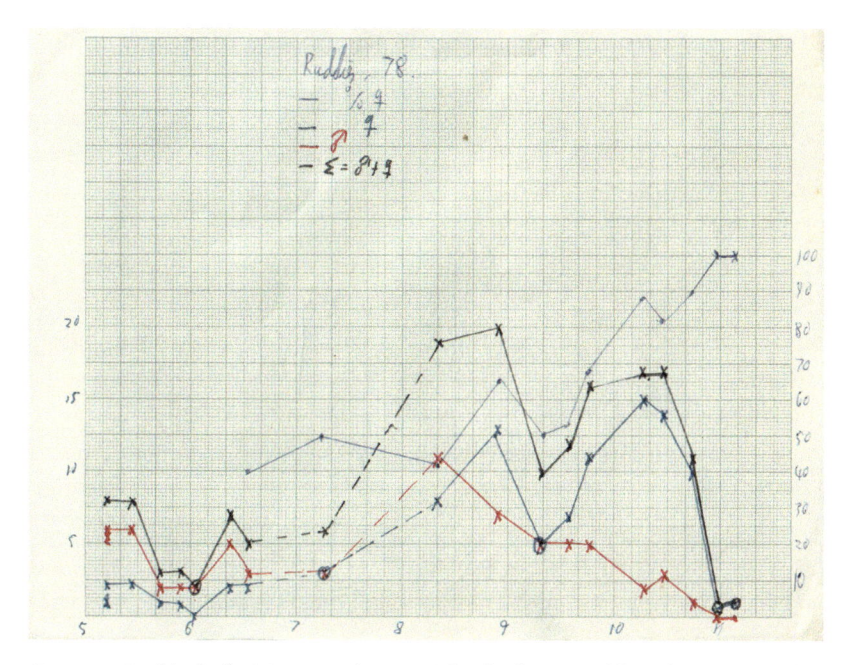

Fig 1.21 Ruddy ducks, Tatton Park 1978. They built up steadily in late summer then all vanished in late October.

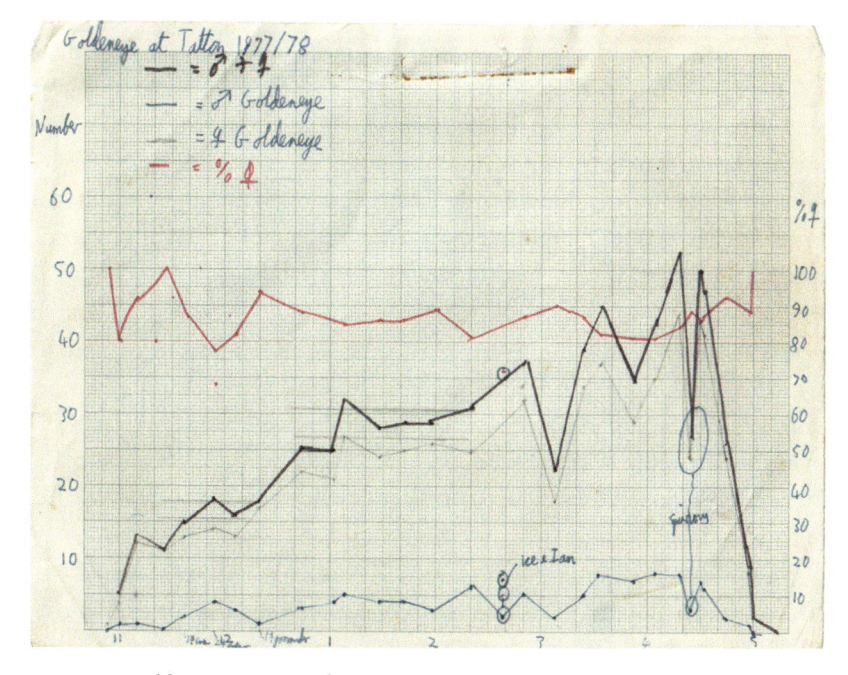

Fig 1.22 Goldeneye Tatton Park 1977/78.

avoid genetic pollution of Spanish white headed duck. I think that's taking purity too far!

The other iconic bird of this swamp wood was the ever-elusive lesser spotted woodpecker. Also reed buntings and reed warblers singing in the reedbed in summer. I did manage to cross the reedbed in summer, though with hindsight I was lucky not to fall through.

After learning to use mask and snorkel in the Mediterranean in the 1970s, I used them in Tatton Lake. There was a 'formal' swimming area on its eastern bank, shallow with low sandy cliffs. I found quite a few flint flakes here and still have them – the lake was/is a recognised site for Mesolithic flints, so I expect that the lake has been there for millennia. Offshore the water suddenly falls away to murky depths about 10m offshore (I saw it), and I am not at all surprised that the authorities banned swimming there. Quite apart from the risk from boats there were banks of weed. A boy drowned in Melchett Mere due to weed entanglement, and it seems only a matter of luck that no-one (AFAIK) died in Tatton Mere. Anyway, we had happy summer days there, and once I swam all the way across the lake from the swimming area.

The main bird interest of Tatton came in winter, when the main lake supported flocks of diving ducks – goldeneye, plus (with luck) female smew. A totally typical winter visit here resulted in a notebook recording male and female goldeneye, plus a 'red head' (female smew). Never a male, until 1979 when one stayed half the summer at Rostherne Mere when I worked there; pity they never bred. Always dozens of great crested grebes, usually a dabchick. Also rarities – a red necked grebe, a great northern diver, and once a flock of black terns on autumn passage. Sand martins in summer, always lots of Canada geese and common ducks.

After Tatton (#1) and Lyme (#2), there were two more parks that we used regularly: Dunham Park (Dunham Massey) and Wythenshawe Park, almost next door. Dunham Park was a short drive, just the other side of Altringham, and for years simply meant a walk in the deer park, followed by a walk out to the canal and a towpath walk back to the car. It wasn't till years later that they opened the formal gardens behind the house, which I have to say are lovely and became a favourite outing with Mum when she was elderly and Dad had died. This park gave us amazing close contacts with fallow deer, also memories of giant *Cardiocrinum* lilies, hobbies flying overhead and a lovely winter garden.

Wythenshawe Park was inevitably a local favourite. For a start we could walk there – indeed push a pram there, which happened every weekend for years, usually pushed by our paternal grandmother 'Little Nan' Flora Shaw, née Wiseman. There was less formal hall than the National Trust properties, but lots of open grassland with copses, plus some nice formal gardens round the house. The tea room even had a couple of stuffed animals heads, though nothing like Tatton Hall. For years I thought it as utterly boring, till I explored it on my own. This meant climbing fences to trespass into every wood and copse on site – at the closest end of the park was / is a big area of fenced-out, overgrown, wet woodland ('Nanook Wood'). It contains a huge steep bank – I think this was an old course of the Mersey. Trackless and clearly unused. I spent ages in there, ticking lesser spotted woodpecker and siskins, plus one memorable May day a male pied flycatcher (a rare migrant, scarce and confined to hanging oakwoods in Wales), perhaps off-target and on passage to some Welsh hills. Last time I checked, this area is now open to the public, with paths, benches and a statue of a frog. (Indeed I first heard a frog croak in this bit of wood, on the amazingly late date of 26 March 1978. In Surrey nowadays they're tadpoles by then.) There is one boggy bit between the football pitch changing rooms and the parkside road where, after a few Psilocybe mushrooms, I saw a woodcock in October 1978. In 2012, while trying to sort out 39FD for sale, I revisited the park and disturbed another woodcock in exactly the same spot as 1978 (same state of mind too). With hindsight, poking around in uninhabited bits of Wythenshawe might have been risky, but the really nasty individuals seem to have little interest in birdwatching, and when you're trespassing you instinctively avoid all vestiges of human contact – I never actually met anyone in there. The park also had greenhouses, not public until later, but when I came home from university (eg Xmas 1981) and really needed to escape the house, the mini botanic garden effect of these greenhouses was a wonderfully welcome relief (even a cactus collection – wonderful). By Princess Parkway is Gib Lane Wood – again full of deep ponds, I think a Mersey food plain legacy (hence 'Wythenshawe = willow woodland'). Also creepy, despite being so infested with traffic noise. There was a gibbet here long ago, and I got a strange spinal tingle there when I went one evening tripping on *Psilocybe* mushrooms.

One other local walk deserves mention – Brooks Drive. Mr Brooks was a rich Victorian Manchester banker who had a drive created from his house in Hale Barns to what is now Brooklands station. (He came from a small village called Whalley, and when he had an estate built in Manchester called it Whalley Range – still there.) Brooks Drive was planted along its length with pine, lime and copper beech – again still there. This passes close to Wythenshawe, and we had a standard short weekend walk up Brooks Drive to a copse called Fairydell Wood. I think this was a wild garden, eg it has clumps of the garden plant pale bridalwort *Spirea alba*, and *Rhododendron ponticum*, but never found out its history. It went downhill once surrounded by new-build houses about 1990. Before these houses, the fields around Fairydell Wood were market gardens, and one day we saw a hare running away there. Not a common animal now. There were also lapwings nesting in quiet, wet patches across the A560 from our house – hardly any nest in Surrey now.

One other favourite haunt of mine needed a bicycle to get there, and with hindsight was a bit of a distance with some risky bits – one furious/terrifying pedal needed going under the M60 motorway junction, for example. Having crossed under the M60 and then over the river Mersey at the Jacksons bridge, you get to Mersey flood plain that has been pretty much let go. Close to a big, deep artificial lake that is Sale Water Park, the northern bank of the Mersey was once a sewage farm but is long abandoned, with vast open areas of coarse grassland. Chorlton Meadows is the name for this area (or Chorlton Ees, an older name), and I heard of it via Manchester ornithologists as a site for short eared owls. That was right: one year in four there were several owls quartering over this riverside grass like huge brown moths. Still one of my favourite birds. I collected their pellets to ID the bones using a key by Derek Yalden at Manchester University, finding huge numbers of field voles whose molars didn't so much have roots as they *were* the roots. Mice had molars with clear roots, field voles *Microtus agrestis* (but not bank voles *Clethrionomys glareolus*) had a zig-zag block that was the same shape all the way down. A few shrew skulls turned up as well. On at least one occasion, Mother found her bathroom sink blocked with fur and tiny bones after I'd been dissecting short eared owl pellets from Chorlton Meadows.

Chorlton Meadows was a really good birdwatching site. It seemed to attract every migrant passerine in the area – never before or since have I been able to count multiple whinchats reliably, but the Mersey valley between Sale and Manchester seemed to funnel them, so I often counted three-four whinchats, along with yellow wagtails, and common sandpipers on some ponds there. Plus really big flocks of finches, tens of thousands, mainly linnets. Short eared owls like giant moths on winter evenings. The best bird there was probably the grasshopper warbler, which sang reliably in summer, and I did get a decent view of one I disturbed in the bushes of the old sewage works. Further east along the Mersey was a great big hole in the ground, used as a landfill site. Remarkably, little ringed plover nested there each year. As one joined Chorlton Meadow there was an area I remember from 1977 to be full of baby shrubs – whips. This is where the whinchats were in August-September and the stonechats were in October-November. I came back around 2012, when Dad was dead and Mum headed for sheltered accommodation, and had a look round some old haunts. Most had not changed much, but Chorlton Meadows had scrubbed up a lot. The hectares of tiny, thin whips had become scrub woodland, maybe 5m tall just like they were expected to. Next to this, a cow-grazed pasture had clumps of *Psilocybe semilanceata* in exactly the same spot as 1977, showing this species to have stable long-lived mycelium (unlike most Psilocybes).

With hindsight, observations from Chorlton Meadows became my introduction to modelling. I recorded chats each visit in summer 1977 and tried to fit a gaussian curve. I knew there wasn't an exact fit for this function but played with some manual iterative algorithms, and predicted that the count should peak at four birds one day in August. I went that day, and only got two whinchats – disappointing. Then, before giving up and going home I went east to tick the little ringed plovers – and found two more whinchat on the fence line by the river, just like the model had predicted. With hindsight this was more luck than validation, but did give me a lingering respect for abstruse mathematical outputs.

There is one set of tangible legacies from our family walks in Derbyshire, which are specimens of the semi-precious mineral Blue John from the Winnats Pass. When I was young, we parked Dad's old Austin at one end of the Winnats pass, went as deep into an open cave as we dared, then I would find bits of Blue John lying around which I'd take home, knowing that this mineral is found nowhere else on the planet. (BTW You are flatly blocked from doing anything of the sort nowadays.) Blue John was unknown until about 1750, became very popular in regency times, then went out of fashion in Victorian times and is now hardly worked, mined or sold at all. See https://www.regencyhistory.net/2014/11/blue-john-britains-georgian-gemstone.html.

Of course, if you chuck money at the internet you'll find Blue John – much easier than Rhynie chert – but even so the stones are worth keeping safe or passing on to someone who knows what they are.

It is IMHO iconically beautiful, with characteristic blue banding in a clear crystal mount. To be pedantically geological, it involves oil deposits seeping into fluorspar (calcium fluoride), and indeed nearby at a site called Windy Knoll is the only place I know where you can find crude oil welling up from the rocks – I had some for a while but it looks like dog poo and smells like bitumen. Anyway, the Winnat Pass / Mam Tor area has both fluorspar and oil, and where they meet creates the mineral Blue John. There is a mine open to tourists called the Blue John mine. One of the most famous icons of (nearby) Chatsworth House is a vase carved from Blue John. To be honest, Blue John isn't much of a gem because calcium fluoride just isn't hard enough – soft, brittle and prone to crumbling, so carving a vase in it deserves immense respect. (They soaked it in resin first – a trade secret.) I found that it was much easier to polish by hand

Fig 1.23 The Winnats pass in Derbyshire, and two hand-polished samples of Blue John I collected there. The right-hand stone looks like a geode but is not, at all. IT IS MUCH MORE SPECIAL THAN A GEODE, IRREPLACEABLE, PLEASE KEEP SAFE OR GIVE TO A MUSEUM.

than the Rhynie cherts (see Whitelands) but as a corollary does not take such a good final gloss. I seem to recall failing to tumble-polish Blue John stones – they shatter immediately.

The pile of bits of Blue John that I accumulated from family walks in the 1970s got kept in a box in my bedroom, then moved to my loft, then ended up in my 'stone bed' – the gravel bed by the pond in 4LW. At one stage I reckoned there was more Blue John lying around in my garden in Dorking than on surface in the Winnats pass! This didn't last. One of the odd effects of the Covid-19 lockdown in 2020 was that I re-found my Blue John and polished the raw pebbles by hand. I dug over that stone bed, and found a few gorgeously banded pieces (one of which I clumsily dropped on a paving slab, making it two pieces). Like the Valley of the Kings, that stone bed has been well dug over for buried treasure! Now all my polished Blue John is (AFAIK) safe, with the sharks' teeth from Malta and the mammoth tooth from Speeton, in the box of fossil treasures in the conservatory.

John Shaw died 3 August 2004, of an abdominal cancer. His ashes are scattered by Brooklawn church (where Mother attended, and ultimately where her ashes were scattered in 2014). John Shaw has no tombstone, but we sponsored two signposts by the Footpath Preservation Society, so John's name can be appreciated by fellow northern walkers for decades to come. These signposts are at SJ74971 85270 (approach from Ryecroft farm to SE) and SK15902 54506 (the Tissington trail in Derbyshire). At that point 39FD lost its guiding light, since all the arrangements, fittings etc in the house were Dad's doing, all the filing systems set up by him. The wiring in the loft was his work before I was born! Elizabeth Shaw died 25 February 2014 – nearly a decade later, but these were uneventful wind-down years. After my father died, my policy was to visit 39FD as much as feasible (given I had a family life and a busy job, plus Manchester was four hours' drive away) and each time spend an hour in the loft emptying out junk. The trouble was that both my parents were WW2 children who knew the meaning of resource shortage. It was unforgivable to waste food or valuable resources in WW2, they grew up under rationing and even got married under rationing, so anything that might come in handy was kept safe, usually ending up in the loft.

To be fair to my dad, when he sold his mother's house 'Lochnagar' in Brooklawn Drive, Withington, he spent hours in his dad's loft, emerging covered in dust with piles of utter junk. He expressed exasperation and amazement that his father, an intelligent engineer, had kept in his loft a sandbag – still full of sand. "I won't have you saying about me what I've said about my dad," he announced, as he vanished into his own loft in 39FD to remove junk. All I can say is that this laudable exercise ran out of steam far too soon, and when Dad died the sheer amount of stuff left was astonishing. The trouble was that 1940s WW2 stockpiling had met 1960 material culture. The complete set of back issues of several railway magazines was fine – people take them. Financial records for an Italian servant they had in the 1950s were fine – straight into the bin. The problem was when things needed looking at and thinking about, or when bits of my childhood resurfaced that I never expected to see again and have no need to keep. A book of animal pictures for before I could read. My 'Bilofix' set, a sort of woody "Meccano". Some remarkable finds like the certificate showing that my grandfather Alexander was the head of the masonic lodge in Aberdeen, a position he had to relinquish on moving to Manchester (showing what a big decision that move must have been). A pair of gardening gloves carefully filed with an A4 sheet of instructions on how to use them. As I said, for several years each visit up north meant an hour in the loft getting junk out. Then around 2012 Mother had a stroke and developed cancer so had to go into a home, so the pressure was on us to empty 39FD for a quick sale. So, I hired the biggest van I could in Dorking, and drove it up to 39FD to empty the loft. I filled this van with utter junk, and took it to the local tip. To find that the van was too tall to enter the standard entrance

Fig 1.24 Loft junk in 39FD garage.

Fig 1.25 The Osteospermum *clone from the garden of 39FD, flowering outside our neighbour's house in April 2020.*

at the tip and had to go round the side with the huge tipper lorries. Then back to 39FD and filled the van AGAIN, back to the tip. Then back to 39FD to fill the van with stuff worth keeping in Dorking (including a middle-aged witch hazel bush that did not survive the transplant but nearly gave me a ricked back from the weight). Was that the end of the junk in the loft? As mother would have put it: "Was it tittle!" I had several more runs to the tip after this, but there was no doubt that the huge van helped break the back of the problem. My final estimate was that in addition to filling the hire van three times, I filled my hatchback car 30 times for runs to the local tip, and that was just emptying Dad's loft. (This latter allocation is more factual than sexist – mother almost never went in the loft. In July 2004, not long before Dad died of cancer, I saw him having to get the loft ladder down for Mother because she could not master using it.)

I didn't have a clean 'leaving home' date for my fledging from 39FD, though to a first approximation this could be argued as 15 October 1979 when I started at Oxford. I had to come home between terms until York in 1982, but really I left 39FD as my home in September 1982 by starting my PhD in York. It has to be said that this 'flying the nest' did not come a moment too soon for either of us – the atmosphere in 39FD was too regimented and WW2 for my liking, and with hindsight my father and I were both strong characters who handled almost everything in life very differently.

39FD was sold in 2015, and the new owners must have spent a great deal of money gutting and transforming it. They even added a fancy bit of ornamental ironwork in the garden – good luck on that staying in place! Last I heard the

Bramley apple tree was still there, but not much else remained familiar looking. I really tried to save the witch-hazel I had planted in front to the lounge window in 1986, nearly rupturing myself to get its stump into the hire van in winter 2014 to move it to a new home in Dorking. Anyone who knows witch-hazels will not be surprised to hear it died of transplant shock (in 2019) but it had a sporting chance, while the flower bed it was in became a car park shortly after the house sale. As someone ruefully observed to me as I bemoaned the changes in my back garden in 4BMC after its sale, "A garden never outlasts its owner".

The only remaining direct clonal connection with the 39FD garden that I know of is a clone of the purple-flowered livingstone daisy *Osteospermum*, I think it may be *Osteospermum* 'Summersmile Magenta' which really brightens up our garden in Dorking all summer but especially in April and May. This cutting came from the garden of 39FD so is guaranteed frost-hardy, while being a South African xerophyte means that it is also very drought tolerant. It easily gets killed by being shaded out, and was down to one clump at one stage, but multiplies up well in bare, sunny spots and should easily outlast me. I am trying to plant it everywhere that will take it for being very pretty, very tough and very weed-suppressing. Yes, a specimen of this plant died of drought in the front garden in 867LB one summer, but at the same time so did specimens of *Haworthia, Gasteria,* and even *Mammillaria* cacti!

CHAPTER 2

M is for MGS

Manchester Grammar School for Boys, 1972-1979

My secondary education was undertaken at The Manchester Grammar School for boys, which was founded in 1515 by a benefactor called Hugh Oldham. This makes it one of the longest-standing continuously functioning educational institutions in the country (if not the planet), 500 years old in 2015, a history of which they are justifiably proud. Its motto is 'Sapere aude' (dare to be wise), and its logo is an owl. All the main fenceposts on the sturdy barrier around the school have this owl, as does its coat of arms.

A couple of asides deserve mention here. Firstly, the owl itself is originally a joke, since in the 14th century the name 'Oldham' was apparently pronounced "Owldham", which is why Hugh Oldham chose an owl as his logo. Similarly,

Fig 2.1 An MGS owl on a fencepost along Old Hall Lane. I walked past many dozens of these each school day.

Fig 2.2 The MGS coat of arms showing Hugh Oldham's owl.

the SI unit of energy (the Joule) probably ought to be pronounced "Jowel" not "jewel" since the Manchester engineer after which it is named would have been called this. Secondly, as an ornithological nerd, I always wondered which owl species it referred to. I am fairly sure that most people connected to the school would point to Minerva's owl, since Minerva (Athene) was the Greek Goddess of wisdom and the school motto is 'dare to be wise'. The owl even got her name – the little owl's scientific name is *Athene noctua*, and little owls were to be seen in the Pennines around Manchester – I had an excellent view of one above Hollingworth Lake outside Oldham in 1974. This tempting logic crumbles on closer examination, starting with the detail that *Athene noctua* lacks ear tufts. More seriously, it was only introduced from France in the 1930s as a pest control agent and used to be known in the countryside as 'the Frenchman'. Professor Ian Rotherham of Sheffield Hallam University remembers when he was a boy in Sheffield the older gamekeepers still referred to Little Owls as "Frenchmen". So there is no way that Hugh Oldham would have been exposed to this species, and I think he was probably referring to the tawny owl (common but no ear tufts) or the long eared owl, a scarce native species of dense woodland, that I did once encounter on Chorlton Meadows in winter 1976. When clearing out my father's stuff in 2005, a cassette tape surfaced that had been made by MGS boys about MGS, years after I left. One of the school's strong features always was encouraging boys to produce media. This tape was by people I could not have met, and the staff they mentioned would mainly be new after I left, so most references passed me by. Two references did make sense to me, and the first was a poke at this 16th century Oldham/owl joke.

Secondly, the motto itself 'Dare to be wise' seems to me to be an oxymoron, even though my father venerated it and saw it as a profound statement of values. In my (perhaps too extensive) experience of taking risky decisions, wisdom and daring are antithetical, at opposite ends of the continuum. For each separate foreseeable outcome (Outcome i) you estimate a probability p_i and an evaluation of its value v_i then calculate over all outcomes calculate sum $(p_i * v_i)$. This is called an expectance, and (for example) shows that when you buy a National Lottery Ticket for 100p you expect to win 42p. It's like flushing money down the toilet, and if you expect to win a lot of money you are deluding yourself and wasting your cash. To be daring you ignore this rationality and go for the high payoffs in the hope they come up – while if you are wise, you do the opposite – calculate expectances and use them as your guides. I think that my father's interpretation of the motto translated roughly as "If petty officialdom mess you around, look them in the eye and tell them politely to get stuffed". He certainly made a habit of this, but whether it counts as "wise" is open to debate since they will inevitably exact revenge. Your best hope is that they over-reach themselves and destroy their own position, like playing a gambit in chess (exactly as happened when the British Oxygen Company under-estimated John Robert Shaw. They double billed him, he faced them down, and won).

There is no doubt that my gaining a place at the Manchester Grammar School for boys was a profoundly significant step, and one that my family very much approved of. My father John Robert Shaw went to MGS during the Second World War, having earned a scholarship (his parents could not have paid), and remained a lifelong supporter of the school and its selective grammar school model. There is also no doubt that the Manchester comprehensive schools were abysmal. The place next door to us, Brookway Comprehensive, was as far as anyone could tell an exercise in crowd control, at the mercy of the most aggressive families on the Wythenshawe estate. My sister Caroline would get off at the wrong bus stop and walk an extra kilometre home to dodge having to walk past the crowd of kids from Brookway school. I know that we can point at the Ashcombe in Dorking (where our children went) as a comprehensive that turned out good pupils with good results, but they mainly came from good family backgrounds. I am not aware of anyone from Brookway school who got decent A levels who went to university (though did hear rumours of one example, a boy who was reputed to hate the place). One of my maths teachers at MGS, Mr Kiltie, took a "promotion" to become head of maths at Brookway. He lasted just one term, reputedly leaving with a nervous breakdown. The famous TV physicist, Professor Brian Cox, went to a similar school to Brookway in north Manchester and got an E at A level physics. I got an A1. Am I better at physics than Professor Cox? No, of course not, but his mark acts a damning indictment of the comprehensive system under the 1970s Labour administration in Manchester. I am sure that a lot of people owe a lot of apologies and explanations for the awful state of public education in Manchester at the time – but am equally sure that they are dead and would anyway have denied all blame.

The people I blame least for the shambles are the teachers, despite them being the usual targets for blame. Left wing idealistic politicians and don't-give-a-damn parents would top my list, but we can never know. I gathered via my mother (who was a teacher and chatted to lots of other teachers) that the Manchester Education Authority forbade comprehensives from any form of academic streaming or selection, because this way you always had a wide mix of abilities in each class. The theory was that the brighter students would assist the weaker ones, sharing their talent and improving their understanding in the process that was later foisted on me by educational theorists as 'group work'. (I did all I could to ignore such daft ideas – that is for the chapter on 'Southlands College'.) It is true that from the axiom of 'Equal Opportunity for All' and the viewpoint of a deontological ethical system (where decisions are assessed based on what goes into them) the pure-equality comprehensive model had a lot to commend it. Many families on the Wythenshawe estate appeared to have low family baselines, and this way their offspring were not selectively disadvantaged like they would have been under a meritocratic system. From the viewpoint of a teleological (=utilitarian) ethical system that evaluates decisions based on their outputs, the system was a catastrophic failure, an embarrassing shambles that must have blighted tens of thousands of lives. In practice the bright students did not help the 'chavs' to advance their academic understanding. Instead, the bright students were harassed by the others physically and verbally to the point that anyone showing signs of interest in a book or obeying a teacher was a social outcast in real physical danger. The education authority rarely supported expulsions. In the face of unacceptable antisocial behaviour that clearly deserved expulsion, education administrators were prone to asking "so if expelled, where will they go? They deserve an education as much as anyone else". (Indeed I have no idea where the airgun-wielding louts of the Wythenshawe estate should have been educated and am very glad I never had responsibility for coming up with good ideas on the subject.) My parents knew all this horribly well, so my sister and I went to private schools (which had the great virtue of being able to expel undesirables at will).

So in late 1971 I had to sit entrance exams for MGS, plus Cheadle Hulme and at least one other selective grammar school. Not one exam, two, both at MGS and Cheadle, an initial straightforward test to filter out the easy failures then a much harder paper to make you sweat. Things like simultaneous equations, that you can't easily crack by guessing values:

$X + Y = 20$, and $2X + 5Y = 64$ – solve X and Y.
(ans: $2X + 2Y = 40$, $3Y = 24$, hence $X = 12$, $Y = 8$)

Anyway, I got accepted at all three places, and went to MGS (at great parental expense). Given that it shaped my interest in science and got me a scholarship to Oxford to read zoology I should be grateful for the experience, and had I gone to Brookway things would certainly have been so much worse. Nonetheless, I hated the place. A persnickety school uniform, four bus rides per day (with an indeterminate wait at a bus stop under the A560 flyover) and two hours' daily homework was bad enough, but I really had problems with the all-male social hierarchies that the place was riven with. Everyone's default position is that you (whoever you are) are below them in the pecking order and this needs to be displayed publicly. In the Docu-drama 'The Crown' about our monarchy, the young Charles Windsor had to go to school at Gordonstoun because his father did, and hated the whole experience. MGS was not boarding, but I felt a strong frisson of recognition. It should be said that there was no actual physical violence, unlike in the comprehensives (you could easily be expelled from MGS, unlike Brookway, and several misbehaving boys just vanished). Once someone said to me "you'd be beaten to a pulp for that in a state school". Objectively we were really quite good in both senses of the word (well behaved and academically bright). Maybe 12-13 year old boys are just incorrigible, but I had a hard time for the first two years, then when big exams started to loom I got on fine. Not so well at first in maths in Y1, which I attribute to an especially useless teacher Mr 'Tweedy' Harris.

One feature of MGS that we all accepted, but which looks slightly anomalous with hindsight, was the system of 'Prefects'. The more reliable six formers were rewarded with a special silver owl badge, called a "prefect", and got used as low-level enforcers of school rules. Most of the time this was trivial, though prefects got to spend the weekend away when "their" class of Y1 or Y2 students went to the school camp in Edale. Two things about the prefect system rather miffed me. Firstly they had their own common room with their own kettle and sound system, and I never got trusted enough to be made a prefect so had no business nipping in there for a cup of tea. Secondly, prefects were used to enforce attendance at Christian assembly each morning, touring the school grounds each morning for atheist assembly-dodgers (like me) hiding in the bushes. The more I think about this policy, the less I like it.

MGS had two very positive features – the out-of-school activities, and the biology block. The school ran treks and camps for the boys, and even had its own hut near Disley (The Owls Nest) where each class spent a weekend. My most memorable experiences were on Scottish and foreign treks. The former we walked through the Lairig Ghru – I saw snow buntings nesting in the scree slopes on Braeriach, above the Lairig Ghru. Foreign trek took me to the Pyrenees. I never really forgave my parents for turning up in our campsite in the Pyrenees (Gavarnie), to check how I was doing. Despite this trauma, the Pyrenees were amazing – we got up Vignemale, almost got up Mt Perdido, saw the Brèche de Roland (pretty), saw my only Egyptian vulture, looked down on griffon vultures circling below us (I love that experience – repeated in the Gorges du Verdon in August 2018), and camped on a glacier (coldest night of my life).

I took biology A level so was in the form based in the Biology Block, which happened to be a repurposed old vicarage in the woodland at the back of the school, inside our formidable boundary fence but by a handy back exit, ideal both for the legitimate short-cut in from the #41 bus stop around 0830 and for sneaking out early hidden by the dense bushes. This was a rambling old building with surprises everywhere, notably the cellar that had dolphins' skulls in recesses in the wall. (David Taylor in his Zoo Vet series of books mentioned being a boy at MGS and seeing dolphin skulls in recesses in the cellar wall.) The big lab benches in our classroom were ideal for pingpong, and generally the atmosphere in my 6th form was better than the O level streams. We rigged up a sound system to play rock music (Genesis and Pink Floyd). One of the rooms, locked when not in use, had been made up into a plant growth chamber, complete with false walls and banks of strip lights dangling from Dexion scaffolds. The false wall was just thin panels screwed on to the same Dexion scaffolding, leaving a gap 30-40cm wide between it and the outer wall of the building, even with a small hatch to allow access behind the panels. This was a wonderful opportunity to vanish. We used some practical work on seed germination to get us a spare key for the growth chamber room, which of course we took home overnight and got cut on the way home. So we gave the key back next morning apologetically, then skived assembly by hiding behind the panel in the growth room which we could now unlock. Once a technician came in to water the plants, but he never had any cause to look under/behind the false wall. And once a prefect touring the site looking for assembly-dodgers (like me) saw my face at the window, and must have spent a while poking around in the rectory. Without the key he could never get into our hideaway, and even with it he'd have to know where to look. With hindsight if he had managed to persuade a technician that he really saw a face at the window it could have all gone wrong, but happily that little ruse never got found out.

There is no doubt that I enjoyed the biology block and A level years far more than the rest of that school. I was quite getting into understanding mathematics at that stage thanks to work, good teachers and a very visual brain. One nerdy achievement I was quite pleased about concerned the counter on cassette players. This was an analogue index of how far through a tape you have gone, based on the number of revolutions of the HIND wheel. This wheel turns faster when its radius is smaller (because the tape is pulled past the reader head at a constant speed, so as the radius shrinks the smaller circle is forced to rotate faster to keep up). The effect of this is that the tape counter is non-linear with distance along the tape. I managed to relate the counter to the tape time, with an equation that had a term for tape thickness. It involved seeing the tape spool at different stages

A Path of 21 Ms

of tape winding as perfect circles, whose difference in area could be divided by thickness to estimate length. Remarkably, not only did the equation work, but with it I could use the counter to estimate the relative thicknesses of different makes of cassette tapes. With hindsight, solving the maths was not that hard, having seen the invariants (1: tape length = running time, 2: counter = radial thickness of the tape spool). The solution is now to get the difference in area between two circular spools of tape, then divided this area by the tape thickness to gets its length, hence using the tape speed of 4.76 cm/s to get its playing time. Applying it to get sensible real-world answers showed real promise. Note that the thickness of the C60 tapes (30 minutes per side) was nearly 50% greater than the C90s (45 minutes per side), and indeed it was mainly the C90s that snapped because they were indeed thinner. All units were cm, so the C90 tapes were c. 12-13 microns thick. Always be clear about units Shaw!

One strange snippet I picked up at MGS was in an informal school mathematical magazine called mathematical pie, that the maths teacher suggested we splash out c. 6 old pence for this little yellow booklet, full of mathematical stories and pictures. Most came and went un-noticed, but one contained the algorithm for getting the day of the week from (almost) any date by a simple mathematical calculation. I learned it, understood it, developed it, and took it with me as part of my mental toolkit for life. Thanks, Mr Jones, for selling me that copy back in 1974!

The calculations all run on the basis of dividing by seven and only paying attention to the remainder. This is called "modulus base 7". An example might

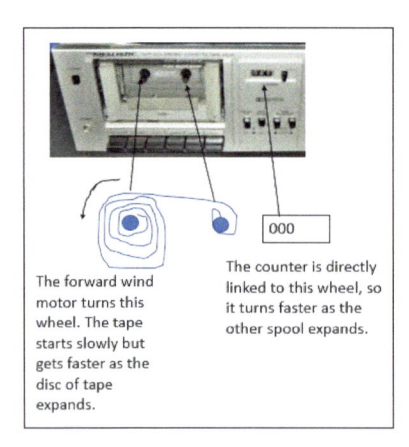

Fig 2.3 Explaining the tape counter problem.

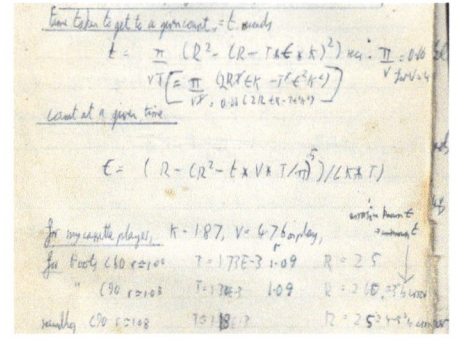

Fig 2.4 And the solution – my tape counter equation.

58

be showing that $\mod_7$ of 8 is the same as $\mod_7$ of 15 = $\mod_7$ of 50 = 1, because always the division leaves a remainder of one. In this case, this would show that in any year, the day of the week is the same 8 days after the start of the year as 15 days after the start is the same as 50 days after the start.

Now you need to memorise this look-up table, which are the 12 "remainders" for the 12 months of the year.

$$033614625035 = \text{Jan}0 \ \text{Feb}3 \ \text{Mar}3 \ \text{Apr}6 \ \text{May}1 \ \text{June }4 \ \text{July}6 \ \text{Aug}2 \ \text{Sep}5 \ \text{Oct}0 \ \text{Nov}3 \ \text{Dec}5$$

Just learn the sequence. It is in fact the modulus base 7 of the number of days in the year at the start of this month.

Just one more hurdle, which is the "year remainder". This is the "fudge factor" for the year in question. So this year – 2023 – is a convenient example, but you should work out for yourself the "year remainder" for the year you are in now. The "year remainder" for 2023 happens to be 6, so for 5 October 2023 (today, so I am sure of the answer!) the calculation is formally

Day = $\mod_7$ (day+month remainder+year remainder),
giving an answer from 0-6.

And the days of the week are as follows:

0 Sunday 1 Monday 2 Tuesday 3 Wednesday 4 Thursay 5 Friday 6 Saturday

Here for 5th October 2023 the calculation = $\mod_7$ (5 [for the day] + 0 [the remainder for October] + 6 [for the year])

= $\mod_7$ (11) = 4 (since 11/7 is 1 with a remainder of 4) = Thursday. You can show that 1st January this year was a Sunday (1 + 0 + 6) = 7 = remainder of zero,
And finally, Christmas this year will be 25+5+6 = 36, and $\mod_7$(36) = 1 = Monday.

For most day-day life I recommend staying with this simple version – just remember what the year remainder is, and you can see the calendar all year! Things get more tricky when you go into arbitrary years, because the "year remainders" are not obvious and get messed up by leap years. The insight I got after hours of playing with these modular calculations set out in "Mathematical pi" was that the easiest shortcut is to learn as look-up tables those convenient years where the year remainder is zero. Now January 1st is a Monday and December 25th is a Tuesday (mod(7)(25+5)=2). These "zero years" are useful anchors and you can navigate your way into an arbitrary year by sequential counting. The anchor point for me was 1979 – that was a zero year. 3 May 1979 was therefore a Thursday (3+1+0 = 4 = Thursday), which was the day Margaret Thatcher got elected and a big fearsome hawk (marsh harrier) appeared at Rostherne to harass our ducks. Symbolic I thought.

This century, 2001 was a "zero year", then 2007, and the last ten months of 2012 (2012b as I think of it), 2018, and 2024a. All the others you can interpolate by 1 each year (because mod(7) of 365 = 1 because 365 = 7*52+1). Thanks, Mr Jones, for a life-changing mental spark!

After two intensive years studying for A levels, autumn 1978 was all about applying for Oxford. The classes were noticeably more advanced, and in university lectures I sometimes realise that I am passing the same tips on to my students that I was given then. A good example is "When writing an essay about an ecosystem, always be able to name one or two iconic species and give their correct scientific names". They did something right, as I sat the Oxford entrance exam in 1978 (harder than A levels), got interviewed by Henry Bennet-Clark and Barrie Juniper, and was offered a scholarship to read Zoology. To be honest, after six years of MGS and 18 years of life in 39FD, going to Oxford looked like the beginnings of the sunlit uplands of Having My Own Life – even now I'd put this down as the single most important transition in my life.

There are a couple of names of boys from MGS that deserve mention. Ian Cropley was easily my closest friend, a lovely chap and keen birdwatcher. It is thanks to Ian that I saw buff-breasted sandpiper on the airfield in the Isles of Scilly (a species of the North American prairie), Pectoral sandpiper at Cley-next-the-sea, Norfolk (another north American peep), and a merlin on Chat Moss one winter's day. A great grey shrike at Pennington Flash and a red necked grebe at Tatton. He got a scholarship to Cambridge to read medicine, became the UK's top expert on Ebola virus, and was the man who told Boris Johnson in January 2020 that Covid-19 was a real danger that should be taken seriously. As Ian later ruefully commented "So that went well then". Ian's voice was on TV in a series about Covid wards, heard saying "The old people up here are just dying". I went to Ian's wedding and he visited me in hospital after my tumour operation in September 2019. He later told me that his experience of dealing with UK Ebola cases was good preparation for being in a London hospital during the exponential phase of the Covid-19 outbreak in 2020.

There was another bird watcher, Nick Oakins, whose family lived next to the dam of the reservoir in Whalley Bridge (which nearly collapsed in 2019). Nick's brother Bill Oakins was a potter and we still have some of his handmade cups.

I spent two years in the same form (1B and 2B) as Dominic Carman, the son of George Carman. (Both have Wikipedia pages.) George Carman was a famous barrister, noted equally for his success rate and his unpleasant personality. George Carman seems to be one of those people like King John of the 12th century about whom all evidence from all contemporary sources all portray him as a real stinker. In George's obituary, colleagues of 20 years trying to say something nice described him as "one of the most difficult people in the legal profession". It seems that at least two paedophiles enjoyed long and happy lives destroying other people's lives thanks to George Carman's skills, though to play Devil's advocate for a Devil's advocate he could have said that everyone is entitled to legal representation and you don't criticise someone for being good at their job. I did meet George Carman once, when I went round to Dominic's big posh house in Withington to swap coins in our coin collections, and can't say I felt any warmth or welcome off him, but that is not much of a judgement. Dominic came chez nous at least once but was never much of a close friend, and his main lifetime achievement seems to have been to publish a book slagging off his father for being a really nasty bit of work. He also lost a deposit and came in 6th place as a Lib Dem parliamentary candidate. Then in the run up to one Christmas decades later Dominic Carmen sent me a letter, having presumably got my address from the MGS alumnus database. Did Dominic try to warm me up by saying things like "Hello Peter, How are you getting on? Have you any news from MGS? I have still got that Napoleonic coin we swapped in 1974. How did Jim Bennet get on after his maths Post-doc in Oxford?". Did he heck! Dominic merely said "Hello Peter, you should buy my new book about my father – it is the ideal stocking filler".

Two masters that stick out (for the good) are Alan Pickwick, who taught me all my advanced maths and basic computer coding, and Keith Neal who was head of biology and taught me all my basic biology. For the not-so-good I must add the experience of sitting in horror watching the Latin master Douglas H. punishing a boy for forgetting his Latin homework by hitting him six times with a slipper. Straight out of Billy Bunter – six of the best. That was legal, official school policy, and came after the boy was given the choice of an hour's detention or the slipper. The atmosphere as a student in Oxford was just infinitely more welcoming and positive. However, MGS did undoubtedly give me experience of mental hardening that proved useful later, notably during the later stages of my PhD. It also gave me a useful minimum baseline for evaluating my well-being in later life – how does my quality of life now compare to being at MGS? (Either it's vastly better now, or something has gone horribly wrong!) I still sometimes revisit the huge MGS assembly hall in my dreams – invariably in bad dreams, where I either lose something crucial and can't find it anywhere, or realise I've no clothes on and the whole school is laughing at me.

CHAPTER 3

M is for "Mere"

Rostherne. My gap year, 1979

Rostherne is a Cheshire mere. Also an NNR, SSSI and Ramsar site, so internationally significant for biodiversity. There are dozens of these 'meres' – small lakes – scattered throughout Cheshire, ice age relics I think, and Rostherne is the biggest, deepest and most northerly, lying just outside Rostherne village itself, just outside Tatton Park. It is roughly circular, and Tatton Mere is longer but thinner hence technically smaller. Rostherne is really quite deep, >30m in the middle, once with a relic arctic fish species recorded (a legacy from the ice age). This relic salmonid is called a smelt *Osmerus eperlanus*, and seems not to have actually been collected since the 1920s and is universally assumed to be extinct now. It is primarily an estuarine species, so how it got there is unclear. It was once netted in large numbers around Easter in the mere. (Ironically, from the viewpoint of global

Fig 3.1 A view The standard view of Rostherne Mere, looking north from Rostherne church. The low building in the middle is the old boathouse.

Fig 3.2 Tom Wall and Gisele when at Rostherne.

biodiversity and a large dose of modern conservation genetics, this extinct fish was almost certainly the most significant species of the site, with its birds being a minor second-rate point.) There are just two Rostherne smelt specimens left to DNA sequence, and being in formalin they are lost. Such isolated populations can be seen as an endemic species now lost to the planet. The main problem with Rostherne Mere that led to its local extinction seems to have been eutrophication. Rostherne Mere also comes with a quaint legend of a mermaid ringing a lost church bell on Easter morning, for which the evidence is precisely nil, as is the underground tunnel to the river Mersey through which she is alleged to swim each year for her annual visit.

My first encounter with Rostherne was an open evening, courtesy of the Hale Ornithologists around 1974, where we crammed into a hall in Rostherne village full of displays about the mere and its ecology, and heard a talk. I was rather enchanted, and we paid to become visitors. The system was that you were ONLY allowed in one place, the observatory, a hut overlooking the lake but several hundred metres away. Luckily this hut had a huge telescope, allowing you to ID a sandpiper at the far side of the lake. (Later some bastard stole it; it was returned but damaged and is now in a locked case, unusable.) To enter the observatory, you went to an outside cupboard in front of the warden's house to sign out the key. You then walked across a field next to Rostherne church, to a little path through the beech trees to the hut.

I got many hours birding in that hut (Dad must have been bored senseless) though few really good ticks: buzzard and siskin seemed good then but humdrum now. Probably the best was a flock of 20+ Bewick's swans one March, on their way from Ireland to Russia.

I wouldn't mention this lake except for the transitional role it played in my life. Having finally left Manchester Grammar School in March 1979 (after a pointless extra term with no teaching, a money-spinner for the school) I had six months to enjoy before starting at Oxford. School friends did gap years or exotic trips, I got on a 'get kids off the dole' scheme as an assistant warden at Rostherne Mere. At the time Rostherne Mere was run by the Nature Conservancy Council, a government agency, and I was employed at the princely sum of £20.55 per week to help the main warden. (I have a letter from my father asking how this sum would affect my taxation status!) The main warden was Tom Wall, who lived in the warden's house with his French wife Gisele, and a cat called Minouche. I liked Tom, and as far as I can tell everyone who ever met him thought the same. I started my first 'job' on 23 April 1979, before passing my driving test, so cycled all the way. That was really hard! In a car you don't notice hills, but going across the edge of Altringham to the Cheshire lanes turned out to have some really nasty hills I'd never noticed before. The worst bit was crossing the Bollin – the bridge seemed to go on for ever. Even the road alongside Tatton Park – flat as a pancake – was in fact inclined uphill, and being a mile long was a muscle killer just before arriving in Rostherne village. One other memory from this short phase was taking a helpful shortcut across fields near the Bollin (not available to cars and saving several miles) and seeing yellow wagtails song-flighting in the grasslands. They were a common bird then – I have not seen one this millennium.

Then I passed my driving test in May 1979, could drive to work, and Rostherne became my life for the summer. Initially it was paid duck watching – we needed accurate counts of all species on site. I still recall the huge buzz of excitement my first day going round a site, no-one else allowed in there, with a 2-way radio!! (Before mobile phones this was like the communicators in Star Trek.) "Patrol calling base – I can see some ducks, Over." We spent quite a while going round the lake in a small boat collecting data on nests etc.

I got off to a good start by finding the roost of a kestrel in one of the ornate gravestones in Rostherne churchyard next door. This produced lots of pellets, some with identifiable contents. After short eared owls I was quite good on pellet contents, showed Tom field vole molar roots, and got a ring from a starling. Another really good 'tick' was that a male smew took up residence on the mere from April-June 1979. Female smews (red heads) were regular winter visitors to Tatton Mere – I routinely expected one or two in the winter flocks of goldeneye, but for some reason males almost never turned up. I have not seen one before or since, nor had the warden Tom. They are really handsome white diving ducks (called "white nuns" by old wildfowlers) with black lines on their plumage; pity it didn't stay or breed. I also had a nice view of a lesser spotted woodpecker there, and there was a good breeding colony of reed warblers in the marginal reedbeds. One of my better Rostherne memories was wading through reed beds (wearing chest high waders) far taller than me to check reed warbler nests with Tom.

One week we got seconded to an NCC project in Edale, staying in the YHA and putting fence posts across a limestone dale. In case that sounds idyllic, remember that limestone soils are about 5 cm thin soil over solid stone, so we were using steel pickaxes and crowbars to smash post holes into the bedrock. It worked, and the post holes will probably be landscape features for centuries. This was probably the time I worked with "normal" (ie not university) people most, as the rest of the team were basically land managers. A chap called Tony Mallett headed the land management team, him plus two lads, who did things like fencing, path clearance etc. To control rhododendron we used 2,4D – agent orange as we knew it – and I recall one of the lads who had white-blond hair coming back from a day's 'rhody bashing' with his hair bright pink from all the 2,4D he'd splashed on himself. With hindsight this looks like a needless risk, though I remember them saying that the herbicide to be scared of was gramoxone (the paraquat really will kill you, horribly). Another job that Tony's team did that looks really odd with hindsight was rabbit control. The logic, I think, is that rabbits stop woodland regeneration, so to help the woods we remove the bunnies. There was also an economic point that farmers had wheat field next to our woods and suffered real loses from damage caused by "our" rabbits. Anyway, Tony et al used to push a material called cymag down the rabbit holes, then tamp soil in behind. Cymag gives off cyanide when in contact with moisture, so the rabbits are gassed. This was standard NCC policy. Cymag has since acquired a bad name for killing badgers slowly, but probably worked well enough on rabbits. We even tried long netting – hang a long net along the hedge between our wood and the field, tied in such a way that it dangles 30cm above the ground so rabbits get out of the wood underneath it, unaware it is there. Then you come along at night and silently untie the strings holding your net up, so it falls to the ground, then you silently stake the net down all the way along its 100m. It is crucial that the net dropping / staking is not noticed by any of the rabbits. Finally, you run into the farmer's field to scare them home, to get netted en route.

So on the evening of the long-netting, we all turned up chez Tom after dinner, and he gave us all a stirrup cup of whisky, then set off for the wood. Somehow, five blokes full of whisky, bumbling around in pitch darkness, failed the "Rabbits must not see or hear anything" test, so by the time we ran around the field to flush the bunnies into the net there wasn't a bunny to be seen. I think one got caught in the net and Tom kept it. I reckon about 500 got away that evening. I did, however, run one over on the way home!

Latterly I spent most of my time helping Tom with his statistics – it turned out that he had loads of calculations to do for the NCC and preferred to outsource them. I'd got A1 at Physics-with-Maths and knew how to work out a Pearson's correlation coefficient using a simple calculator, so Tom jumped on the chance. The data were based on crude weather data like 'degree days'. I correlated duck counts with these met data, and found no correlations of any interest at all. This combination of heavy manual work, birdwatching and statistical calculations suits my temperament well, so I look back very fondly on my time with Tom Wall at Rostherne.

To recall this summer, I just need to hear some of the album that took over my head that summer – Joan Baez love songs. I borrowed it from Wythenshawe

Peter Shaw

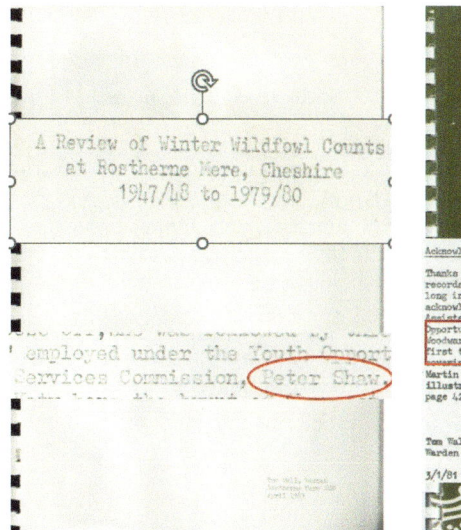

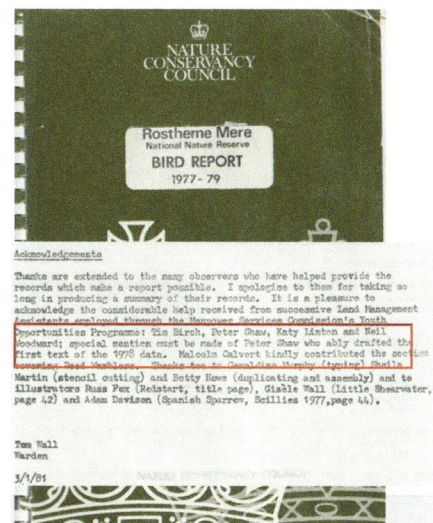

Fig 3.3 Detail from a write-up of Rostherne duck counts by Tom Wall.

Fig 3.4 I got a mention in the 1979 bird report!

library, taped it (of course) and found its songs stuck in my head. 'Sad eyed lady of the lowlands', 'Sweet Sir Gallahad', and more. The looming event was going to Oxford in October – after 18 years of the unquestioningly WW2 atmosphere of 39FD I just couldn't wait to get away, to get some personal liberty. There was a period in summer 1979 when I did calculations like "if I went backwards in time, as far as Oxford is forward in time, that would be my fist day at Rostherne – that's so soon!!" Slightly worryingly for a pre-cannabis phase I also really got into Planet Gong: the Flying teapot and Angel's Egg. Tony Mallet (land manager) had a dad in Knutsford who was immensely proud of his Bang & Olufsen hi-fi, so I visited him and got him to play the first side of the vinyl album 'Angel's Egg' by Gong. I certainly enjoyed the experience, though it clearly wasn't his cup of tea and it would have sounded much better stoned. Another hypothetical counter-factual.

[A curious little-known postscript concerns the song "Sweet Sir Gallahad" mentioned above. I assumed it was traditional, but in fact was written by Joan Baez about her sister Mimi, whose first love Richard Farina was killed in a motorcycle accident, having written many songs including one I discovered a few years later in my PhD – Reno Nevada – covered by the Pentangle. Mimi found love again, Joan celebrated this new happiness. Knowing this makes the song more special IMHO].

Then, September 1979, I waved goodbye to Rostherne, and headed off shortly afterwards to St Catherine's College Oxford for three years of solid zoology – well, three years of solid student life anyway. The last thing I found of any interest there was a mass fruiting of the giant puffball *Calvatia gigantea* on the south-western boundary of the site. Fried up with bacon it is still the most delicious wild fungus I have eaten, and the mycelium is probably still there!

Tom moved on to become warden of the Stiperstones (Shropshire), before retiring and writing a series of readable and erudite books about Rostherne, and other national nature reserves (Wall 2014, 2019 a; b). Remarkably I re-met Tom and Gisele in June 2022, and was honoured to stay a night with them and to be taken round the Stiperstones by Tom. He is still a better birdwatcher than me, picking up a singing reed bunting 100m away. With a little collective effort we were able to recollect the names of people I had not seen since before starting university. I was so immature then!

CHAPTER 4

M is for the Metazoa

Oxford University, October 1979-August 1982.

As a preface to this outpouring of undergraduate exuberance, I have to admit that I probably messed around more than now looks laudable. However, by way of justification that I wasn't totally wasting my time, I can claim to have used my Oxford lectures and tutorials extensively in later life, unlike the vast majority of undergraduates in the great majority of universities and subjects. For two decades, the 'Animal Biology' lectures I gave to Roehampton undergraduates were heavily based on the same lectures I received as a zoology undergraduate in this phase of my life. I suspect very similar, but since I lent my entire folder of three years of handwritten notes to someone who never gave them back, I cannot actually prove this claim. (The chap in question was most apologetic when he found out 40 years later and even went through his old stuff looking for them, sending me a scan of them as proof he still had them safe! Thanks, appreciated, if perhaps a little late for preparing my own lectures.) Similarly, my experience of Oxford tutorials shaped my approach to the tutorials I gave in Roehampton in later years. I was especially impressed by the tutorial environment of my personal college tutor Dr Henry Bennet-Clark. It was a c. 5m square office in the concrete of the Tindbergen building, piled high with dusty old tomes and home-made engineering kit to advance his research on insect flight mechanics. My offices in Roehampton were smaller, similarly piled high with not-quite-so-dusty middle-aged books and interesting specimens, fossils and skulls etc, but never had quite the same gravitas as Henry's. Once, about 2015, I was doing a PhD upgrade interview on behalf of a colleague, Robert Busch, a Cambridge biochemist (and one of the cleverest people I have ever worked with), who later said that the whole process just remined him of a Cambridge tutorial. I took that as a great compliment. At a college reunion in 2022, two of my close friends in

St Catherine's (who had attended state comprehensive schools and lacked a lot of background) both told me that my involuntary tuition had saved their degrees, though at the time I was simply being me, chatting about biology and maths without any pretensions to being a saviour.

I started as an undergraduate at St Catherine's college, Oxford (henceforth Catz) October 1979, after a summer at Rostherne and some birdwatching at Cley with Ian Cropley. To be honest, the undergraduate experience was deliberately a bit of a sausage factory, with far less scope for independence than at postgraduate level. This means that the course structure really isn't worth going into in detail. Suffice to say that the first year was common across Zoology, Botany and Agriculture & Forest Sciences (being roughly a hard A level standard – I hardly learned anything new in that first year) followed by a really intensive two years all about the metazoa – multicellular animals. Plenty of vertebrate study certainly, but it was here that I glimpsed the vastness of "the invertebrates" (a useless catch-all name – some animals in your own phylum, such as sea squirts, are invertebrates!).

Dominant memories from this are of liberation, being alone – free at long last – in my little room 4/11 in Catz, playing Hawkwind "Hurry on sundown" as the winter sun set. I saw Hawkwind – featuring Tim Blake and recorded in the live79 album – in Oxford November 1979, comprehensively stoned with a well-known college neo-hippy. She drove me to Shotover Hill one dawn to pick *Psilocybe semilanceata*. We still swap Xmas cards; she is now happily and respectably married in South West England.

The zoology building itself (the Tindbergen building), shut down totally as an asbestos emergency about 2017 and is demolished. As students we had tea and doughnuts, admiring butterflies and fish. Once an old man wandered in to meet someone – that was THE Charles Elton, one of the doyens of academic ecology. (Whenever anyone says, correctly, that it is more carbon efficient to be vegetarian than carnivore, the underlying science goes back to Charles Elton. Ecologists talk about 'Eltonian pyramids' of energy flow in ecosystems) The collection of invertebrate specimens was amazing – it wasn't till I taught the same material myself at Whitelands that I realised that not everyone has such good specimens, eg intact deep sea crinoids (+their parasitic polychaete worms, the myzostomids). *Limulus* (king crabs, not crabs but large chelicerates unchanged since the Ordovician) collected 100 years ago, etc.

Key people from Oxford must include Sally Thorogood (my cosmic twin), who read biochemistry, and with whom I shared a house in 1980/81. (When Ian Cropley met Sally and heard of this, he said to her "You have my commiserations". Ian shared a tent with me around the Pyrenees so is entitled to claim experience.)

Fig 4.1 My cohort of zoology undergraduates, outside the Tindbergen building 1982.

> Key to the Oxford zoology UGs 1982: numbers refer my overlays on the photo
> 1 = me   2 = Tim Guildford   3 = Rosie Hails   4 = Phil Sterling   5 = Neil Nightingale

Another key person from those days is of course my brother-in-law, John Shelvey, who read botany with Mark Hirst, and was initially a beer drinking/punting colleague long before marrying my sister Caroline. Jon Mortin (from Buxton, who also went to MGS – I saw him in the MGS biology block about 1978), also read zoology at Catz, did a PhD in fossil inverts and became a Buddhist country recorder. Being Buddhist means he won't kill springtails so I can't guarantee many of his names.

I was in the same undergraduate cohort (the 1979 matriculation cohort of the zoology programme as administrators would see it) as some seriously impressive people. The list includes Tim Guildford, Rosie Hails, Neil Nightingale and Phil Stirling.

Tim Guildford URL: "https://www.zoo.ox.ac.uk/people/professor-tim-guilford#/" won the Christopher Walsh scholarship to stay on and do a PhD in Oxford zoology, becoming one of the foremost experts on sea bird navigation. Among other remarkable things, Tim's team showed that if you temporarily inhibit the sense of smell of a tube-nosed seabird, it cannot navigate over the vast oceanic distances. Yes, tube-nosed seabirds navigate oceans by smell.

Rosie Hails URL: "https://en.wikipedia.org/wiki/Rosie_Hails" became a professor of mathematical and conservation biology at Imperial. Then head of

A Path of 21 Ms

science and conservation for the National Trust, and received an MBE for services to conservation.

Neil Nightingale URL: " https://en.wikipedia.org/wiki/Neil_Nightingale" became a wildlife film producer for the BBC, and his remarkable wikipedia entry makes David Attenborough's productivity look just average.

Phil Stirling was always fascinated by moths, was curating his moth collection in his rooms in New College, is a regular writer about moths and runs the Dorset moth group. The picture of Phil curating moths is 2021 but reminds me greatly of him c. 1981.

I lived in Catz itself Y1 and Y3, but lived out in 15 Boulter street in Y2. Bought quite a few cacti then, of which one survives, *Gymnocalycium quehliahnum*, from the Waterperry stall on covered market about 1980. I know it flowered April 1982, my finals year.

To be honest, not all my memories of that period are as sharp as they should be due to widespread availability of cannabis. A lady called P. showed me the way, and transformed my life. Thanks for ever. When one of my school biology teachers visited me in Catz to introduce nice young MGS boys to a 'successful' alumnus who got the coveted scholarship to Oxford, my window ledge was full of *Cannabis sativa* plants. The master giggled slightly, but otherwise said nothing. Rumour had it that he had previously been required to change school in a hurry, having been caught growing cannabis plants in the school greenhouse. I liked him – he was excellent. I found myself repeating his advice on revision tips to university 3rd year undergraduates. There was at least one more window ledge full of weed in St Catherine's each year I was a student – with hindsight this looks rather blatant. A year later, a friend Nick got a formal ticking off from his

Fig 4.2 An Oxford punting party c. 1981. I am in the middle left, with the most hair!

72

tutor Barrie Juniper for his window ledge of weed being directly over the college entrance, the first thing to greet all visitors. Given this rather easy-going attitude, it must have been an irrational fit of paranoia that inspired me to get rid of some plants into a local churchyard in summer 1980, presumably on the basis that (1) people in college were bothered about weed, and (2) no-one bothers looking in churchyards. Both assumptions were wrong. So I carried some plant pots of pot plants along Manor Road to Saint Cross churchyard, and stashed the stash somewhere in the tombstones, where Kenneth Grahame ('Wind in the Willows') is buried. With the benefit of hindsight, the harvest was doomed and hopeless, but one learns from experience. This led to an unfortunate evening when a friend Mark and I tried to reclaim the stash. Again, I'm not sure why, and again the wisdom of the plan looks flaky with hindsight. We waited till nightfall, filled up a bong with some top quality resin, got well stoned then set off to the churchyard to grab the booty. Number one difficulty was that I couldn't remember where I'd put the plants. Number two was that we didn't have a torch. Number three is that I think someone had already spotted a pile of new pot plant pots in the tombstones and snaffled them. So we bumbled round the tombstones in pitch blackness for half an hour, tripping over tombstones and brambles and not finding anything remotely interesting. Luckily no one noticed us! Back to college for a beer and a rethink. I put this on a Facebook post, in which someone applauded the Catz tradition of seditious behaviour:

(Catz Gaudy Facebook 7 March 2021) "How many windows full of weed overlooking the playing field has Catz sprouted in recent years? When my alma mater Manchester grammar School (AD1515 and not much advanced since . . .) sent a group of Oxbridge wannabes with a biology master to come and visit a "successful" MGS alumnus (me) in a real Oxford College in May 1980, my entire view over the fields from 4/11 was occluded by a wall of weed. Luckily the biology master in question had already been forced to change school after growing the same species of weed in the school greenhouse so just smiled and carried on as though nothing was amiss. I really don't know if the chinless wonders who accompanied him understood what was going on, and suspect they didn't. That was the same old-school visit that I got Mark H to show them the Botany genetics garden. So we walked behind the botany building, hoping that the impact of a recent couple of joints on our behaviour wasn't too obvious, when we turned a corner to see a building site. Mark's ensuing sentence deserves to be immortalised: "This is the world famous Oxford botanic genetic garden. Oh dear, someone appears to have dug it up!" I am afraid to say that I collapsed in hopeless giggles, meanwhile the chinless wonders from MGS looked utterly uninterested in a shambolic meltdown unfolding under their noses."

(From some Facebook posts about 2021)

Jonathan Mortin
I remember a certain Peter Shaw demonstrating his trick of attaching a long strip of toilet paper to the ceiling in a darkened room and then lighting it at the bottom (ie the base . . . nobody's bottom was involved!).

Peter Shaw
Wasn't it a candle lit at both ends, tied by a bit of cotton to a ceiling lamp? There is an elegant self-stabilising effect in that the candle end which dips lower melts faster, then the two flames circle each other faster and faster until plummeting in a ball of waxy flame onto the carpet. What could possibly go wrong? With hindsight, this jolly jape left a legacy of a ball of waxy mess in the carpet that stayed a long time afterward as a memento of the experiment. Or was that toilet paper pyrotechnic something else again?

Jonathan Mortin
It was definitely toilet paper. Have you forgotten the trick!? It has left me with a lifelong fear of darkened rooms and long sheets of toilet paper

Peter Shaw
Gosh – I had forgotten this and had no idea I had burned this trauma into your nervous system! I thought that any residual scarring I caused your soul was just those mushrooms.

My main tutor was a man who I have venerated ever since my interview in November 1978 – Dr Henry Bennet-Clark. A redoubtable bearded man with strong leanings towards the engineering mathematics of animal bodies, his speciality was arthropod locomotion including the energy storge within flea bodies and the cuticular deformation used by the diptera to rotate their wings. (The flight mechanism of endopterygote insects like flies is remarkably indirect, with muscles not attached to the wing but instead deforming the thorax to make the wings move.) He was good enough to sell me his elderly Ford Escort 1100

TFC975P to me for the trifling sum of £100 in September 1982, which utterly transformed my life as a PhD student in York. In honour and gratitude, I always called TFC975P "Henry". Henry had a top speed of 55 MPH, but held a great deal of storage space – wonderful. I could not have made my PhD work without that car. Henry taught me the basics of car maintenance (eg setting the timing by seeing when the points let go of a fag paper!). Henry TFC975P ended up in Dorking scrapyard in 1986 with 110,000 miles on the clock and I still miss that car – if I lived in somewhere like Arizona I'd have kept him out of nostalgia.

Fig 4.3 Dr Henry Bennet-Clark.

Richard Dawkins was active teaching in the department at the time, and his book 'The Selfish Gene' was a key reason for my wanting to go to Oxford. I'd put as high on my list of lifetime slips was failing to get Richard Dawkins to autograph his book in a lecture. I had the opportunity in January 1981, when Richard gave us lectures on animal behaviour.

I also received a term's worth of tutorials from his wife Marian Stamp-Dawkins (URL: "https://www.zoo.ox.ac.uk/people/marian-stamp-dawkins-frs-cbe#/ or https://en.wikipedia.org/wiki/Marian_Dawkins", also in animal behaviour. She was lovely, very interested in farm animals' welfare (how do you ask a chicken if it is happy?) and never mentioned him. One of the more sensitive undergraduates observed at the time that Marian looked like she had a sad air about her, like she needed a hug, but as she was probably going through the early stages of divorce at the time (they split legally in 1984), a certain lack of chirpiness might be expected.

Although he was a botany tutor, I regarded Barrie Juniper as a co-tutor since he was also based in Catz and taught us first year modules. Barrie is best known for his work on the history of the cultivated apple, which seems to have come from the Tien Shan mountains in China, and undergone evolutionary selection pressure to taste nice to bears and horses. After his death in January 2023 I learned that he had saved the college gardens from certain embarrassing failure

A Path of 21 Ms

by looking at the landscape plans for the college drawn up by the all-controlling architect Arne Jacobsen. (Who had even insisted on designing not just the buildings but the beds, the cutlery and the mains sockets!) Jacobsen had specified plants that he knew grew well in his native Denmark, not understanding that many of them were in the heather family ericacea. They are well known (by ecologists and gardening cognoscenti) to be calcifuge – they die if exposed to limey soils. The problem seems to be that high levels of calcium interfere with their uptake of ions of iron (Fe^{2+}), going yellow with 'lime induced chlorosis', then slowly dying over many ugly years. Barrie (then a PhD student – describing himself as "the lowest of the low") had to tell this bad news to Jacobsen. The

Fig 4.4 Prof. Barrie Juniper of apple fame. RIP 2023.

news was not well received, but the eventual planting choices that the two men agreed to worked admirably well, leaving the college with distinctive, individual and lovely gardens that have aged extremely well. There is a bust of Barrie's head in the gardens of Saint Catherines, as well as two memorial apple trees. He may be seen on this link, showing his characteristic quiet erudition in his favourite apple orchard in Wytham. (Barrie Juniper "The apple orchard": https://www.youtube.com/watch?v=lz1oc-LJmnk).

I missed several significant opportunities as an undergraduate, of which number one would probably be failing to train in the Shorinji Kempo dojo in the Catz squash courts, despite Sally Thorogood (brown belt) telling me I really should. Yes, I should have, dammit. I later went on to get 2nd dan in Shorinji Kempo (see chapter 10) and trained with people from the Catz dojo, such as Chris Lloyd and Lucy Keppel-Palmer (later Jones). Lucy (Agriculture and Forest Sciences, matriculated 1980) went on to get 2nd dan blackbelt in kempo, while being a professional herbalist specialising in Tibetan healing (and raising a family). She threw me around on blackbelt courses years later.

Two other Oxford connections should be mentioned, both of whom re-appeared in later life. One is Dr Steve Head, who was the demonstrator who taught me most of what I know about invertebrate

Fig 4.5 Dr Steve Head.

zoology. He researched red sea corals, and some of his specimens are on display in Oxford museum. Steve turned up later as director of the charity "Pondlife", whose staff came to 'my' nature reserve Inholms Clay Pit to advise on our ponds' biodiversity. He went on to run the Gardeners Wildlife Forum, again advising on techniques to optimise biodiversity. I gave a talk to this forum about springtails – see this link (http://www.wlgf.org/june%202015%20wlgf%20conference%20 proceedings%20soil.pdf).

Steve was instrumental in helping me re-establish contact with Henry Bennet-Clark in 2022, after 23 years of retirement. Unsurprisingly Henry's university email bounced, but Steve knew the phone number.

The other is the famous mammologist David Macdonald, who set up and ran 'Foxwatch'. At time of writing (2022) David Macdonald is still active, running 'Wildcru'. An ex-zoology student Anna Nesbitt (see her dormouse picture in the section on Roehampton field courses) went on to volunteer for Wildcru. I worked for David July – August 1982 after graduating, driving round Oxford all night in a converted taxi with a radio antenna on the roof. The idea is that you get a fix on a fox's transmitter, draw a line on a map, drive off, get a second line, and where the two lines meet defines where the fox is. I mainly followed a fox called Maynight. I never really took to being awake all night, and my sleep was messed up for weeks afterwards. People thought the van was a TV detector and sometimes ran out with a TV licence in their hand. ("Thanks, but I'm after foxes.") On the plus side I saw Oxford as few other people do, empty and haunted by foxes and badgers. It was very quiet between 2am and 4am. I followed them as they entered a garden then heard the clatter as the bin lid came off (a badger trick). I saw a big German guy called Heribert jump out of a moving Land

Fig 4.6 Professor David Macdonald (and his dog 'Fly', who hates badger fleas). Again thanks to David for kindly supplying me this lovely photo.

Rover (that he was driving at the time) one night in Wytham woods to throw himself on top of a badger to put a collar on it (The badger got away, saving Heribert some nasty bites). Heribert went on to greatness as the Director of the Berlin Wildlife Institute. I had to collect fox poos for David's research, recording their location and smelliness – the rucksack I used for this became so foul smelling that it got banned from the student house I shared. Having a car meant I could take friends out to visit the local countryside, like Woodstock – when my mother was dying in an old folks' home north of Oxford in 2012, I realised that by going there I was revisiting villages that I had last seen in 1982 driving friends for a picnic in David Macdonald's fox van.

Fig 4.7 The Foxwatch van. Plus fox. Thanks to David Macdonald for kindly digging out this old photo.

It was in Henry Bennet-Clark's office in the Tinbergen building in South Parks Road, Oxford, that I had a chance meeting that has quite changed my life. It was spring 1982, and Henry asked if I knew what I was going to do when I "turned into a butterfly" (=graduated and left Oxford). Of course not. He told me of an old acquaintance of his, Michel Usher, who needed a bright student for a PhD on springtails in York. Was I interested? I knew about the evolutionary history of springtails (going back to a famous fossil *Rhyniella praecursor* in the Rhynie chert – see the chapter on Roehampton for more), and pretended to be enthusiastic. Henry believed me, tipped the wink to Michael Usher, and my future was set on course.

This is how I ended up working on springtails – Collembola. Maybe I should have inserted this Collembola text in my next chapter since this line of research started in York not Oxford, but it all came out of this moment in Henry Bennet-Clark's office in Oxford in 1982. I will not go into technical details here, but suffice to say at the time we all thought that Collembola were wingless soil insects, the commonest of the apterygota. Collembola are found in every garden soil and woodland leaf litter, flightless but often able to jump many body lengths with a unique organ (the furca = pitchfork) evolved from fused crustacean abdominal legs. Almost right, but since then detailed DNA sequence analyses show that they are not insects – their Devonian marine ancestors were a different group of marine crustacea to the insects (though to be honest pretty close. Both groups evolved out of a Devonian shrimp similar to the modern *Artemia*.) At the time we thought there was one fossil Collembola species in the 400 million year old Rhynie chert – now I think we have 4 species of Collembola in the Rhynie chert (see the chapter about Whitelands college for more about the Rhynie chert). These all look remarkably like modern forms – unchanged for 400 million years, even longer than dragonflies. One of my better claims to fame is that I have added nineteen species of animal to the UK list. All overlooked Collembola of course. (*Calvatomina superba, Calvatomina rufescens, Dicyrtomina violacea, Fasciosminthurus quinqufasciatus, Hymenaphorura nova, Entomobrya imitabilis, Entomobrya intermedia, Desoria trispinata, Heteromurus major, Isotoma riparia, Isotomurus unifasciatus, Katianna australis, Katianna schoetti, Lepidocyrtus nigrescens, Parisotoma ekmanni, Sminthurides bifidus, Sminthurinus alpinus, Sminthurinus minutus, Sminthurinus reticulatus*). Plus got DNA or photographic evidence of another half dozen or so, new to science! In each case someone else collected them but I added the name to the UK list. This is how I became the national expert in Collembola, the UK recorder for the group. I have run identification courses for entomologists for the Field Studies Council (Preston Montford many times, Juniper hall once). Probably the most memorable was the course I ran for Scottish soil biologists of the James Hutton Institute based in Mar Lodge in Braemar. Mar Lodge is a Victorian hunting lodge full of deer skulls – over the breakfast tables and in every corridor. It is famous for a dance hall full of 2400ish deer skulls – see https://www.youtube.com/watch?v=bqQ1OhW9rc8 (if you don't mind a really creepy dance venue).

I arrived there by train (+hire car), a rucksack full of Collembola in tubes, to find a vast old building (much like portrayed in films about Hogwarts) and no way in. Not a soul in sight. In the end I knocked on the door of a courtyard next door, which (by luck not good judgement) was indeed where I ran the course. There was a moments silence, then some door banged deep inside the old building, and a big hairy bloke came to the door, with another scary big hairy bloke behind him. They were ghillies, professional deer hunters. Both had huge sharp knives on the belts to garroch (eviscerate) red deer in minutes, but what really freaked me out was that both had hunting rifles casually hung over their shoulders. You might expect that level of armaments in the remote hillybilly regions of Arkansas, but in the UK while preparing for an academic course on microscopic soil creatures it rather disturbed me. Either man could easily have killed me on the spot, and my tiddly little pen-knife just was not in their league. "H.H.Hello – my n.n.name is D.D.Dr Peter Shaw and I am meant to be running an ID course here tomorrow" I stammered, hoping to sound cool and confident. Remarkably, not only did they not attack me, but they knew all about the course and had been delegated to help me set up the microscopes etc. Getting the extraction facilities set up was like a "now get out of that" exercise, featuring some desk lamps on dodgy extension cables shining on soil samples perched on aluminium foil in old cut-out drinks bottles. But it worked! The experience was also memorable for my getting up before dawn to see black grouse dancing in the dawn light at a lek in Glen Lui 11 April 2011. Mar lodge gave me a bedroom but no breakfast facilities at all, so I made do with a cup of tea in the dark. Also the only time I have visited Aberdeen (where my father grew up), and seen the Shaw family grave in Aberdeen cemetery. Someone had put fresh flowers in it – I never found out who, would love to know.

But to get back to Henry's office in Oxford in spring 1982, I have often been asked "how did you get into the Collembola?" I reply with candid honesty "Back in 1982 I had the choice between a PhD on the Collembola, or long-term unemployment". Sadly, all true, though I am pleased to have followed that path. I could have added a quip about "M is for the Mesofauna", but decided against it.

Anyway, it was at the instigation of Henry Bennet-Clark that I applied for my PhD place in York. Henry warned me that Michael Usher wouldn't let me play around as much as he would have – fair warning. With hindsight I would reword this slightly – Michael Usher wouldn't have let me play around at all if he had any idea what I was actually getting up to in my spare time! Still, this was one of the most important developmental decisions in my life, and leaving Oxford in September 1982 to start a PhD in York, driving Henry's old Ford Escort up north, was easily among the best things I did in my life.

There was a podcast of me talking about springtails at:

http://www.uk-wildlife.co.uk/ep80-springtails-aka-collembola-with-dr-peter-shaw/

CHAPTER 5

M is for Mycorrhizas (and Merlewood)

York, September 1982 – September 1985, The PhD years

In which I get a PhD, a first love and first job, but lost a millicurie of $^{14}CO_2$ in a train and sailed a bit close to the supervisory wind.

Although the length of time I was a student at York and Oxford was about the same (three years), I find that I have far more to say about York, since undergraduate courses are always something of a sausage factory, putting so many students through such a detailed syllabus that you dare not give them many choices. By contrast a PhD is wide open – each student forges their own destiny. I learned so much more about everything in York – Oxford was the effervescence after years of repression in Manchester; York was me becoming an adult.

Before going too far into the experiential side, I should explain a minimum about mycorrhizas. Not only were these the subject of my PhD, they were also the subject of the preceding PhD in Michael Usher's lab (Roger Finley, who went on to work with David Read in Sheffield), the subject that got James Merryweather his PhD,

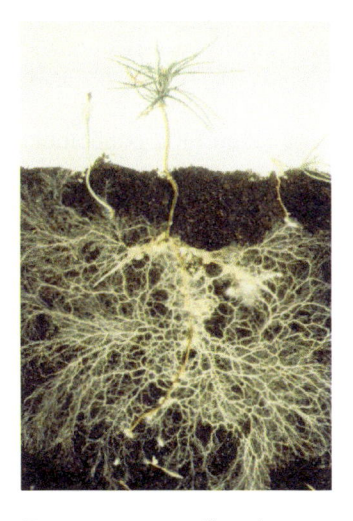

Fig 5.1 A pine seedling showing ectomycorrhizal infection on its roots. I needed and used baby trees like these, pleading some off David Read in Sheffield. Not my photo, but looks much like my better microcosms. Might be Paxillus?

Fig 5.2 York University, Central Hall.

and got me more publications out of the CEGB's air pollution work than any other single topic. A mycorrhiza is a symbiosis between a plant and a fungus, in which the plant supplies the fungus with chemical energy (sugars) and the fungus acts as an extension of the plant's root system to collect nutrients (NPK etc), water etc. For current purposes there are two main sorts, loosely called "ectos" and "endos" or "VAM" by the cognoscenti. Ectomycorrhizal fungi are found on tree roots, sheath the root like a condom, surrounding the plant tissue with a surprisingly thick mesh of long, thin fungal cells. Although this goes inside the root it seems never to penetrate inside plants cells, merely pushing between them. The root pushes out against the wrapping and ends up looking swollen and deformed, 'coralloid'. Ectomycorrhizas spread their spores by macroscopic fruit bodies, usually mushrooms (though truffles are also ecto, ascomycetes so an independent evolution of the state). Well known genera of ectomycorrhizal mushrooms include the boletes *Boletus* and *Suillus* (mainly good to eat), *Amanita* and *Cortinarius* (mainly VERY BAD to eat), and *Paxillus* (see below). Endomycorrhizas ('Vesicular Arbuscular Mycorrhizas') are very different. They are found on herbaceous plants, are almost universal, and do not sheath the root so are much harder to see. They do in fact penetrate into plant cells (hence 'endo'). Their spore bodies are <1mm across buried in the soil, but the spores produced are (relatively) huge and persist a long time in soil. This is an ancient symbiosis: Something looking like VAM fossilised on roots of *Asteroxylon* in the Rhynie Chert 400MYBP, before plants evolved leaves. Look at the short, fat roots of bluebells and ask yourself how these can possibly explore and exploit remote pockets of soil nutrients? (Answer – they don't, they subcontract the work. Short, fat roots are usually heavily infected with endomycorrhizal fungi.) All my research has been on ectos, always on forest trees and usually by counting their mushrooms in the autumn. This is why I was employed by the CEGB to count mushrooms (in an air pollution experiment). I first met endos when teaching soil biology around 1994 – one of my key lifetime observations is that there is nothing like having to teach something to force one to learn about it! Boil bluebell roots in KOH for 10 minutes then stain with cotton blue and examine at x400. You might even see a tiny intra-cellular exchange site called an arbuscule with care and luck.

Back to York: I started at York University in September 1982, with a zoology degree, an elderly Ford Escort estate car, and a PhD place to study "Interactions between Collembola and the ectomycorrhizal fungi of lodgepole pine *Pinus contorta*" in a NERC CASE studentship jointly with ITE Merlewood (late lamented). CASE schemes were meant to be university with industry, but somehow my supervisor Mike Usher persuaded NERC that ITE was industrial. I know industry, and ITE wasn't!

The logic was simple and solid. We know that many trees depend on ectomycorrhizal fungi for nutrition, and that their soils are full of Collembola. If the Collembola were eating the fungal hyphae in the soil, they would effectively steal the plant's sugars and downgrade any mycorrhizal benefit. This is exactly the effect shown by exposing leek plants to endomycorrhizal fungi and a springtail called *Folsomia candida* (see Warnock Fitter & Usher 1982). Indeed, the springtail reduced benefits, and a follow-on PhD by Roger Finlay found non-linear (parabolic) responses to changing springtail grazing density. So, my PhD was set up to see what effect Collembola had on ectomycorrhizas under field conditions.

Studying what Collembola overlapped with ectomycorrhizal fungi in the field was the easy bit; the hard part was recreating the interaction in controlled conditions. It is remarkably hard to get mycorrhizas to form on sterile trees in the lab, considering how hard it is to stop them forming in the field! I tried various methods, none very successful. This was partly because the fungal supervisor John Dighton wasn't very good at it either, though better than me. I pleaded with David Read in Sheffield to give me spare mycorrhizal seedlings (he did – saving my thesis), and used his kit to measure radio label in springtails. Or rather, not. One time I turned up in Sheffield by train with a tube of about a millicurie of radioactive bicarbonate solution to dispense $^{14}CO_2$ onto my minitrees. Then David Read measured it, and found no radioactivity at all. Amersham International did say something about buffering the pH in the tubes, but somehow I missed that detail and the radioactive CO_2 all gassed off, probably in the train over from York (while warm and shaken). David's advice was to say nothing, as there was no real danger but if British Rail got wind of the release of a radioactive gas on a train they'd have a national-scale meltdown. Men in NBC suits with Geiger counters ordering commuters off the train and waving plastic sheets to move the polluted air while journalists look on, all for teeny (<micro-grey) levels of exposure. It would have been picked up by Fox News! Instead, we decided to say nothing, and have a beer, or two. David was keen that all his lab staff (and students, and visitors like myself) accompany him to a Friday lunchtime drink in a local pub. David Read became FRS and is one of the most impressive people I have worked with, and that bar is set high. I also giggle at the thought that when I came to visit David Read in 1984 I dumped my old banger of a car in a handy empty space outside some big old building on the edge of the university. It turned out that this was Sheffield University Senate house, that I had absolutely no business parking there and that the only reason the space was empty was that the VC had gone off somewhere and no-one else was entitled to park there. If they could have clamped me they would have, but clamps were not available then, so I left Henry in this helpful space before cheerfully driving back to York with a load of mycorrhizal seedlings and no idea of the magnitude of lèse-majesté I had just committed. (Later on, Roger Finlay found out and said: "You parked WHERE?! No one is allowed to do that.")

Back to the PhD. Did Collembola demonstrably impact tree health by grazing on ectomycorrhizas? To precis a summary of the abstract, the little blighters refused to do anything of the sort, apparently starving rather than eat some hyphae, and taking up no radio-label I could detect. This is fine for a PhD, a perfectly good answer for which I got the PhD after a viva with a few sweaty moments. The external, Tony Warwick, was fine. Alistair Fitter was fine and fair but made me sweat in the viva. I remember squirming as he asked me what my "killer photo" of a springtail eating a mycorrhizal root actually showed. "I looked long and hard at this," he said, before pointing out that you couldn't actually see what the tiny white blob was, let alone what it was doing. I'm sure it was *Onychiurus armatus* (now called *Protaphorura armata*, and undoubtedly a taxonomic quagmire in need of DNA revision) having a snack of hyphae off an ectomycorrhizal root (justifying my whole PhD) but accept that image needed more faith than science should ever require! He also spotted the pseudo-replicated statistical analysis I used, and I am ashamed to say that I was doing what Michael Usher told me. Not actually true and I am sure Alistair knew it, as he raised a quizzical eyebrow and said "and how SHOULD you have done it?" (Luckily I knew, had done it, and it was non-significant dammit.) For decades afterwards I used this as an example to PhD students of why you should NOT have your supervisor in the viva. They cannot defend themselves when used as a scapegoat for some slip! (Standard policy now is contrary, and supervisors normally attend viva, but policy on this varies between universities.) Obviously, I did not want MBU in my viva, and had he been there he would certainly have said something about my inflated degrees of freedom.

Back to York. In York I was based in Alcuin College. (Alcuin of York was a teacher to Charlemagne, a Yorkshire man who was highly regarded in European court and who helped smooth over a 9th century trade dispute.) One day I got a postcard addressed to "'S', AD062 YO1 5DD". Since YO1 5DD is the university, this became Alcuin College D062 room of Peter Shaw. The sender was an Italian marine biologist, Romano Baino, who was a close friend for my first year. He did the MSc in biological computation till May 1983, came to Grange-over-Sands and took the photo of a limestone pavement; I even stayed with him in Genoa in 1984, earning my keep by importing a ZX Spectrum computer – cutting edge stuff (32k memory and all DIY BASIC coding!!), and not then easy to get in Italy. Romano turned up in 2021, advising on marine conservation in Tuscany (eg see Mancusi et al 2023), and producing a remarkable calendar that recreated famous artworks as photographs. In later life his email signature was Euler's equation, which as it happened I introduced in "Planet Nauru":

$$e^{(i*pi)} + 1 = 0$$

This is my favourite equation as well! We re-met in my place in Provence in July 2023, and got on ever so well just like we used to. By then we had both looked Death in the eyeballs courtesy of serious illness. (And our wives got on happily as well, finding multiple funny little similarities in their lives).

I kept this same room for the three years of my PhD. With hindsight I pushed university rules to their limits since I sublet it without telling the college, and kept Henry in the staff car park just outside my window. Just before leaving York, I got a £5 fine for using the staff car park without permission, but having used the same space since September 1982 I ignored it and have heard no more. Having a corridor full of students gave plenty of opportunities for social life. One girl, Jane Tyler, had previously taught English in France, and told me the correct colloquial for "I only smoke spliffs" – which is 'Je ne fume que les petards', which arguably proved crucial in initiating my relationship with Catherine in 1987! Less positive for relationships was a first-year philosophy student opposite, Duncan K., a self-professed anarchist (from a rich and powerful family, of course). He got into the habit of taking a tab of LSD on his way into a tutorial. This wasn't quite as daft as it seems since there is about an hour's lag before the trippy effects kick in, though mixing psychedelics with tutorial guidance isn't generally seen as good practice either by academics or acid heads. So it was my luck that Duncan had a tutorial the day I finally managed to persuade Yvonne to come round for a cup of tea. Yvonne Nicholas was finishing a PhD on plant genetics, a pretty, shy, delicate girl with a gorgeous smile, long curly black hair and a proven record of turning heads among staff as well as PhDs. So Yvonne sat down on my bed, smiled sweetly, I switched the kettle on, then there was a loud knock on the door. Great. It turned out to be Duncan, fresh out of a tutorial (though I only discovered that bit later). He wore a balaclava, a superman cape, and was carrying a large hunting knife. Waving it around making silly noises trying to scare me – the twit. He could have got shot if he'd tried that in the 2010s. Anyway, I knew it was Duncan, could see the knife wasn't sharp enough to worry a banana and that Duncan would have been pushed to worry a wet newspaper, and Phil Hunt had been showing us knife defences in aikido. So I said "Hi Duncan", got him in an arm lock (ikkyo or tembin), took the knife off him. I remember my actual words: "Duncan: I have got your knife AND I've got you in an arm lock. Now go away and play somewhere else", then threw him gently out in a heap in the corridor, chucked his knife after him and slammed the door. I turned round to restart the conversation about Yvonne's studies on the genetics of *Plantogo coronopus*, to find that Yvonne had to go. Anywhere, immediately, and never came back. Obviously worried about who else she might meet around me. Not even my least successful date (that was Samantha and the grilled mouse – see chapter 8).

While settling into York I missed some aspects of Oxford, obviously the settled social life and less obviously punting. Despite this, moving to York was one of the best things I ever did, giving me a fresh new outlook. Coming from Manchester helped – Oxford felt southern, York felt more northern than Manchester. Proper local accent, walls and buildings over 1000 years old. A vast lake full of ducks. I also had something transformational – my first car! This was sold to me by Henry Bennet-Clark as a farewell to Oxford gesture (£100 – I got that back at scrappage three years later). This was a mustard-coloured Ford escort estate TFC 975P, a big car with a 1.1L engine and 80,000 miles on the clock. This car was in fact vital to my PhD as it carried me and lots of kit (including a Tullgren funnel apparatus) between York and Grange-over-Sands, which is where Merlewood was based. "Henry", as I always called TFC975P, was wonderful in the horizons it opened up. Not speedy though – above 50mph the whole thing juddered alarmingly, and 55mph was confined to the long downhill stretch of M62 from Huddersfield down to Oldham. Preferably with a stiff easterly wind. Henry had no built-in radio so I used a Walkman to play cassette tapes. I still recall the wonderful buzz of freedom setting off from the University on a weekend to drive into the North York Moors (or the Yorkshire coastline) with Grateful Dead's 'Box of Rain' belting out on headphones from my Sony Walkman.

Henry had so many holes in his bodywork that it was a full-time job filling them in with the finest Polyfilla that Halfords could sell. I did most of the rest of the maintenance too, and with hindsight it's more by luck than actually knowing what I was doing that I got away with it. Anyway, I got quite expert at setting timing angles with a cigarette paper (when the paper is released from the contacts, that is when the spark would form). I really dislike the way that modern cars are designed to prohibit DIY – some need a garage set up to change a lamp bulb, whereas Ford escorts are delightfully simple to take to bits. A bit too simple the day I took the carburettor to bits . . . One scary day I was tinkering with Henry in front of a farm in Grange-over-Sands, when the farmer ran over and switched off the ignition. I had disconnected the petrol pump, then (oops) squirted petrol over the engine, which ignited. Luckily Mr Brocklebank noticed before I did, and it all burned out harmlessly. This story was in the back of my mid about 1987 when I found my next-door neighbours lodger in Barley Mow Court working outside my kitchen on his car fuel supply while smoking a fag (as I tactfully pointed out).

My PhD had two supervisors, as is normal. Michael Usher (henceforth MBU) was the York supervisor, John Dighton represented ITE Merlewood. John Dighton covered the fungal side of the project at ITE Merlewood, MBU the Collembola from York University. Michel was the senior, both in age and in research supervision experience. He ran his lab with a metaphorical rod of iron – one of the few people who scared (still scares) me. A predecessor PhD student warned me – "Michael is not very sensitive, but he will stay up half the night to give you feedback on your thesis when you need it – which is what you want in a supervisor". It was all true. In fact, about 2015 when the Bumblebee Conservation Trust had a meeting at WWT Barne Elms and MBU chaired this meeting, I was terrified that I might turn up late. I imagined him waiting on the door saying "Shaw – you're late". Obviously I wasn't and he didn't, but by then I was a well off blackbelt with two grown kids and more than 20 years' university experience – and still felt like a naughty schoolboy. So you can imagine how he scared me when I was, if not actually a naughty schoolboy, certainly sailing a bit close to the wind at times.

I should add that MBU taught me most of what I know about multivariate statistics – and that was enough to write a university textbook on the subject (Shaw, 2003). His understanding of PCA gave me the insight to write code in BASIC (on my home computer, a long-forgotten make called a dragon 32 after its "massive" 32K internal memory. Remarkably I was able to dust off a paper print out of my York BASIC code, re-type it by hand, and thereby run PCA on undergraduate data when I started at Roehampton in 1992 and their implementation of SPSS lacked this analysis.) When I told MBU about my coding project, he didn't say "What on earth for? You will take weeks of coding to get an analysis available in our mainframe packages" as most supervisors might have done. What he actually said was "Be sure to extract the eigenvectors of the correlation matrix, not the covariance matrix. Makes the interpretation much easier as the values are not dominated by the commonest species". He was right, of course. Oddly, when the PCA algorithm was encoded into the statistical language R, the default setting is to use the covariance matrix, the "wrong" option (at least for ecologists, though apparently not for mathematicians). It was 30 years later I was examining a PhD thesis for Royal Holloway and was puzzled why one of her PCAs was utterly dominated by the signal from the chironomid flies. Then I remembered MBU's advice, and during the viva established that indeed the student had used the R package and its (incorrect) default setting, and chironomids happened to have been very common in this samples. When running PCA in R, always add this switch ("scale = TRUE") to the command line:

> Answer <- prcomp(datamatrix, scale = TRUE).

Much later on in a tutorial I was showing my two supervisors some analyses on the mushrooms under my different ages of lodgepole pine trees in Spadeadam, using two fancy analyses. One was a standard diversity index (the Shannon index, also known an entropy to some statisticians), the other was my favourite ordination PCA. PCA lets you see a big multivariate data set as one picture, and is a standard useful tool. I found that the second axis of my PCA correlated surprisingly well with the diversity, and suggested that somehow the PCA was detecting diversity. MBU looked hard for a moment, then burst out laughing. "No, that's the arch effect again". One of the little known artefacts of almost all ordination analyses is that when you apply them to an ecological succession, a progression from the community found in a young site through middle aged sites to the species mix on an old mature site, when comes out looks like a capital letter "U", the arch effect. So this distortion is maximum about the middle of the succession. (See Shaw 2003 for an explanation – it is a meaningless artefact, simply reflecting distance conservation within a mathematical space). Also ecological diversity habitually peaks mid-succession. So what I got was two uninformative artefacts interacting, nothing profound. What was profound was that MBU spotted this arcane explanation in under a second. I should add that he was also a superb field botanist, correctly identifying rare bog plants bog rosemary *Andromeda polifolia* and Cranberry *Vaccinium oxycoccus* under my pine plantations from just some small sad twiglets. And remarkably, in 2023 (40 years later) Michael sent me a dataset of spiders from forest plantations across the British Isles. I still had access to statistical analytical power (the free but challenging language called "R"), analysed the data, and we got out a new publication (Shaw & Usher, 2024). Fifty-five woodlands, two hundred species, a year of laboratory time and months of coding and the conclusion is that there is a strong climatic gradient, with the north west of Scotland having very different species to the south east. (Perhaps more surprising was how much richer the spider community became as one heads south and east. My intuition might have suggested the opposite.) This was a satisfying experience for both of us.

It has to be said that MBU scared me throughout my time in York, to the extent that I now realise that I even tried to avoid walking within sight of his (second floor) window – perhaps an over-reaction with hindsight. There was one worrying interlude when MBU would certainly have terminated my career if he'd looked into his NERC-funded growth chamber down the corridor in the top floor of the biology block. I had a collection of clonal lines of *Cannabis sativa* (grown from seeds I'd brought from Oxford) growing under lights in a wardrobe in my room. The college were paranoid about any dodgy electrical appliances – didn't like me having a kettle, as the bursar told me. Mercifully he didn't follow the maze of power cables that sprouted out of the one plug in the wall, because the multiple extension cables plugged into extension cables gave a surprisingly good demonstration of exponential growth, feeding something like 6 Hi-fi boxes plus computer stuff, plus a mysterious side cable which dived under the carpet into the wardrobe, where I dangled some lights and ran them on a timer switch, plus a peristaltic pump automatically feeding in water controlled by a second timer switch. This worked superbly well and by adjusting the timer switches you make the plants flower (11 hours light:13 dark) or not (13 light:11 dark), and get the water level just right. The university would have had kittens, justifiably, so obviously the timer switches were set so the wardrobe was dark when the cleaner came, but I lived in dread of an electrician having a proper look. Years later I found myself outside my old room on a return visit to York, and found it had been knocked through into some conference facility. Sort of sad, but really not my problem, and I giggled at the thought of workmen puzzled by the strange holes bored into the old wardrobe frame when they finally cleared the building out.

Anyway, one worrying day the college authorities told me that they were going to change the carpet in my bedroom, so needed the room emptying for a few days. Worse, if that were possible, is that I had to be away for a few days at a conference then. The clones seemed doomed, and with hindsight I'd have been better off restarting from seed in the new year. But I really valued that clone "Shiva" and didn't want to lose it. Shiva was complimented by Walter Appleby, an authentic long-haired Vietnam draft-dodger on a post doc from California to study plant genetics and to photograph English formal gardens. (He got top marks for the year with no apparent effort when he absent mindedly signed up for a third year molecular genetics module). Walter looked very much like a ginger-haired version of Jerry Garcia of the Grateful Dead, whom he had seen (while stoned of course) with Jefferson Airplane in San Francisco in 1968. Walter didn't so much dodge the Vietnam draft as (in his own words) "turn up for the interview so stoned [I] had to shut one eye to see double". Quite an achievement for California in the 60s, so when Walter said he really liked Shiva I knew that clone was worth keeping. I knew that MBU had his own plant growth chamber down the corridor, that he had no use for in his current research. It was a long shot, but really the only hope I could see. So I borrowed a big trolley from the Biology department, and commandeered an Italian friend Romano Baino, another keen devotee of my weed (who went on to run marine conservation in Italy). We waited till dark, loaded all my plants onto the trolley and pushed it across campus – luckily no one said anything. The Biology department was empty and locked, and no security guards turned up, so we got up to the second floor, into the growth chamber, and stashed the plans under the lights. I went off to the conference, leaving my room as tidy as I could and my wardrobe as full of clothes as I could. Came back a few days later to find a new carpet in my bedroom, MBU's growth chamber full of happy healthy plants, and generally life ticked over just fine. But my heart really was in my mouth next time I met MBU lest he say "Peter – I happened to pop into my growth chamber a few days ago and do you know what I found?" This never happened, life ticked over just fine, a heart's beat away from meltdown. Shiva lasted nearly a decade, as a clone line under lights, until I sold 4BMC, and finally got killed by a hungry badger in the CERL nettlebed in 1992. (That's another story.)

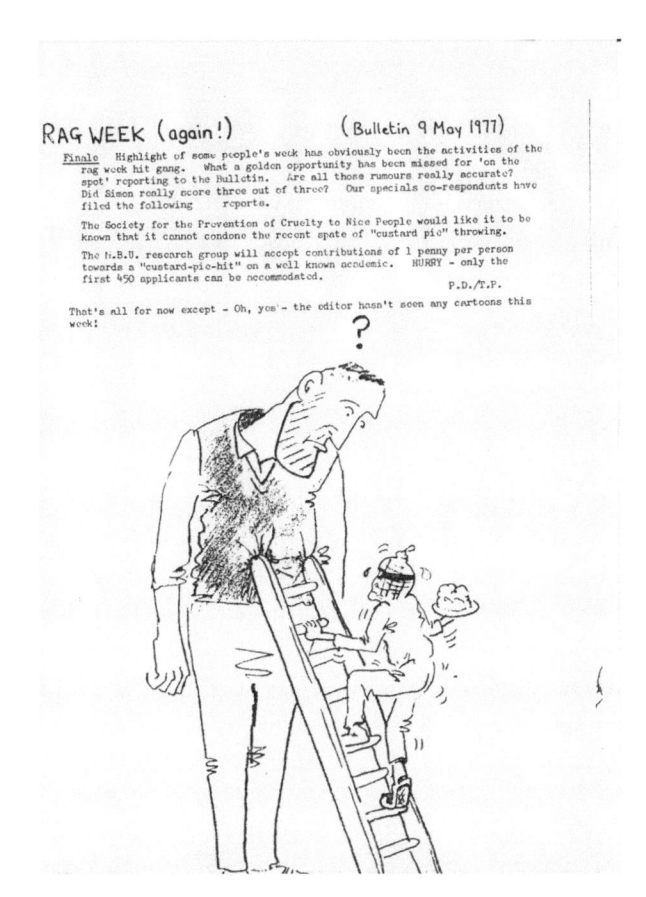

Fig 5.3 Cartoon of MBU by Nev, a technician who later went freelance and gave us Peppa pig!

MBU was never a sensitive soul, with a bit of a reputation. One story – before my time but the stuff of departmental mythology – is that during a rag week about 1977 someone had the bright idea of taking out 'contracts' on lecturers; pay enough and someone wearing a balaclava throws a custard pie at them in a lecture. It sounds like a bloody awful idea, with hindsight. Needless to say, enough people clubbed together to fund the 'hit' on Michael Usher, who duly got splatted in a lecture. He then had a full-on sense of humour failure and chased the girl across campus to detain her and invoke university disciplinary codes. This incident got immortalised in a cartoon in the 'Biology Banned book'.

The next lab to ours was run by Chris Rees (RIP 2023), an amiable chap who handled things differently. Firstly, he kept a bucket of water in his lectures to soak any attacker. Secondly, everyone liked him so he didn't get 'hit' anyway.

Michael Usher was fascinated by Antarctic soil biology, had collections of Antarctic springtails and mites (helped by a post-doc Roger Booth) and a flightless fly *Belgica antarctica* (helped by a post-doc Marion Edwards). He collected spiders from the Falklands, adding a Gondwanaland connection. I started in September 1982, not long after the Falklands war of April 1982. Michael Usher was a leading light in the local conservative party, so kept a close eye on the military progress in the Falklands. This involved taping a map of the Falklands to his laboratory door, with daily updates on the progress of 'our boys'. Such a public display of military nationalism was always asking for trouble in a university environment, and sure enough one day one wag scrawled "Los Malvinos" over the map, which went down in departmental folklore as having annoyed MBU more than anything since the 'hit squad' attack. No-one ever confessed or got found out, so someone got away with that massive lèse-majesté.

Fig 5.4 Professor Michael Usher.

As is normal for PhDs I had to upgrade about halfway in. This means that you initially get registered for an MPhil, and have to convince a committee that you are worthy of being registered for the full PhD. I had to jump through hoops like we all did, had an interview with Alistair Fitter, got upgraded. Not worth mentioning except for its explanation by MBU. Before the sequence kicked off, he called me into his office and explained that he didn't really agree with the process but that we had to go along with it. He looked me sternly in the eyes, and said something like "This process is to allow the timid spineless staff to get rid of inadequate students by hiding behind the committee. (In a slight mimic falsetto voice:) 'I hate to lose you but the committee says you have to go because the regulations say so'. (Change to a deep sergeant major voice:) 'If I think you are not good enough, I will look you in the face and tell you to go.'" A long pause . . . "'As it happens I don't think that you are weak enough to be removed just yet, so I am going to suggest that we enter you for the usual upgrade process'." I left his office, rather shell shocked. A bit later the chap I shared an office with, Richard Jefferson, said, "Did he do that bit about saying he'd throw you out if you weren't good enough? He does that to everyone."

One curious parallel between myself and Michael Usher is our interest in quarries as nature reserves. Michael got PhDs to study this – I shared a desk with Richard Jefferson, still an active conservation writer – who studied the recolonisation of Yorkshire quarries. Richard Jefferson was out in a disused Yorkshire chalk quarry one day counting his seedlings when a loudhailer voice told him to put his hands in the air. He looked up to find a police marksman pointing a rifle at his chest. Someone had seen Richard with his quadrats and flower books and called the police saying he was in the uniform of the IRA and on some terrorist training camp. In his PhD thesis Richard improved on the usual acknowledgements section with a "No thanks to the following:" list. I forget the details but it certainly included: "No thanks to the man who put his bee hives on top of my experiments. No thanks to the man who called the police saying I was from the IRA". Such an inspirational idea, pity it never caught on!

A previous one of MBU's PhD students, Terry Parr, studied Collembola in a particular quarry called Wharram Quarry, still a Yorkshire Wildlife Trust reserve, finding *Brachystomella parvula* in the youngest soils closest to the working edges. I have become warden for Inholms Clay Pit, while MBU became warden for Wharram Quarry. (He later told me that when he left York to move to Scotland he gave the records and archives of Wharram Quarry to Yorkshire Wildlife Trust, who lost all trace of them. This story haunts me.) Unlike Inholms Clay Pit, Wharram is hard, dry, bare limestone, and the orchids are bee orchids. (Old quarries are good for orchids.) The orchids come and go with succession, and at one stage in the 1970s the Wharram bee orchids were being shaded out. What happened next went down in Yorkshire conservation legend – I heard a version from Ian Rotherham in Sheffield some 30 years later. MBU got a contract with someone with a JCB, and employed them to scrape the entire quarry floor bare. This was rational, was defensible, did work, but maybe should have been explained to the management committee before rather than after the event. It seems that everyone else involved with Wharram Quarry YWT reserve turned up on site to discover the whole reserve bulldozed flat, with especial emphasis on the orchid areas which had been hammered. Different versions of the story used expressions like "had kittens" and "apoplexy", and even MBU made some cryptic comment about getting complaints from "Job's comforters".

So the bulldozing did what it was meant to, which is to reset the succession. The following year the bulldozed areas were smothered in a spiky biennial called Weld *Resedea luteola*, from long-dormant seeds, which formed an impenetrable metre-high forest the year after. None of this pleased the managers at YWT one little bit. But then the Weld died off (it's a biennial), and in the thin turf that replaced it were hundreds of bee orchids. It was entirely rational to reset a succession in a successional system like a brownfield site. I had this story in mind when I got SWT to excavate insect cliffs at Inholms. When SWT – and MVDC – asked what I wanted for the site I said I wanted it bulldozed flat. It never happened, of course, but I got two new cliffs. I made a point of emphasising the need for resetting successions in my Roehampton conservation module, though whether anyone actually listened remains to be established. The logic is inexorable – some life forms only survive in early successional habitats, in whatever succession you are looking at. This is a plant succession, the most familiar sort, but you also get successions in mushrooms and springtails (and on decomposers of dead bodies and pretty much any other group in any other unstable habitat). Always, to encourage early successional species you absolutely must have early successional habitats. In the case of land plant successions, this of course means physically creating early successional habitats. This requires destroying something existing and stable, unavoidably, as space is finite. Following this logic, I have found myself telling Lee Valley Park Authority around 2003 that they should bulldoze a few hectares of their native woodland and smother it to at least 30cm depth with the industrial waste PFA, to kill all underlying plants and restart the succession. Otherwise, they would lose their nationally famous orchid colony. They did no such thing (of course), and duly lost their nationally famous orchids. In the chapter on Inholms Clay Pit, I reprint an email to Mole Valley Council in which I lament exactly this temperamental behaviour of orchid colonies.

For two autumns (1982 and 83) I was based at ITE Merlewood, in Grange-over-Sands. ITE (Institute of Terrestrial Ecology) was set up as the research wing of the Nature Conservancy Council (NCC – they ran Rostherne). A few years after I left, ITE got merged with the Institute of Hydrology to make CEH, the Centre for Ecology and Hydrology CEH). This required me to live in Grange-over-Sands for two autumns, to collect field samples for lab work in York. Merlewood was an old hotel rather unconvincingly repurposed as ecology labs, with faded posters about soil organic matter mineralisation rates. The staff were permanent, went home to family each evening, leaving transient students like me with no social life whatsoever. Having done a couple of autumns' fieldwork there, I treasure the quote from a CERL colleague (Keith Brown) about Merlewood: "It's got so much dead wood it's a fire hazard". Rather unfair – some really good researchers came through Merlewood (Richard Bardgett and Phil Ineson, among others).

Views of ITE Merlewood:

Fig 5.5 ITE Merlewood as it was in 1982.

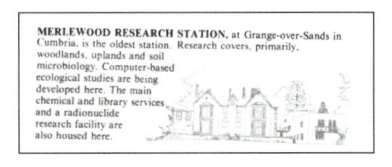

Fig 5.6 A NERC leaflet about ITE Merlewood.

It was in Grange-over-Sands more than anywhere else I had real problems with boredom and loneliness. I did not have a computer with me – the horror of it! I had bought a Dragon 32 and enjoyed writing BASIC code, but had unwisely sent it off for an upgrade and it took ages to come back. No PC, no TV, no humans my age, alone in an old farmhouse on the edge of open moorland. Nearest pub a mile away, the road such a poor track I was scared for my car's suspension. I did have quite a few cacti, remarkably – how they ever survived Springbank farm is a wonder.

The landscape around Grange was undeniably pretty, in what George Monbiot calls a "sheep wrecked" way. In other words, lots of heavily grazed grass. The area was notable for some stunning natural structures called limestone pavements, one of which was photographed by my Italian friend Romano Baino. These are thought to have formed under woodland, and to get to Merlewood each morning was a 5km walk through Cartmel woods where this process was/is ongoing. Later I saw a similar outcrop by Hutton Roof with tropical ecologists called Mike and Helen Hokpins. Much later I had a tiny version of the same thing in my garden in France.

Fig 5.7 The Grange-over-Sands limestone pavement, sun after rain, photo by Romano Baino.

So, from October 1982 to December 1982, and again from October '83 to December '83, I lived in Grange-over-Sands, had a desk in ITE Merlewood, and used a Merlewood car to drive to my field site in the borders near Hexham. The site was called RAF Spadeadam. It was an RAF site not because of planes, but because of the former 'Blue Streak' missile project which was based there. Next to one of my clumps of lodgepole pine was a surface-to-air missile. Fierce-looking except that the nose cone was bent out of shape, suggesting it was symbolic purposes only. I did get stopped and questioned regularly for driving around RAF roads in a mustard-yellow Ford Escort with so many spots of Polyfilla it looked like it had smallpox. One day I was unlucky enough to turn up for my weekly collection of Collembola and fungi when Greenpeace had – for a weird reason – imposed a 'peace blockade' on the site. "Hi I'm an ecologist please let me in" doesn't work then, and I spent half an hour on the phone to some colonel, assuring him that I had signed the Official Secrets Act (true – ITE demanded it) and I only wanted to collect soil insects, not interfere with any of their operations or . . . Eventually I was let in, and so grateful to the blokes who spoke up for me that when I wrote the work up (Shaw & Usher 1997) I put in a specific note of thanks for the guards that day. (The editor queried this, until I explained that the kindness of the RAF guards saved the statistical integrity of my PhD sampling design.) Years later, in 2012, that acknowledgement in that paper got me an invite from the RAF to revisit to recheck the Collembola at Spadeadam. As a minor aside, I missed a neat trick one day at Spadeadam – my worst missed opportunity in the York years. I always talk to security staff – they know the wildlife on site far better than the managers – so made a point of getting the RAF staff at Spadeadam to talk. They had literally nothing of interest to do since Blue Streak had shut down a decade before, so welcomed the diversion that I presented and always chatted. One day in 1983, one old bloke with a proper north-eastern accent, who lived in a remote house in a remote valley on the Spadeadam site, said he knew where there were Viking runes carved on stones somewhere on the Spadeadam moors. He said someone from a university was on the case, so I asked no more, being keen to get on with my work and back to the lab for the hour setting up the soil samples rather than spend another half hour listening to a bored bloke rabbit on. Pillock, I should have asked him for the full details. In 2012 when I returned there, staff on site were all new and while entirely helpful and friendly, they politely did not believe me when I said there were Viking rune stones on site. Nothing noted online, of course. I am sure these carved stones exist and will be re-found one day, just wish I'd kept the knowledge.

Before going on to York, I must observe that Grange-over-Sands was the most dismally damp and dreary place I have ever had the misfortune to live. In two autumns, I counted one day when it wasn't raining at least some of the time. Henry would only start if you kept a dry newspaper under the bonnet each evening. Sometimes he'd hit a puddle, stop a while, then the heat dried the spark plugs off and he'd start again. The farmhouse I rented in 1982 was surrounded by fields, and as autumn turned into a cold soaking winter, every mouse in the area decided to move in with me. I had mice on the kitchen shelves and mice scampering around the living room. I really hit my limit when one ran up my trouser leg without warning, then when it realised its mistake, it ran down my sock. I killed it by hitting this scratchy lump in my sock, and started investing in mousetraps. I was SO glad to be back at York in a big, warm accommodation block with female humans instead of mice. Some students really enjoyed being based at ITE Merlewood,[1] but I was too used to university levels of social life for the under-30s, and Grange-over-Sands just wasn't. It is supposed to have the highest average age in the country by virtue of being a retirement town – plausible, though why retire somewhere cold, cloudy, rainy and universally steep?

Clearly York required a total kickstart of my social life. Most of these have gone the way of casual college contacts, but a few have proved noteworthy. Starting with a classic hippy-looking couple – he had long blond hair and went round in a black cape, she had long black hair and was into artistic expression. Deb and Mark. Mark Cahill and Deb Weinstein. Mark did physics, did a PhD in physics at Canterbury, I'm still in email contact with him – he ran IT at Bath University. Mark spent hours writing computer code for fun, like myself. We spent hours talking about coding (in DOS BASIC!) and about our computing projects at school. Deb started an English degree but dropped out, couldn't solve a linear equation, but was very intelligent, inquisitive and well read, and liked plants. (She would be fully entitled to say that I worried too much about linear models, needed to explore artistic expression but was quite good with plants.) I popped round to get stoned with them most weekends, often with other members of the alternative scene. It was Deb and Mark who introduced me to Phil Hunt, hence aikido. They came see me in Grange-over-Sands – we did mushrooms (*Psilocybe semilanceata*) in Cartmel woods. I got briefly much closer to Deb after they separated, March 1985, shortly before leaving York. I can see that Deb must have been a bit of a challenge to live with. After her marriage to a long-forgotten chap called David they went on honeymoon camping in Scotland, and David got a tick *Ixodes* embedded in his scrotum. Sadly common, easily treated by twisting it out with tweezers. Deb decided to burn it off with a lit match. The marriage did not last long after this. Later in York she found a young hedgehog, dying piteously in her garden, and decided to rescue it. Of course it was infested with ectoparasites like hedgehogs always are, so she put it onto her duvet and covered it in flea powder, at which point all the fleas and lice abandoned ship for a safe new home in the duvet. Her relationship with Mark didn't last well either, and of course the hedgehog died shortly afterwards of dehydration from a nasty bout of diarrhoea (again not an asset in anyone's bedroom). When I took Deb to see a Bruce Springsteen concert in Leeds in summer 1985 I rolled up at her place around 4pm to find she was still in bed pondering breakfast. (We had no tickets and crashed a hole in the fence, of course.)

The other very significant person in York was a post-doc in John Lawton's lab working on extra-floral nectaries in common vetch *Vicia sativa*. She was (Dr) Suzanne Koptur, again someone I am still in regular contact with. Suzanne is a tropical forest ecologist, who did her PhD in Costa Rica on the 'extra-floral nectaries' of *Inga*. This needs a little unpacking, and actually turns out to be about a profoundly interesting question in botanical evolution. *Inga* is a genus of tree that grows in Costa Rica. It is distantly related to peas and beans (Fabaceae), though *Mimosa* trees are evolutionarily closer and much more obviously tree-like. *Inga* produces sugars (like all plants) and has organs that secrete sugary juice, called nectaries. Most flowering plants have nectaries, inside their flowers, to make a sugary reward for pollinating insects. Wind pollinated plants do not do this AFAIK, as it would be a waste of energy. Literally, a waste of the chemical energy that the plant has slowly accumulated from hours of sunlight. Evolution selects against wasted energy, as a gene for wasting energy will on long-term average lose out to an allele that invests that energy in the future of the gene line. But *Inga*, like many other plants, has nectaries on its petioles and leaves, just pumping out energy-rich sugars for the world to enjoy. Why? It was suspected that these attracted ants which in turn protect the tree from herbivores. It is well established that ants like sugar, and that some trees have a special relationship with ants (read up about ant-acacias), so the idea had some merit. But this would open a much wider question, since extrafloral nectaries are quite widespread in the flowering plants. Maybe they all do the same job, effectively payment to a band of hymenopteran mercenaries who keep herbivores at bay – for a fee of sugars? So, Suzanne tried to keep ants off *Inga* trees by various cunning methods, and showed more herbivore damage where ants were excluded. This was a nice result, and with potential to become a more general result. Scientists always like general results, as they represent a new way of looking at the world and one that may well be copied down the academic generations. Your hope is that future PhD theses will say things like "nectaries were ablated by the classic methodology of Koptur (1982)" etc. (More usually it's along the lines of "The basic method of Shaw (1985) was improved by . . .") So Suzanne collaborated with one of the most eminent UK ecologists, John Lawton of York University, to see if funding could be found to replicate these experiments on the extrafloral nectaries of a convenient UK plant. By some path I will never know, they obtained NATO funding for Suzanne to spend a year in the UK on a post-doctoral fellowship, studying a native UK plant called the common vetch *Vicia sativa*. This has really big, easily visible nectaries on each leaf base – a taxonomic feature of the species – and is common enough to find in every garden. The funding was forthcoming, Suzanne arrived in York in January 1984, and the rest, as they say, is history.

It was in January 1984 that Suzanne Koptur turned up in Alcuin College, also based on the same floor in the biology block as me, with a year to fill and knowing no-one. I'd been in York for a year, giving me some apology for settled status, and somehow I summoned up enough courage to ask her out. Thankfully we got on well, and by Feb 1984 we were actually in a proper relationship. My first. It sounds hackneyed, sorry, but it's true that the experience of falling in love for the first time as winter turns into spring is such a wonderful state of being that standard adjectives just don't do the job. Needs new words for a new neuronal state (I have seen the word 'liminence' used in this context,

Fig 5.8 With Suzanne, North York Moors Railway c. May 1984.

as a noun – the state of being – not an adjective). Once in a lifetime – thanks for the experience, everyone should feel it before they die. Just about then there were snowdrops in flower as we walked into York (also a pretty little annual called Spring Beauty *Claytonia perfoliata*) and somehow I looked hard into them for the first time. Even now, seeing their delicate white flowers still reminds me of that time, and these pretty and tough little bulbs have cropped up in later life as a recurring theme in my gardens (see also 'Whitelands'). I didn't know that simply being with someone could be such a powerful experience. We drove out to the Yorkshire Dales or coastline every weekend, watching puffins or curlews while sharing a picnic – Poivre Boursin maybe. We took a ride on a steam railway, went to folk clubs, and generally enjoyed each other's company. I met her mother and sister when they came over – played backgammon with her mother, and think of her each time I roll a double 1 (she emphasised how much she valued rolling a double 1). They were of Bulgarian descent, with family stories of life in Bulgaria. Suzanne and I shared an allotment behind Heslington Hall. Some things like bee borage worked fine, but the rabbits ate anything tasty. It is amazing how much time and effort you can sink into an allotment without getting much food back, but as a shared experience it was lovely. She puzzled me with the description "croquettes" for dead seedlings, derived from the diminutive plural noun of the verb 'to croak' – to die, hence croakettes. Suzanne was friends with two tropical ecologists who happened to live in Lancashire – Mike and Helen Hopkins, living in Hutton Roof, a small village not far from Grange-over-Sands. We went over and stayed with them for a few days. I got a giant pea pod off them (*Entada scandens*) that I used for years in my lectures on tropical island ecology. Later, Mike Hopkins turned up as a collaborator with one of our PhD students, Adrian Barnett, also an Amazonian biologist. Small world!

Suzanne's supervisor was Prof John Lawton, who was eminent then and became much more so later, heading up NERC and advising the government on scientific matters. He features in this Radio 4 biopic: https://www.bbc.co.uk/programmes/b01d0rtj

His relationship with my supervisor MBU was professional rather than warm. One evening Suzanne entertained John to a meal in her flat, and of course I was there knocking back the wine as well as the others. After a bottle of my homemade elderberry wine, my sense of politics

Fig 5.9 Professor John Lawton, Suzanne's supervisor.

and tact (never well developed at the best of times) evaporated badly, and I remember saying to John Lawton that meeting Michael Usher when you're stoned is a horrible experience. John flashed back: "Meeting Michael Usher when you're not stoned is a pretty horrible experience too."

So, Suzanne's post-doc ended in Dec 1984, then I drove her down to Heathrow. We stayed overnight in Whitelands College Gilbert Scott building (staying in the room of my sister Caroline, not knowing I would teach there 15 years later), and finally said goodbye at the Heathrow security desk. We next met at a conference in Oxford in 1988. I discovered Jan-Feb 1985 the symmetry of the pulse of happiness from starting a relationship; which is of course the pulse of unhappiness when it ends. I think it is quite plausibly mathematically symmetrical if you visualise the first differential of some vaguely square-wave time-dependent 'happiness function'. A big pulse above baseline (the steep rise at the start) seems to be matched by a similar later drop (the negative gradient at the end as you return to baseline). Whatever, I have to admit that being left alone to get on with my thesis was just what I needed to get the blasted thing finished – either mope, or keep busy by working on chapters, so I worked on chapters.

Life in York in 1985 had some upsides. For a start I had a car and a whole student accommodation block to myself out of term time. Into which I generally settled in and made myself at home, even buying my own fridge in the kitchen next door, with a padlock and big chain round it. The first time Deb looked at the chain she smiled knowingly. Unlike home, it was full of undergraduates all term (they transformed the local social life for the better) but conference goers out of term (who didn't). You had a building full of accountants / OU students / balloonists / Samaritans / whatever with lots of alcohol and two days to pretend they're students again. I had a thesis to finish and needed my sleep. I think one party of balloonists caused me the most sleep loss (drinking till about an hour before dawn, then they vanished and just as I was drifting off to sleep their blasted and surprisingly noisy balloons drifted over the accommodation block, one at a time, just as the dawn was coming up. Or maybe it was having the room above mine full of >20 Samaritans dancing the Hokey Cokey at 3am, the floor shaking while I worried about the PASCAL code to write data to my appendices. I should have told them they were making me suicidal, though psychopathic would have been more accurate.

About this time Mark and Deb split up and in March 1985 I was able to take Deb out a few times, collecting plant fossils on the coastline near Scarborough. The Hayburn Wyke – well worth a visit. Host to fossil cycads and 2m high horsetails in the cliff, but horribly easy to get cut off by the tide. When I took Tobias (who later put a poisonous mushroom *Paxillus involutus* in a pizza – see below) and friends fossil hunting there, we got cycads and horsetails but had to climb out over boulders as the tide was about to cut us off. James Merryweather told me of the place, its fossils, and warned me of his multi-hour wait with armfuls of wonderful fossils on the crumbling cliff to escape. While hunting Mesozoic invertebrates in the Yorkshire Cliffs, I found the milk tooth from a baby mammoth, in the boulder clay overlying the fossil beds at Speeton (near Bempton Cliffs), still one of my most treasured possessions. I briefly entertained the idea of a 100MYA dinosaur tooth but that was impossible – reptiles have simple peg-like

Fig 5.10 Paxillus involutus, *the common roll rim. This toxic ectomycorrhizal fungus cropped up in my experiments, and on a friend's table.*

Fig 5.11 Mammoth tooth from Speeton, Yorks boulder clay 1985.

teeth and this was unmistakably highly folded, exactly like an Indian elephant (and from the much younger, overlying ice-age debris).

James Merryweather deserves an individual mention. He was in the university as a key technician in Biology, but this was almost a side-line when set alongside his other activities. He was also an expert in medieval music, playing bagpipes in a medieval re-enactment group called the York Waits. He did a PhD with Alistair Fitter on the VA endomycorrhizas of "Pretty Wood", Yorkshire. See Merryweather (1993). Among other findings he showed that infection with different species of VAM profoundly affected the biology of common woodland flowers, altering things like flowering time as well as nutrient status. I find these responses amazing, and not mentioned in basic teaching on mycorrhizas. After retirement to Skye (hence 'Blue Skye Thinking'), he went on to become, among other things, a UK expert in pteridophytes (publishing a highly praised field guide to UK pteridophyta in 2020). Ironically for someone portrayed as 'The Provider' of York teaching labs, he has done what he can do to be the scourge of creationists. At one stage I sent a "readers' letter" to a minor Scottish provincial newspaper about some anti-evolutionary outburst by some west coast minister, inspired by James. I forget the details of the situation, and doubt that I caused that vicar to lose his faith, but I really do not support misleading kids about basic scientific facts. The Presbyterians of the Scottish Isles have traditionally been especially fiery – the "Wee Frees" as they dislike being called.

It was during January 1985 that I found that I really missed Suzanne rather badly. To set the situation in a wider context with the benefit of hindsight, the

Fig 5.12 The cartoon about James Merryweather.

Fig 5.13 James Merryweather in medieval garb.

final write-up stage of a PhD is always such a traumatic and tense time for almost everyone almost every time, that this added stress probably didn't take my dopamine circuits down much further than they would have been anyway, though I don't think that was quite the answer I was looking for at the time. I even made the bad mistake of saying to MBU in his laboratory one day that I wanted to fly out to Miami to see Suzanne. I'm not telepathic and human facial expressions don't always make much of an impression, but I do clearly remember his face contorting in a strange way, less frown and more snarl, and flushing a few shades pinker than normal. I remember him snapping, "You will do no such thing. Your priority now is to finish your PhD thesis, nothing else. Plenty of time for jetting off to see girlfriends once that is done." Annoyingly I have to concede he was right. So I stayed in York, wrote my thesis, and spoke to Suzanne by phone. It is astonishing how quickly old coin phones swallowed silver coins on international calls! RSI from feeding in 10p pieces as fast as they would go in. It should be noted that the job in Miami International University that Suzanne landed in 1984 has turned out to be a good position and her job for life, so York can be said to have shaped her life too, also very positively. Suzanne later married a nice man called John – we've met once in Kew Gardens when they came over. They have a son, we swap Xmas cards, and everyone's life has ticked on just fine. And I still think of the York spring each time I see snowdrops.

Thus it was that, almost exactly 30 years later, I could pass on Michael Usher's sensitivity and guidance on PhD supervision to a PhD student of my own – let's call her Louise. Probably my most academically brilliant of my PhD students, always turning in lovely writing based on good research. This did not always equate to a corresponding level of internal happiness. Always a sensitive soul, her equanimity resembled the bloom on a peach (but without the same durability). Louise lived with a man who sounded rather tedious to me (eg he refused to drive on a motorway so to go long distance they went across country on minor roads for hours and hours), but about whom she talked quite a bit. About nine months before her thesis was due, she walked into college looking like a poster child for PTSD. I'm not very good at faces but she took the hangdog look a few steps closer to blind horror. It turned out that her man had ended their relationship, and she would have to live alone. She was distraught. So here was my chance to show that

I had learned from my brush with MBU, and was a caring, supportive supervisor. "That's almost exactly what happened to me. It was just what I needed to get my thesis finished," I explained supportively. "You too – exactly the opportunity you need to finish off your thesis – nothing to do but feel awful and mope or write up – so logically you get on with writing up. In the meantime, chuck him out so you can carry on living in the same place while you write up. At all costs, keep on with the write up." So she did the exact opposite – moved out of their former flat into some student accommodation in Reading, and got signed off sick. As she wailed in a subsequent supervision, the corridor she found herself on was full of loud reggae music and cannabis smoke. "Yes, that was exactly my experience," I smiled happily, thinking nostalgically about the social life in Alcuin D block in summer 1985. Sad to say, I don't think she ever really forgave me.

Apart from finishing my PhD thesis (submitted one week before the 3-year deadline – YES!) I did one other really useful thing in 1985, which was to apply for a job as a research scientist with the CEGB at CERL. This gets a chapter to itself ('CERL'), but the interview was May 1985, in my York phase. So I saw the advert in New Scientist, put in the application, got called to interview, got the train down to Leatherhead, stayed with Gwen Hack ('Aunty Gwen' but in reality a Whitelands College friend of my mother's) who also lived in Leatherhead, along with my Godfather Howard Hack, a CEGB engineer. I dumped my rucksack chez Gwen and passed her my suit and shirt, then sat down with a cup of tea. A few minutes later Gwen came in looking worried. It transpired that although I had my suit and white shirt and clean shoes, I had somehow left the suit trousers back in my bedroom in York. Jacket and underwear would not be the interview look I had in mind. Happily, her next door neighbour's son was about my size, so I passed the CEGB interview in a borrowed suit. I quip that I owe my entire career to Gwen, but actually I do think that I really was on the cusp of blowing my one good chance, so the logic stands. Sad but true, Gwen improved my employability in one 30-minute period more than Michael Usher did in three years!

Before moving on from my formative years in York, I wish to mention three York-related anecdotes that have stayed with me. About snowdrops, toxic mushrooms and night-flowering cacti.

Galanthus nivalis, the snowdrop, one of my favourite flowers, is probably native to Turkey but has been grown over here since at least Medieval times. It is noted for tolerating the coldest weather, and naturalising well. It is very bad to eat, so that one of my abiding horticultural nightmares is that a snowdrop bulb gets into my garlic patch. The bulbs and leaves look almost identical. You'd never know till you got sick. Not, thankfully, dangerously hospital-level sick, but a really sore tummy for a few days. So before adding any soil to my vegetable patch I check it very carefully for bulbs. One experience from my weekend walks round Yorkshire came to define a snowdrop legacy in all 'my' plantings. This concerns a pretty little lake called Gormire, about 30km north of York (near to a REALLY STEEP road called Sutton Bank). It has its own wikipage https://en.wikipedia.org/wiki/Gormire_Lake I forget all but a few key details – I was walking near there with a friend called David Gibeaut, who came over from California with Walter Appleby. H*e* researched plant physiology on a post-doc, and helped Walter tour English gardens for his photographic survey. (Before leaving, David and Walter hired a car and in their words, "We did Scotland. Then Wales, then Cornwall". Americans don't worry about long drives. When they returned the car a week later the lady at the car hire return gasped and triple checked the mileage before asking them where they had been.) So David and I were walking by Gormire and found by the path a crumbled down remains of a stone cottage. No roof tiles, just a few crumbled walls and the clear remains of a front door, maybe last used by a Victorian shepherd. By the remains of the front door was a huge flourishing clump of snowdrops. Quite apart from dating this visit to February 1985, this observation made a profound impression on me since it showed snowdrops easily out-lasting a stone structure. They are effectively immortal. So, I have made it my business to encourage snowdrops wherever I can, getting annual satisfaction from watching old clumps re-appear in the same spot at the same sort of time year after year after year. The new Whitelands College has lines of snowdrops in front of the main building after I rescued them. The old Whitelands gave us dozens of snowdrop clumps that now adorn the Holmwood Park estate – both on my land and in public areas. None in the wild areas of the claypit I hasten to add – they are technically aliens, though with a long pedigree of escaping from English gardens. Each February I keep an eye out for escaped snowdrops coming up in local hedges to be "rescued". This is legitimate – technically they are invasive aliens to be removed, and they are readily transplanted in March to somewhere more welcoming.

So, onto mushrooms. Or toadstools if you prefer – the distinction is a semantic quibble, they're fungal spore-shedding structures. Not the magic ones in this chapter, just toxic ones. One minor skill that came out of my PhD was identifying fungi in the field. To be honest, I've been doing that since Rostherne in 1979 (nothing like eating them to make you check ID), but my PhD required me to survey ectomycorrhizal fungal carpophores (=mushrooms under the pine trees) so I got quite good. Good enough that I've eaten 14 wild species and not poisoned myself yet, though I shouldn't raise a hostage to fortune. I can see the epitaphs now: "In his autobiography, Dr Shaw who has just died horribly of mushroom poisoning, boasted of having eaten 14 wild species and never once poisoned himself". So it was that one day in autumn 1985 I popped into a friend's house, and saw some interesting mushrooms on the kitchen table. "Toby," I said – for the friend in question was called Tobias – "why is there a *Paxillus involutus* on the kitchen table all chopped up? You do know, don't you, that is reputed to be deadly poisonous?" I could have said much more since I have worked a lot with *Paxillus involutus*, the 'common roll rim' mushroom – photo above. It is a facultative ectomycorrhizal that appears early in ectomycorrhizal successions. For a review of ectomycorrhizal successions and an example from the Liphook forest fumigation experiment, I refer you to Shaw & Lankey (1994). I grew it on agar for infecting sterile pine seedlings, and it behaved well compared to *Amanitas* or *Suillus*. I have seen it on decaying logs, clearly living as a saprophyte, so it is easy to grow, unlike late-stage successional fungi like *Amanita* or *Cortinarius*. It probably isn't as toxic as it sounds, since it is common widespread fungus that has been sometimes been eaten (supposedly in eastern Europe) after boiling and throwing away the water. If you do this with some *Amanitas* you will die slowly, horribly and inexorably. *Paxillus* does not have this reputation, more that it causes cumulative haemolysis, so you could probably survive a small exposure. Anyway, Toby's girlfriend Sally-Anne pulled a bit of a face and the mushroom that was intended for their home-made pizza got chucked out quickly. I quip that my mushroom PhD gave Bedales school their Head of Physics, though this is probably an exaggeration.

I retain one very tangible legacy of Michael Usher's laboratory in York, which is a cutting of the cactus he had brought back from his time in Ghana. Michael Usher spent a while in Ghana before starting at York – I heard the name "Ashanti" mentioned, and know he published a few papers on termites and termite protection. Anyway, he came back with a 'moon cactus', *Epiphyllum oxypetalum,* a queen of the night that grows REALLY big! It was grown as a hedge plant in Ghana. Michael grew it up the lab window – easily 2.5m high. When it grows it puts out long thin shoots 1-2m long, effectively a cactus evolved into a liana. No-one would grow it for its growth habit, which is incorrigibly inelegant, sticking out oddly shaped stems at odd angles. You grow it for the flowers, which are huge, nocturnal and perhaps the most beautiful thing I have ever seen.

The biology of all the true *Epiphyllums* is the same – they live on leaf mould up trees in the jungle, and need to attract bats for pollination. So, in cultivation they need warm conditions and acid, organic soil – leaf mould is best and free. Quite tolerant of drought, but they do not need it, unlike desert cacti. Then one day a small scaly bud appears in what looks like an old leaf (it's a stem in reality). This gets bigger and bigger until maybe 25cm long, curved so it's sometime called the dutchman's pipe. It swells for several weeks, then one day you see some paleness showing inside the bud – watch it every hour every evening! It will open at dusk, and suddenly become huge and intensely white. To attract every bat in the jungle it emits a powerful but lovely perfume, a distinctive fragrance. More than once this plant has flowered un-noticed on some window ledge, but just after dusk the whole house starts to smell of the fragrance, so I knew it had flowered. In Costa Rica, it is recorded that humans can smell the fragrance 100m away in dense jungle.

This plant first grabbed my attention in September 1985, when I had finished writing my PhD thesis but still had to assemble it. Word processing was in its infancy at the time, and the entire department **shared one word processor** (!) that couldn't handle images and got indigestion if you asked for page numbers. On this machine I once saw someone lose six months of their life, when their entire thesis (which was just on one disk) suddenly corrupted. (ALWAYS have two copies.) This machine had a sign-in sheet, which was fully booked not just 9-5 but fully booked 0200-0400 Sundays. When I used this machine, each time that I went to the toilet some poor soul would usurp my place. Rather than argue whose thesis time pressure was the most mind bendingly urgent, I used to modify one crucial system file before heading off downstairs for a wee. The knack was to drop down to Unix then rename some crucial system file like ALPHA.EXE to something else similar looking before heading off – 'OLPHA.EXE' did the trick, for example. The 'alphachronic' (properly called the 'Alphatronic') was so notoriously temperamental that no-one thought it odd that the system flatly refused to load. "Yes, useless thing, it said that to me too – still I'll have one more go with it" was the best way to be left alone with a crippled word processor. Then, when all was quiet, I used unix to rename the system file to its correct title, and hey-presto it all worked again. (In case you are interested, the way this worked involved a setup batch file called something like INI.BAT containing text saying "alpha.exe" to launch the word processor package when the disc was first inserted. I could have altered this file too, but didn't dare because this could have made the system totally unusable, which would probably have caused about half a dozen nervous breakdowns and made me public enemy number one. I always left it working AOK.)

So by September 1985 I had all the pages of a thesis, and all the diagrams, but no page numbers. Also, my artistic skills are so limited that each diagram and figure had at least one duff copy, blurred or stained or some such. The solution – to the problem of ensuring that the examiners see only good copies – was to create 3 piles of the pages, number each by hand (OK, actually by typewriter) and ensure that the duff copy was in the thesis I kept myself. I duly got out three copies of everything, sat down in the lab after dinner, and started sorting, piling and typing. Sound easy, but all such sorting jobs are non-linear (quadratic generally) with number of cases, so a thesis of 300 pages is 9* longer to sort out than a mere 100 pages. In other words, it was a huge job. About 1am I found that not only was it a huge job, that I was winning, but also that the lab had the most amazing smell. This was an *Epiphyllum oxypetalum* flower that had 'chosen' to flower that evening. Maybe my leaving the light on late forced it, though I like to think that it was cheering me on. Subsequently it has often timed its flower well, including "predicting" one baby and two marathons, among other special evenings and memorable events.

Fig 5.14 The York clone of "Queen of the night" Epiphyllum oxypetalum, *July 2022.*

CHAPTER 6

(M is for Megawatts. 660MW to be precise. See below.)

Central Electricity Generating Board years 1985-1992.

One of the more unusual parts of my life was also one of the best for me, in terms of both academic and personal development. I was a research scientist for a national government-owned body, the Central Electricity Generating Board = CEGB. In this role I have visited about 10 power stations, stood inside cooling towers, explored the industrial archaeology of old ash dumps, got my only paper in 'Nature', along with most of the better publications on my CV and certainly anything to do with SO_2 or O_3. Also my first book, "The Acid Tests", a monograph about the entire corpus of biological "acid rain" research funded by the CEGB and its successors.

It may be an indicator of a left-wing government, when state-funded state industrial outfits spawn incongruous academic appendages. About 1994 I was briefly expected to collaborate with academics working for the philosophy department of the Moscow Steel institute, for reasons I never understood. (Nor ever visited, though got to Heathrow one day to be told at the check-in desk my visa was invalid.) Thus the CEGB was set up by a left-wing Labour government post-WW2 (along with the NHS) as an engineering establishment dedicated to keeping the lights on across the UK, and the CEGB spawned a research laboratory called CERL (Central Electricity Research Laboratories). This looked at high voltage transmission systems, was based in Leatherhead, and which soon ran out of space in its little triangle up against the railway line so expanded onto a bigger site nearby, and expanded into power station chemistry. From the 1950s to the 1970s the Leatherhead laboratories were world-leading for their research into power station chemistry and transmission systems. After privatisation, when the site was sold, I heard it said that the accountants talked to the wrong people to evaluate CERL. They asked power station managers, who didn't talk to anyone from "the boffin hole" (their name for the site, not ours) from one year to the next. They should have talked to power station chemists, who were on the phone to CERL on a monthly basis. They even employed biologists – initially to advise on chlorination regimes to control mussel fouling in coastal power stations (which BTW is a real and serious problem), but around 1984 'Acid rain' became international news, and they started employing biologists to undertake pure academic research on acidification. Thus it came to pass that I got employed by the state electricity producer to count toadstools in a remote woodland!

Back in York in 1985, the end of my PhD was in sight, but my future was not. I found an advert in New Scientist for a soil microbiologist with the CEGB, and thought that my PhD in soil fungi would be close enough to apply. In fact, I had only ever counted toadstools, but it was a long shot that might be worth a go. To my astonishment they employed me, to help their biology team on a big new air pollution experiment.

The background is that in the early 1980s there was a considerable amount of media attention given to some new pollution effects in quite remote 'pure' parts of Europe. Specifically, fish deaths in acid lakes, and a mysterious dieback of some forests, mainly in high altitude parts of Germany. This 'Neuartigewaldschaden' = 'new type of forest decline' made trees go yellow prematurely and lose needles. The idea was that this was caused by long-range air pollution by SO_2 from coal, especially UK power stations that mainly burned coal at the time. Other governments were pressing the UK government to retrofit SO_2 scrubbers, which would have been spectacularly expensive, running into billions I was told. At the same time the science linking our SO_2 to their diebacks was frankly inadequate, an embarrassing mismatch between claim and evidence. So the CEGB ran research on whether its emissions really could be guilty of causing forest dieback in the Alps. This used in-house research employing a whole team of top scientists, and me. We were housed at CERL, the Central Electricity Research Laboratories, on Kelvin Avenue, Leatherhead. (Yes, Kelvin after the same Lord Kelvin who gave us absolute zero. Thermodynamics matter hugely in power station design.)

Nowadays this would not happen – a state-run research centre. There is a small biopic about the site, called "From Shed to watersheds – the history of CERL" (Ian Mogford, 1993 https://www.amazon.co.uk/CERL-shed-watershed-Ian-Mogford/dp/0951717227.)

In summary, the oldest labs went back to the post-war electricity board created by Attlee, which did research on transmission gear in the brick annexe passed by trains up to London. This cramped site was kept on for materials testing (including a scanning electron microscope, which I burned out on first use), but the research arm expanded to employ about 1000 people and a budget that must have been well over £1 million p.a. The whole CERL site had central buildings full of engineers, plus an idiosyncratic little building at the edge of the woods that held the biology department. (A recurring theme!) Initially the CEGB employed biologists on things like anti-fouling in pipes (sea water inlets can be utterly blocked by mussels settling, and loose autumn seaweed often shuts down coastal nuclear plant by blocking inlet filters). Then in the 1980s came along 'acid rain'. The public concern was about low-level effects: if you extrapolate from lab experiments in which wheat is exposed to SO_2 (that show a roughly linear increase in stress/damage with increasing SO_2, say in the 10ppm-100ppm range) to national wheat yield multiplied by 10ppb (=0.01ppm) that SO_2 actually is most of the time now) to find a huge financial cost.

As part of this we ran outdoor fumigation rigs, exposing plants to SO_2 etc in the field, not on pots, with controlled gas levels whatever the weather (except for a cut off at high wind speeds). This technology was developed in a field rig at Littlehampton Glass House Crops Research Institute (GCRI), with a circular array of nozzles releasing SO_2 in a crop in the field. There were multiple such rings, each controlled by a macsym computer to release SO_2 upwind on the plot and in larger amounts when the wind blows faster. The SO_2 levels were not constant, as they would be in a lab chamber, but fluctuated minute on minute, following values in a published SO_2 data set from near Birmingham. In other words, the pattern of peaks etc was wholly natural because it followed a real data set.

When this was run at Littlehampton, there is a photograph of the field showing big green circles against a backdrop of yellow leaves. SO_2 was proven to delay senescence, so was actively GOOD for the plants and their yields. This

Fig 6.1 A photograph from the Littlehampton field fumigation experiment, showing SO_2-treated plants to be green in a field of yellow, due to a reduction in leaf surface microfungi. The green pipes released the pollutant gas.

A Path of 21 Ms

turned out to be because the leaf-surface fungi were much more sensitive to SO_2 than wheat ever was, so the gas acted as a fungicide. Yeasts were especially sensitive – and Romans knew to burn sulphur in wine barrels to sterilize them.

I think that this work impressed Peter Chester and Walter Marshall, because it utterly undermined the argument that one can use linear approximations to estimate damage from low levels of SO_2. The response to SO_2 had a turning point around 100ppb where the fungal control was more beneficial to the crop than the metabolic load caused by the gas itself. Without Littlehampton, Liphook would never have happened. (As an aside, Andy McLeod once said that the same linear response logic was always applied to predicting the effects of low doses of ionizing radiation, and that this assumption should also be regarded as unreliable in the absence of good empirical experimental evidence.)

This same technology was deployed in conifers in a wood on 'Ironhill', near Liphook, Hants, henceforth just 'Liphook'. The site had 20m diameter circles of gas release pipes, with sample tubes everywhere (to allow feedback). It was physically hard to pack these huge circles into one patch of lowland heath, so in the end we only had seven plots. This gave us an awfully bad statistical design, essentially an unreplicated 2x3 factorial with an extra control plot. Remarkably, we manged to analyse this, but only because the ozone treatment did apparently nothing so we used that as a replicate. I should add that the treatments were SO_2 at three levels (ambient, ambient +10ppm, ambient + 20 ppm) crossed with O_3 at two levels (ambient, or ambient x1.5). The O_3 treatment was hard to set up but did nothing, interestingly. When setting up the O_3 generator, Andy McLeod

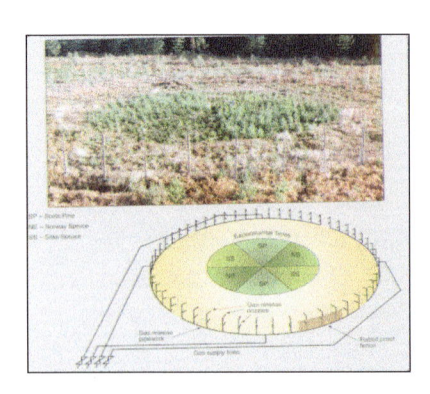

Fig 6.2 The layout of a plot at Liphook.

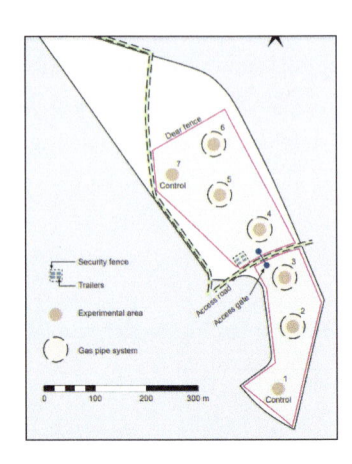

Fig 6.3 The layout of the seven plots at Ironhill, Liphook.

Fig 6.4 Gas release pipes around a Liphook plot. Gas was released at two heights to give a near-flat horizontal profile.

Fig 6.5 SO_2 tipburn on Scots pine, plus the sleeve of my Barbour jacket.

decided to catch the pollutant gas in a dustbin full of activated charcoal, to be sure none escaped into the woodland. This was a splendid example of mis-reading the real danger. O_3 – ozone – is highly reactive and an oxidant, yielding oxygen. Charcoal is carbon, which gets hot when it oxidises – we call it burning. So the dustbin full of charcoal caught fire within a minute or so of having O_3 pumped in, and they were just lucky it burned out harmlessly instead of wiping the entire site.

The Liphook site had seven circular plots each with Scots pine, Sitka and Norway spruces in paired blocks. They were planted in 1985, a bit before I started there, and when first seen they were tiny – about 20-30m tall. Each year we measured each of the 4100-ish trees, collected stem run off, soil water, foliage chemistry . . . in fact, everything we could think of. I was in charge of soil fungi, and (astonishingly) no one mentioned DNA. I spent many hours in the tea cabin at Liphook, mainly chatting to the technician Ken Alexander. No-one was ever as good at getting handling devices to behave themselves as Ken was. The team of Andy McLeod and Ken Alexander made the CEGB fumigation rigs work as a national level resource. Scientists from Imperial College came to CERL to get tips on handling pollutant gases at the ppb levels needed to emulate reality. Ken came to CERL from the Marie Curie, a cancer-research institution, and recalled the shock he had on his first day at going from the nanogram precision of molecular biochemistry to Joan Rippon giving him a bucket of dilute sulphuric acid to pour on the soil in an experimental lysimeter. Ken came with a rich fund of colourful stories, all, I fear, true. Nowadays one doesn't work with live rats, or if one does they are disposed of after death in a 'whole rat homogenizer' – a muscular blender that turns a dead rat into a liquid pulp that one flushes away down the sink. In Ken's day they used lots of rats at the Marie Curie and put the dead ones into a bin. So, one day Ken had a good idea. You can easily flush rats down the sink once they are finely powdered. However, rats have spent something like 400 million years evolving to NOT crumble into dust on contact, so they need some persuasion. Every science student knows that rose petals crumble to dust after exposure to liquid nitrogen at -196C, so why not repeat the experiment with *Rattus norvegicus*? So, Ken took a dead lab rat, immersed it in liquid nitrogen until it stopped fizzing, and took it out a literal stiff – probably mechanically stiffer than any dead rat has been before or since. Then the clever bit – hit frozen rat really hard with a hammer to fragment it. Do you know what? It worked! The rat disintegrated explosively into a cloud of fine dust. What happened next could have been predicted. The rat dust blew around, because that is what fine dust does. Then it settled, surprisingly widely around the lab. Then the rat dust thawed out and turned back to a thin sticky layer of finely minced dead rat. Which stayed there, decaying slowly and odiferously for weeks. And of course the fine dust penetrated deep into every crack before thawing and settling. Another good idea Ken had was to get rid of a load of unwanted hydrocarbons by burning them in a large metal skip, a long way from anywhere. I gather this was official advice from the fire brigade. Unfortunately, some of the labels had come off and it was a bit of a guess what got chucked in. The energy content of burning hydrocarbons is scary – think petrol – so it's not obvious what could make it worse. The answer is that a powerful oxidising agent could make it worse. One bottle that got chucked it had the label dissolved off by the acid, but Ken thinks it was perchloric acid. This is one of the most powerful oxidising agents going, and when mixed with hot hydrocarbons the energy release is likely to be spectacular. Ken described this unknown bottle going in, making a really strange glugging sound, quite unlike the hiss of the Winchesters of gallons of (highly toxic) benzene. It made an ominous glug, like a giant waking up. Ken and colleagues just had the sense to dive face down when the whole skip exploded, with an eruption of flame that involved the Marie Curie subsequently compensating allotment holders 100m away for the tops of their cabbages being burnt off. I probably spent more time chatting with Ken over a cup of tea, and less time collecting data at Liphook than ever claimed on my time sheets!

Other key staff who deserve to be mentioned include the section head Mike Roberts (TMR for T.M. Roberts but the T was never used), who left to run ITE Monks Wood and was succeeded by Richard Skeffington. TMR went on to run the government central science laboratories, and is the only person to interview me twice for two different jobs. (1st at CERL in 1985, 2nd for a position in Monks Wood in 1992 after CERL melted down. I didn't get the 2nd job, deservedly.) Both TMR and Richard Skeffington came from the illustrious stable of Professor Tony Bradshaw in Liverpool. TMR ran air pollution experiments looking for "invisible damage" to plants, making him ideal for acid rain research. Richard worked on the revegetation of China clay spoil mounds in Saint Austell, including some very significant findings showing that ecosystems need to accumulate a critical mass of fixed nitrogen before woodland can develop. The china clay work came with a good selection of anecdotes, mainly about what happened when non-scientific site managers had "good ideas". One such good idea was to graze the spoil mounds with Soay sheep. The is not totally daft since it has been known since 18th century research that sheep grazing improves soils fertility, and Soay sheep are an especially hardy lineage. Unfortunately, they are also especially bad at staying in well behaved flocks and especially good at jumping fences, resulting in all the sheep escaping within minutes, then grazing flower beds and back gardens all over Saint Austell. I gather that the entire staff spent the best part of a day rounding up errant stray sheep from back gardens all over the town. Then one manager learned that the difference between a mature soil and industrial waste was that mature soil has a higher carbon content, so he had the brilliant idea of adding the carbon directly in the form of pure sugar. He bought out pretty much the entire stock of sugar in the Saint Austell supermarkets, and added sugar like a fertilizer to the grass on the mound tops, in amounts corresponding to the carbon content of a woodland soil. Anyone with chemistry A level would know that soluble sugars create a high osmotic pressure (unlike dead leaves and insoluble humic acid molecules), sucking the water out of plant roots. This was lethal, and meant that the "restored" plots promptly died, visible at some distance, with the 'high' treatment plots appearing to be covered in golden syrup. Probably the soil microbial community had a huge density of the fast-growing saprophytes known as 'sugar fungi'. After privatisation Richard went on to become Professor of Geography at Reading University.

One more CERL researcher I worked with was Dr Keith Brown. He came with a rich collection of anecdotes of varying degrees of plausibility. My favourite comes from his time as a PhD student at Hull, where the Professor of Biochemistry (Edwin A Dawes) was also a member of the Magic Circle, performing a repertoire of illusions, some of which featured a tame white rabbit, that really did pop out of a hat etc. It was a docile, well trained creature that knew to stay quiet inside the Professor's jacket during the performance. It was housed in the departmental animal house, along with the lab rats, rabbits etc that were standard in those days. One day one of Keith's PhD colleagues needed some rabbit liver enzymes, so went down to the animal house, collected a random white rabbit, killed it and removed its liver for in the name of Science. Then someone gasped in horror. "Do you know what you've done? That was the Professor's magic rabbit! Better replace it fast before anyone notices." So the Professor's tame rabbit was replaced by a random white bunny, and no-one was any the wiser. Until, of course, the Professor's next public performance which was ruined by a frantic rabbit-shaped bulge kicking and scrabbling inside his shiny coat, as people looked on perplexed.

Keith went on to manage research at Harwell nuclear labs. In the later days as privatisation loomed, all CERL research staff – myself included – were required to return monthly statements about how much time we devoted to each job code. They imposed something called matrix management, meaning that we had to make sure the totals added up roughly correctly from the viewpoint of two different sets of managers. I think that the idea was that this made it too difficult to fiddle your data, compelling you to be honest. I also think that the brains behind this genius plan must have been a humanities graduate. Of course I wrote a little computer code that took as its input what I was meant to do, then gave outputs that added up to the correct totals from everyone's point of view. Then carried on doing exactly what I fancied, of course. The warning sign should have been that my answers were perfect – maybe I should have added some random noise for verisimilitude, but no-one said anything. Except years later, when Keith was running staff at Harwell. He told them my story, followed by a stern admonition: "If I catch you doing this you are in BIG TROUBLE!"

So, my contributions to the Liphook forest fumigation experiment were varied. At a practical level I quantified leaf decay (using litter bags), counted toadstools, and generally kept an eye on the trees. I also wrote and ran the database then identified each of the 4000ish trees and their associated square metre of soil. (AFAIK this database worked just fine, no clashes or misallocations, despite being written in an obscure mainframe language called APL where each command is a unique symbol and the code looks like Egyptian hieroglyphics.) It was while poking around aimlessly one day keeping an eye on things that I first spotted some odd damage that turned out to be sulphur dioxide damage on the Scots pines. This should not have happened – we controlled the SO_2 levels carefully and they never got into the hundreds of parts per million that were known to cause visible injury. We were looking at high levels being 40 parts per billion – ppb not ppm. The pines had no business getting burnt by this, but the evidence was overwhelming (twice as much damage in the high SO_2 plots as in the low SO_2

plots and none at all in the control.) After three years of data collection we had an answer. Firstly, it was only a select group of trees that got burnt needles. We knew each tree's history, and saw damage on the same few trees each year. So it was a genetically coded sensitivity, perhaps low levels of some anti-oxidant (that never got tested). Also, the damage varied from year to year, with some plots having more – or less – damage than was expected based on previous results. This gave us enough data to hunt for correlates of these inter-year differences, and it turned out after some fairly chunky multiple regression analyses that the best predictor of damage was average SO_2 level in the week when buds were first bursting and the new needles first emerge into the air. Having stated this it sounds like "Duh – obvious" but in fact the tests involved assembling each 1 day SO_2 means for 7 plots for 3 years, then all 2 days means, then all 3 day means, then all 4 day means . . . then ask SAS which set come top in a stepwise multiple regression. Stepwise MLR has gone out of favour with the statistical community for philosophical reasons, but worked like a charm in this case. (See Shaw, Holland, Darrell & McLeod 1993.)

By counting the ectomycorrhizal toadstools, I got a lovely successional change in the toadstools as the trees grew. In the first two years under tiny whips we mainly produce the little pinky-brown toadstools of the deceiver *Laccaria laccata* and a few of the bigger Brown Roll Rim *Paxillus involutus,* along with the brown crust of *Thelephora terestris* – earth fan. As the trees got over a metre high more fungi appeared, boletes like *Suillis bovinus* (and its parasite *Gomphidius roseus*). By the end of the project we had Fly Agaric *Amanita muscaria* and Cep *Boletus edulis* along with various *Cortinarius* and *Suillus* species. In 1990 the experiment ended and the CEGB was privatised. I quip that the new shareholders in National Power failed to see how my counting toadstool enhanced the performance of their shares, so the counting ended. Except that it didn't, as I left in 1992 to work at Roehampton, and (thoroughly enjoyed) going back on site for a few more years continuing the surveys. I had to (1) confine myself to Scots pine sectors as the spruces were impenetrable, spiky and low in fungi, (2) use a machete to carve a network of paths inside the Scots pine sectors. I assume that they are still there. It all got written up – to summarise seven years' work and more, there was no evidence that SO_2 or O_3 affected the ectomycorrhizal fungi at all, but species and age of tree made a huge difference, with a clearly defined successional sequence running roughly *Paxillus* + *Laccaria* to *Cortinarius* and *Amanita*. This is not mycologically surprising, but it has been a nice data set to compare multivariate analyses. (See Shaw Dighton & Poskitt 1993, or any of the multivariate analyses on this dataset in Shaw (2002).)

As well as fungi I ran the chemical analyses of foliage. The main result was unexpected, showing that the spruces had more nitrogen in the SO_2 plots. As known in 1955 London when hospitals opened bottles of ammonia to counteract the SO_2 levels, sulphur dioxide reacts VERY FAST with ammonia gas and pulls down a dust of ammonium sulphate. (My only Nature paper was this – McLeod et al 1990.) Less surprisingly, we got clear soil acidification and leaf damage in the SO_2 plots, but not in O_3. In the end, power stations were retrofitted for SO_2 removal, and I think that the clear evidence that SO_2 always acidified soil contributed to this change of heart. We never recreated German forest dieback, but it was later shown by Mike Roberts that we could not have done so. It was caused by acid rain leaching magnesium out of the thin poor acid soils, leaving the trees acutely magnesium deficient. This deficiency almost never occurs in the UK as enough magnesium falls in rainwater, due to sea salt. We had soil lysimeters in place before and after the famous storm on 16 October 1987, which showed that a clear spike of sodium (and magnesium and chloride and sulphate) appeared in the soil water on 16 October and migrated down roughly 1m in 6 months.

One of my less successful lines of research involved trying to measure the impacts of air pollution on soil respiration. This could have worked, maybe should have worked, but ran into the sands of statistical noise. The logic is simple: we were studying the impacts of air pollution on all aspects of ecology within our woodland circles. One of the most important biological functions of any ecosystem is the transformation of carbon atoms. Plants take them in from CO_2 in the air, turn them into biological macromolecules, release them as dead material (leaves etc – food for decomposer microbes) or as food for animals. Either way the carbon atoms get returned to the air as CO_2, having spent a sojourn immobilised

Fig 6.6 The Solardomes, for exposing plants to accurately controlled levels of pollutant gases. These geodysic greenhouses survived the 16 Oct 1987 hurricane unscathed.

Fig 6.7 The 'Excess Nitrogen Rig' where Emma Wilson and Richard Skeffington experimented on the responses of young conifers to additions of nitrogenous pollutants/fertilisers.

inside some biological molecule inside some life form. In most woodlands most of the time, most of this return comes from the slow decay of leaf litter in the soil, along with roots, dead seeds etc. (A fire does the same job but much more quickly.) Soil is effectively alive and breathing, taking oxygen from the air and exhaling CO_2. It is just that the metabolism comes from countless cells of fungi and bacteria, not from the body of one animal. We know from various classic studies that pollution reduces decay rates. For example, leaf litter has been shown to be deeper in woodlands near a heavy metal smelter because the leaves in the soil are mildly toxic, so decay less than at a clean site. (I was told of a naughty chemical researcher who killed a neighbour's garden tree by injecting it with arsenic. It went orange and died in weeks, so he swept up the orange leaves and said nothing. A year later when he dug over his compost heap the leaves were perfectly preserved, orange intact and undecayed, preserved by their high arsenic content. This is not a good idea at all!)

So I was tasked to measure the soil respiration – the CO_2 release – from each of the experimental plots at Liphook, in the hope of finding reduced respiration in the high SO_2 plots. This was probably really happening – the key researcher in the field was Phil Ineson of ITE Merlewood who had shown convincingly that the deposition of SO_2 reduced respiration in experimental microcosms. All I had to do was make this work outdoors at Liphook. The technology is simple and well defined. CO_2 is well known to selectively absorb infra-red radiation, making it a heat trapping gas. (This effect was first documented by the great Swedish chemist Svante Arrhenius in 1896, and of course predicts that as atmospheric CO_2 increases, average planetary temperatures should be expected to increase.) The kit to measure CO_2 is called an Infra-Red Gas Analyser, henceforth IRGA, and is a standard bit of kit used by plant physiologists as a standard tool. What could possibly go wrong?

What can go wrong is that IRGAs work very well. Too well in fact, they are really sensitive touchy devices, and the levels of CO_2 coming off soil are never very high. So I took the IRGA out into the wood, put it on the soil, and it found nothing. Then I put a cover over the sensor, and it gave me some numbers. Then a gentle wind blew and the numbers changed utterly. Then a tiny whisp of my mammalian breath wafted past the sensor, and it went off scale for five minutes, before setting down to find nothing. In fact I think I spent a week fiddling around with the wretched thing and never got one measurement that I had any faith in, let alone dared put into a dataset for a publication. I took my experiences to Phil Ineson, revisiting ITE Merlewood for the first time since my PhD. (It had not changed at all in the intervening three years as far as I could tell). Phil laughed, and said something to the effect of "now you know why I run IRGAs in the laboratory not the field". He told me a wonderful story that gives you some idea how fussy they are. He had to run his IRGAs in a sealed microcosm in a sealed lab, letting them settle down for a hour before recording data. Then yes there was a clear effect of SO_2 to reduce respiration. But every afternoon about 4pm the data went skew-wiff and took about 30 minutes to return to sensible values. This became such a regular feature of Phil's day that he looked into it. It turned out to be because the air for the microcosms was sucked in from a tube on top of the Merlewood roof, three floors up in the Lakeland air. Every afternoon about 4pm one of the cleaners stood in the courtyard for his cigarette break, and his smoke (being hot) rose. As traces of this hot air went over the rooftop, a tiny percentage of its molecules got sucked into Phil Ineson's air inlet, then back down two floors to the microcosms, where the IRGA promptly went off scale. I gave up trying to measure CO_2 in the field, instead taking samples back to the laboratory. Even there, merely having a human nearby was ruinous, because our emissions dwarf soils' production by several orders of magnitude. I finally got access to a locked laboratory that I could keep to myself, and by sealing the place overnight I actually got some sensible answers. Not many, but enough to calibrate a far easier enzyme assay (Fluorescein di-acetate hydrolysis – see Stubberfield and Shaw 1990). Using this I was able to show that adding nitrate-rich acid rain promoted leaf decay (as any gardener could have predicted), but I never found any effect of SO_2 (Shaw & Johnson 1993). That's how research works!

CERL did solve the cause of German forest decline, thanks to Mike Roberts getting some sabbatical time to pull threads together. His publication (Roberts Blank & Skeffington 1989) showed clearly that the problem was due to simple magnesium deficiency due to prolonged acid leaching of low-base soils. Interestingly, although this solved the mystery with a simple model that fitted all the evidence, it left all sides able to claim a degree of vindication that their original claims had some validity.

Since leaving CERL (as I continue to think of it – to be pedantic, at time of its dissolution the site was called 'NP Tec') almost no-one in academia has contacted me about the Liphook work. Just one statistician who wanted to have a crack at some new analyses on ecological data and wanted my toadstool successional data. What I do still get people contacting me and asking about came out of a sideline, assisted by some supportive managers. This was my interest in 'PFA', a.k.a pulverised fuel ash. This is a grey powder resulting from burning coal dust in a modern boiler (where temperatures are >1500C). It is also called fly ash, as it flies up chimneys. It would make washing go black miles away, so legally must be captured at the chimney base and disposed of. In practice, this meant dumping millions of tons of the stuff, either in lagoons or man-made hills.

The first time I met PFA was a memorable day, 27 April 1987, when I signed out a CEGB pool Sierra to drive to a meeting at Rye House power station, something to do with meeting staff from the London HQ team who wanted to explore 'creative conservation'. Certainly, the CEGB land resource had huge biodiversity potential, and Rye House was a good example of this. The power station was newly shut down – it was an old coal-fired plant, always low down the merit order so only called up at times of peak demand. I heard tales of chemical engineers weeding flowerbeds all summer, for want of anything else to do. The PFA from its 40 years or so of operating life had been dumped on waste ground behind the site, along a lane with the delightful name of 'Ratties Lane'. Sounds horrid, but the PFA had undergone natural regeneration, with no plants added. It became birch/willow woodland with orchids and other wildflowers, especially clovers, vetches and melilots, in abundance in the open glades. The site was fascinating, trying to understand how such a complex mix could develop on raw industrial waste.

In fact, this example was quite typical of what PFA does when left alone, and why I like it so much. Orchids and the trees (birch/willow) all have light windblown seed, evolved to colonise transient bare soil such as this. A minimal soil profile develops (an organic mat over native PFA, showing no worm activity, probably too saline for them). Where PFA formed vertical banks, sand martins and kingfishers drill nest holes (PFA is ideal for sand martins – soft to dig but doesn't collapse). With the hindsight of years exploring old PFA dumps, orchid woods and sand-martin cliffs are the iconic examples of interesting biodiversity from power station activity. The soil profile in the old PFA woodland was weird – a mor profile with a thick thatch of organic matter but in a calcareous soil – due to lack of earthworms (due in turn to salt toxicity in the PFA).

Fig 6.8 The brick-red form of the early marsh orchid Dactylorhiza incarnata coccinnea *on PFA in the Lee Valley (Northmet pit).*

Fig 6.9 The soil profile on old PFA at Rye House power station 1987. Note the brown peaty surface layer, which should not have been there!

Fig 6.10 Southern marsh orchids Dactylorhiza praetermissa *on PFA at Drax power station.*

All the evidence was that the peculiar properties of PFA faded away with natural weathering, and were a property of its high salt and free oxide content. Over ecological timescales these are evanescent phenomena, washing away or absorbing CO_2, leaving a boring, slightly alkaline, silty sand of no special interest beyond its history. PFA is ecologically odd in its first two decades, roughly. The Lee Valley got me in to look at their famous PFA orchid beds, which have absolutely nothing special about their soil any more. Fifty years of washing in nitrogen-enriched river water turned an extreme, infertile, alkaline industrial waste into a boring semi-fertile silt. My advice to restore the orchids? Dump more PFA. Did they? No. What happened? The orchids died off, just like I said they would.

Out of this I persuaded managers at Drax and Tilbury power stations to let me try some 'naturalistic' mixes on PFA mounds there. The design I used was statistically flaky, especially at Tilbury, but I do think that it was my introduction of soil that introduced *Dactylorhiza* orchids to both sites, including the early marsh orchid *Dactylorhiza incarnata*. I seeded the biggest colony of early marsh in Essex when the Tilbury PFA experiment was peaking around 2004. I also "had" some good ticks of saltmarsh plants (*Spergularia, Atriplex, Chenopodium*) on PFA and FGD gypsum at Drax and Tilbury. This is due to the salinity of fresh PFA. The high temperatures cause some silica spheres to melt, blow up like balloons then set hard; these tiny hollow balls called cenospheres (a.k.a. floaters) float on

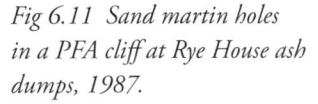

Fig 6.11 Sand martin holes in a PFA cliff at Rye House ash dumps, 1987.

Fig 6.12 A floating island of PFA cenospheres at Welbeck c. 1991.

water, and these build up where PFA is dumped in water. I saw one site (Welbeck near Leeds) where a metre-deep cover of cenosphere had broken up into multiple floating islands on a lake about 100m diameter, whose positions all changed each time the wind blew. All had rounded edges like dodgem cars, from decades of bumping into other islands. I stood on a few.

The Welbeck floating islands are gone now, tidied away. It is typical to see brownfield sites as needing tidying up, but often the best thing is to leave them alone for nature to exploit the space like it would before humans came along (while protecting the industrial archaeological features). I am especially fond of an industrial waste called Leblanc process waste, which was a major feature of the industrial NW in Victorian times and supplies a bare chalky soil quite different to the acid soils of the industrial NW. Leblanc sites are very few, oases of orchids and calcicoles in millstone-grit landscape. There are five in the world. A sixth in Newcastle was "tidied up" by the council around 1995.

On the basis that work isn't done till it's written up, I wrote up the Rye House site in a paper in the Journal of Applied Ecology (Shaw 1992), and the general PFA succession in British Wildlife (Shaw 1994). The long-term experiments at Drax and Tilbury became classic salami science, generating multiple papers as new data came in. Key papers are Shaw (2009a; 2009b). The PFA succession panned out pretty much as expected, with salt-tolerant plants replaced by grass and nitrogen fixers and a big but brief display of *Dactylorhiza* orchids. What was not expected was the discovery that the conservation interest hung on longest in the geographical centre, because the biodiversity interest lay in early successional plants (orchids, halophytes) and this 'young stage' was displaced by brambles and scrub that came in around the site edge. I have a photo showing some orchid

A Path of 21 Ms

Year	Df	Di	Dp
1995	0	1	4
1996	0	7	1
1997	2	12	3
1998	0	6	6
1999	0	13	5
2000	0	27	51
2001	0	112	256
2002	0	110	320
2003	1	149	259
2004	0	126	610
2005	0	135	1030
Mound 1	2	23	30
Mound 2	0	535	1986
Mound 3	0	28	349
Mound 4	1	5	6
Mound 5	0	103	417
Mound 6	0	4	17

Abbreviations: Df: *D.fuchsii*; Di *D.incarnata*; Dp *D.praetermissa*

Fig 6.13 Counts of Orchids on PFA mounds at Drax power station. Mound 2 was pure PFA.

Fig 6.14 Early marsh orchid Dactylorhiza incarnata *in 'hollow centre' in the Tilbury PFA plot. This was about year 12.*

spikes in a "hollow centre" at Tilbury, with the thin bare soil of brownfields surrounded by taller coarse grass, mainly *Festuca arundincea*.

I counted literally thousands of marsh orchids on 'my' trials at Drax power station. The table shows the totals. The mounds got smothered by the inexorable advance of the Barlow ash mound after 2005, though there is a mini-mound set up west of the main Barlow mound that might still have a few orchids. Of course, if anyone were to ask me how to create a nature reserve from PFA nowadays I would have to say "don't do it!". Not because of the PFA (which is fine), but the CO_2 that coal unavoidably belches out.

It is through this work I can visualise carbon deposits, because at big coal plants like Tilbury there would always be a HUGE area (over 200m * 200m) piled a 5m deep with coal. That's the coal heap, the stockpile. Once at Blythe power station, around 1990, a botanist called Richard Smith looked at the vast coal mound and said to me "This is King Arthur's doing" (referring to coal stockpiling around the miners' strike led by Arthur Scargill in 1984).

That is what bulk carbon looks like – you can see it as huge brown/black deposits. Like peat bogs or the leaf mould in forest earths. Pedants might point out that it can be white – calcium carbonate such as reefs – but whatever, the point is you can see bulk carbon, it's not magically invisible like CO_2. As part of my angst about the runaway greenhouse effect I have found myself trying to visualise what a gigaton of carbon would look like. A Gigaton of pure water would be a cube of side 1km, so imagine a cube of water the height of three Eiffel towers. To see a gigaton of carbon in the form of organic matter (eg wood), we need to increase the size of this to account for the lower density of wood and its containing more than just carbon. So imagine a pile of solid timber 1km high by 1km wide by about 4km long – that holds roughly 1 GT of carbon. We need to be stashing multiple gigatons of carbon each year, and keeping them safe for the geological future. Consider the political problems this will generate!

Just to set a baseline, my years in the CEGB taught me about a standard feature of UK coal fired power stations. They consist of "units", each with a boiler that burns coal dust, and a chimney ("stack") to vent the exhaust gases. (Drax, the biggest, had six such units.) All over the UK each such power station had each unit powered at 660MW. This is a useful baseline to bear in mind when considering energy schemes. (Assuming a typical household's power demand peaks at 30KW, this means that one such power station unit could support 22,000 houses.)

Fig 6.15 A PFA lagoon by Didcot power station, June 2009. Grey = PFA, yellow is a field of melilots Melilotus (legumes or fabacae, typical of old PFA sites).

A Path of 21 Ms

I must add a mention of the CERL badgers. Behind the biology labs was a decent expanse of woodland alongside a stream, the Rye brook, flowing towards North Leatherhead. I loved this pocket handkerchief wood, maybe 2ha, about 200m × 100m. The trees were all middle aged oak, but the flowers included primrose *Primula vulgaris*, wood anemone *Anemone nemorosa* and native bluebell *Endymion non-scripta*, also Spurge laurel *Daphne laureola*. These together say clearly "Ancient woodland". In fact, I gather that there may once have been a manor house near there abandoned around the 13th century, raising questions over the standard 'ancient is pre-1600' rule. There were badgers in a sett off an earth bank right in the core of the wood. I knew the holes well, saw the footprints, but it wasn't till one day, maybe July 1990, that I came back from PFA at Carmarthen Bay but stayed late on site, and climbed a tree opposite the badger sett in the oakwood. Sure enough, a badger stuck its head out and gave me a good view. It then made a warning yelp, vanished, and not a badger emerged the rest of the evening.

I got the CERL natural history group to cough up some money for a garden shed, which I set up overlooking a well-worn badger path near the labs. I made a point of putting out peanuts each day, which badgers love. So do blue tits and foxes . . . I put peanuts under an upside down saucepan, with a brick on top (to keep foxes out). Each day the pan was turned over and the peanuts gone. The badgers' technique, I later saw, was not to flip the brick off but to dig out the soil around the pan until it fell over, which did work OK, but took much digging. I think badgers enjoy digging – it's not work, it's fun!

The CERL badger featured below ate my peanuts every evening, just in front of this garden shed we had put up overlooking the oxbow in the stream. I wonder if the hut's still there. I left it there intact with a combination lock on the door in 1992, but have subsequently forgotten the combination! It is symptomatic of how CERL worked that I was unable to get the garden shed 'properly' illuminated because that would have needed a proper 240 power supply properly installed in a waterproof setting with a properly installed cable crossing from the Biology block across woodlands and a track, which would need a trench and planning permission, but if we

Fig 6.16 A CERL Badger, enjoying some peanuts.

really wanted it we could consider putting in a formal plan to a site committee who might raise the matter with the council planners . . . Yeah right, that's not going to happen. So I went to Dorking scrapyard and bought a headlamp and old battery from some dead old banger for a few pounds, then wired up the headlamp through an old dimmer switch I'd dug out from somewhere, put a red filter on the lamp (badgers ignore red light) and dangled the lamp from the flimsy ceiling of the barely-waterproof lean-to using some old string, giving us an illuminated badger food supply whose brightness could be adjusted, faded in gently to avoid stressing them. Not that badgers are particularly sensitive to light, if there are peanuts on offer! With this setup we could sit in comfort and see badger cubs knocking over the pan for their daily peanuts each evening. I even have video somewhere. One of the best things I have done in my life.

One thing academia has been good for is getting me to invent bits of kit for specific measuring purposes. Some of them actually worked. Not all, the nadir being a badger detector I created in CERL that consisted of a balloon connected to a pen recorder on a clockwork timer mechanism, the idea being that the badger's weight would squash the balloon and deflect the pen, showing me what time it emerged. You won't be surprised to hear that no part of this cunning plan

fig 6.17 A publicity shot for National Power featuring me and a badger cub.

Fig 6.18 Me with some Snakes Head Fritillaries Fritillaria meleagris *on the CERL haymeadow c. 1990. A haymeadow species, but more gardening than conservation I fear.*

actually worked. The badgers refused to go near it, and a subsequent trial using myself in CEGB boots jumping on to balloon didn't move the pen. Oh and the clockwork mechanism jammed.

Next door was a wildlife rescue charity Wildlife Aid, run by a Simon Cowell (not the TV personality namesake). CERL had a little contact with them latterly, when I got to meet a badger cub.

One more interesting thing we did at CERL was running one grass bank near the biology labs as a hay meadow. The key activity here is to cut and remove the hay. The meadow was about 100m along and about 30m down the slope, and with a hired Allen Scythe I cut the whole thing in one lunchtime. It took five of us a week just to pull the hay down the slope, let alone remove it like the books said. I also got some calculations showing that to seriously reduce soil NPK levels we needed to remove mowing annually for about 100 years. I am sure it's just a coarse grass bank now, maybe with that *Fritillaria meleagris* I planted!

Anyway, by 1991 it was obvious that the CEGB was gone (split into NP and PG, plus the National Grid network, with the taxpayer keeping nuclear plant). The minister in charge of the CEGB sell off was Cecil Parkinson, who hadn't the first clue about engineering but achieved fame after a fashion by getting his secretary Sarah Keays pregnant. And used the courts to keep quiet about it. This was, of course, satirised by some of the wags in CERL.

You hear gossip in industrial canteens, and more so when beering with blokes you will never meet again on the mandatory 'Power Plant Appreciation Course' that we all had to go on. For years I kept a folder they gave us on this course explaining how the merit order worked (National Grid keep baseload on 24/7 and call up less efficient power stations as the frequency falls <49.9hz). One chap, a wannabe manager, told me that the then-head of CEGB – Walter Marshall, Lord

Fig 6.19 A mickey-take of Cecil Parkinson and Mrs Thatcher about CEGB privatisation.

Marshall of Goring – had called Margaret Thatcher in early 1984 to announce that every power station in the UK was stuffed to the gunnels with fuel in every nook and cranny, so now would be a good time for a coal strike. So, she shut down some minor pit, and Arthur Scargill fell for the bait, starting the national coal strike at the beginning of spring 1984. (He should have waited till winter.) The power stations kept on working, the lights stayed on, Scargill lost. Later, on 16 October 1987 when an unexpected hurricane shut down the South-East (and all phone companies stopped billing for the evening as the billing systems couldn't cope), it was Walter Marshall who called Thatcher to say he was blacking out the whole of London. He then blacked out London, leaving one unit at Tilbury to do a 'black start' for the first time in UK history. (This means starting a major power station while not connected to the grid – needs a gas CCGT to supply the initial power. The whole power supply to London depended on one car battery starting up one diesel engine powering up a gas generator powering up the coal feed system for the 660MW coal boiler). For this impressive performance, Walter Marshall (a national level chess player as well as a top-level nuclear engineer and keen nuclear advocate) was rewarded by Thatcher by a kick in the teeth – his CEGB was dismantled and Marshall had no further role.

Walter Marshall can be seen on YouTube alongside a trial hitting a nuclear fuel flask with a train (https://youtu.be/ZY446h4pZdc?si=4zvXFclVj8ihxLYr) or search for "Train test crash 1984 – nuclear flask test".

(Having seen the video you will appreciate the joke when Walter Marshall – in debate with Arthur Scargill – said that he (Walter Marshall) would get in the fuel flask as long as Arthur Scargill drove the train.) I think that Walter Marshall's reputation has grown with the passage of time, but suspect that there are some people out there (notably devout anti-nuclears) who would disagree.)

I was not on the list to be made redundant, but instead to be transferred to Swindon to work in the NP offices there, which was actually worse. After seven years at CERL, I had put down roots deeply. NP would help me sell my house, but not to find a new martial arts club or girlfriend, nor were the CERL badgers going to go with the rest of us. As much by luck as anything else, a lectureship came along in a geography and environmental science department at the Roehampton Institute of Higher Education. I knew the place and one person there – Jonathan Horner – as I had given a talk about CEGB research to his pollution module. A long shot but worth a go . . . and to my astonishment, Roehampton offered me the place. I got no redundancy, as I should have gone to Swindon. The shutdown / transitional phase was quite traumatic as the whole CERL site was being dismantled, with NP and PG bickering over any valuable asset but a thousand people looking to lose their jobs. It was an open secret that lots of tools / chemicals / books were evaporating off site, some with permission, others less so, and my car was searched, fruitlessly. (When I ghosted glassware to the Roehampton labs I found a way through the back of the car park over a pedestrian walkway that bypassed the CERL gate and its guards, so for a short while my routine was to arrive punctually, load glassware into my car so it went to a university not into a skip, have a mid-morning sandwich at the CERL canteen, then drive the kit up to Roehampton, before returning the same secret way and driving offsite through the main gates, to be searched.)

Shutting down CERL felt a lot like selling off a family house, full of memories and little secrets. I have to express criticism of the people in charge of dissolving the laboratories, since they clearly gave little or no value to the intellectual legacy of the site. I was appalled to learn that the main microfiche archive of all the CERL reports was lost presumed trashed. Someone found the microfilm archive, microfiches of every significant document produced by the hundreds of scientists going back to the 1950s, including potentially stuff about the building of Magnox reactors. This entire archive got put in a skip and was never seen again. Just maybe the main files got backed up in the British Library, but no promises. This shows the wisdom of the policy in the Biology Labs that each internal research document should have a matching external publication in a public journal – to the utter horror of some senior managers who much preferred secrecy. I once got a formal ticking off for sending a document about orchids on industrial waste deposits (PFA) in the Lee Valley to the Lee Valley Park Authority – shocking behaviour, I know. Entertainingly, since I 'leaked' it by putting the LVPA onto the formal circulation list that HoD signed off without looking, there was nothing anyone could actually do to me. I smile at the thought of someone in the CEGB planning dept getting hold of that circulation list and spitting tea all over his desk saying "they sent this to WHOM??". Come to think of it, I suspect that some CEGB work on *Legionella* bacteria in cooling towers may have vanished at privatisation. I kept some back for years in my loft, but eventually I decided that these results were not concerning enough to be worth keeping.

More or less the last thing I did at CERL was to top up my badgers' peanuts at about 1630 one afternoon near Christmas (Dec 1991 – dark by then). As I was in the badger hut getting the nuts, the badger cubs of the year were scratching at the outside of the hut. I really missed those badgers. It helped my peace of mind a lot that my next employer – Roehampton – also had badgers! (In fact, the closest I ever got to a wild badger was probably in Roehampton, not Leatherhead).

> **No relief**
>
> The article by Terence Kealey ("Does government support damage your research", 26 September) makes privatisation sound like a blessed relief, escaping the miseries of state support for the joys of the free market. I can only assume that the author has never actually undergone the experience.
>
> The Central Electricity Leatherhead in the 1950s by the nationalised electricity company, the Central Electricity Generating Board (CEGB). At their peak, the labs employed over 700 staff and undertook research on a wide range of topics from "near-market" subjects (such as power plant efficiency) to the biological effects of power station emissions.
>
> The team in which I was involved was largely concerned with research on the effects of air pollutants on ecological systems, and set up two unique long-term outdoor experiments (one on crops and one on coniferous woodlands). The work was of undoubted scientific value, producing papers in many reputable journals. Contrary to Kealey's statement that "employees of all nationalised monopoly industries are badly treated", conditions of service and staff morale were both excellent.
>
> The CEGB was split up for privatisation in 1990, with National Power inheriting the Leatherhead site. Within a month of the companies being floated, National Power announced the cessation of in-house research and the closure of the Leatherhead laboratories along with extensive job losses. Not only was academic research (such as on air pollutants) terminated, but so was the kind of performance-related research that Terence Kealey's article implied should benefit from new-found freedoms.
>
> Under the new regime, personnel matters were handled with great insensitivity, and those of us who managed to find jobs elsewhere all took pay cuts. Privatisation was one of the most unpleasant experiences of my life, and New Scientist does the scientific community a disservice by publishing articles suggesting it to be a panacea.
>
> Peter Shaw
> Roehampton Institute
> London

Fig 6.20 This appeared in New Scientist – and speaks for itself.

I later sent a letter to New Scientist about the experience, in response to some inane article about free markets and research. Pleasingly, both times that I got a letter in New Scientist they gave me a dedicated cartoon! I decided not to mention the two suicides we had in the biology team about this time.

As a corollary, the CERL years 1985 – 1992 gave me a good CV and much irreplaceable experience. I kept up the long-term monitoring of toadstools at Liphook and orchids at Drax and Tilbury for years after, but ultimately once I lost the industrial contacts, I could not keep up the research. Air pollution rigs in particular need a critical mass of expertise and kit that is difficult and expensive to create. Once I left CERL it was back to the Collembola!

I want to digress for a moment about life at CERL. It was always a solidly industrial site, with engineering 'rigs' simulating various aspects of power station design. There was a whole field fenced off devoted to testing really high voltages, over 200KV. If you drive from Esher to Leatherhead you go under a high voltage power line as you pass your closest to CERL. You may wonder why there is such a high voltage spur into rural Surrey with no other big transformers or HV demand. The CERL high voltage rig is why! The site was a full community, c. 1200 people, missing only the sleeping facilities. It had a canteen with a lovely view over the site, though rather less lovely food. Plus a separate buttery where I enjoyed buying a mid-morning sandwich and soup. It had a bar, and for a while it was standard for staff to sink a beer or three before driving home. One senior engineer put his car into the elegant blue lagoon outside the front of CERL after too many beers between work and driving home. (He got billed for the crane which pulled his car out and for the change of water his oil leak required, and in my opinion was lucky not to get busted for DUI.) The site had its own martial art club (giving me my 9th kyu in Shotokan and a red strip on my white belt), its own wildlife group and its own monthly newsletter, to which I contributed articles on the plants and animals of the site.

One of the features of the site was the 'heavy gang'. They were workmen and the initial idea was to have a team of obedient strongmen on instant standby to help the boffins make their clever experiments work. That was the theory anyway. They were based in a walled compound at the far bottom of the site, even lower down the site than the biology labs! To get them to do anything you had to persuade their boss, Dave Roberts, that the work really needed doing and that his lads were the people to do it. To get to Dave you had to tiptoe in through his high gates and across the yard where his blokes were playing cards, and wait to be invited into the inner sanctum. I am sure Dave Roberts was a lovely chap, but was big bearded and muscular and his gang of strongmen appeared to be scared of him, so I tried to keep out of his way. Section heads were timid to enter alone; as a mere Research Officer I never dared. The only time he'd seen me do anything of note was to burn out his cement mixer in the first 30 seconds of operating it. (Hint: switch it on then fill it with the heavy material ONLY once it is turning. If you fill it up with heavy stuff FIRST and turn the motor on SECOND, the motor burns out terminally and embarrassingly. "Have you never used a cement mixer before?" they said in astonished horror as a cloud of blue smoke came out of the silent, immobile engine windings). So the discovery I was grilling a mouse for a hungry 3m python to impress his daughter Samantha came as a bit of a shock (see BMC).

One gentleman who had originally been in the heavy gang – let's call him Cuthbert – epitomised all that free-market gurus despise about the public sector. He was with us in biology only because no other department wanted him. The heavy gang refused to have him as they wanted blokes who pulled their weight rather than swinging the lead. Cuthbert had been tagged onto multiple laboratories and teams at CERL and was always sufficiently incompetent that was sure to botch any job, so got pushed off elsewhere. Cuthbert's ability to mess up a simple job was impressive. On one occasion while he had been passed to the Biological Laboratory he was given the job of writing some labels for samples of wheat from the Littlehampton field fumigation rig. All he had to do was write the codes on the paper labels, peel them off the plastic backing and stick them onto a sample bag. What he actually did was to peel the paper labels off first then stick them to a wooden desk, then write the codes on them, then pull them off the desk and stick them to the sample bags. There was just enough sticky left on the paper that it stuck to the plastic bags, but once the bags were packed with wheat and on their way back to the laboratory the labels all fell off, leaving Andy McLeod with an utterly useless bag of wheat samples and a totally wasted day. He would routinely turn up late, do naff all and leave early, having smoked a few fags along the way. It transpired that Cuthbert had somehow persuaded a manager to sign for him to some in and work at the weekend. Who, how or why was gullible enough to sign this off I will probably never know, but I assume they didn't actually know him very well. So, Cuthbert's little earner was to come in through the security gates on Saturday morning, get signed in, then climb over the back fence and nip off back to Leatherhead to earn cash actually doing some work somewhere, before climbing back over the fence and being signed out on Saturday afternoon, having done exactly nothing. I would love to know how he finally got caught out, but even though CERL was a big site he couldn't realistically expect to vanish for six hours every Saturday without anyone noticing. So when he was finally rumbled, HR punished him with the stiffest penalty in their rule book – Cuthbert was suspended on full pay for a month, while he doubtless earned cash doing manual work in Leatherhead, before being brought back and foisted on the biology team as being the only ones not to have actually rejected him yet. In a commercial outfit he'd have been sacked years ago, or busted for fraud. As an aside I have to respect him for getting over that 3m boundary fence each weekend, because I had him down as far too unfit for anything of the sort. I have nipped over that fence a few times in dubious activities like clandestine badger watches, and it was always a challenge for me!

CHAPTER 7

M is for 'Made it!'

Roehampton

Even when I had a good job in the CEGB, I hankered to be back in a university setting, and a couple of times applied for a position that would have involved a pay cut, just to be in a university. Happily, I was always rejected! In the end the closure of CERL forced my hand and coincided with a vacancy in Roehampton, that I succeeded in getting. This was only a college of higher education at the time but became a university shortly afterwards, so that lifetime ambition was fulfilled. It also gave me some of the richest and most rewarding experiences of my life, and taught me a great deal about all sorts of things, about humans and computer coding as well as springtails and lecturing. I moved between two colleges and two departments in this time, so describe them separately.

Roehampton 1: Southlands

With hindsight, I was pushing my luck a bit in 1991 when I applied for a lectureship in environmental science at Southlands College, Roehampton Institute of Higher Education (RIHE). OK, I had a PhD plus seven years of diverse research in pollution-related matters, but I last lectured when I gave a talk about acid rain to the 'Pollution' module run by Jonathan Horner, of Southlands College. Maybe that was an asset after all, especially as Jonathan was on my interview panel. (I'd also picked up a huge statistical problem in his PhD thesis – pseudoreplication – that both supervisors had missed, but the external examiner had not). Much to my surprise I got the place, and started in Southlands College on 1st April 1992. The brief was to create new modules on soils and on energy, two things I did know a lot about, and most of summer 1992 I was writing new lectures. (This takes a long time; I estimated roughly eight hours' typing for an hour-long talk).

The environmental studies programme was based in the old Southlands College, on Wimbledon Parkside (running along the northern edge of Wimbledon Common, almost opposite the Windmill) and on Inner Park Road. The building was built for exiled nobility from the French Revolution – I recall very faded gilt mirrors, and an elegant circular hole between ground floor and 1st floor that was fashionable around 1800 but condemned as a fire hazard by humourless fire chiefs, who had it blocked up. There was a huge cypress in front, about the same age I think. Needless to say, the academics were not based here, but housed in a functional but Stalinist concrete building at the opposite end of the site. Overlooking the Argyll estate, it was common to have undercover police ask to sit in our lab looking out of the window at the behaviour of some local underworld bigwig. I had a tiny office to myself, next to the prep room where technicians (Katharine Lankey and others) prepared chemicals and kit for practicals and projects. The other side of the prep room was Anne Robertson's office, with the

Fig 7.1 Southland college, 1992. We were based in the new building on the left.

Fig 7.2 The main Southlands building 1992. Old, elegant and impractical. A recurring theme!

convenient extension of x3456. Being the next academic along, my office was 3457, and we both kept these same extensions till retirement despite several further moves.

The Head of Department was – let's call him Mike. I never worked out how he got there, lacking as he did any worthwhile publications or much sign of university-level knowledge of chemistry, biology or statistics let alone interpersonal relations, but we were stuck with him as head of EGS (and similarly stuck with Tim as head of Geography) until a new professor called Vince came in above both of them and sacked them both. Some anecdotes from then do reinforce the worst stereotypes about idle academics. I had been used to being at work in the CEGB at 0830hrs. I found this a natural behaviour, so got into Southlands at 0830 on 1st April 1992, to find the building deserted, not a soul in. A few faces appeared mid-morning, and about lunchtime Mike rolled in, saying "I never expected to see you here, Peter". Mike seemed to have been widely disliked by all staff who knew him. Meanwhile, Tim ran a field course to Barbados which geography students went on and staff pleaded to help with. He had no publications of note, and refused point blank to help me create a new module on energy policy.

Apart from my lectures on soil and energy, my memories of EGS give a high profile to field courses – see the section on field courses below. EGS was split between Environmental Studies who went to Sheffield, and Geography who went to exotic islands, initially Barbados then Malta – Gozo. I went on the Sheffield course several times. This ran in summer, so allowed me to count my orchids at Drax power station then meet students in Sheffield to teach them about lichens. We generated one cool dataset, concerning the dissolution of marble tombstones by 'acid rain' air pollution. The key agent was SO_2, which also kills lichens. I got students to measure the extent to which lead letters, once sunk flush with the surface of marble headstones, stuck out. On stones from Victorian times the letters actually fell out – >6mm stone dissolved away. The rate of dissolution was almost steady with time, and worst in the city centre exactly as you'd expect. I used this in a later book on multivariate statistics to exemplify a multiple linear regression model. I could run a lichen day only because I had been on an FSC lichen course, and supervised a PhD on lichens (Simon Ellin and Mark Seaward at Bradford University). I'm still not confident though – needs chemical tests and microscopes, which isn't easy when you've a hundred bored undergraduates in a heavy shower guessing which *Lecanora* they've found. Everyone found more lichens in the cleaner air, which was the point of the exercise! One graveyard, after we'd got back on the coach and counted students – proved to have one student fast asleep behind a distant tombstone. (I have always been paranoid about counting students back in since then!)

In many ways Southlands was a transitional phase, as I still maintained CEGB research sites (Tilbury PFA, Drax PFA/gypsum, Liphook toadstool surveys) while looking for a future.

Part of this future was domestic. At home, my girlfriend Catherine (see "Martial arts" and "1986 and all that") had graduated from Oxford and started working as a probation officer. We also engaged with scuba diving, so it was that we were doing an air-sharing exercise under Swanage pier in September 1992 when Louise's DNA had just come together. That could have gone badly, but was fine.

Come October 1992 and we knew of Louise being due, so grandmothers had to be visited. We went to Manchester – Dad was delighted, Mum slightly horrified and asked when the wedding would be. Made sure that her mum, 'Big Nan' Bessie Kershaw, found out from her first. So we went up to Big Nan in Royton, still at home then, who was also delighted. As we got in the car to drive off, her next door neighbour (75 years old if a day) ran out remarkably fast, knocked on the car window and asked when the baby was due.

Neither of us are in any way religious, so we got married in Epsom registry office 11 Dec 1992 (see "1986 and all that"), and honeymooned in Maubec. Meanwhile, Southlands moved to a new, purpose-built site on the main campus next to Digby Stuart college, and I have to say that this made sense. The old Southlands was utterly isolated from the rest of the university, too far to walk but with infrequent bus connections. 'We' (EGS staff) were told we'd move into a dedicated lab in the new Southlands, and even helped design it. It is still there, and used. Not by us! At the last minute (in 1997) we were moved instead into Whitelands College instead. A colleague, Jonathan Horner, had just bought a flat next to the new Southlands, and never really got over the change of plan.

Whitelands

I should say that Whitelands has such a large part in my life that I still try to pop in to the lab most weeks, and really enjoy doing so. As I noted to an ex-student (overleaf), going into Whitelands feels like coming home.

A Path of 21 Ms

> ### Email to ex-student
>
> Dear [snip]
>
> Yes, I retired July last year. Though I say so myself, the timing was good. Teaching through covid would have been a nightmare, I'd planned to go anyway, and this way they gave me a good payoff:-) In fact I still pop into the lab most weeks to work on my research – springtails. Most people on the Whitelands Biology staff still remember me, and I really deeply enjoy being back there. I park in my usual spot in the car par, next to some mistletoe I planted about 2010, walk in past the snowdrops I planted in 2005, past the JCR logos of badgers (from my badger watches in 2006 that inspired the students to name the college cat Badger!) It feels like coming home.

My family has a long connection to Whitelands College. My mother (then Bessie Kershaw) went there 1946-47 learning to be a teacher. I understood she took home economics though the legacy papers we unearthed in the loft refer to history and craft. A check of the Whitelands College archives with archivist Gilly King found that Bessie Kershaw had been the secretary of the International Society in Whitelands, though Mother claimed to have no recollection or understanding of this when I told her! Then my sister Caroline went to the same college, same Gilbert Scott campus, also to study home economics, from 1981-1984. She also spent a short while in Leeds on a teaching placement in 1984, and one evening in Spring 1984 she had a meal with Suzanne and I in Suzanne's post-doc flat in York. (Suzanne and I stayed in Whitelands in December 1984 before she flew home, not knowing I would teach there 15 years later.)

Fig 7.3 The Gilbert-Scott building of Whitelands college

So when the Southlands transfer fell through in 1997 and we got reassigned to Whitelands, I was probably happier than anyone else. My family college, plus a transfer to the biology department – a perfect fit! (Colleagues in human geography were much less happy, and had all left by 2004.) In the end, literally, I gave the last ever lecture in the EGS programme about 2006, a final lecture in my energy module (in which I foresaw problems from CO_2 and its control). This was the only time I have ever brought a bottle of champagne to circulate after a lecture! After that, myself, Anne Robertson and Mary Mackenzie transferred to the Whitelands Biology dept and everyone else needed a new job. Suffice to say that the apparently quiet world of environmental studies had shown me more about human fissiparity than I ever wanted to know.

I settled down in Whitelands happily, giving zoology lectures much like I received at Oxford about 1980, same topics too. We were based in Gloucester Court, a new annex away from the main Gilbert Scott building, greeted by an elephant skull in the foyer. The staff offices here were a good size, and the whole building was overshadowed by a big *Magnolia soulangeana* tree whose giant pink flowers covered the building and dominated the view from some rooms for a week or so each Easter. With hindsight, having the tea-making facilities next to the Electron Microscope (and its supply of Osmium tetroxide) and a human skeleton may have violated one or two H&S regulations, but no-one seemed too bothered. The elephant skull was bought by the founder of the Whitelands zoology collection, one Felix Pfeiffer. The Felix Pfeiffer collection contained many more interesting specimens, including quite a few human skulls. Supposedly during the 2004 college move, documentation turned up that one of the skulls was a soldier killed in some pointless war somewhere and donated to the college by his father as a memento.

The main disruption came in 2003/04 when Whitelands moved campus from the 1920s Gilbert Scott brick / parquet building that my mother stayed in (then cutting edge new), that my sister Caroline had stayed in (then rather dated), that I stayed in when taking Suzanne to Heathrow in 1984 to say goodbye, to an 18th century stately home on the edge of Richmond Park, elegant but impractical. (See what I said about the original Southlands, and spot trends.) At least this was walking distance from the main campus, while Sutherland Grove Whitelands needed a car or bus. Formerly this was called Manresa House, before that stately home to Lord Bessborough. He gambled away all the family money and sold the house to the Catholic church, and it was used to train Jesuits for more than 100 years. (At this point I always used to wag an admonishing finger at visitors on a college tour and say "Let that be a lesson to you all, never ever gamble

A Path of 21 Ms

Fig 7.5 A cast of a human skull in the Felix Pfeiffer collection – from a photo used in our publicity.

Fig 7.4 The Magnolia soulangiana *which enlivened our view from Biology each Easter.*

money".) Hence Manresa, after the founder of the order of Jesuits who came from there. Gerald Manley Hopkins was a resident here – famous for his semi-religious nature poems such as 'Windhover'.

The closing down of the old Whitelands in 2003 left a sizeable legacy of treasures to safeguard, starting with the gardens. (In case this sounds like theft, I must point out that the site was substantially bulldozed by its new owners – flats for the rich, not for students). The flower beds had many snowdrops, which I did my best to rescue in 'Snowdrop season', March 2003. These ended up in my garden at Holmwood Park, and ultimately in the new Whitelands College. I also gave loads away to staff as memorabilia of their old college, and I am sure many of these snowdrop clumps will way outlive me. I also rescued a pampas grass *Cortadeira* which got planted next to 4LW, next to our neighbours' (#6LW) parking space where it survived for a few years. The other plant from the old Whitelands was less of a good idea! One flower bed, under the flagpole, was full of winter flowering heliotrope *Petasites fragrans*. A sweetly scented winter flower memento of my old college – what could go wrong? The warning sign was the way it filled out the flower bed! So I carefully planted a root in my garden, watered it in, then admired how well it took. In fact, it was the most aggressive, invasive nuisance I have ever planted – even worse than the creeping comfrey *Symphytum grandiflorum* which otherwise smothers all in its path. *Petasites* tramples over *Symphytum*, invades lawns, is immune to drought and all other extremes. The flowers are quite nice in winter, it's true, but that was one mistake of an introduction. (As a botanical aside, you can see this plant all over the UK by roadsides where people have thrown out garden waste, and each time it is the same clone, a male from North Africa I think. Coldharbour Lane, south of Dorking, is lined with this same clone.)

Aside from gardens, the materials to be rescued were mainly biological samples. Obviously the teaching collection – the Felix Pfeiffer collection – came over safely. But there was much more. At one time Whitelands Biology taught modules on fossil plants, though this was well before I started. This left a remarkable collection of plant fossils of various qualities. I had intense memories of hunting plant fossils on the Yorkshire coast in 1985, *Ginko* and *Cycas* for example, so knew what to look for. The trays of material students had found on field trips in the 1970s were rubbish, literally, low grade coal measures stuff. Drax Power Station burned hundreds of tons of better material each hour! But some of the fossils were wonderful. I later learned that some key lecturer long ago was married to someone from Kew and somehow got hold of some nice spares.

By far the best discovery in this batch was a shoe box at the back of a cupboard full of low-grade student collections of crumbly sandstone and the odd almost-recognizable conifer needle. The box was labelled 'Rhynie'. I said something unpublishable when I read that, because the Rhynie chert is the most amazing, wonderful and inaccessible plant fossil deposits. It would be fair to call it the Burgess shales of the colonisation of land by plants, and is dated to about 400 million years ago. It is a lagerstätte – one of the elite of global fossil sites, where everything is preserved in microscopic detail. I think the official date is 390MYBP, for what difference that makes. The story is that an early swamp got inundated with silica-rich volcanic water that turned rapidly into chert. This is effectively flint, glass, SiO_2. And very hard. What is special is that when it is polished very fine, and you can see individual plant and fungal cell walls. This is true of both the Rhynie stones I rescued from near-certain destruction, you can see the vascular bundles in the roots of *Rhynia* (smaller stone) and of *Asteroxylon mackei* (larger stone), plants that had not yet evolved leaves. The same deposit held the first ever springtails – from three different families according to Penny Greenslade, but the usual name is *Rhyniella praecursor*. My stones do not seem to hold any

A Path of 21 Ms

Fig 7.6 Rhynie chert, found while clearing out Whitelands. Each black line (c. 2mm thick) is a fossil stem of Rhynia, *a land plant so early it lacked leaves (but had a vascular system whose cells are perfectly preserved and clearly visible).*

Fig 7.7 Whitelands has a long-standing tradition that the students elect a 'May Queen'. These photographs are Victorian/Edwardian era May Queens.

animals, sadly, despite some mind-blowingly beautiful plant cells. The smaller, better stone also has stems of Rhynia easily visible like back spaghetti. I spent a whole winter polishing this stone by hand with sandpaper of increasingly fine grain, ending with cerium oxide (jewellers' rouge). Those stones are many hours of hand-rubbing, since the chart is literally as hard as flint. The result is both beautiful and scientifically valuable. I regard this stone as the most special item in my possession – my ownership will only be a tiny transience in its existence on earth, and it really must be kept safe for a proper museum – NHM, Oxford or Liverpool would be my suggestions. This is because of the back-story.

About 1910 a Scots geologist called William Mackey (commemorated in Asteroxylon ***mackei***) was indulging his hobby of collecting stones from around Scotland – especially from stone walls. He collected some odd-looking stone in a wall near the village of Rhynie, near Aberdeen, and saw strange details. So he took it back and polished it, to see astonishingly finely detailed plant fossils. He came back and found the main deposit, under metres of overburden hundreds of metres away – it was such an unlikely event that this deposit was found and recognised. The entire deposit is tiny, under a hectare, under soil, under a private field whose farmer is not noted for welcoming spade-wielding amateurs. You can't buy lumps like this, even on the internet, though I found one microscope slide on Amazon. So as far as I know that lump of stone is the most special, irreplaceable and scientifically valuable item on the estate. You just have to be a fossil-plant nerd to appreciate it.

The new Whitelands building – Manresa or Parkstead House – has legacies of the Jesuits, like carvings on the walls – IHS Jesu Hominem Salvator (Jesus who saves men), INRI Jesus Nazari Rex Judei (Jesus of Nazarus King of the Jews) for example. The site came with a number of Jesuit burials in front, which had to be moved to a fresh interment at the back of the football pitch.

We moved into the new site in January 2004. I was pleased that in front of the main building was a grassy area full of bulbs, snowdrops and crocuses. So I was horrified to find a bulldozer scraping them up in Feb 2004 – I barged into a meeting with the head of college to ask for a delay while we dug up the bulbs. I got a couple of hours, long enough to dig up most of them with help from Mary Mackenzie. Luckily snowdrops transplant well. When all was over, we replanted the bulbs in a new pattern, and they have come up every spring since, faithfully recreating the meandering path I whimsically created. And the purpose of the bulldozing? To put down a wildflower meadow. You couldn't make it up. Not that any meadow plants ever came up – the site was unsuitable, too shady.

The site came with the remains of the temple where Lord Bessborough blew his cash gambling. Oddly this structure was covered in soil full of a blue bulb. I though it to be *Scilla verna*, but the anthers are spiral so it's *Chionodoxa*. I rescued them and they now grow among the snowdrops – lucky, as the temple got moved to the bottom of the site.

The Manresa building came with a magnificent chapel, which should have been left a chapel. It even has a minstrel's gallery at the back for the Jesuit choirboys, now oddly repurposed as a meeting room. For some reason someone decided to build a new chapel outside and use this (leaky, cold and high maintenance)

Fig 7.8 The Manresa temple, plus its Chionodoxa.

Fig 7.9 "My" snowdrops line the way into Whitelands main entrance, Feb. 2020

old one as a lecture room. This was one of the sillier ideas of the whole college move since the Manresa chapel had the worst acoustics of any building I have ever had to lecture in. Something about the high ceiling and low side walls and curved back wall seemed to swallow and mangle sound. You could stand at the front of the class, put up an OHP, talk slowly and loudly and literally students in the front row could not make out your words. This wasn't just me – Prof Stuart Semple, who has a loud, clear voice and doesn't mince his words, described the hall as useless and refused to teach there. In the end they put PCs in there and kept it as a quiet work space.

And after this move? Basically, my professional life toddled on year by year – I carried on teaching in the Biological Sciences programme, convening especially the Conservation Ecology module that drew heavily on my UK-based experience (see Rostherne, CERL and the chapter on Inholms Clay Pit). I celebrated my 50th birthday in Swansea University by running the last ever Whitelands field course to Swansea, ending a tradition going back to the 1970s. Field courses have been such an important feature of my university life that I mentioned them in my 'thanks and goodbye' email to the department (see below), saying how they would make a chapter in my autobiography. Having said this, I thought I'd better do exactly that! See, therefore, the sub-chapter called "Field Courses". We usually brought along one or two PhD students to supervise. One undergraduate I would like to mention was an ornithologist called Richard Bufton. He came in as a mature student, big and bearded looking just like David Macdonald in Oxford, and was a brilliant birder. He ran bird ringing sessions in college, added Brambling and Chough (!) to the college list. No-one else would I have believed, but he lived for a while on a remote Scottish croft with choughs flying around. (They also had an escaped puma that slept in their barn – it eventually died there and is retained in a Scottish museum.) I oversaw Richard's project on his pet subject – ring necked parakeets *Psittacula krameri*, mapping every one of their nest holes in Richmond Park. He went on to get his PhD in Ring necked parakeets, and is undoubtedly the UK expert on these invasive birds. I still have his undergraduate thesis on them somewhere. See https://www.newscientist.com/article/mg24532770-600-little-green-invaders-how-parakeets-conquered-the-world/

Part of my day job was to oversee the administration of the paperwork around all our PhD students. For many years every PhD application in the university had to be approved by a central committee (called RDB = Research Degrees Board), on which I sat. I even chaired a meeting briefly when Ann Maclarnon was late. RDB has been described as the committee from Hell, though that is a bit harsh. It certainly used to involve us reading, understanding and assessing every PhD in the whole university, and the range alone made this hard. Then there were a few bitter clashes of epistemology. Notably the Sports Psychologist who wanted to use hypnosis to boost performance (fine) and lined up athletes to take part (fine), but came up with a design that lacked a control group, let alone randomisation. This is first year undergraduate stuff, taught at A level. No control group, no estimate of effect size, no philosophical possibility of knowing whether your intervention has actually done anything. So I did all I could to get the design corrected, starting with face-to-face chats with the staff member (who insisted that by using qualitative analyses these objections can be sidelined. They cannot). In the end I got RDB to block the PhD until it included a valid statistical design, at which point the staff member withdrew the application and went to a place somewhere else. Last I heard she still hasn't got a PhD – information I have had to gather second hand since she never acknowledged my existence thereafter. I used her case anonymously for years afterwards in my MSc statistics lectures (in the lecture on experimental design, emphasising the vital importance of control groups and randomisation) as an example of incomprehensible stupidity – why on earth NOT have a control group?

The new Whitelands College came with a nicely wild, overgrown area that had a pond, grass snakes, foxes, badgers, and whitethroats in summer. One badger got so predictable in its path and timing that I ran a badger watch that basically involved everyone standing in the car park at dusk. Along came a big adult male badger in broad daylight, took one look at 50 students pointing at him and ran off again, but the logo stuck and the college student body sticks a badger on everything. The black and white cat who adopted college was called "badger". I like to claim some responsibility there! Certainly the closest I ever got to a live wild badger was when I was up a big laurel bush at the edge of the car park and a badger stood directly underneath me. Years later my daughter Louise was at Twycross zoo, when an ex-PhD student of ours called Emily Bethell came along to discuss research. "Once I was in Whitelands car park at dusk and someone invisible called out my name. It was your dad up a tree doing a badger watch," she said. "Yes, that would be my dad," said Louise.

I got my 25-year clock in 2017, and my plan had been to do one final year of normal teaching 2020/21 then take my pension early at 60. Things did not work out quite like that, due to two different medical issues. Firstly, I started becoming dizzy and sick in 2019 due – it transpired – to a tumour (a 'choroid plexus papilloma' to be exact – not as dangerous as some brain tumours, though still deeply undesirable), which was removed on 3 September 2019. In the aftermath I was signed off work sick till end January 2020, by which time the key modules had already started so needed a new convenor. A post-doctoral researcher stepped in to convene these (dissertation and Conservation Ecology). His name was Nacho, a Spanish freshwater ecologist for whom I have a great deal of respect (I was internal examiner for his PhD and know that he knows more about coding complex anova models in R than I do). So when I formally returned to work in Jan 2020 I had almost nothing to do. Then we had the international calamity of the Covid-19 pandemic, which shut the university from March 2020 and led to such a predicted financial meltdown that the university leant over backwards to persuade people to leave. I had to surrender my driving licence due to the tumour, and was given the option of taking a lot of money to retire a year early, or come in by train to somehow teach courses with students not allowed in coughing distance of other students. The emails below convey my decision-making process, which was clear. I really hate the phrase "no brainer" in the context of someone cutting a hole in my skull to remove nervous tissue, but you get the idea. So I jumped before being pushed, and formally retired on 31 July 2020. They sponsored a patch of Woodland Trust in Kent on my behalf, which really touched me.

The day after I retired, my son Alex was 25. Tempus fugit.

Whitelands archive – emails around my retirement in 2020

Dear All

This is a small circulation list, personalised heads-up on something that will doubtless become widespread public knowledge soon, and which someone paying close attention to my situation might have predicted as an obvious move.

The explanation I sent to Caroline (below) is pretty self-explanatory, and in summary I have spoken to HR yesterday about taking severance, and been made an offer I am minded to accept. There are no guarantees of anything yet, but for what it's worth I therefore expect to leave formally on 31 July, which will obviously affect both our offerings and your loads next year, something that sits heavily on my conscience. I have hopes of being offered some kind of honorary position so UoR can associate our lab facilities with the national Collembola recording, in which case I will make a point of letting you know in advance and seeing you over lunch on days when I come in to sort out springtail samples. In the long run I'll need to set up a lab in my spare room but this will take a lot of planning negotiating, and then shopping for kit.

More immediately I need to make sure my list of jobs expected of me gets flushed out. As far as I know my main "Get on with it, Shaw" type job is assembling a list of next year's dissertation projects, for Y2 students to choose between. [snip]. If there is something else that you know of that I'm expected to do, please tell me!

Just to say that if things had panned out more normally I'd have stayed on the last year gladly as you have been the loveliest bunch of colleagues I've ever known. I could not have wished for either nicer or brighter or more interesting people, an honour to work with, thanks. I had a good idea to invite everyone over for a BBQ this summer, then thought about 2m separation. Our garden table is not that big! When I am again allowed to get people round a table in my back garden, I'd like to run a day where I take you round Inholms Clay Pit LNR then do beer & BBQ later chez nous. It doesn't sound like a lot to ask, but might not work out until 2021 at this rate. You'd all be very welcome whenever.

Further afield, I expect to be in France quite a lot, and would love you to come and visit us out there. Sorry, "there" is Saint Maximin near Aix en Provence. We have slept 8 people in the house, though with quite a bit of multi-occupancy in bedrooms. The algorithm used to be easy: Easyjet from Gatwick to Marseille, hire car at airport or I give you a lift Marseille to Saint Maximin. Neither Easyjet nor my driving licence are showing any sign of life at the moment, but one of these days it will be possible and you'd be very welcome.

Thank you all again for being great colleagues

Kind regards

Peter

A Path of 21 Ms

From: Peter Shaw
Sent: Wednesday, May 13, 2020 10:30 AM
To: Caroline Ross
Subject: Re: workload for next year

Dear Caroline

[snip] I may as well put my cards on the table now since no-one benefits from prolonged uncertainty. The background is that it is almost exactly a year since I started feeling sick and dizzy and losing weight, which should have been sorted out by cutting a lump out of my left vestibular system. The operation went well I am assured (. . . though if that was 'going well' I never want to experience 'going badly' . . .). I am still rather dizzy and wobbly in the morning and, worryingly, am still losing weight, and had planned to retire in July 2021 anyway. I am genuinely worried about how the rest of my life will pan out, and not particularly worried about the rest of my career. I have no driving licence, cannot get it till December, and if DVLA swap notes about my scans with the Marsden I am pretty sure they will never let me drive again. I have bought a folding bike so I can get to/from the train without a 493 bus, but it is unstable with tiny wheels and each time I ride it I fall off. I have fallen into several ditches around Dorking, which is inelegant but merely trivial. Falling into the path of a 493 bus would be less trivial, though it might update my health worries.

So I am expecting to ask Owen today about severance options, and to be honest I do not expect to return to teaching this autumn. I doubt I would teach / convene / mark modules next year. I realise that this makes your life harder, both personally and in requiring my colleagues to work extra to cover for me, and this had been playing on my conscience, but ultimately I only have one life and don't know how much of that I've got left. Sorry.

Kind regards

Peter
Dr Peter Shaw

Peter Shaw
Wed 7/29/2020 8:59 AM

Dear Caroline *[nb my HoD not my sister]*

The obvious day to wave goodbye would be this Friday 31-7-20, both as the end of the week and of the month and of my career. Before lunch? Names definitely to invite include Anne, Lauren +JL, Stuart, Dan + JR, Mary Mac, Todd, Garry, Colette, . . . and you of course. Gosh – Anne and Mary were there when I started in 1992. It's more a case of wondering if there is anyone in the dept. I don't want to see, and happily there isn't (though there are one or two who have sailed close to this classification in the past . . .) If people cannot make Friday morning, Monday 3-8 or Tuesday 4-8 would be good fallbacks.

I'm sure there is someone really obvious I've missed out, sorry. I'm afraid that I'm rather losing focus on work issues and timing – as I ran down forest tracks off Mt Aurelienne 3 hours ago the sun was rising over the pre-alps. I had hopes to glimpse a wolf again – no luck, but a hoopoe by the vineyard was a nice bonus.

Thanks for everything. See you soon

Best

Peter

From: Peter Shaw
Sent: Friday, July 31, 2020 4:28 AM
To: [snip]l; Suzanne Koptur
Subject: Peter Shaw Not goodbye but Au Revoir

Dear All

Today 31 July 2020 is officially my last day as an employee of Roehampton, having started on 1 April 1992. Sad, but all things must change and there have been so many changes in my/our circumstances that this seems to me to be a rational decision. I've got my 25 year clock, marvellous memories, great colleagues and (to the best of my knowledge) lots of happy ex-students. Recollections of the field courses alone would be a full chapter for an autobiography – wrynecks and dolphins in Gozo, choughs over sand dunes in Wales, and vast heather moorlands near Sheffield come to mind immediately.

As the email subject explains, this is not 'Goodbye' so much as 'Au revoir', happily. For a start I am very pleased to have been offered an honorary position as Reader (thanks everyone), and will continue to be UK recorder for the Collembola, so people using the 1st floor laboratories can expect to see me, every now and again, looking down a microscope at springtails. I will carry on PhD supervision, though not start anything new.

Apart from this, I expect to spend the rest of my time (as long as my health holds up) oscillating between Dorking (Surrey) and St Maximin (Provence), and will always be delighted for ex-colleagues to visit either place. Drop me an email on PJA_Shaw@yahoo.com and see where I am. Currently you can also text me on 07415 740557, but mobile numbers move on as contracts change or (as happened) phones get hacked. Currently it looks like we will be in France till October then Dorking for a while, but plans evolve as circumstances change.

Plan A: In Dorking any weekend I would love to take you round the nature reserve for which I am MVDC warden – an ex-quarry called Inholms Clay Pit, which is very pretty despite its name and just 5 minutes' walk away. Box Hill is next door too. If you enjoy jogging I am always delighted to take anyone any time for a run to the Leith Hill tower (the highest point in the south east and about an hour's run away) then back through sunlit pines along the Greensand Way. I am sure it is the prettiest running available anywhere near Roehampton, with sandstone hills covered in heather, bilberry and pines that could be on Speyside rather than Surrey. (Or just drive there and have a picnic?)

Or Plan B: If you find yourself anywhere near Marseille or Aix en Provence, come and see us in Saint Maximin. Symmetrically there is a quarry nature reserve next door, and the local mountain (Mt Aurellienne) is about an hour's jog away, though unlike Dorking I've seen wild boar and wolf in the woods, and we get short toed eagles rather than buzzards. So far most visitors have skipped this energetic option in favour of lounging by the pool and walking into town to see the Basilica, a 12th century edifice that proclaims itself to be the 3rd great tomb of Christianity on the basis of a skeleton alleged to be Jesus' girlfriend Mary Magdalene. In the absence of C14 dates and DNA sequences I don't believe a word of it, but I always was an old cynic and it is a magnificent building. The Camargue and the Mediterranean are both about an hour away so there is plenty to do. Like I said, just drop me an email to check the situation.

Otherwise, it just remains to me to say that it has been an honour, pleasure and privilege to have worked with you all. I could not have wished for a better working environment, thanks again for everything and I look forward to seeing you again in Roehampton or elsewhere.

Kind regards

Peter Shaw
Dr Peter Shaw
Reader in Zoology

Field Courses

Preface: It might seem odd to have an entire chapter about a series of undergraduate modules that were never large in the credit structure, 10 or 20 credits out of the 360 needed for a degree. I wouldn't waste time and effort listing the minor first year modules I helped teach, so why go on about the field courses? There are two different reasons. Firstly, these are the events that stick in your mind years after the students have moved on. Around May 2019 I found myself driving a minibus along the M4 towards Wales with Mary Mackenzie, then head of the UoR technical team but also a friend and colleague going back even further at Roehampton than I do. We started digging out field course stories, and realised it was a rich vein, even excluding some of the more extreme behaviour over which a veil should be drawn.

"Do you remember the time you reversed the minibus into that Range Rover?" and "losing a student in a Maltese hotel as the taxis were waiting to take us all to the airport home?"

"We still owe that campsite money for turning up with a load of students unexpectedly."

"That wryneck in Gozo?"

A Path of 21 Ms

"That osprey on the Axe estuary?"

"That dormouse half-asleep in its nest?"

"Were you there when Jonathan fell out with Liz?" etc.

Secondly, in my retirement farewell email to the Whitelands Biology dept on 31/07/2020 (printed in the chapter 'Whitelands') I quipped that "the field courses alone would make a chapter in an autobiography" – thereby setting myself a challenge! So here goes – I list them in chronological order: Sheffield, Swansea, Malta/Gozo, Morganhayes Wood (Devon), and Orielton (Wales). Before that I had experienced quite a few field courses, but either as an undergraduate (being taught) or a PhD student (either helping the York course, or collecting my own data for my own thesis). In the CEGB we went to remote sites often, but almost always to a power station to inspect something on CEGB land. We did get away to 'inspect' what looked like forest die-back in South Wales, suspiciously close to some of the little surviving heavy industry in the Wales M4 corridor, and got a 'jolly' to visit Loch Fleet in Galloway, to admire a huge outdoor CEGB experiment treating different catchments differently to offset the effects of acid rain. For the uninitiated, a 'jolly' is time spent away from home and from the office looking at something for no better reason than 'familiarisation'. On the Loch Fleet jolly, I learned a bit about catchments, and a lot about multi-padlock chains. (One gate, far out in the moors above Loch Fleet, had a long chain with two padlocks on it, the idea being that they run in series so both key owners can get through. I still remember the chap grumbling about the time someone connected the second padlock in parallel, meaning that the gate could not be opened, and a 10 mile walk across boggy moors was unavoidable as there were no mobile phones.)

The courses described below all involved me teaching undergraduates while employed by Roehampton, and each time their aim was to collect primary data which undergraduates should analyse and write up for their assessment. Unless otherwise stated (notably the Devon wood) we were taken to the accommodation by coach and to the sites each day by coach. This has given me an abiding fear/dislike of waiting for coaches, since there is naff all you can do if they run late. One especially memorable morning in Orielton, the coach to take us home was 90 minutes late due to some admin mistake, the long pause being interrupted by the arrival of the ambulance to take a student away for urgent surgery, having collapsed in agony overnight (testicular torsion, I gather, which is as painful as it sounds). Habitually in Swansea the coaches would be just late enough to get my blood pressure up. Once in Orielton the coach driver was Polish and as far I could tell only spoke Polish and Welsh. I tried to enquire about equipment transfer in

English, French, German and Italian, and someone else chipped in with Spanish and Russian, all to no avail. In the end we took the minibus as well, to carry kit, needlessly as it happened. One of the few times I really got cross with students was when a Welsh coach driver put the squeeze on us. Welsh coach drivers seem to be a breed apart, or maybe I have just been unlucky that they always double book our days with school runs. I have seen a Welsh coach driver tell Prof Robertson and soon-to-be prof Lewis Halsey that they would have to lose the final sampling point of the day because the students' lunch overran and he had a school run to do. So, two professors put in their place and an entire module's assessment had to be altered because of a coach driver insisting on doing his job. On one day that got seared into my memory, a sand dune day at Orielton, the coach driver had told me firmly that he had to go and do a school pickup at – I think 1500hrs. We had finished data collection well before then, and were all heading back to the coach, but some girls started playing in the sea. I think they had really not seen the seaside before and it was a lovely sunny day and a wonderful experience. Unfortunately, their play was making US ALL late and I knew damn well that the coach driver would just go, leave us to walk the 15km back home. This would stop us ALL doing the group presentations on which the module assessment depended, so we HAD to go. (If that assessment were to have been invalidated, the consequences could not be sorted out until the exam board next June, and might carry over to affect everyone's graduation the year after.) And the silly girls wouldn't shift, standing in the surf and taking selfies. I couldn't physically drag them out of the waves or lose my job on an assault charge (and anyway there were about four of them). So, I stood next to them on the beach with a loudhailer saying they had to move on, and still they didn't go at first. Mindbending. I still do not think that they understood the magnitude of the situation.

One of the truisms that stuck with me – You really get to know people on field courses, how they really tick. Sometimes you become very impressed, other times less so.

I must emphasise that the technical support team is utterly vital to holding a field course together. Unfairly, if they do their job well (as they always do) they don't get noticed, at least by the students. The behind-the-scenes planning, counting and preparing are a constant full-time job that appears to happen by magic. I was lucky to spend many field courses with Amanda Morgan, a keen birdwatcher who retired to a lovely place in Suffolk near Minsmere, but tragically died too soon thereafter. She was inspirational in her support of FSC identification courses, including the hoverflies which she brought to Roehampton. All the hover flies on the Inholms Clay Pit species are ID Amanda Morgan. The other key technical support person on many field courses was Mary Mackenzie, who was well in place when I started at Southlands, and had risen to top position (richly deserved) by the time I retired. Mary was a cartographer by training, and taught at UG or MSc level anything to do with maps or mapping or GIS, effectively acting as a lecturer. Rather better at it than many lecturers IMHO, having seen plenty of both! Mary is also a keen horse rider, maintaining a beloved horse called Sherbet while overseeing the university technical team (by a lot of hard work!).

Each year we also co-opted PhD students to help on the main undergraduate teaching field course – Swansea or Orielton. One was memorable both for her excellent field botany, and her ability as a 'card sharp' to give out the correct 'random' playing cards to reluctant students to ensure that they worked in the groups we chose, not the ones they chose. Mike Terrington and Emily Hay were not PhD students, but came along and helped a lot anyway!

Brockham Quarry

This was not so much a field course as a half-day excursion, showing the first-year undergraduates the process of ecological succession first-hand. The visit was to the conspicuous white chalk cliffs on the southern face of Box Hill. These were exposed by the mining of a Victorian/Edwardian lime workings. This left a magnificent cliff face, a relic railway line, some derelict lime kilns and a series of areas that had been exposed as bare chalk at different ages in the past. One might imagine that bare rock exposed by heavy industry would be an ecological disaster, and perhaps for a few decades that is how it looked. But of course this is exactly what happened in each of the 17(ish) interglacial warm periods during the Pleistocene, and of course "Nature" comes straight back in. We could see the mix of grass clovers and orchids on the younger areas (much like you see on abandoned power station wastes, for exactly the same reasons), and young woodland on the railway track (dating the woodland phase to about 1870). I have several very positive, happy associations with this field site (quite apart from the convenient fact that it is almost next door to my house, less than an hour's jog away).

It is worth mentioning for three reasons:

1. This was my backyard stomping ground when I lived in 4 Barley Mow Court. As I said to the students: "I came here a lot in my happy bachelor days, so when I tell you that the old derelict buildings are really dangerous you had better believe it." It is true – twice I was poking around in the old kilns and realised that I was standing on top of the roof of a long-abandoned

lime kiln. There was a void at least 3m deep underneath me, and if the old brickwork crumbled, I would just disappear and probably not be found till someone noticed a bad smell. So, I tiptoed off back to the edge, back to solid ground, and made a mental note not to do that again. When I first explored this patch in 1986, the old beehive kilns had their original beehive cowlings, then very decrepit and crumbled. These got fixed later.

2. This was a research site of mine. Not very high profile, but I have published two papers on this successional sequence, one on the plants and one on the springtails (Shaw 1999 and Shaw & Buckhoree 2001). Zia Buckhoree was a student who collected Collembola from different aged regions here and found a nationally scarce species called *Folsomides parvulus*, typically associated with seasonally dry habitats. (He was also the one who declined to have someone keep him company during field work on the grounds that he was a blackbelt and took his own chances. My sentiments exactly, though the paperwork in the event of a cliff fall would have been messy.)

3. Peregrines nested there. Most visits we saw at least one peregrine overhead, often a male and female together. One visit I took the students out of the quarry by a nifty little back way – which involved a short vertical climb that nearly defeated quite a few of the less fit townies – and while waiting for wobbly students to get dragged up a steep bank we watched a male peregrine just sitting on the cliff watching us. Supposedly released by a local falconer I discovered years later, perhaps explaining its tameness near a group of humans.

Fig 7.10 Floral survey in Brockham Quarry 1998.

Millport 1983

This was run by York University and I was helping as a PhD student. The other assistant was a PhD student called Yvonne Nicholas – see 'York'. Worryingly, the undergrads drank the island pubs entirely put of one particular whisky – Laphroaig – but I was innocent in that case! It deserves a mention not so much for what I contributed (more I fear on the social side than the academic) as for what I saw there. Millport is on the west coast of Scotland, an island with a long-standing research station which is an outpost of the University of London. That July the Chancellor of London University decided to pay a visit to inspect their facilities, so they came to say Hello. The Chancellor in question was Princess Anne, so HRH Princess Anne toured our lab one day. The module convenor, Christopher Rees (whom everyone liked – again see 'York') expressed his opinion of the monarchy by arranging for the undergraduates to spend the day dissecting fish guts for intestinal parasites. So we had trays of fish guts, lots of nematodes and a few cestodes (tapeworms) and acanthocephala (thorny headed worms) on display when HRH circulated. The general consensus was that she took it very well and asked sensible questions, while her posh equerries looked thoroughly sick and green. This gave me a very worrying few moments because we knew the police would search the area for IRA bombs, and I was worried that they might turn up the home grown weed I'd brought along to keep me going for the week. Luckily, the police who checked our fish lab were even less keen on inspecting things than the equerries and didn't check the old rucksack under my bench. Also luckily they didn't have a sniffer dog, though there were certainly an abundance of smell camouflages on the air, since the rucksack in question was my fox poo rucksack (see 'Oxford') and the whole lab reeked of elderly fish. Anyway, I was very glad to see HRH in person since her arrival meant the Isle of Cumbrae police went back to whatever they did on a small island with no crime of note. This was also the field trip I saw my only basking shark, a monster with a triangular fin in a bay on the west of the island, fireflies in the bushes and luminous plankton flashing in the sea at night. Lovely memories of a lovely place.

Sheffield 1992–1997

My first experiences of teaching university residential field courses came when I joined Environmental and Geographical Studies at Southlands College in April 1992, and I was required to come along on the annual field course to Sheffield in June. Given that the corresponding Geography field course involved flying to

Barbados, Sheffield sounds rather dowdy and humdrum by comparison. Actually, I really thoroughly enjoyed the Sheffield courses (barring the odd low point like students getting stuck in lifts or being sick in my toilet block!). This was because it felt like going home, in several senses.

Firstly, literally, since leaving York in 1985 I l had lived in the SE near Dorking, and rather missed my Manchester roots. I am adamant that people in the Surrey commuter belt are generally less open and welcoming to strangers than in the ex-industrial north. I missed the Pennines, post-card perfect though Leith Hill is. I had been working at power stations in the north – notably Drax, but also West Burton, Carrington (RIP), Fiddlers Ferry, Meaford and more, and always found a cheery bluntness about power station engineers and land managers that you simply didn't get in southern commuters. I had experiments on enhancing the biodiversity of PFA (fly ash) at Drax power station that I enjoyed monitoring, and Sheffield is (moderately) near Drax. So by going on the Sheffield course I could pop in to Drax on the way, collect data, say hello to my experimental plots, then spend a week drinking beer with students. Oh, and maybe teaching them a bit of my knowledge of plants and birds (which comes as naturally as breathing) as well. Paradise.

We stayed in the halls of residence of Halifax Hall, University of Sheffield. (Close to the botanic gardens, and with lovely old landscaping.) Decades later, Mary Mackenzie still drank her tea in Whitelands out of a Halifax Hall mug, dating from this course. Central Sheffield was slightly familiar since I had visited the same part of the same university in 1984 for my PhD, pleading mycorrhizal pine seedlings off Professor David Read, who in return insisted that I come with him and his entire lab down some pub for a beer or two on Friday afternoon. The connection between him and me was his post-doc Roger Finlay who was my immediate predecessor in Mike Usher's lab in York doing a PhD on springtails and fungi. Anyway, this meant that I thought I knew Sheffield. And each time I drove round Sheffield I got more-or-less lost, but always eventually got back somewhere helpful. Years later I took my daughter Louise to Sheffield for her undergraduate degree, and sure enough I kept on getting lost but always eventually got back somewhere helpful. Louise observed that at one point while I was trying to show her Sheffield city centre we went past some border immigration control post, bizarrely. I think Sheffield planners have tried to make the city centre as car-unfriendly as possible, to encourage use of public transport.

Anyway, once we had all settled in Halifax Hall we had coaches taking us out from Halifax Hall each day and enough food and beer on campus that we did not need to explore far from Halifax Hall. A name that must get mentioned here is (Professor) Ian Rotherham of Sheffield Hallam University. Ian is a wonderful combination of deeply erudite – especially about his chosen subject of landscape history – but also a top notch botanist and a superlative networker who really enjoys getting academics together for seminars or conferences on a wide range of subjects. Ian has written some excellent popular books about Sheffield's wildlife based on his articles for the local paper as well as editing several highly respected academic journals. Check for the references I list that have Ian Rotherham as an editor! I mention Ian Rotherham since he gave us an evening talk each time we brought undergraduates to Sheffield, plus suggested interesting post-industrial sites we could visit. We got to survey some fascinating utterly derelict canal-side warehousing that Ian tipped me off about that I'd never have dared enter otherwise. The successional sequences as plants return to ex-industrial land are fairly predictable, but often feature some interesting or unusual species mixes.

Ian would turn up for an evening talk with a carousel of slides. NOT PowerPoint slides on a memory stick, but celluloid slides that you project upside down onto a screen. The carousel held about 50. Ian really enjoyed his work and could spin out anecdotes about each one and the people behind it (eg, just by way of example: Ian told us how the council once paid a self-styled archaeologist to excavate and interpret deep holes in the local woods (finding nothing of note) instead of asking Ian, who had records showing not just who, when and why, but even how many beers per day the labourers were paid for these 'white coal' pits (etc). Wonderful, but by this stage the students were flagging badly. You couldn't blame them – after a day running around the Pennines in full sun followed by a lecture on statistics and a quick beer, we packed at least 50 of them into a small dark room and gave them a lecture by someone they didn't know on a subject that to be honest most of them probably weren't as interested in as Ian was. You could see the poor little things wilting and dozing off as the room warmed up. A few of the keener ones in the front rows did their best to stay engaged. Then came the point of mass panic, as Ian finally got to the end of the final slide in his carousel, and people started to clap their hands in the traditional lackadaisical way that means "thank heavens that is finally over, now please shut up and go away", only to see Ian get out a second full slide carousel.

Ian could validly observe that – in his enthusiasm for urban ecology in Sheffield – he was the bearer of a longstanding flame. The best-known Sheffield urban ecologist was Oliver Gilbert, best known as a lichenologist. He was also a keen urban botanist who advocated studying the 'recombinant' ecosystem that arises when urban 'wasteland' gets invaded by urban plants. He found and publicised the famous Sheffield fig trees, and even found a good word to say for Japanese knotweed *Reynoutria japonica*. At the Oliver Gilbert memorial conference in 2019 arranged by Ian Rotherham, I gave the talk reviewing Oliver's urban floral work and how it had informed not just my research on PFA management, but the national thought processes about land evaluation for biodiversity. (See Shaw (2021).) Both these eminent men were connected to our department, in a roundabout sort of way. Ian's connection was via a colleague who lectured in EGS called Jonathan Horner. I think they studied together a long time ago. Anyway, it was Jonathan who introduced Ian Rotherham to our EGS course and led to me giving a good few talks to conferences at Hallam, either about orchids on fly ash, invasive fungi on woodchips, or invasive Collembola in England. Look for references where I cite Ian Rotherham as an editor. Oliver Gilbert's connection was via a technician we had called Chris M., whom I gather was one of his daughters-in-law. Certainly he came into the bar in Halifax Hall one evening about 1993 to chat amicably to Chris. I wish I'd realised the significance of this and made more effort to grab the chance to say hello. I treasure a copy of Oliver Gilbert's book "The Lichen Hunters" autographed by him.

I had to earn my keep on this field course, and after my first year I earned this by teaching two "days". The first was my lichen day, where we visited churches along a pollution gradient and collected data on the lichens and the tombstone erosion. My qualifications for this day were, to be honest, somewhat flaky since I am not at all sure that my lichen IDs were reliable. NOT in the league of Professor Oliver Gilbert, at all. I had been on a weekend lichen course at FSC Preston Montford, paid for by the CEGB, of which I remember mainly how cold and uncomfortable the bedding was and how many little grey crusts turned out to be different species given enough microscope time and chemical tests. I had co-supervised a PhD on lichens (Simon Ellin), though never felt my contribution to it to be particularly satisfactory. Even so, I am sure I knew more about lichens than the undergraduates – even now I have yet to meet one undergraduate whose lichen IDs I believe! Plants yes, birds yes, even fungi, but not lichens. Soon the Sheffield lichen transect we started by a city centre ex-church called St Georges, finding almost no lichens, then ended up in a lovely clean air site at High Bradfield out to the west, an old churchyard next to a derelict motte-and-bailey castle where every stone was festooned in lichens. Better. I got them to measure the degree of protrusion of lead letters in marble stone. At burial the lead letter is flush with the stone, but as the stone dissolves away the lead letters stick out. You would predict that if acid rain (SO_2 etc) were constant over time the degree of exposure of the letter will increase linearly with time. By comparing the slopes of this graph in a clean and a polluted site you should see it is steeper with

A Path of 21 Ms

the more pollution, as more acid + more time = more stone loss. This worked stunningly well, so much so I used it as an example of a multiple regression model in my book on multivariate statistics.

Away from my lichen day, the Sheffield courses were really nostalgic for me at several levels. Quite apart from my newly-created experiments at Drax power station, I had deep family roots in the North. Not only were my mother and father both still alive in the North, but Mother's mother (Bessie Kershaw née Holland or 'Big Nan') was, at least until July 1997. The last time I saw her was June 1997, about a month before she died in a rest home in Sale, near 39FD. I came over to see her from the field course in Sheffield. That same visit I had driven to Kinder Scout, and walked up to Kinder Downfall (see '39FD'). Picking up on the way a wood warbler singing on its wooded slopes (a remarkable shivering trill), and a whinchat by the car park. This visit up north in 1997 was not just that last time I saw Nan – or any grandparent – it was also the last time I have heard a wood warbler or seen a whinchat.

Fig 7.11 A wet lichen day at High Bradfield church near Sheffield

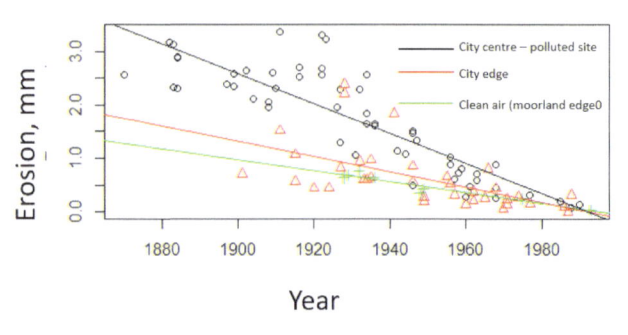

Fig 7.12 And the data generated that day: Erosion was fastest in the polluted site.

Fig 7.13 A typical scene from the Ladybower day – students following streams across vast upland catchments.

One of the 'days' was to investigate the biota and hydraulics of a well-known beauty spot called the Manifold Valley. Classic Karst landscape with limestone cliffs, crystal clear streams, caves and a dry river (flowing only in winter). This day was led by our freshwater ecologist Anne Robertson, who took the students along the main riverside paths and to 'Thor's cave'. The odd thing for me was that this same spot had been a popular weekend outing for the Shaws in the 1960s and early 70s. I clearly remember my father parking his old Austin near a bridge over a dry riverbed, and little me being amazed at the idea of a river that only flowed in winter. Then one day around June 1994 I realised that I was standing on exactly the same bridge looking at exactly the same dry riverbed, except that the adult next to me was not Dad towering over me, but my (roughly same age and height) colleague Anne Robertson. That was a strange existential bump there as my body image updated itself!

Fig 7.14 Students doing a floral survey at Wakefield PFA site c. 1995. Note the bare grey PFA and the abundance of clovers.

I managed to combine this course with my CEGB research by taking students to Wakefield PFA dump, called the Half Moon, SE352206, and get them to survey the site for conversion to a nature reserve. Although this does not sound much fun, in fact old PFA sites can be lovely and this one was carpeted with orchids, a range of clovers (including hares foot clover *Trifolium arvense*) and a really pretty little asteracea called 'fox and cubs' from its intensely foxy orange flowers *Hieraceum aurantiacum*. The site was odd for having open patches of totally bare PFA among the orchid/willow scrub, not a feature I have seen elsewhere, plus a solitary heather clump looking out of place on an alkaline site. Its biodiversity was enhanced by a small lake among the ash mounds, plus a nearby canal – ideal for kingfishers. I had previously communicated with a former site engineer whose daughter did a project on the orchids at this site, so knew it was worth a visit, and as far as I could tell the students all enjoyed the day. Not a claim I always make – see "sand dunes" below!

The day that sticks in my mind from the Sheffield course was both the most fun and had by far the most potential to go wrong. (It didn't, thankfully.) A hydrological geographer called Rod Ward sent the students off to quantify water flows in the catchment of the Ladybower reservoir. They threw dog biscuits into the streams to monitor flow rates. They were dropped off at various spots around the entire catchment and told to be back at this same spot at a set time, then off they went, unguided and unsupervised. And they all turned up, present, correct and unscathed – with hindsight we could easily have lost some students if the weather had turned bad. I thoroughly enjoyed marching out on the heather moors, just like the Shaw family did 20 years before. Above Ladybower reservoir is a structure called Alport castles, which are not castles at all but frost-shattered millstone grit. So we marched out onto vast open moors, heather almost all the way to Sheffield. Walking there with students, in the sun, with a redstart singing in some woods, made me think "I'm being paid for this – jammy git!". On the way there the first time, Rod Ward got the coach to stop at a crucial hillside, got the students out and asked me to explain the landscape. No warning, but he dealt me an easy hand! To one side was all millstone grit, acid soils with dark brown heather; the other side of the valley was limestone karst – alkaline soils picked out with the bright green of grassy meadows. Once you knew the geology, its impact was easy to see and explained the whole landscape structure. Luckily, my dad had showed me exactly this before I was about 10 years old, in more or less the same spot!

Malta / Gozo 1997–2002

This field course was primarily a geographical course, chosen for its human geography as much as its physical geology. These were impressive experiences, and I have seen on Malta what is arguably the oldest building in the solar system, but in terms of wildlife or natural processes the interest was underwater rather than above. There are two key features which intersected here, both highly geographical. Firstly, the geology consisted of hard limestone above soft blue clay, with a tendency for things to crumble away and for water to be strictly limited in where it could be found. Secondly, it was a small island that had been hammered by *Homo sapiens* since the dawn of history, with very little vegetation cover, mainly urban areas or bare limestone. Just the year before I went, they introduced planning laws for the first time – before that it was like the Wild West, alarmingly literally. Lots of hunters and guns, journalists getting killed, just missing the horses (as there was no grazing for them). I hated the Maltese tradition of using caged birds to call down migrant birds moving between northern Europe and Africa, to kill them. The EU tried to stop it. I sent a letter to the PM about it (gosh that will have shaken him!) but AFAIK it is still going on. There are a subset of Maltese people – whom I mentally parody (perhaps unfairly) as under-educated and over-patriotic, the Maltese version of Trump supporters – who support shooting any bird overhead, who tried to keep tourists away from their shooting grounds. I also think that these are a vocal minority, and this pushes the limit of how far an external body like the EU has any business interfering in traditions. But hang on – those are OUR migratory birds, so we do have a moral right to intervene.

Anyway, apart from this, the Malta field course was primarily an exercise in human geography – people visited the freeport (HUGE container ships), made notes about the tourist areas, town planners and such like. We visited a hotel built directly by the sea on a bed of blue clay. The clay slipped and the hotel is a ruin, of course. Never build on Maltese blue clay! I did teach a day, in which we visited the wildest place I could find on the island, a coastal headland called Il Qarabbah. Here the cliff had crumbled so much no one built there and we could see the different successional stages of the post-collapse plant communities. The taller Euphorbias seemed to take centuries to come in, while caper appeared quickly on the cliff faces (yes, caper as in the pizza ingredient, the pickled flower buds. All round the outside of the walls of the Vatican you can see self-sown caper plants too). I saw the ornamental bush *Convulvulus cneorum* growing wild by the sea at Il Qarabbah, rather small and stunted. I have found this plant is exceptionally drought-tolerant, and having seen it surviving on bare limestone just above the salt zone of the southern Mediterranean it's not a surprise!

This is not going to get me much sympathy, but from one point of view the Malta field course acted for me as a subsidised diving holiday! I'd take my wet suit etc but hire heavy kit and a companion out there, and go diving offshore. Nothing deep – the Mediterranean is fairly shallow there with lots of amazing underwater cliffs and caves. While quite a few of the dives were humdrum, some were among the most memorable and intense of my life. Top two on this list would be the time we were diving between Malta and Gozo, when there was a bizarre loud whistling click that seemed to come from inside of me, then a big grey creature appeared – had a look at us – and whizzed off. I had been checked out by a wild dolphin! The dive leader was very happy too – not a common event. Then there was a time in Gozo I dived the blue lagoon. This is a lake-like bay, slightly green because of low salinity, which is almost but not quite cut off from the open sea. The connection to the sea is a narrow fissure that cuts directly through the headland to the open sea beyond, and the dive involves entering the (green) lagoon, swimming through the narrow dark cleft at about 3m depth to the open sea. The lagoon is OK, the open sea is good, but the middle of the tunnel is utterly wonderfully amazing for the experience of swimming through a just-about wide enough dark tunnel watching the green light (from the lagoon) fade to a dot behind you while the deep blue of the open sea starts as a blue hint ahead and opens up into a full sunlight – a typical deep blue Mediterranean seascape. There are fish (eg the dark red cardinal fish) that habitually hang out in Mediterranean caves, and there were shoals of them in this passageway. THE scariest dive of my life was here too. We dived Valleta harbour to look for plastic explosives. That was the safe bit. The dive leader announced he has been in the Maltese special forces – with hindsight I doubt Malta has special forces and rather doubt his connection to reality. Anyway, we dived 'The Maori', a WW2 wreck, saw yellow plastic explosive, came out for a chilly lunch, then returned for a "quick dip in the harbour". Nothing to see except flat mud. The only place I have seen the solitary coral Cerianthus alive BTW. We dived directly into the busiest part of the harbour, just as a big ferry was coming in over our heads – heaven knows why and we could have been killed. I am sure that if anyone had panicked and gone up in a hurry they would have been minced by the big propellers. The throbbing was incredibly loud, going straight through you, and my only thought was to lie flat on the bottom and wait for the danger to pass. Easy in a woodland, not so easy when diving on a flat muddy bottom. So eventually the ship passed over, the throbbing faded, we got out and I wrote a letter of complaint to the dive outfit. Other Malta dives had me in an underwater cave being washed back and forth by the swell – which sounds fun except that the tunnels were lined with nasty sharp spined sea urchins Diadema that would go straight through a wetsuit, so it was a bit like an arcade game, being swung about in an unfamiliar tunnel while dodging dangerous obstacles! No true reef forming corals here, but excellent limestone scenery. I was shown a vent of hot (volcanic) water, and a cave where a whole group of divers had got lost in the murk and drowned – there was an underwater memorial outside. I wasn't so keen about being taken into that fatal cave at the end of the dive when air was getting low (that's how they all died), but we got out AOK.

Fig 7.15 I put Fungus rock, Gozo on the cover of my textbook, for no good reason except how nice it looked!

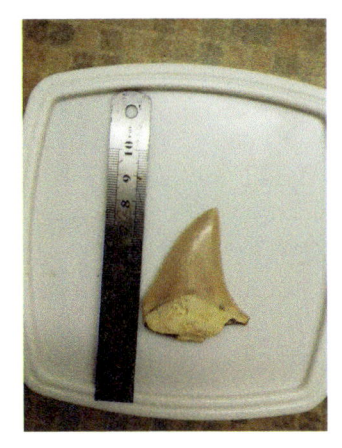

Fig 7.16 The Carcharias *tooth I found in a limestone boulder in Malta.*

Fig 7.17 The Azure window, Gozo. We walked over this 4 April 1999; it collapsed March 2017.

After the main course on the main island of Malta, we had an 'advanced' field course on the adjoining island of Gozo. Much as I disliked Malta as an island, Gozo gave brief moments of unadulterated magic. For a start, the diving was wonderful – the tunnel through the headland alone was remarkable. One day Mary Mackenzie and I saw a strange brown bird in the scrub, which perched to show its contorted neck. Not wounded, but a rare woodpecker called a wryneck, with the wonderful name of *Jynx torquilla*. We took students to a bay where the whole cliff face was covered in an endemic plant, a species of 'everlasting',

Helichrysum melitense. [Melitense means 'of Malta' in Latin.] Non-biologists wouldn't know their significance, but remote islands often evolve local endemics found nowhere else and highly vulnerable to extinction. We read about them in Hawaii, St Helena etc and here we had an authentic island endemic just above our picnic spot! Next to this was a spot called Fungus Rock, named for the famously rare 'Maltese fungus' *Cynomorium coccineum*. This is not a fungus but a parasitic plant, like *Rafflesia* or *Orobanche*, which used to parasitise sun rose *Cistus* bushes there. Long extinct there, of course. The Knights Templar sold it as a cure for venereal disease – which it wasn't, of course, but it was a good money spinner for them. Another never-to-be repeated experience was when we walked out over a natural bridge called the azure window (which collapsed a few years later). The experience so blew my mind that I put it on the cover of my book on multivariate statistics.

Inevitably such a holiday destination inspires holiday-like behaviour in students, with at least one case of a student who somehow ended up in the wrong room then oversleeping, so when the taxis came to take everyone to the airport to go home, he had just vanished. In the end, the rest of the students went off, the hotel staff searched their empty rooms and found him in the nick of time.

One oddity about Malta is that it is famously rich on fossils of sharks' teeth. I gather that the Maltese authorities don't like you taking them anymore, so I am in company with David Attenborough in having an illicit but beautiful shark's tooth from Malta, found by me, sticking up out of a limestone boulder. Clearly from a great white. In Gozo there was a black line in one cliff which was pure sharks' teeth – little brown teeth of sand sharks, I think.

Swansea 1997–2011

The Swansea field course was a long-standing tradition within the Biology Department, going back to the 1970s. At one stage the entire assembly of biology teaching staff were expected to attend, even researchers into African primates (like Caroline Ross). The final day involved students inventing and performing their own projects, which is an excellent plan pedagogically since it forces everyone to wake up, think and communicate. It was a bad idea in all other respects, since no-one knew in advance what projects would be done or how, so the policy was to cover all the bases and bring all equipment that could possibly be used. The course ran in mid-September, just before term restarted, and the technicians traditionally spent the whole summer packing up the equipment for the field course. Some kit was obvious – portable meters to measure pH or salinity, for example, quadrats to quantify flowers, or keys to churchyard lichens. Some less obvious, like binoculars. Some not at all obvious like gardeners' bulb planters (to collect soil cores) and soil sieves (to extract cockles from saltmarsh mud). The logistics of the week were complicated by the way that the 'lichen day' (run by Nigel Reeve, the hedgehog expert) was spread over the whole week, so each day on the way to or from the field site, the coach would have to stop at one or more church yards to gather more lichen data. This sort of on-off learning makes for complicated field notes that are hard to write up. By the time I started going to Swansea, the course had been de-staffed and simplified as far as possible, and we dropped the lichen day (to no-one's regret).

My contribution was to introduce a 'sand dune day'. This involved taking the whole student group on a classical 'psammosere' = sand dune succession. The location was Whitford dunes, at the south-western edge of Swansea bay. I really liked this day, because it was a lovely spot which generated really nice data. We started at the furthest point out, the upper edge of the beach where annual plants (notably saltwort *Salsola kali*) popped up in the salty sand. Thence we walked inland, through the "embryo dunes" of marram grass through the flower rich "fixed dunes" to pine forest. As long as the weather behaved this was a lovely day – a brisk walk down a hill overlooking the Gower with the sun reflecting off the bay below, then out to the edge of the tide and back through flower-rich pastures. The fixed dune stage is really pretty, with carpets of wildflowers like Birds foot trefoil *Lotus corniculatus*, rest harrow *Ononis repens* and wild pansy *Viola tricolor*. Often pyramidal orchids *Anacamptis pyramidalis* and marsh helleborines *Epipactis palustris* too. It could become very hot on a sunny day, with surface soil temperatures that we measured >30C (soft and sandy as well as warm – lovely to lie on after a picnic). The final stage was a pine wood, which is cheating since it was planted while the rest of the sequence was authentically wild – happily no students complained. The plants behaved just like they had read the books, with saltwort at the edge of the sea, being replaced by marram grass tussocks being replaced by flowery sward being replaced by woodland. The soil also followed the textbook prescription, being pure sand at the edge of the sea but becoming more organic rich and acidic as we moved inland, leading to a clearly different soil under the pine trees (with a surface brown layer of old needles). I can't help thinking it is such a nice sand dune system someone should write it up properly, but our data were never really solid enough for a publication. I know too much about the botanical skills that went into those data, and think of my favourite acronym from the early days of computing: GIGO (explained in the appendix).

The downside of the Whitford sand dune day was that it was physically challenging. I would have thought nothing at the age of 10 about the walk we all did down that hill, out across the dunes for a picnic in the marram clumps then back up the hill to the waiting coach. By contrast, some of the students had real problems with this, being quite unused to physical exertion. One of whom (it turned out) only had one lung, and that lung suffered from impaired function. We only discovered this when she all but collapsed on the way back up the hill to the coach and we had to carry her up. The near-total lack of cover made it fiercely hot on sunny days, but even more fierce when a westerly gale was blowing rain horizontally out of the Irish sea. When a sand dune day goes bad it goes badly bad, because the un-hardened townies suddenly come face to face with the reality of being fully exposed to the wind and rain while having to focus on collecting data, and all with a group they didn't choose and for an assessment in >4 months' time. I have seen students just walk off from their group in a huff, yelling as they marched off that they didn't want to be here anymore. (My thought bubble went something like as follows: "You and me both, dear, but TINFA so beeping well get on with it".) This is when you find who didn't pack a raincoat – there's always one.

I also picked up the Swansea field course 'Bird Day', which should have been money for old rope since I knew more about birds at primary school than the whole cohort of students knew together (most years anyway). The day involved visiting WWT Llanelli, and studying the captive ducks. Llanelli WWT staff even gave the talk for us, supplied the ducks for us; it was a lovely place that even sold sandwiches for lunch. What could possibly go wrong? I reman slightly haunted by a 'good idea' I had once, the trauma being justified since I broke the cardinal rule of 'Always check it out on your own first'. The idea was to get students into the mood of bird watching by using the woodland by Swansea University (called Singleton Park), to introduce woodland birds. So we trooped off into a wooded glade nearby, I sat everyone down, and explained how woodland birds need to use sound rather than visual displays so that songs and calls were really important. So, let's all sit still and silent, and all listen very hard. The warblers will have stopped but we can still hear the subtle quiet contact calls. So we sat still and quiet and listened

Fig 7.18 Ochre deposits, Pelenna bog, near Swansea, caused by leachates from an abandoned coal mine.

hard, and a big dog appeared, started barking and playing with the students. Sigh. His owner finally vanished into the distance after what felt like ages, and I tried to sound enthusiastic: 'So can we hear any little "seep seep" contact calls?' Just then one of the gardeners turned up in a tractor, a very slow and very noisy tractor that drove past us at a leisurely pace. Very leisurely. Eventually the cacophony moved on, and I tried again. "Let's listen very hard," I yelled, trying to sound enthusiastic. That was when, just across the boundary fence, a contractor started emptying one of the university skips (waste containers), which seemed to have been full of old cookers and metal sheeting because the racket was incredible and just kept going on and on. I should have given up there and gone to WWT Llanelli for lunch and some ducks, but I had another good idea to try out. The year before, I'd seen a section of cliffs near Llanelli full of sand martin nest holes, which is both a lovely sight and a good source of data. I had spent a while explaining what data might be collected here. So we got a coach to drop us off nearby, all marched along to the sand martin cliff, to find that the council had deemed the whole cliff unsafe and concreted it over the previous winter. Sigh – back to the tame ducks. On the plus side, I did get to see wild spoonbills at Llanelli, and once an African spoonbill that might even have been wild.

Cottshayne Wood, Devon

This was the most personal of the field courses, and genuinely led to some long-lasting friendships, involving not just 'us' but between our undergraduates and Christina Bows, the owner of Cottshayne Wood (also known as Morganhayes Covert). It arose from a personal friendship between Christina Bows and an EGS colleague, Karel Hughes. Karel was interested in satellite imagery and GIS modelling, not a biologist, but she saw that her friend's wood had immense pedagogical potential. This is because of its history, of which Christina's ownership was merely the most recent in a long history. The wood is all on an acid north-facing slope, some quite steep, near Axmouth and Axminster in Devon. The grid reference is SY224936, near Colyton in East Devon. It is 11.6 ha of which 6.5 ha had been planted with Douglas Fir *Pseudotsuga menziesii*, Sitka Spruce *Picea sitchensis* and some Western Hemlock *Tsuga heterophylla* in the 1970s. (The neighbouring farmer J.W. remembers the wood before most of the conifers were planted, as a "place of magic, full of willow warblers and bluebells".) It is ancient woodland, once and future dominated by oak, but in the 1960s most of the native trees were cut down and replanted with conifers. This was a common event then, inspired by memories of wartime shortages leading to bizarre tax incentives to plant with conifers. In the CEGB forestry work I met an old forester who remembered being called by top brass from some big accountancy firm one March and being told "You MUST get these trees planted by the end of the tax year. Money no object, just do it". That was normal. So Cottshayne Wood became solid blocks of conifer monoculture, with a few uncleared strips of old wood left more by accident than design. Then Christina acquired it and started getting the conifers out, to burn in her wood stove. This was nowhere near as easy as it sounds since the trees were >10m high with >30cm diameters, growing in boggy land on a slope and producing a resin that blocks chimneys. Anyway, she did it with a local farmer, his heavy horse and a special burner, and set about restoring the wood to its 'native' state. We were able to compare conditions in the conifer blocks with the recolonisation of the newly cleared areas. Even the least perceptive student saw immediately that the conifer blocks were densely dark and deeply shady, with no ground plants, but the cleared areas were light and full of young trees, brambles and many other plants. The contrast was clear and massive, though devising good projects was less easy that it seemed since the regrowth was spectacularly impenetrable. We had to use heavy kit to get in to survey the dormouse boxes. One student's feedback form said of this module: "Most memorable feature of the learning experience – waving around a six foot machete".

Each year we came we could see that more conifers had been cleared out, and the bare soil left behind was turning back to woodland much as it would have done about 10 KYBP. In theory we had a golden opportunity for long term monitoring, which is what Christina wanted. In practice there was a subtle pedagogical problem here, which is that we left the students to devise their own projects and sampling protocols. Yes, we did show them what had been done previously, but then they had to come up with their own plans. The students stayed in the Youth Hostel in Beer (honestly, that is what it is called – there is even a Beer pleasure gardens!) and spent the evening planning their data collection. At least that was the idea, and maybe actually happened. The trouble is that each year they did something different – as you would expect. So when I tried to write the work up as a unified body of results (after the module closed down and my career was doing something similar), it quickly became clear that the data sets just could not be merged in any meaningful way. I wasted hours trying to get something accepted by British Wildlife about all our data collection in Cotteshayne Wood, but ended up with just a write up about woodland soils for schoolchildren. I think that this was inevitable, and if you want a publishable dataset you employ people to do what you choose in a pre-defined protocol each year; don't let them

Fig 7.19 The Devon dormouse – photos by Anna Nesbitt.

choose. But if you want them to learn about planning for themselves, you let them make mistakes and end up with unusable data.

This field course only involved two nights away, with one day of serious data collection plus time on the second day before going home. We did hire a minibus but preferred students to use their own cars – as did the students! Getting the minibus up the steep angled drive to YHA Beer was an annual driving test. A key feature of this site was the (almost) eternal campfire burning in the main clearing, around which you could generally find a few students sprawled. Another feature were the dormice, which liked the impenetrable bramble scrub and made nests in there. If you gave them plastic nest tunnels, they used these, so we surveyed dormice by looking into plastic nesting tunnels with an endoscope. This is the only place I have actually seen a live wild dormouse. A student called Anna photographed a sleepy dormouse clambering off up into the brambles when disturbed, looking bleary eyed and a bit grumpy.

From an academic viewpoint, the management of this wood threw up several philosophical conundrums. As is so often the case in biodiversity conservation, the solution starts off easy, obvious and simple, until you start looking at the evidence. I think it is fair to say that Christina's initial take on the wood was an emotive one that deep dark aliens are smothering our native sunny wildwood and that this is a BAD THING. If we can arrange it to be returned to the wildwood with native species that had been there since time immemorial this would therefore be a GOOD THING. (Sorry for the passing dig at '1066 and all that'). So the solution is easy and obvious: to make the site more biodiverse, cut down the alien dark conifers and replant with native trees. And this is exactly what Christina started to do, and initially we supported the logic wholeheartedly. So I can tell you what you get when you clearfell sitka (etc) on this Devon soil. The soil starts off bare with a scattering of tall, thin, wispy broadleaves (oaks and birches) that hung on in the shade and were left uncut. The bare soil explodes into life the next year, especially foxgloves, and what happens next depends on your grazing regime. For the first section that Christina had cleared, she took the advice of the Forestry Commission, who insisted on having a deer-proof fence around the whole section. Otherwise, they explained, deer would eat all the saplings. So, a 2m-high fence was put up around several hectares of land (this is seriously expensive as well as hard work), and the deer stayed out. And inside the deer fence was the most humungously dense thicket of scrub and brambles, which certainly included young trees and certainly gave the dormice a good home, but made all survey/management work very difficult indeed. Subsequently Christina just didn't bother with the deer fence, and the cleared areas ended up more open and more accessible but still with lots of young trees. In fact, I am quite sure that planting trees, at least in UK woodlands, is a waste of time. Trees come in anyway, in their natural succession, birch and willow then hawthorn and oak. You don't need to deer fence unless it's a commercial crop as the trees come back from browsing. I have seen this same effect on brownfield sites repeatedly – leave land alone in the UK and it becomes woodland. Don't pay people to dig holes and plant them, leave the wind and birds to do it for free. (Clearly in a garden where you desire exotic species this won't work.) We had projects comparing the deer-grazed and fenced areas, and there is no doubt that the deer grazing opened up the scrub. Whether that is good or bad depends on how you define good or bad, and the impact of the deer would certainly be modified by introducing a predator like lynx or wolf.

Before going on to the conifer birdlife, some other birds from Cottshayne deserve a mention. One visit, on our first few minutes there, we walked into the wood to hear a commotion overhead – a hobby (a small falcon) was mobbing a larger peregrine falcon. Another time we saw an osprey hunting for fish in the Axe estuary, and my last (?ever) sighting of an English spotted flycatcher was in Christina's wood. It used to be that spotted flycatchers were common and ospreys nationally notable – it's almost the other way round nowadays.

So how about the conifers – were they really evil incarnate? In a word, no! There are certainly places in the UK where any conifers are bad for global biodiversity (eg the Flow country, where nesting waders hate forest edges), but in this site there were some species strictly confined to the conifer blocks. These included fungi – there were far more mycorrhizal fruitbodies (*Lactarius*, *Russula* and *Cortinarius*, for example) under the conifer monocultures than under the oaks. There was a truly odd fungal mycelial mat under some marshy Sitka stands unlike anything I have ever seen elsewhere, but I have read about such things in the Pacific NW of Oregon. It needed a DNA test to see if it was actually a new species or just an odd growth form. But the group that swung Christina's opinion was the bird life. The conifer blocks ALONE held goldcrests, coal tits and crossbills. Not surprising – any bird book will tell you these are species of coniferous woods. We had a few bird-surveying projects, plus we later got MSc students to analyse GIS data based on several years' CBC data from Cottshayne Wood showing clearly that removing conifers also removed goldcrests and coal tits. Maybe blackcaps too. In the end I think our data persuaded Christina to leave some conifer stands, because their continued presence undoubtedly enhanced biodiversity. What is the optimal balance of tree species can now be seen as a philosophical question – what do you mean by the "best" woodland community? The most species? The most native species? Most nesting birds? Most similar woodland community to what it would have been 3000 years ago? Most similar to what it would have been 300,000 years ago? All these answers mandate a different management target and all are justifiable.

Christina used this wood to throw a party, a magical experience since the main woodland glade was decked out with lights, and the food and drink were excellent. In Tolkien's "The Hobbit" there is an account of Bilbo and his companions, lost in Murkwood I think, blundering into a party thrown by the wood elves, encountering a circle of lights and laughter in a deep dark wood, which vanished as soon as seen. This woodland party was as close to that as I'm going to get! (Key differences to Bilbo's encounter included the fact that Christina's party didn't vanish in a puff of smoke when entered, and that there were no giant spiders nearby. Nor dragons guarding gold loot in the distant hills . . .) Camping in the nearby field was OK, but waiting to drive to the local town to use a toilet the next morning was a bit of an ordeal! I gather that Christina sold the wood in 2019, and wonder if I'll find out what happens to it next.

Orielton 2012–2019

By 2011 we were getting quite fed up with the Swansea field course. Not, I hasten to add, the days themselves, but the welcome supplied by the university. For longer than anyone could remember we had been welcomed by the biology department who let us use a laboratory for our practical work (eg measuring diameter of cockles or osmotic pressure in *Salicornia*). This welcome grew thinner, and in 2011 we were forced out to use a top floor chemical laboratory. Quite apart from anything else, our bedrooms were at the top of one accommodation block, the lab was at the top of another building half a kilometre away, and the lifts were unreliable! Word in the SCR was that Swansea biology department had their eyes on national status based on molecular work, and old fashioned field ecologists leaving muddy boots in their labs just wasn't part of their business plan. Maybe there was a genuine concern about DNA contamination, or maybe someone left and a new broom swept clean. Things just got less and less convenient. By way of example, we had to get the security staff to open buildings for us each evening for the evening lectures, which never used to be a problem, but somehow we ended up hanging around for ages before each evening lecture, while someone went off to find someone who had the correct swipe card. The lab we ended up working in had the most horrendous collection of chemicals, including nitric and perchloric acids on open shelves. I cannot emphasise enough what a nasty liquid perchloric acid is – both a strong acid and a powerful oxidising agent. Ken Alexander – who invented the -196°C rat aerosol – was convinced that perchloric acid was the mystery ingredient that caused his skip of burning wastes to explode, leaving the Marie Curie with a bill to replace the field of cabbages 100 yards away whose heads were burned off (see "CEGB"). If any student had taken the top off the perchloric acid bottle I'd have evacuated the lab and hoped no-one got their lungs burned out by its vapour. So, we took the hint, and found another Welsh field station which actually welcomed us. No surly porters, no endless climbing up and down stairs, no jars of lethal liquids lying around, just our own private manor house for a week and dedicated staff who wanted to help us and knew about the local biodiversity.

This new field course venue was FSC Orielton, in Pembrokeshire. This was based in a manor house while our laboratory space was in the stable block, and was vastly more convenient than Swansea University. I am not sure that the students appreciated the change as much as the staff, since they slept in communal dormitories, unlike the en-suites in Swansea. Rather too much staff time was taken up resolving disputes along the lines of "I want to share the dorm with him (/her)", or "don't want to share with them". To solve this, I wrote computer code to come up with genuinely random allocations, with a stern 'no switching rooms' rule. This was far better than allowing cliques to develop. There seemed to be a regular tendency for the Islamic students to do all they could to end up sharing with other Islamic students, then making others in their 8-person dormitory feel unwelcome. A strict enforcement of random allocation was the best solution here. Remember – we are all equal here, no-one is any more special than anyone else. (As I made a point of saying loudly and publicly on a few occasions.) Likewise, each day the students were required to collect data (eg % cover of plants in quadrats) in 'groups', usually 3 or 4 students working together. The obvious solution is to say to them "form yourselves into groups", and this is also one of the worst solutions. Students quickly condense into cliques, don't mix, end up in the same cliques each day, and the wastrels end up with the wastrels and waste everyone's time. So, each day I wrote special R code to come up with a different allocation of students to groups each day, to enforce social mixing. I think this was an excellent solution, since no-one formed cliques, and no-one had the painful social pressure of having to say "please can I work with you?", because I told them all who was working with whom. (I know from painful personal experience how hard this request can be.) Everyone learned how to work with other people, and the wastrels were quickly identified by the hard-working students. Since I controlled the allocation list, I could check immediately if anyone had tried to switch groups to work with their friends. If we had queries about some data, I could dig out my R output and see who was in (eg) group 7 on sand dune day. The only people who didn't like this were the wastrels, who found they had nowhere to hide. At least one feedback form complained about the random allocation, saying they wanted to be able to choose their friends to work with. (Tough – life isn't like that! We later used this as an example for senior management of our degrees making students ready for the world of work.)

Orielton Manor was once owned by a famous Welsh ornithologist Ronald Lockley (https://en.wikipedia.org/wiki/Ronald_Lockley) who write a book about the house and estate (Lockley 1977), as well as others about natural history of Skokholm island, and the Private Life of the Rabbit (inspiring 'Watership Down'). He also advised on an award-winning film about the private life of gannets (https://www.youtube.com/watch?v=lN_doZVuWEY).

Curiously, in his book about Orielton, Ronald Lockley mentions a previous owner Cyril Mackworth-Praed. He was a keen birdwatcher, friend of Julian Huxley, and such a good sharp shooter that he pruned tall cypress trees by shooting their tops of with a rifle! (See Lockley 1977, p. 14, p. 28.) Their son Humphrey Mackworth-Pread was my wife's landlord when she lodged in Hyde farm on the edge of Headley Heath (see chapter 8).

Just as the Manifold Valley in Derbyshire brought back some childhood memories for me, so did Pembrokeshire. Not Orielton itself, but we had holidayed just 10 miles away in Saundersfoot, every August, for quite a few years. With hindsight, that week in Pembrokeshire was our shot of sunlight for the whole year. Anyway, when we took the students to a lovely beach called Manorbier next to a lovely old castle called Manorbier, I got a real sense of déjà vu, as I really had seen that exact spot before. The castle, unsurprisingly, appears not to have changed much since I saw it aged about 12. The beach seems different, now that I am taller than most of the stones! We had to get students and equipment down the cliff here, an exercise which really separated the mountain goats from the sofa-slouchers! (Routinely there would be half a dozen girls who clearly did little outdoor exercise and literally needed hand holding to help them walk down a crumbly shallow cliff). Another lovely local spot from childhood was Bosherston Lily ponds, long thin lakes of crystal-clear water full of waterlilies, though we never found an excuse to take students there. There is a well-known seabird colony and tourist attraction nearby which I remember from years before, Stack Rock and the Green Bridge of Wales. Stack Rock has even popped up in my dreams on occasion, even before rediscovering it at Orielton. These are both cliff features, roughly halfway between Orielton and Saundersfoot. Stack Rock is a huge rock monolith just offshore covered in hundreds of nesting guillemots and razorbills, very close and very easy to see, but very safe since there are 100m sheer cliffs on both sides. The Bridge is pretty much what it says – a natural bridge. Much like the Azure window in Gozo, and doubtless also doomed to collapse into the sea after a heavy storm.

Fig 7.20 Stack Rock, Pembrokeshire. The dots are nesting auks.

There was one thing about using Swansea as a field course base that worked far better than the corresponding day at Orielton, which is the sand dune day. Whatever else can be said about Swansea University, the Whiteford sand dunes were text book. There were sand dunes in Pembrokeshire, but nothing as good, nothing that went all the way from tidal sand to pine woodland. We visited a lovely Pembrokeshire sand dune at 'Freshwater West', and saw some of the typical plants and land forms, but the data were never as good as from Whiteford. In particular, Whiteford had a clear soil profile developing, with a transition from pure sand at the young edge into an acid brown humus stratum over yellow sand in the oldest areas. Freshwater West dunes had no such soil and no pH shift, no woodland and almost no orchids. (Probably just too young, a mere few hundred years.) Otherwise lovely, with gannets hunting offshore, buzzards, kestrels and the odd peregrine overhead, really big, steep dunes and (most years) lizards and slow worms. Once we heard a weird laughing cawing noise, and a deeply black crow with wide blunt wings flew over – Arthur's crow, a chough. This is our rarest crow, with a uniquely blood-red bill and legs, typical of cliffs in the Celtic fringe, with an indescribably wild call, the essence of western cliffs.

Although I can understand that the students were less than keen on sharing dormitories, staff did rather better and I used to quip that Orielton gave me my own personal spiral staircase. It also came with a handy badger sett nearby. I saw badger cubs before dinner time a couple of times, having obviously not listened to their badger mummies about being a nocturnal species. Setting up a remote camera on this sett gave cute films of four cubs playing. Overlooking the sett was a collapsed lime tree that one could easily walk up to, sit on the remains of the root plate and wait. One evening with Stephanie Bird and Astrid Willener (PhD students along to help), we sat up this tree and had badger cubs literally underneath our feet in the late dusk, only weeks old and still blunt nosed. To get to the local pub (The Speculation, or "The Spec" to locals) we walked past a lake that used to be a duck decoy. This was a large-scale netting off bits of the lake so that ducks could be gradually scared into a tunnel from which there was no escape, traditionally for food (but now for ringing). The Orielton book describes hearing otters whistling in this lake, and one evening walking back something made a strangle whistling call in this lake edge. Someone hoiked fresh water mussels out of the lake and left their shells by the path. I'd love to be sure it was otters, but may be wrong!

As a sad postscript, FSC Orielton never recovered from the 2021 COVID pandemic and closed in 2022. Ronald Lockley would have been very saddened, as was I and all who had taught there.

Fig 7.21 A selfie showing "my" spiral staircase in Orielton, my final visit, May 2019.

CHAPTER 8

M is for Marriage!

1986 and all that (From bachelor to retirement)

After leaving York in 1985 I lived as a bachelor in the Dorking area, first renting a small space in lodgings opposite the Gatton Manor country club, then in 1986 I bought my first house. This was 4 Barley Mow Court (henceforth 4BMC), and is strongly associated with working in the CEGB. Thereafter I got married, we moved to Pixham Lane to rear our two children, thence on to North Holmwood. I describe these phases separately:

4 Barley Mow Court

By a combination of a good job, family money and a bit of luck I managed to buy my first house in April 1986. This was 4 Barley Mow Court, south of the A25 by Pilgrims Way cottages and neatly between the Betchworth landfill site and the Betchworth haulage yard (Atkinson's haulage). I had two bedrooms, a tiny kitchen, poky living room and a bit of a back garden, for the princely sum of £42,000. Laughable now, but seemed a lot at the time. Somehow I also afforded a nice 'new' car – an Opel Manta. The engine wasn't as great as the bodywork promised, but it was a lovely machine that I thoroughly enjoyed driving. Looked good outside the house too!

4BMC was kitted out with old Kershaw family beds, an old Kershaw cooker, and old Shaw sideboard, but to be fair a new sofa. I celebrated the new house by buying a new duvet from M&S – that felt rather special.

For a while I had a pet python in the house, inspired by my astral twin from Oxford Sally Thorogood, who bought a baby Burmese python from Mark Harman (as in Harman's antiques in Dorking), and it grew well from 20cm to a couple of metres. Sally moved to the north almost exactly the same time

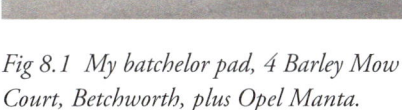

Fig 8.1 My batchelor pad, 4 Barley Mow Court, Betchworth, plus Opel Manta.

Fig 8.2 My python, climbing the staircase in 4 Barley Mow Court c. 1988

I moved to Leatherhead, so I also popped into Mark Harman and got a small Burmese, plus some frozen chicks. I called the snake Shibboleth, for its ability to tell people apart ('yuck' vs 'wow'), and have to say that as far as a large python goes Shibboleth was extremely good tempered. He only bit me once when over stimulated by the smell of freshly warmed mouse, and even then he didn't mean business. Although he had a heated cage, I left the glass door open so he had the choice. Inevitably he'd ignore the heater and curl up behind the sofa. Snakes convert rodent meat into snake meat very efficiently, and it wasn't long before it was a rat a week, then you'd see the python head sticking out one end of the sofa and the tail out the other.

The slight trouble comes when they shed their skins – the eyelids glaze over and they can't see, so get tetchy. A bath helps a lot. So about 1988 I was on my own in 4BMC trying to give Shibboleth a bath to help skin shedding, when Shibboleth was about 4m long. I came to the uncomfortable realisation that (1) he was stronger than I was, and quite beyond my ability to impose control, (2) this had hardly started yet. London zoo had a picture of this species of python killing a leopard, and I remember thinking "Hmm – leopards kill humans, and pythons kill leopards. Doesn't that suggest that you shouldn't argue with them?"

Indeed I later learned of amateur snake keepers killed by 4m pythons, though not (AFAIK) Burmese; an African python has certainly killed its owner, and I wouldn't trust reticulateds either.

It probably shows that I'm not much of a natural romantic, but I had hoped that "come and play with my python" might work as a chat up line. It didn't. There was one exception, about which I giggle each time I see a skip lorry around Leatherhead. The connection is the name of the waste disposal company, D Roberts. Dave Roberts, for it is he, used to work at CERL as the head of the heavy gang (qv). As well as keeping the heavy gang on their toes, Dave had a daughter called Samantha who earned money as a cleaner in the biology building. She was a pretty young woman, I didn't know who her dad was, so I arranged to work a bit late and asked Samantha if she'd like to come round and see my python. To my astonishment, she did. I thought I'd show her the feeding activity, so prepared a frozen mouse.

The problem is that the meat must be warm, both for safety and because the snake only swallows warm food, and (astonishingly) microwave ovens were not widely available. Given they were invented in the 1940s this seems daft. Anyway, I had to use standard oven facilities to thaw out frozen rodents. Normally I'd use a long slow warm in a low oven, but that took ages. So I put the dead mouse under the grill, and set it at a low heat. This was a much more focussed heat source than usual, so within a few minutes of me pouring Samantha a cup of tea the whole house developed a faint but distinct odour of dead mouse. Then slightly grilled dead mouse. Then the whole house smelled of cooked dead mouse, Samantha made an excuse and legged it. Perhaps wisely – the python could smell dinner all around it, but the only new food item in sight was Samantha on the sofa – it could have gone badly. She didn't just leave the house, she also seemed to move her office cleaning duties, never returning to the biology block. Presumably Daddy had a word with someone.

So I had a 4m python to rehouse. Luckily I happened to have stayed in contact with the 'Greater Manchester Zoological Society' – ex staff of Belle Vue Zoo who wanted to restore the zoo. I do not recall how I picked this contact up – probably pre-Oxford. The editor of their little journal was a former reptile house manager called Clive Bennet, and he was delighted to take the snake off my hands. So one day about 1988 after a CEGB work Xmas party I set off to Manchester with Shibboleth, and his heated case. The idea was to leave the snake with Clive in north Manchester, having stayed the night with Mum and Dad in Wythenshawe.

The standard way to transport large non-venomous snakes is in a cloth bag, so I used an old pillow case. With hindsight, a part-rotten old pillow case from the damp of Royton was a bad choice, though the magnitude of the error only came to light on the M6 in Birmingham, one of the A38 junctions. Which is where, about midnight and to be honest driving a little above the speed limit in my new Opel Manta, I looked down at the gear stick. Where there should have been a gear stick was the head of a 4m python, its tongue flickering at me as it tried to work out what to do next. It's one of those flashbulb moments I'll never forget. If Shibboleth had decided to explore the mechanical responses of the steering wheel, or my neck, things might not have gone so well. As it was I was able to pull off onto the A38, stop the car, get me out, get the snake in the boot in a new pillow case, and no policemen came along, to my immense relief. The next morning Mum noticed a strange big pillow case in my bedroom but luckily decided to leave it alone – it had about 10Kg of cross python inside.

So I got away next day and hit the motorway to north Manchester, giving Shibboleth to Clive Bennet, who had a selection of heated cages with snakes and lizards around his house. (In the Zoovet books by David Taylor, Clive Bennet gets mentioned as the Belle Vue reptile keeper who reared two starving alligators rescued from a Manchester night club called "The Garden of Eden". This same nightclub featured an exotic dancer with an anaconda, and the nom de guerre of Miss Seksi.) He told me stories about reptiles and the zoo and north Manchester, and one story stayed with me. He had a son, a young Bennet boy, who when much younger was playing in the streets of north Manchester when he was offered sweets by a fat lady who asked him to get in her car. He ran away. She was Myra Hindley, and the next day she caught, tortured and killed another child, same streets, also called Bennet. (He is still somewhere out under Saddleworth moor.) This story came back to me many years later, when the handyman who regrettably pumped foam into our walls was called Steve Downey, from Accrington. Myra Hindley's most famous victim, Lesley Ann Downey, was his family, his niece. My father treated some of the policemen involved in the case as dental patients, and described them as being still traumatised by the experience of hearing the notorious "Lesley Ann Downey tape". We call it PTSD nowadays.

Anyway, after the snake was given away (ending up in Paignton Zoo, I gather) more people visited my house, and I switched to keeping guinea pigs. We have very fond family memories of a guinea pig called "Snuffles" 1972-1979, and I do like their little squeaks. They are apt to smelling a bit though!

4BMC came with a once-in-a-lifetime chance, in that there was land but no garden at all, the garden was all to play for. It was only about 4m wide and 12m long, with just a wire fence between us and neighbours, but it was mine and it was a blank canvas. To be pedantic it wasn't so much a blank canvas as a large

A Path of 21 Ms

lump of concrete, the gas supply from the previous buildings, but a stern letter to the council got the builders in to smash up the cement. They chucked the cement over the fence, into the nettle bed on Atkinson's land, where I expect it can still be found.

I had fun that first summer – 1986 – planting the whole site with night scented stock. For a few weeks the evening scent was magical. Then I dug it in as a green manure.

The main features of this little garden were a pond and patio by the house. I did both – the pond liner was some super-tough Gundle landfill liner "thrown out" by the CEGB after our using it at West Burton power station. (Again I expect that the 1000 tons of FGD gypsum on a Gundle landfill liner will still be there if you look, for many years into the future.) Somehow some of this thick tough black liner got rolled up and taken home. In fact, a second roll got carried through the CERL boundary fence, and into the farmer's pond near the crematorium. So that my first December in Southlands I sneaked off early one day, parked in Leatherhead crematorium, nipped over the road and fence so got to the pond. It was almost dark by then (. . . that's why I chose December . . .) but light enough to find a 3m plastic tube in a pond edge. Then carried the rolled up plastic back to my car, where it became the pond outside 1CC (and is still there AFAIK).

So 4BMC had a pond, and I managed to beg frog spawn off some locals, so had tadpoles in my own garden!! Anyone can do that – success is when adults return to spawn. Thus it was that two years later, March 1990, when the adult frogs did indeed return to spawn, I felt like a proud father. That was fine, but it was a mistake to share this enthusiasm too literally. I ran into the main bedroom to announce the good news to my new girlfriend Catherine. "I'm a DADDY," I announced proudly. It took about half an hour before Catherine actually accepted I was talking about frogs not a clandestine girlfriend, and she never really forgave me for the shock. My sister said, "I'd have chucked the spawn down your pyjamas if I'd been her." Fuss fuss – that's native biodiversity doing its bit.

I stayed happily in 4BMC until Catherine moved in (after Oxford) and got pregnant with Louise. At that point it was obvious we had to sell up for somewhere bigger, even though the housing market had just crashed (for no apparent reason). To cut a long story short we sold the house in the nick of time, moving into 1 Chester Close, Pixham Lane in June 1993, a week or so before Louise was actually born. Given the long timescales on house moves that was sailing a bit close to the wind! I sometimes pop back to Barley Mow Court to re-visit my former garden. The pond is long gone, but a few of my plantings of trees and shrubs in the front have persisted, notably the paperbark maple *Acer griseum* in front of the kitchen window. Between the end house #2 and the haulage yard is still a narrow pathside strip planted with 'Elephants ears' *Bergenias* and a pine tree. I planted them – the *Bergenias* came from Belvedere in Swanage, the pine tree was a spare from the Liphook forest fumigation experiment (see "CEGB").

The French Connection

This extensive and important phase in my life is easily the best known by others, as it was shared so intensely with the rest of the family.

Several strands came together to make this work at the start. A key facilitator was the local Friends of the Earth group back in 1986-87. This seems an odd choice for an air pollution scientist, but I had been in contact with FoE because of my research interest in forest die-back, and I wanted to meet people. Nowadays a quiet evening alone at home sounds like paradise, but as I was still freshly out of university, the prospect of a lifetime of solitude in the Surrey commuter belt seemed a wasted opportunity, so I tried joining things. Via Dorking & Reigate FoE I ended up meeting a local couple called Paul and Maggie, who ran 'Oakwood Organic Farm', a smallholding between Leigh and Gatwick. (I also met a chap called Griff Wilter, the local coordinator, who turned out to know Rana Marrington – a close friend from later years.) Paul Brown was local stock – his dad was a lecturer somewhere in south London – but Maggie was (very) Irish. They aimed for self-sufficiency in food and selling the surplus to generate an income. Being peasant farmers is never easy, especially on weald clay without chemical fertiliser. When there are only two of you, you're doing well not to starve. To buy their produce you had to stop your car in a random country lane near(ish) to a tiny hamlet called Leigh, marked, if you looked hard, by a hand-painted sign stuck in a hole in the hedge. If you let the sign lead you off the road, a small muddy path led you towards a rather derelict-looking caravan. At this point a large Alsatian would appear and run towards you, barking. The idea is that the dog was friendly, Paul or Maggie would emerge from the caravan and offer you a cup of tea, then you could buy some organic potatoes or whatever. Not surprisingly, they sold nothing at all this way, though a few settled locals supported them. When eventually they gave up on living in the Surrey commuter belt, and moved to Maggie's native Ireland (plus small child) they showed the same entrepreneurial spirit. They had a small holding supplemented by income from a B&B. The location was amazingly remote – Mizzen Head, as far south as you can get in Ireland. The B&B was not advertised online, or anywhere else. If

A Path of 21 Ms

you happened to be in the southern tip of Ireland and tried to drive due south until you went off the southernmost cliff, then about a kilometre before falling off the cliff you would pass a small hole in the hedge, and if you stopped and looked hard you might see a tiny sign saying "B&B". (When their neighbour had not moved it, to keep the area quiet, as happened regularly.) Yes, that was Paul and Maggie's advertising, and it worked as well as it did in Surrey. Last I heard they were getting divorced but could not afford to live apart. Sad, but I couldn't help thinking that they were their own worst enemies.

Back to 1987. I got to know P&M well, including helping them on their farm. One day they had to move a small herd of young cows from one field to another. The sort of thing farmers do on a daily basis, would barely rate a mooing sound in the Archers. Not so Paul & Maggie. The cows were to be driven by humans along country lanes to the new field. Even P&M realised this could go badly wrong, so we did it at dawn around midsummer, in other words hideously early. Even so, the cows were up for a bit of fun, and didn't stick to the script. One especially big posh house near Charlwood had a small gap in the elegant hedge around their immaculate back lawn, through which 10 or so excited cows piled in so they could run around on the turf a bit. I will never forget Paul dancing on this banker's lawn, as the sun came up, trying to chivvy cows back onto the public road through the hole they had squashed in his ornamental hedge. We got away without the police being called, but I do wonder what the owner said when he saw the state of his lawn over morning marmalade.

So when Paul & Maggie invited me to a Halloween party 31-10-1987 I expected it wouldn't be run-of-the-mill. It was thrown by someone they somehow vaguely knew called Lucy, whose hobby was adopting Down's syndrome boys. She had several, and seemed to be doing a good job with them. (Though how they will cope without her remains an open question – not my problem thankfully.) Lucy also happened to know a musician called Richard Allen, who came and brought along his ex-girlfriend Catherine. My first substantive memory of that party is people introducing themselves, and someone saying in a very French accent "I am Catherrrrrine Neubert" (she rolled the R, something I cannot do). We got chatting, and Richard stayed quietly out the way. She smoked a fag and asked if I smoked, so I dusted off a phrase from York "Je ne fume que les petards". (Thanks, Jane Tyler, life transforming.) She was delighted, so I was delighted, and the upshot was she agreed to come round in a couple of weeks. . . . And she did come round, but not until she got lost on the Betchworth lanes, had to find a telephone box to call to ask where I was, and I realised how much I had been gutted by the thought that she'd let me down. An oddly intense reaction after

184

years of such experiences . . . So we kept on seeing each other. Then went on holiday together, first to Maubec. I am sure that having a villa in Provence does wonders for cementing relationships 😊

I don't want to write anyone else's biography for them, but it is a useful family record to note that Catherine came with one strong UK connection in addition to a great many French links. Her mother's family came from Swanage in Dorset, and Catherine had spent pretty much every childhood summer in Swanage with her mum, dad and sisters. The story is more complex – originally the redoubtable Grandma Dorothy Gossling came from east London, but their first child, Elinor, had a weak chest and got respiratory infections due to the shocking air pollution there at the time. This was before any controls on coal fires, and the sort of SO_2 levels that killed thousands of people in 1952 were not queried (ppm rather than ppb levels). The doctor told Don and Dorothy Gossling to be nice to Elinor as she would not survive another winter. Don asked whether she would survive in clean air, and the doctor said probably, yes. So Don gave up his job in London (a banker) and moved to Swanage. He got a banking job for a while then they ran a guesthouse 'Belvedere', where Elinor grew up, and the Neubert family stayed each summer. Later the Gosslings were instrumental in saving the Swanage steam railway, and when she coughed (which was a lot) I used to quip that was the cough that saved Swanage railway. In French hospitals doctors used to call in juniors to see her lung damage – you just don't see it like that nowadays!

Belvedere (Seymer Road, Swanage) was a lovely if rambling multi-storey house with a big garden, very convenient to stay in (if perhaps not very warm or dry in winter). It came with many stories, as Don and Dorothy were both strong and intelligent characters. Don was an inspector for the scouts, who had strong local connections being so close to Brownsea Island. Dorothy was very musical, obviously a born organiser, who helped run the Swanage Operatic society (AKA Gilbert & Sullivan). And the 'Belvedere singers', and a Sunday school as well as a guest house. The guest house required three months of solid work and nine months of gentle preparation, which sounds like a pretty good life, but busy in the season. Breakfast, elevenses, lunch, high tea, dinner, and bedtime cocoa every day – just endless. The dishwashing sounded endless too, especially when everyone had to have a separate dish and knife for the butter (etc). The big round table in our living room came directly from Swanage, and is known to have seated 14 people at a time (not all adults, but even so . . .) The *Acanthus spinosa* and *Yucca gloriosa* in our garden in Dorking are both cloned from the Belvedere garden in Swanage. (I lovingly nurtured that *Acanthus*, to discover it is an invasive

Fig 8.3 Grandma (Dorothy) Gossling showing the Acanthis spinosa *in the garden of Belvedere about 1989.*

thug that regenerates from root fragments and smothers anything nearby. It hasn't taken to Provence as well as I expected.)

Although Belvedere in the 1950s sounds in many ways quaintly idyllic, Swanage was a small society where everyone knew everyone, so social relations could be fraught. Elinor Gossling got her first degree from Exeter and had vague plans for something post-graduate. However, she went on an exchange visit to Paris, went to a dance at an Anglo-French club, met a tall Frenchman who talked a lot about de Gaul but was a rather clumsy dancer (Jean, of course). To cut a long story short, they married hastily a little while later, Elinor moved to France, and that's how the Neuberts became Anglo-French. Elinor's younger sister Catherine also got accidentally pregnant, producing a son Toby who was immediately taken for adoption. He turned up again years later – pretty much about the time Catherine Gossling developed cancer – and he became a leading light in the Ancient Yew Forum. Catherine Gossling married a school pottery teacher Leslie Gibbons, lived in "The Owl Pottery", and produced two daughters Sharon and Carol. In the small world of Swanage all this inevitably became widely known. This all probably explains why Elinor Neubert toured French schools teaching about sex and contraception, to the intense embarrassment of her daughters. At one stage I was shown the "sexy bus", a second hand bus kitted out for driving round France giving out advice on family planning. Although an impeccably well behaved and respectable lady, Elinor had some brushes with the law in France, where demands for family planning were seen as seditious by the (predominantly) Catholic state. At least once Jean had to bail his wife and daughters out of police custody (to his annoyance) after the CRS turned up at some pro-choice rally. As a curious aside, all the active members of French family planning groups are from protestant backgrounds, and they constitute a real and historically oppressed minority, about 1% of the population. The French still refer to la Galère – forced service rowing boats imposed on Huguenots (they worked till they died hence "C'est la galère" means it's really hard work). When on holiday in the Ardèche we had to make a pilgrimage to a remote refuge where Huguenots hid from Catholics, including a wine barrel that doubled as a pulpit and a Bible with some slightly different form of words that upset the Catholics. (French Catholics address their God as "vous", while Protestants prefer "tu".) I am always horrified by human fissiparity and the fuss they make over fairy stories. The other theme is that the first child of protestant family-planners in France tended to develop a bit of a complex that their mothers wanted them dead. "Look at me – I was lined up for a PhD in Exeter and I had to have you instead." Not that anyone actually said that AFAIK but I can see it's not a boost to your self-confidence.

Back to 1987 . . .

Catherine Neubert was renting a room in an old farm house called Hyde Farm, in Headley, shared with Rana Marrington among others. The landlord was Humphrey Mackworth-Praed. The name is worth watching out for, not only distinctive but distinguished. The Mackworth-Praeds were eminent early naturalists and got mentioned in "Orielton" by R Lockley as previous owners (see "Orielton", chapter 7). I think that he was involved in protecting a population of 'wild' martagon lily near Mickleham, and certainly he conducted his business meetings walking on Headley Heath. An exemplary landlord AFAIK. We still have photos from inside Hyde farm, featuring Catherine, Rana Marrington, and a dentist called Kate Negri (a lady with a taste for MG sports cars who was taught by my "Aunty Gwen", Gwen Hack).

Catherine then worked at a photographic developer company called Durst, on the Longmead industrial estate in Epsom. Durst UK was up against the likes of Kodak and Fuji, but its entire turnover was a fraction of their R&D budgets, so her job was never secure. Durst came with some interesting international features, such as a head office in Bolzano (= Bozen, the bit of Italy where everyone is blond and speaks German). There were international conferences, which led to Catherine once being stranded in No-man's land between East and West Germany, after one border guard played hardball about the import/export paperwork. On another trade fair she needed to show her passport for each visit to the toilet!

When that job folded in 1988, she found a new job in Leatherhead with Dean & Wood, who distribute refrigeration equipment. Dean & Wood were probably the more secure as a position, but the management were sexist and old fashioned, the job tedious and unrewarding. I got invited to the 1988 Xmas party, where the creep of an MD called a round of applause for how lovely all the women looked – yuck. In the evenings Catherine took to volunteering with ACP – the Alternatives to Custody Programme, aiming to redirect young local ne'er-do-wells away from criminality. She got a great deal of satisfaction from this, and decided to try for a qualification in it. In the end she got a Ministry of Justice sponsored place at Green College Oxford to do a CQSW (Certificate of Qualification in Social Work), 1989-1991. I quip that my Oxford scholarship got me £60 per year, whereas hers kick-started her pension with two years of proper pension contributions. Do the maths!

Green College Oxford (now known as Green-Templeton) was just lovely, with the college holding the former Ratcliffe observatory, which is now the college canteen. The most elegant student dining in Oxford, I reckon! The whole gardens were also beautiful, with a live-in gardener who wrote erudite articles on garden design for the college newsletter. (The gardeners at CERL were good blokes who knew their stuff and worked hard, but couldn't have written a review of historical approaches to naturalism in garden design to save their lives.)

Catherine's tutor was the dean, Colin Roberts, son of a Merseyside docker who rose to dean of an Oxford college by hard work and brain power. One of the lads on Catherine's course had a dad who was a Merseyside docker; in fact his dad had worked alongside Colin. So, when he was late for a lecture, Colin Roberts the dean went to the student's bedroom door and knocked him up to get out of bed and on with the day. I have to say that this goes against the general 'stay away from students' private lives' principle that tutors should generally follow. Catherine came from the French university system where everyone is eligible but space is tight, so the system is geared to getting rid of students. Individual support? People who know who you are? Forget it. In Oxford the college dean knew Catherine by name and bought her brandies in the college bar, as well as running individual detailed tutorials exploring essays in analytical depth. Totally mindblowing by comparison! So by 1991 Catherine Neubert MSc Oxon. was qualified to start work as a probation officer or a social worker. Shortly afterwards some minister – maybe Kenneth Baker? – removed the requirement for a CQSW from the job description for POs or social workers, effectively demoting an entire generation. Anyway, Catherine started work as a PO in 1991 and continued doing this until retirement in 2017.

After Oxford, Catherine needed a home in the SE, and moved in with me to 4BMC. The python had gone then, replaced by guinea pigs. I have a flashbulb memory of hearing that Catherine's sister Sophie had just given birth to her first son Eliot, which was August 1990, in my bedroom in 4BMC with two guinea pigs squeaking happily. Strangely I don't remember any problems with smells or noises from having two piggies next to my bed, though they must have scampered, nibbled and squeaked all night. Since I had two bedrooms, Catherine (always a sensitive sleeper) just slept in the rodent-free room. Apparently around July 1991 I was heard to say something along the lines of "now I'm 30 it's time to copy my DNA". I'm sure it wasn't quite that blunt. Anyway, about August 1992 we agreed that maybe contraception could be sidelined. I know it was about then because shortly afterwards we did a BSAC dive test under Swanage pier that involved buddy-breathing. This requires two people to share one air supply (... it can happen ...), and it was only later that I realised that my holding too tightly to my air supply could have cut oxygen to the newly conceived Louise. Happily, all went well under Swanage pier, and Louise was subsequently born 12 June 1993 AOK. Actually she came out rather late (c'est la vie) and rather fast (in desperation we tried cod liver oil which worked terrifyingly well), but after a brief medical flurry all was well. It was a life-changing, once in a lifetime experience to hold newborn baby Louise in my hands and look in her eyes. She looked back.

One other very significant event took place on 11 December 1992, which is that we got married. This was in Epsom registry office, with a reception in the Bookham Grange Hotel, on the edge of Bookham common. The wedding was, of course, memorable. The mind-bending few minutes when it looked like the father of the bride might be late (he wasn't). The entrance of our two surviving grandmothers. My father playing the accordion watched admiringly by Sophie's son young Eliott. The chef at the Bookham Grange was French and used some truffles Jean brought over along with Chateauneuf-du-Pape from his favourite supplier Henri Petrucci. Overall a good experience. Yes, Louise was there, but not yet emerged!

Some of our wedding photos.

Fig 8.4 Our two grandmothers – Bessie Kershaw (L) with the fur hat, Dorothy Gossling next to her. John Shelvey (R) and Howard Hack (L) behind.

Fig 8.5 Epsom registry office 11 December 1992.

A Path of 21 Ms

Louise was born just before midnight 12 June 1993, and (as any parent will tell you) life is never the same afterwards. Sleep is the number one change – I kept on seeing hours of the night I'd only heard about before. Catherine had mastitis so we needed bottled milk (formula). I really don't recommend it, because then the father can take turns overnight!

You have no idea how much a baby turns your lives upside down. It's not just that you don't sleep, it's that every priority, aim and hierarchy in your life plan is shredded. You want to do what – sleep? Relax? Dream on, you're not that important, someone else is. Like a fool I agreed to be equipment officer for the dive club in 1993. That lasted a few months but I simply could not justify it and didn't pull my weight. We had sold 4BMC and moved into 1CC by then – the house was plenty big enough with one baby. So, Louise grew up, and charmed all who met her.

Fig 8.6 Eliot Roynette listens to John Shaw's accordion after the post-wedding meal.

To be honest the years 1993 – 1999 are a bit of a blur. I thought we'd got the hang of babies, until Alex came along. (This was a calculated decision, having seen how my parents were unhappy to have no siblings.) We lived in 1CC, we spent as much time as we could in Yerres or Maubec, but also went to Manchester (for my parents) and Oxford (Caroline and John). Alex was born at East Surrey on 1 August 1995, by a planned induction. Louise's birth had scared the medics (glad I didn't understand at the time) so Alex was an induced birth. We had to be in East Surrey Hospital early, and I went for a dawn walk that day. As I walked into the local woods (by Betchworth golf course) I saw a hobby, a scarce summer falcon, very fast and a very good flier. Yes, I took that as a good omen.

With one small child and two organised adults you can just about maintain a life. We both even worked full time. Once Alexander was born, 1 Aug 1995, simple domestic survival became a top priority end in itself. Things like – both kids liked a bottle of milk, which had to be sterilised each time in our dedicated steamer, but the teats we gave to Louise (nearly 2 ½) had to have a much larger hole than the ones Alex (just a few months old) could cope with. We needed

Fig 8.7 Catherine, Oxford October 1989.

Fig 8.8 The Shaws, at the wedding of Catherine's sister Sophie July 1996.

two collections of plastic teats with different sized holes, and woe betide anyone confusing them. One night in two of sleep, one in two on milk duty. Our new house, 1 Chester Close, Pixham Lane (henceforth 1CC) had carpets down everywhere, which rapidly smelled of old milk. (Carpet in the toilet too – I put down lino there quickly, and found it was a much bigger job than expected.) It had a huge front garden (the Judas tree and rowan tree I planted are both still there) but a stupidly small back garden, just a lawn plus narrow flower beds. I have maintained birdwatching notes for most of my life, and among my most treasured possessions is my card index of bird records. It goes back to my earliest notebooks around 1970, and has things like the first swift / swallow / redwing each year. This goes back to my childhood and I still keep the records, on old computer punch cards. Except from 1995 – 2017, from Alex's birth to his leaving university!

At the time we lived in 1 Chester Close, Pixham Lane RH4 1PP, which was just up the road from the 'Pixham annex' of St Martin's school. So of course Louise started there. Years later this annex was sold off, and years later I had the odd experience of an aikido course in the same room that Louise learned basic schooling (with a 4th dan called Hashimoto Sensei – I learned a sneaky counter when clashing swords high above your head). Alex didn't go there, only because we moved to 4LW in 1999 when Alex was <4 years.

We moved to 4LW June 1999, bought off Mrs Elaine Gould, and it has to be said it was a very stressful phase of life. Selling houses, chains of vendors, huge amounts of money – horrible. I have a fond memory of a tiny Alex carrying some pots of honeysuckle cuttings into Mrs Gould's garden a few weeks before purchase. The same honeysuckle that still smothers the cherry tree in the corner by my garage came from that cutting, which fragrances the patio next door for Cathy and Trevor to enjoy on summer evenings. Oddly, Elaine Gould knew 'Aunty Gwen' (Gwen Hack) somehow, and Gwen had seen our house and garden before we bought it. The 'Queen of the night' cactus celebrated our arrival by flowering!

Mrs Gould celebrated by taking all the curtains with her so I had to not just buy curtains but the support rails too or no-one would have slept the first night. (With hindsight that was desperately tight because we could only start curtain shopping having moved in, and the walls in 4LW are pathetically soft, more like cardboard than plasterboard. Somehow I got them to stay up.)

4LW came with a designer-designed garden, of which some features remain. I profoundly disagree with some of their choices, notably the heathers in all the flower beds. *Calluna* is a plant I know well from acid free draining sandy soils – pure infertile sand, washed in acid if possible. The soil in 4LW is a heavy alkaline clay that waterlogs half the year – *Calluna* never had a chance. The cherry tree closest to #2 is utterly tedious too, but a useful hammock mount! The Leylandii hedge is their fault too, and never really had a chance against the woodland edge. It is doomed to get thinner and leggier over time, because it regrows badly from old wood. I have underplanted it with hollies, to fill in the gaps with a true hedging plant as a gradual process over decades.

Louise never ceases to remind me that the nasty gap in the right hand edge of the *Leylandii* hedge is when I burnt the hedge down, c, 2011, during Louise's A level revision. True, though ignition was 48 hours after the BBQ ended (I put embers on the compost heap without soaking them first – one was glowing and ignited the dry moss which ignited the hedge). At the time I quipped that it should be healing over nicely by the time Louise did her MA. In fact, it still hasn't healed over years after Louise got her MA – hedges are like that. I replanted the gap with holly and firethorn – tough, fast and tolerant of heavy cutting. And very spiky too. And I added as many roses to the far side as I could get – subject to the description of "very large", "vigorous", "invasive" etc. Each end has a 'Rambling rector' – notoriously spiky and invasive, while in the middle a giant red pillar rose has colonised a hawthorn bush, and out-grew a bindweed one summer. The idea is to discourage visitors from climbing in. Or "To keep out the hordes of greenhouse effect refugees mid-century" as I once explained it, rather melodramatically.

Some features were good – the maple at the bottom left of the garden has grown well and gives superb colour every autumn. There was a dinky Japanese maple on the bed I call 'snowdrop promontory', but it got a rot and died. (So I replanted with the witch-hazel from 39FD, which died in 2019. So did the "Charlotte Russe" – that spot seems cursed.) Probably the best individual feature that Elaine left us was the pond next to a gravel bed. The pond is surprisingly deep and as Elaine said the frogs spawn in it each year (late February). Typically about 30 frogs turn up, and some years the entire water body seems to be frogspawn by March. Unsurprisingly, lots of tadpoles follow. The gravel bed was just tedious white gravel, but proved to be very useful for my habit of picking up interesting stones. So I kept finding boxes with stones that took up space in my loft. They're stone! So I put them into the stone bed by the pond, and they have rather built up. I really like the effect. With a few old shells, an authentic amphora fragment and a seaside plant called thrift (*Armeria maritima*) there is a curiously coastal feel about it. This is where I realised I had more blue john lying around than on the Winnats pass where it came from, and in the Covid-19 lockdown of 2020 I took out each stone here and washed it (finding several lumps of blue john that got polished).

There is a strong argument that the section covering Catherine's time as a probation officer should be the longest one. It was the key 25 years (1991 – 2016) in which our kids became adult and I developed my career as a university lecturer. I am sure Catherine would have a great deal to say about this period. Some key aspects of this – Maubec, Inholms Clay Pit, Roehampton – have got their own chapters in this book. Many of the stories from the Surrey underworld are best left for Catherine to tell. A few, anonymised, have high entertainment value, such as the twit who left his footprints at the crime scene so ate his shoes in police custody. "Yes, ossifer, I always eat my shoes when I get hungry." The twin who visited his twin brother in jail and swapped clothes to let him home for a night – only to realise (too late) that you need to know how meals, cells and toilets work in jail.

I am afraid that my viewpoint was hearing years of grumbles about the unending burden of dodgy IT systems and (generally) poor management. Balancing two jobs and two small kids was so intense that the only way to cope was strict scheduling. Catherine worked full-time for a short period but mainly worked part-time. My being away two evenings a week (Shorinji Kempo at the Tolworth dojo) needed very accurate timing. Of course the kids had music lessons, Louise did Brownies then Guides, Alex did football . . . Looking back I am not sure how we coped. Parents make a fuss about the empty nest when kids leave for university, but it sure makes life easier.

One event that really deserves recording was how our daughter Louise got us a visit to meet the Queen, Elizabeth the Second no less. Louise was at primary school at the time, and unknown to us had been entered in a national competition to write a poem for the Queen's 50th jubilee in 2002. Winning entries got to visit the palace for a royal reception. Louise aged eight duly wrote a little poem that got submitted by the school, and came second nationally in her age group. So the school was told that Louise, her family and teacher were invited to a reception in Buckingham Palace! We duly turned up in our Sunday best, Louise plus her brother, Mum and Dad, grandma (my mum) and the teacher Mrs Pidgely who had set the project up. We were met in a grand room in the palace, duly got to shake hands with HRH plus the Duke of Edinburgh. The Duke came over well to us – he tried to help Louise find a vegetarian nibble. Overall, a remarkable experience, from a sweet little poem. (We still have the booklet of the winning poems.)

Although anno domini would have forced our retirements anyway, events certainly speeded the process up. In Catherine's case the catalyst was a series of reforms introduced by Chris Grayling. Even by the standards of Conservative MPs, Chris Grayling was cursed by the inverse Midas touch, epitomised by a

Fig 8.9 HRH gives Louise her award.

Fig 8.10 The Queen and Prince Philip with the winning children – Louise is first on the left.

weird contract to ship vital supplies in from the EU by a company with no ships using a standard contract from a takeaway pizza outfit. Not surprisingly his 'improvements' to the criminal justice system were catastrophic. Clients had confidential meetings to discuss burglary and drug abuse in Costa Coffee or phoned in to assure untrained staff that they were doing fine thanks. I think at one stage probation officers were communicating by yelling through people's windows. "Hello Jason, how is your opiate habit and wife beating this week?" as the neighbours all listen in. It is symptomatic that Catherine was officially retired while at her desk in a prison and was not told of this, so she was in fact uninsured and had no business being there.

An email from years later sets the scene well

Email 2022

Dear [snip]

It was indeed the impact of Failing Grayling which brought on my decision to leave. I am pleased to report that my office, Redhill had the dubious privilege of serving his constituency. With our union, Napo, as Vice-Chair for Surrey I led a demo and blocked the traffic in Epsom. It did not do much good but it was great fun! When I retired I was asked what my greatest achievement was by my SPO and jokingly said "blocking the traffic in Epsom High Street". I then received a letter from the CEO of South East probation thanking me for my 25 years and stating, yes you have guessed it!: "I understand your proudest achievement is blocking Epsom High Street."

So, Catherine retired, grumbling about the criminal justice system, in 2019 and I retired (primarily on medical grounds) in July 2020, sunning ourselves in Provence at the time. Louise and Alex had left home to live with their partners, and our life involved an oscillation between Dorking (for medical check-ups etc) and Saint Maximin (for the sun and the sea). Wherever I happen to find myself, I have a garden that will absorb any spare time I can give it, plus I have land nearby that needs my attention to keep back the brambles, plus collect data (the claypit in Dorking, the local garrigue in 867LB), plus I have files to create on my computer. Now retired, Catherine makes money and keeps mentally active by running online French conversational classes: I quip that she is actually getting paid for doing what she most enjoys doing anyway, which shows excellent planning. I have done a little examining of theses and reviewing the odd paper on springtails, and have managed to carry on popping into Whitelands laboratories to check springtail specimens for other researchers.

Finally, just for the record, I would like to take the opportunity to stick in a few "Been there done that" memories of family holidays in this period. Growing up in Manchester, family holidays were Wales or Scotland, while Catherine's mainly involved oscillating between Yerres and Swanage. Our kids got to see a bit more of the planet! Without attempting a definitive list, some of the best pictures come from Cambodia 2013 and Kenya in 2009. Alex and Louise did not come to Peru in 2017, though Louise did visit Machu Picchu before we did, and Alex has toured South America pre-Covid.

Fig 8.11 Ta Prom temple, Cambodia 2013.

Fig 8.12 Champagne breakfast after balloon flight over the Masai Mara, Kenya 2009.

Fig 8.13 Lake Nakura, Kenya 2009. Note the 10,000 flamingos.

Fig 8.14 Peter and Catherine, Machu Picchu June 2017.

CHAPTER 9

M is for Mitosis

My tumour

Take it from me: you want brain surgery like you want a hole in the head.

So a life-changing event came along in 2019, just one of those things where the backgammon game of life throws a double 6 against you. Maybe my bad fall in June 2014 that tore my right shoulder was a harbinger since it was caused by my left foot suddenly collapsing. Maybe my hopeless balance on the Garlaban in early April 2019 was a warning – whenever the ground was not flat, I had problems with balance.

I ran the Brighton marathon in April 2019 with no problems, apart from missing the bus back so had to walk another couple of km, but in May 2019 found that I was getting two unfamiliar new symptoms. At night when I had a single light source (eg a torch) I saw two images, and could not get them to align. Coming back from moderate jogs I became dizzy, nauseous and physically sick. After the second time, I decided to pop in to see a doctor. She heard about the nausea and dizziness and diplopia, she looked into my eyes and saw something she didn't like at all, and told me I wasn't going into work until they had ruled out a stroke. So I got scanned for a stroke, and it wasn't. But the doctor there said she didn't like the look of something about my auditory nerve and requested an MRI scan. This took a few days, but did find a lump that shouldn't have been there.

To cut a long story down to size, this proved to be a brain tumour, but a reasonably low grade one and a very uncommon pathology. A choroid plexus papilloma in the 4th ventricle I gather. So I was told it should come out, and basically got the year off on sick leave. The operation was on 3 Sep 2019, and some idea of the experience is conveyed in a work email listed below. I could go on.

Six months later we re-met the surgeon, Mr Simon Stapleton. Catherine asked him how big the growth had been. Simon flicked through some scans. I had this down as a pea-sized lump, maybe a large baked bean.

"It's about this size—" he held his finger and thumb well apart – "say about the size of a walnut." That took the wind out of my sails.

Email to Antonia Ford, a work colleague, 26 Sep 2019

[snip]

My situation is as follows. Brain tumour removed 3 Sep 2019, am assured all went as well as possible. All I can say is that I'm glad not to have encountered an unsuccessful procedure, as this one has clearly damaged the nerves to the left of my face leaving me with a bad case of diplopia. "Your hearing is probably a lost cause," said the consultant cheerfully yesterday. Thanks, a clear case of the cure being worse than the disease! They still plan to run a lumbar puncture to look for loose choroid cells in my spinal CSF, yippee.

Anyway, what I see as the huge improvement is that I am now home, after > 3 weeks sleeping (or rather not) in hospital beds with no blanket let alone duvet but lights on all night. Bliss! I had thought that I could exercise my legal right to self-discharge any time but everyone else but especially family members declined to play along, doubting my ability to behave safely. In St George's I got off on the wrong foot by pinching a portable IV drip stand to give me the stability to make a run to the toilet instead of pushing a button to request help like they told me. It worked like a charm, but when I came out there were several nurses gathered round the door glowering. After that it was like being on suicide watch, each time I got up off the bed I'd have a few nurses eyeing my every move. Anyway after a nocturnal transfer to East Surrey and in a second ward, I finally showed two occupational therapists that I can stand up on one foot with eyes shut for 5 seconds, correctly answered the question 'Would you carry a pot of boiling tea on a slippery tray around your living room?' (Hint: they did not advocate the plan) I got my discharge papers and slept in my own bed last night. After being shaken awake each night at 0400 hrs to have a blood pressure cuff inflated on my arm, I was beginning to feel stuck in a Kafka-esque nightmare with no prospect of escape. Highly not recommended.

Email to Phil Collins ex-PhD student

26 June 2020

Dear Phil

Many thanks for the PDF. [snip] I had a mild lingering concern that someday someone might say "I don't believe you, please show me a copy". Not that anyone pays anywhere near that much interest in me. For years my CV listed a conference proceedings paper with my name on, given by a colleague from Powergen, from a waste disposal seminar in Germany in 1992 (. . . yippee . . .) that indeed if challenged I'd have had to admit looked flaky. Then two months ago in the pile of CEGB archive papers at the back of my loft I found a copy! The wider scientific community was unstirred by my review of orchids on power station waste dumps but I do feel slightly better about my CV claims now.

As to how I'm doing in myself, I'd say "As fine as can be expected". You may not know that I have had a deeply troubled year due to a medical issue. It was May 2019, a bit after the Brighton Marathon, that I started getting dizzy and sick with double vision. I saw my doctor who packed me off to hospital for a scan that same day (thinking I was having a stroke). It turned out to be a low grade tumour roughly where my left ear enters the brainstem, which had to come out, and out it came on 3rd Sep 2019. Although they left most of my CNS alone and assured me it all went as well as can be expected, it was a profoundly debilitating experience. In the aftermath I couldn't tell which way was up and my 2 eyes wouldn't coordinate to lock onto any image. Explaining, I think, why everyone then treated me as a 2 year old for a few weeks, to which I took badly. I hate lying still in bed so kept on trying to stand up and do exercises. I hatched a creative plan to borrow a 5-wheeled drip stand so I could get to the toilet without either falling over or asking a nurse, about which they were thoroughly miffed when they worked out where their drip stand had got to. I learned later they sectioned me for my own safety for some reason – didn't know they could do that without explaining. I'm not sure who was the more relieved to get me out of St George's, me or them.

Once home they shipped me off by ambulance each day to expose my head to hard gamma from a cobalt 60 source, leaving me with a (small) bald patch and weeks of nausea. Thankfully that ended in December, and

> I notionally returned to work in February. In fact Covid-19 then shut the uni so I have been pretty much stuck at home all this academic year. I have requested taking voluntary severance at the end of July, so won't be going back in. I will need scanning for life now – all I can say is that the post op scans have all been clean of returning cells so far.
>
> Apart from this I'm doing fine, though can't get my weight back up. I'm on a "2 breakfasts and sticky toffee pudding" diet, which suits me well. I am running on Leith Hill every few days (doing good distances – see screendump), and keeping an eye on "my" nature reserve Inholms Clay Pit which I think you visited. In fact my biggest single daily job is collecting beer cans etc from the clay pit. I make a point of popping round each afternoon with a bulging bin bag each to every group I see saying "You'll take your litter home won't you?". It seems from everyone I have heard from that the countryside is being plagued with visitors who know nothing about how to behave outdoors. Holmwood common next door reported someone opening gates to let cows loose because "they looked like they wanted their freedom". I keep finding 5cm grey gas cylinders in the litter, which I assume are laughing gas N_2O – though the youngsters in the clay pit always look innocent and baffled and deny any idea what such a thing might be, presumably thinking I was born yesterday. It was spliffs when I was their age . . .
>
> The next question is when we can get to France. In theory I could pack the car and set off to live in Provence for the rest of my life. Reasons not to do so include, in no particular order, Inholms Clay Pit, medical appointments here, the French lockdown/quarantine regulations and the fact that DVLA won't give me my driving licence back. They are VERY touchy about brain tumours because of the risk of seizures, and I can see the logic. This December is my chance to re-apply.

Writing with the benefit of 18 months' hindsight, I am compelled to see my operation on 3 Sep 2019 as an end point for my previous life, a marker of the beginning of the wind-down phase. I never really worked again, and it was more than two years until I next drove a car. My balance is shot for life, and my left ear doesn't work and won't work again. (I have quipped that I will never dance the sugar plum fairy again, leading at least two physiotherapists to ask me about my ballet dancing career – showing good training but poor understanding of my

A Path of 21 Ms

jokes. The only person who actually described me as doing the dance of the Sugar Plum Fairy was a karate Sensei in Leatherhead, describing my attempt at kihon kata in unflattering terms.) The experience has taught me a lot, mostly stuff I would be happier having never known. I have never known any pain equivalent to the post-operative pain in the muscles that hold my neck up. They had to be sliced open to access the skull, and the medics warned me that they might sting a bit. "Burn with unendurable agony" might be closer to the mark, the only time I have pleaded with a nurse for morphine. Morphine is remarkable for its effect on pain – after an hour of having a blowtorch play on the cut muscles of my neck, one suck of a blue morphine-based ice cream and the pain just stopped, so I dozed off for a happy snooze. I can understand why they were cagey about giving the stuff out though – powerful magic.

There was one light moment, of spontaneous happiness and relief. It was in St George's, and the physiotherapists wanted to check whether I was fit to be transferred to a more general ward closer to home. So they gave me a "Montreal cognitive functioning test" or whatever it is called. Where are you, what date is it, what day of the week, who is Prime Minister? Catherine was sitting in, observing. Then they showed me a drawing of a two-horned rhinoceros that lacked the heavy body plates of the Indian rhino, so must have been one of the African species. The trouble is that both black and white rhinos can look like that and have two horns – it's the upper lip that distinguishes and that wasn't shown. So I looked puzzled and worried, and eventually said, "Obviously you want me to say 'African Rhino', but the question is which species?" At this point Catherine and the nurses laughed out loud and looked happy. It turned out that they thought I was unable to identify a rhino at all and faced a lifetime of debility, then suddenly clicked that my problem was the species-level ID, not the nature of the beast. They then showed me a camel, but camels are easy as they have one or two humps and this had one, so I told them it was a dromedary. They decided I was fit to be released to East Surrey hospital (to everyone's relief).

That wise songstress Joni Mitchell said "You don't know what you've got till it's gone", and I certainly learned that. All my life I had looked at one thing with two eyes and saw one thing – not something I'd ever queried. Then for six weeks post-op I saw double. Two suns, two dots in the sky for each bird. One day I found that although I was walking past the edge of a table, my eyes assured me that I was walking through the table. (Maybe a lifetime of magic mushroom experiments provided me with useful experience that allowed me to look at this anomaly calmly as an interesting experience, rather than a cause for panic?) The surgeon said give it six weeks, and almost to the day after six weeks my eyes re-aligned. I have never taken optical alignment for granted again. I knew I liked sleeping in my own bed, but hadn't realised just how important it was to me until I'd been in hospital beds for more than three weeks – lights on all night, nurses checking your blood pressure every four hours, a kafka-esque nightmare. The first things I saw when I got out of the ambulance that took me home 21 Sep 2019 were the flowers of *Cyclamen hederifolium* welcoming me home, and these suddenly rose in my estimation to being really valuable low-key perennials.

The aftermath of the operation was, I am assured, wholly successful, but there was lingering nervous damage. My left ear is disconnected, and for a while the muscles for the left side of my face were under-stimulated, causing a mild facial palsy. My lips didn't seal properly on the left side for example, which remined me horribly of my mother's father, George Kershaw, who had a stroke and lived for a decade crippled. This asymmetry can be seen when I got my French passport, though it is not marked. To be fair to the NHS they spotted this and acted to fix it, by some minor surgery on my left eyelid to tighten it. I think it was called a Mullerectotomy, and to be honest when the doctor said "this procedure is well tolerated" my heart sank and the last thing I wanted was having to tolerate anything surgical. It was November 2020, a half hour procedure with local anaesthetic at a "Centre for Sight", and involved some crucial tiny muscle being stapled to somewhere new on my skull. Ugh – I only discovered that weeks later when a nurse explained why I had strange aching feelings in my bone, which made no sense for an eyelid operation. For weeks afterwards there was blood in my tears, which may sound romantic but is not at all, since what actually happens is your vision goes cloudy then your pillow goes messy overnight. As I grumbled at the time as I wiped red tears off my cheeks – "An iatrogenic injury to cure an iatrogenic injury". All true, but to be fair everyone has said how much better I look now with a symmetrical face. I was in denial of my facial asymmetry before, but the universal agreement is that it is fixed and no-one would know just by looking. The last bit of evidence of the operation will come when I am cremated, when a lump of titanium will turn up in the ashes, having held my skull base together for years.

The other legacy, which future researchers will think positive, is that the experience has really focussed me on future-proofing what I want to leave to others after I die. This book is one such. The setting up of wills and powers of attorney is a slightly chilling and expensive process, but worth doing. I remain slightly haunted by the solicitor going through her questions and getting to "And what should happen to your money if you and your wife and children all die together?", asked with a breezy cheerfulness to which the honest answer

"I don't care" isn't quite good enough. I have tried to arrange the card indexes etc for Inholms Clay Pit to be archived in Dorking museum, and left detailed instructions on which stones and which plants are special. You just know it will go wrong on the day, but hopefully we can keep >75% saved for the future.

As for an overview on life, it certainly got me thinking. It confirmed my long-standing view that when evaluating the quality of a life you need to include an index of happiness as well as simple longevity. Objectively I was only in hospital beds for a bit over three weeks, which is probably quite short by some standards. I have never been so glad to get out of anywhere ever, and that even includes Manchester Grammar School! Even more glad to leave the public ward behind than Latin homework, which set a previous new low. If that bed-rest had been the prospect for the rest of my life I'd have thought something along the lines of "Thanks, but no thanks". I can see a simple, intuitive mathematical model here which helps focus my evaluations. It does involve having a Y axis which is some composite "happiness function". I am sure some people will profoundly object to condensing down the diversity of experience into one index, but actually that is pretty much how evolution has configured our behaviours – animals maximise activity in some "happiness" circuits, associated I think with the neuro-transmitted dopamine. In theory we could use a net dopamine flux as a surrogate for happiness – or just ask the person because they will know damn well. Whether or not they dare admit the truth is another question, of course! So let's imagine a graph showing your 'happiness function' against time. It will not be flat, but will unavoidably go up and down. The "up" phases will be matched by equivalent 'down' phases, simply because you can't have an ever-increasing index based on an objective measurement. (This is roughly why Siddhartha Gautama, the first Buddha, taught that all life is suffering – you cannot expect to be happy all the time.) The y value of the blue line in the diagram below spends about as much time (=x axis distance) going down as it does going up, unavoidably. (Note that here I am looking at the rate of change of the physiological state, the gradient of the line. This is how our nervous systems work – we note the rate of change of sensory channels rather than their absolute value.)

Then along comes some bad experience, dropping happiness way down into absolute negative values. Active unhappiness, which is almost certainly a different neurotransmitter in a different circuit. You know when it's active and you want anything to stop it. Being stuck in a hospital bed in a public ward with the lights on all night and a nurse measuring your blood pressure every four hours including 4am – just an example of an experience that gave full-on negative scores. Shown in red opposite.

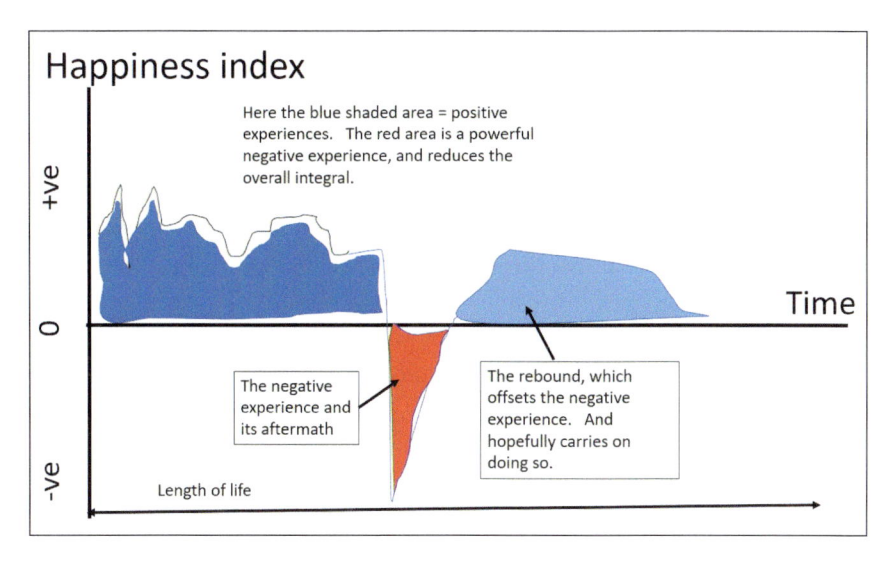

Fig 9.1 A simple model visualising lifetime happiness.

So hopefully after the negative experience ends, things return to something better, and happiness goes back up. I want to have some confidence that the rebound area will end up offsetting the bad – that the area under the pale blue curve will at least equal the red area below the line. One of the consequences of my surgery has been to make me ask myself "Is my quality of life into the positive?". This in turn has made me ask myself hard what experiences really do score a big positive in my valuation system.

Two such are clear: running in quiet woodlands as the morning sun comes up always scores a really big positive. This is true for Leith Hill in winter, and Mont Aurelienne at dawn in summer. Swimming in warm, clear water with shoals of big and tame fish is another – the Mediterranean has fish reserves like Cary-le-Rouet where Sophie and Eric swim weekly and where the fish are just wonderful. (It was only when I swam in a heavily fished bay in Antibes and saw barely a fish that I understood the contrast.) I get nearly as much of a pleasure kick from just being in a landscape I know and manage – my nature reserve or one of my gardens. They become a 4-dimensional visionary model crossed with a set of personal anecdotes – looking at each plant as an old friend, with shared stories and a predictable future trajectory. Visionary doses of *Psilocybe* score highly positive too, but you can feel quite peculiar for a few hours.

The corollary question – what gives me a negative score? – is a wider subject, but strongly depends on the degree of control of my life I have. Thus, I really suffered in hospital in various ways, all inherent in the situation. I really cannot cope with needing to ask for help to go to the toilet – that immediately drags my life score down into the red. My leg muscles really hurt for lack of exercise – I need exercise every few days, and if I am unable to get enough movement again, I'll plummet into the red.

I need a personal space to withdraw into, and a public ward is not one. Away from being institutionalised, there are a few other things that have ruined bits of my life when younger. I hate human hierarchy-conflict, having to face people down who are adamant that they are better than you are (while I tend to lack such certainty). Not a problem now I'm an adult, but it sure gave me hell all the way through school as boys are incorrigibly aggressively hierarchical, especially in an all-male school. Our Brexit-associated clown of a Prime Minister Boris Johnson epitomises the sort of aggressive absolute assertiveness that elbows its way to the top in all-male schools, and I'm far, far happier being on my own with wildlife than with them.

So finally, the most important question, and the one that I don't actually know the answer to. How does one evaluate this happiness function? This leads me onto what I call the "Rat paradox". This concerns the well-established observation that it is possible to implant electrodes into the correct region of a rat's brain, a reward centre, and wire up a Skinner box so that the rat can push a lever and get a jolt of pure "reward", whatever that might be. I suggest it looks like a belt of pure happiness to the rat. So the rat keeps on pushing the button, and stays there till it dies of dehydration. My question is "Was that a happy rat?".

If we look at a graph of its happiness against time, we have whatever its day-to-day happiness cycle is, probably connected to food or social activity, and it will have an average value. Hopefully >0, but that is not a given. The way it is calculated is to ask what rectangle has the same area as your messy function. The area under the graph is meaningful – the integral, the sum of all individual moments. The rectangle corresponding to this area is the area divided by the length of the Y axis – here, how long the animal lives. You get the "average" (a weighted mean) as the integral divided by the Y range. This is the height of the rectangle that has the same length and area as your function.

Now let's visualise what happens when the rat ends its life in a short block of solid 100% saturated happiness. This is shown as a big blue rectangle, running from "entry into Skinner cage" to "dies". This will inevitably pull up the overall average, and if we work out the average the way we did before this end-of-life experience greatly adds to the integral but adds little to the time divisor, so I expect that almost every time a rat that dies this way has a higher lifetime average

Rat's happiness index

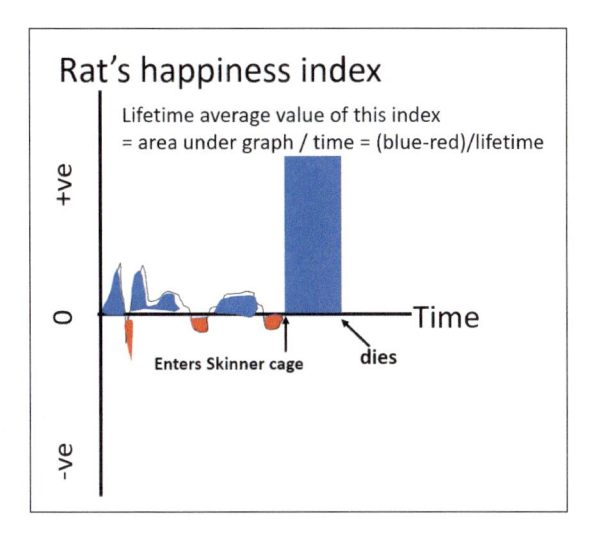

Lifetime average value of this index
= area under graph / time = (blue-red)/lifetime

Enters Skinner cage — dies

Fig 9.2

happiness than a control rat that lives to its full age of two years ish. So it is a happier rat? Its average happiness is above the population average. A shorter life with fewer achievements maybe, but perhaps happier.

Which rat would you choose to be? Yes, me too. Now apply that logic to humans!

Beyond the rhetorical flourish, this question might inspire the mathematically minded to muse on what function you actually want to maximise. Is it total length, total time above the line, or how about the average value? I can see a strong argument that this average value would be a good thing to optimise. On that basis, the rat who pushes up its happiness function with electrodes wins since it will have the highest average (any low scores will pull down the average). A Buddhist friend disagreed, saying the short-lived rat would miss fulfilling its karma. I don't know how to model that!

CHAPTER 10

M is for the Martial Arts

Introduction

In this chapter I review my experiences and personal highlights from engagement with various martial arts. After reading this you will know why I own a black belt with my name in Japanese, have the *Hoi* (ceremonial gown) of a Zen Buddhist priest hanging in the wardrobe with my suits, and why I visualise a ball of light in my centre when jogging. It also explains why I address mountains in Japanese, and count in Japanese when doing repetitive exercise. Oh, also how a man has died while fighting with me, and how the chief clothes buyer for Dorothy Perkins facilitated the relationship of my life.

A few terms need explaining. All budo martial arts operate on a hierarchical basis with an instructor or *sensei* ('master' but who can equally be female) who instructs *kenshi* (=students). Your progression is defined by gradings, which are (dreaded) tests in which Sensei plus helpers set you tasks and judge your execution of them. Typically in karate and kempo you are told the Japanese name of the technique, then you show how well you can do it. Nicola's aikido gradings were less rigidly defined, often just defining the attack (maybe each person takes it in turns to come in with a *jodan zuki* = punch to the head), and left you to find suitable techniques. If you pass the grading you go up one level. This often means a change in belt colour, though the details vary greatly from system to system and shisekan aikido has only white belts, up to black belt. The different belts on the way up to black belt are called kyu, and they decrease with elevation so my 1st kyu in aikido was one below black belt, and my 9th kyu in Shotokan is one up from the bottom. Black belt is not regarded as a kyu but a Dan grade – 1st dan. Dan is a step, and the image you need is of a staircase. Black belt is getting to the first step on the staircase, it is a beginning not an end. In Shorinji Kempo, 1st Dan took me six years, 2nd Dan took me an additional 11 years.

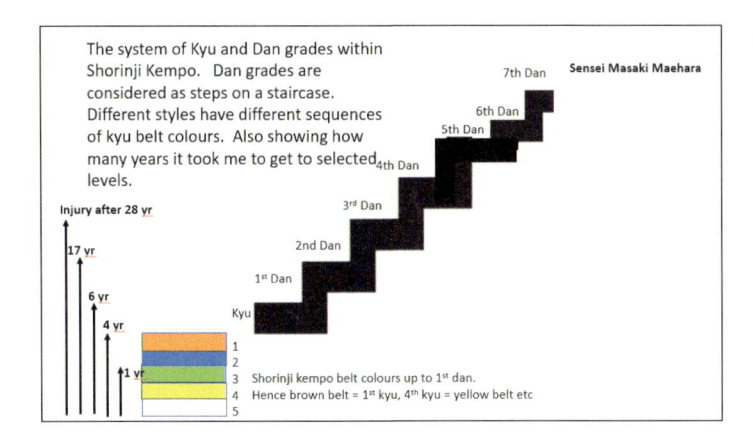

Fig 10.1 The system of Kyu and Dan grades within Shorinji Kempo. Dan grades are considered as steps on a staircase. Different styles have different sequences of kyu belt colours. Also showing how many years it took me to get to selected levels.

Each successive Dan grade gets harder and needs more time and dedication than the previous. I was training for 3rd Dan for 12 years but did not get to the standard before a shoulder injury intervened. Sensei Masaki Maehara got to 7th Dan. That is mind-blowingly elevated – there cannot be more than a few dozen 7th Dans in anything anywhere ever!

Back to my personal history

Although I'm a pretty peaceable sort of chap, I have followed several martial arts for solid blocks of time throughout my life, though this probably ended with my neurosurgery in 2019. Certainly all the rolling (=somersaults = ukemi) that were such a feature of kempo and aikido really don't go well with a shot vestibular system that leaves me dizzy whenever I move my head too fast. So for the time being this is a retrospective.

So I have stopped training, and hardly ever actually used any sort of street fighting techniques in real life (though see the York University chapter for what happened when Duncan did too much LSD in his tutorial). Anyway, three decades of my life (start 1986, end 2019), two evening away from home each week for a good 30 years, all for no observable purpose – was it worth it? Happily, I regard this an investment in my personal development – not wasted at all. Quite the contrary – it has been a very positive feature, though rather hard work to mix with a young family. Just for a start it was excellent keep-fit. To varying extents, all the systems involved intense aerobic exercise. Judo involved pushing my limits of strength (which to be honest have never been outstanding), both karate and kempo had bouts of 'randori' – punching and kicking for several minutes, really intense. Aikido much less so, though that was only the last decade of my training career and partly overlapped with kempo, and even there the free form techniques were so tiring that you could hear people breathing very heavily after just a couple of minutes.

Martial arts helped with the transformational development of my self-image, superimposed on the normal maturation processes. As a middle class nerd growing up surrounded by the feral youth of the Wythenshawe estate, it has to be said that I wasn't at all self-confident. Probably with good reason. When I spent a few weeks in 39FD in 2004 as Father died, I realised there was a cul de sac on the council estate next door (off Fern Bank Drive) that I had never dared walk into as a kid, due to my perception of the aggressively hostile nature of the families who denned down there. I told myself that this was the 21st century, I'm a 40 year old blackbelt with kids, you can't have no-go zones 100m from your doorstep – and generally don't be silly, Peter – so I walked in there just for the experience, and had no encounters to report. But it makes the point about how the local estate seemed physically threatening for all our childhood. Even in Oxford I felt quite brave going out and around town on my own, though I got the hang of it soon enough. By contrast, nowadays I find it quietly reassuring each time I go round Inholms Claypit with a bin bag asking kids to take their beer cans away, that I can tell myself that I am a 2nd Dan black belt. Mind you, the fact I habitually carry a two-foot machete does wonders for the self-confidence too.

Martial arts training has led to a literal transformation in my self-image, the image I see of my body in my head. For example: When I am running down some remote slippery hillside, I visualise my solar plexus chakra as a ball of light and try to push that ball of light forward in a smooth straight line. This came out of my exposure to aikido, but sounds so much like new-age twaddle that you may think I've been too stoned too often on too many mushrooms. Seeing light emanations from your solar plexus while running through woods on Psilocybe mushrooms – straight out of Carlos Castenada, and his yaqui guide Don Juan who said almost exactly this sort of thing. Bear with me – this comes from the intersection of several things, one of which are the equations of Newtonian mechanics. For a start, I know perfectly well that chakras don't exist any more than souls or angels, and that Castenada was a fraud. (See the chapter on magic mushrooms.) I don't think the yaqui culture says anything about chakras, or that Don Juan ever existed. But I do think that a body – any body, including cars and stones – continues in its motion at constant speed in a straight line until acted on by an external force – this is Newton's first law of motion. (Physics pedants may observe that in an inertial reference frame like gravity, the 'no external force' model involves constant acceleration due to the force of gravity multiplied by sin(theta) – true but usually ignorable as offset by the energy losses in my muscles and joints.) I do also think that the motion of my body can be approximated as being a point of mass at my centre of gravity – this is basic mechanics, the Centre of Gravity (CoG). And I know far too well that I developed a bad tendency to slouch (bend my head forwards) in Wythenshawe, probably as a reflection of low status in the pubescent-male hierarchy, and that after tumour surgery in September 2019 my left ear stopped talking to my central nervous system, leaving my balance ruinously damaged. So how does this all fit together? It turns out to be an easy command to issue to my CNS – "Visualise a ball of light in your midriff" – this just pops up in my self-image. Maybe that is why the 'chakra' meme persisted. Then by seeing this ball of light, I automatically focus my attention on my centre of gravity (CoG), rather than my head. Focussing on my head's balance seems intuitive – at least to me – but is actually a lousy engineering solution since it is the CoG that matters. By keeping my CoG moving in as close as possible to a straight line means mechanical stability, avoiding the sort of lateral forces that take me off balance. I have used this principle equally when trying to come to terms with going downhill on a new electric bike with small wheels and lousy stability – as long as your CoG is going in a straight line at constant speed you should be fine; it is when you try to change any of this that you fall over. Also, by pushing my centre forward when running, this forces my spine and my head to go vertical – it is when my head slouches forward that balance can fail in a split second. Plus, this posture change is good for my spine anyway – always lift with a straight back. It's not magic – clearly sheet ice or sloping wet clay will see me slide and fall, but this rather cosmic visualisation certainly helps me, especially running downhill. See it as a simple technique that simultaneously optimises my management of my nervous system and my body at two different levels. I like quasi-mystical techniques that work because they are actually rooted in experimental science – the intersection of cool and nerdy! See also *juji gote/nikkyo* below.

So, where to start? I first met the idea of martial arts training when at school, of course. A boy in my class was doing judo, and I was envious. When I was about age 16, my mother decided to get me out doing something more social than birdwatching (?why?) and got me on a tennis training course, at the Royal Northern Tennis Club, which is apparently famous in such circles, founded by Fred Perry I think. I could hit the ball fine but wasn't wild about it. Then she asked me what I wanted to do next, and I said judo. Mum took one thought at the idea of her beloved son being thrown around by Wythenshawe thugs and packed me off on another tennis course, which I pretty much refused to cooperate with. I got a few months' judo training with a club in Sale leisure centre before university, and enjoyed it far more than tennis, but discovered that I lack the "win at all costs" mentality that you need to grade at judo. This was Summer 1979, shortly before Oxford, so I did a bit of judo in Y1 and Y2 at Oxford, but it was more brute force than technique. I did enjoy throwing around a zoologist in the year above me called Nigel Varty, but never graded.

While at Oxford I shared a house with Sally Thorogood, who tried to get me to attend a new martial arts class in the Catz squash court, called Shorinji Kempo. I never went along. Looking back at Oxford I see a few huge missed opportunities, and this was one of them. (Sally did tell me to go and had been right. Mea culpa.)

In York, once I got to know a few people outside of my lab, I spent time in the company of one Phil H., a student of philosophy. He was also into aikido, and showed us some techniques. (Again, see 'York'.) I did attend a few aikido classes in York University, but never really clicked with it. The attacks in particular seem very slow and predictable (. . . with hindsight, yes of course that is how you train!). I did come to proficiency in the wrist lock (or rather family of techniques) called *nikkyo* in aikido and *juji gote* in kempo – you can drop someone on the floor like a tasar, using the sudden pain in their wrist bones. To emulate this, stretch your right hand in front of you with the thumb down and little finger up. Now pull the arm in, keeping the little finger uppermost and horizontal – your right elbow now sticks out to the side and your arm is shaped like a letter S. Now push the back of your right wrist into your tummy button, and if your little finger is raised, a sharp pain appears in your wrist. This is two carpal bones being pulled apart, not actually dangerous (never causes medical probs AFAIK) but is so fast and painful that it seems like magic. Or like Captain Spock in Star Trek, to give a dated analogy. You visualise driving a sword into their 'tannen' = centre of gravity = solar plexus chakra, and the sword blade runs parallel to their little finger, but its energy comes from your intention. As they drop forwards try to flip their elbow forwards so that you pin them face down. I sometime entertain passing daydreams of saying to someone foolish enough to grab hold of my collar "I'm a Zen Buddhist – careful, I might zap my ki energy into your tannen chakra" before dropping them on the floor, screaming.

There is an interlock in my life between the martial arts and CEGB chapter, which is that the CERL facilities in Leatherhead included a karate dojo. This ran after work in the dining hall, and was a Shotokan dojo run by a nuclear engineer called Phil Shire. I went along for several months in 1986, and passed a first grading. When I did aikido we wore pure white belts, but the one I use has a faint red line at one end where repeated washing in various machines have failed to dislodge the residue of red ink. This red band was my 9th kyu in Shotokan – I smile quietly to myself each time I see it. Despite this I never really got on with Shotokan as it was all 'Goho' – punches and kicks. To be honest, you can't get much detailed skill in these, just accuracy and speed. I knew from aikido about the 'Juho' techniques of twisting and throwing, and shotokan just wasn't teaching these. After Phil Shire got a new job at Sizewell B, the dojo needed a new instructor, and we invited a few in to put them through their paces. One was the scariest fighter I have ever encountered – in his introductory session we were taught how to get your fingers behind someone's windpipe, so it can be snapped and they drown in their own blood. Another seemed to personify egocentricity. Sadly, it has to be admitted that ego-inflation is a bit of an occupational hazard with Senseis across many martial arts – I have become sensitive to this and intolerant of it. I don't know who they got to teach the dojo next, as I decided it was time to take up Sally's suggestion of the local kempo dojo. One day in September 1986 I did two hours' Shotokan at CERL, then two hours' kempo at TRC. No doubt, I enjoyed the kempo session more, so that became my hobby.

I should introduce the martial art of Shorinji Kempo, since it came to dominate my non-work life for years, and is little known outside Japan. First the odd name: the "po" equates to the "do" in judo or aikido, and roughly translates as "the path" or "the way" (as in Jesus said "I am the way," etc). "Shorinji" comes from the Japanese adjective meaning "Of Shaolin", while "Ken" is a fist. So the name translates fairly well as "The Shaolin temple way of the fist". Henceforth I call it kempo for ease of typing. Very much like aikido, Kempo was founded in the aftermath of WW2 by a charismatic teacher who had been inspired by the

Fig 10.2 Doshin So Sensei the founder of Shoriji Kempo.

Fig 10.3 This technique is common to kempo – as here, demonstrated by Paddy throwing Kevin Wheelan – and judo; Ippon sei nage. We did use a mat for this, unlike most of the throws!.

teachings of Chinese Buddhist-related fighting systems focussed on the monks of the Shaolin temple. While aikido was founded and taught by Sensei Morihei Ueshiba, Kempo was founded and taught by Sensei Doshin So.

On his death, oversight of the system passed to his daughter, also called So Doshin, who has seen me once at a training camp, but if she remembers me at all it will be as the chap who REALLY messed up his kata with Sensei Maehara. Some public failures should best just have a thick curtain drawn over them.

Kempo is explicitly a self-defence system whose axioms start with the model that someone is attacking you so you must stop them, ideally using weak points to apply non-damaging pain (though to be honest the hard techniques look just like karate at first sight). For a system which is deeply rooted in Zen Buddhism, it is highly structured and rigidly hierarchical (like all martial arts AFAIK). When I told a friend from York that I had passed a written exam in Zen Buddhism, he replied that under his understanding of Zen Buddhism it would have been equally valid to submit a blank sheet of paper. Maybe valid, but no black belt for you until you jump the hoops! Kempo can be seen as a 50/50 fusion of karate and aikido, and about half the techniques are punching/kicking ('*goho*')while the rest are locks/throws like aikido ('*juho*' – not a spelling mistake, not Judo, though from a similar etymology). Kempo emphasises use of pressure points and weak spots on the body, many of which are shared with acupuncture meridians. All I can say is that when an expert gets his hands on them you really feel it. One senior Japanese kempo instructor was known to keep a cocktail stick in his belt, then demonstrate the exact location of pressure points by pinning someone immobile before applying pressure with the point of the stick on the exact sensitive spot, though I could never get this sort of precision. (As a small aside, lots of pressure points fail to work on lots of people, due to small individual differences in the layout of superficial nerves. By contrast, the wrist lock I call *juji gote* works on everyone every time.)

It wasn't until I lived alone in 4 Barley Mow Court that budo training became more than a passing time filler. I knew one person who lived nearby, my Oxford cosmic twin Sally Thorogood who started Kempo at Catz, then on graduation moved to a job based in Horley (relatively next door to Dorking, at least by comparison with Yorkshire), and who still trained in Shorinji Kempo under Sensei Graham Nabbs, pictured below. She moved to the north, near Blackburn, about the same time in 1985 that I moved from York to Surrey, so couldn't fix my social life but put me in touch with local kempo trainers. (To be honest, my life was terribly short of female company, and a martial arts club seemed like a plausible place to meet a girlfriend. It could have worked out.)

Fig 10.4 Sensei Maehard demonstrating gyaku gote on Sensei Chris Lloyd at TRC. You start with a flick to the eyes before applying the wrist lock.

Sensei Graham Nabbs always found girlfriends via Kempo – the only person I know for whom you could honestly state that he apparently only ever dated Scandinavian black belt women.)

I ended up in the Tolworth dojo, inspired by a black belt called William O'Brien, who owned a furniture company Sven Christiansen and epitomised the 1980s yuppie persona. Like Sensei Nabbs, he never seemed short of female company, though being a managing director and a millionaire who dressed like one and who drove a Porsche everywhere probably helped. (He obviously knew his stuff – he recognised a chair that Sally rescued from a skip at Saint Catherine's as being authentic Arne Jacobsen, which it was.) The overall instructor was Sensei Masaki Maehara, Japanese-born in Hiroshima not long after The Bomb. His English was never fluent, but his training and abilities never ceased to impress me (. . . and I'm not easily impressed). Sensei was 6th Dan in 1985, getting 7th Dan and chief European instructor a few years later. Profoundly impressive. Also able to write all the Japanese character sets, and Chinese ones and Korean, and fluent in Italian as he was chief instructor for Italy. Generally, he just showed us beginners' stuff, but he also taught advanced features on international black belt courses. Things like taking a real knife ('a live blade') off an attacker while throwing them. I've only seen two people do that convincingly, Sensei Maehara once, and an aikido instructor called Stan around 5th Dan (who took a proper Japanese sword off an attacker while throwing him). As a sad coda, Maehara Sensei died in March 2020 aged late 70s, probably associated with Covid-19 though I do not know this for sure.

One of my 'lightbulb moments' was the first time I met a white belt kempo throw called gyaku gote, administered by a black belt called Sensei Tony Moody in TRC in my first few weeks there. I dutifully grabbed Tony's wrist and swung

Fig 10.5 A scan of my shodan obi. I gather this Kanji text says "Tolworth Peter".

a punch at his head. There was an amazing blast of pain in my wrist, and somehow I hit the mat 2m away, to be pinned face down. I know what he did, know how to do it, have taught dozens of beginners how to do it, but still look back on the encounter as an amazing/ shocking experience.

Before moving on from Kempo instructors I should add the Yin to his Yang was Mizuno Sensei, another Japanese 7th Dan instructor based in London. I got the impression that Mizuno was tougher than Maehara, but maybe just more prone to showing what he can do. I remember well what happened when Mizuno used me to demonstrate a throw at a summer camp. I didn't know I could fly so high or fast, but he lifted my arm behind my back and I hit the crashmat several metres away. Reminded me of the high jump at school, except that I hadn't jumped. (The knack to making this work is to hold their wrist 25cm above the spine, and bend it up the back at just this distance to find the line where the shoulder absolutely will not go, then put your weight exactly on that line, aiming to get them forwards rather than up. Sensei Nicola Endicott used to tell me off in aikido when I did anything vaguely similar, saying I should put them down gently, not fling them across the dojo.)

Back to Mizuno Sensei – about 2010 there was an internal fission in kempo, splitting on Mizuno Sensei. Last I heard UK kempo is split with (roughly) a Mizuno branch and an official branch. Tolworth dojo remained official. Sadly, the evidence especially from karate and aikido is that martial arts undergo multiway splits like religious sects do, like languages do, like galapagos finches do, like any other replicator system is liable to. Purists might observe that kempo and aikido are themselves splits off ancestral Shaolin teachings.

Back to 1986. I had nothing else to do at home – no need to write a PhD thesis, all my computer coding was done at work on CEGB mainframes, I can't stand television, didn't know any neighbours, there was no internet only Ceefax, so I went to train in Tolworth Shorinji Kempo dojo twice a week. It helped hugely that, after two hours' hard sweating, we'd retire to the Tolworth Recreation Centre (TRC) bar for a beer and a laddish chat about fighting, or cars, or women, or booze, or – you get the idea. With hindsight it was rather male dominated, though females were very welcome and some did turn up for a while. I dived into the mindset and training materials for kempo, and moved up the rankings.

Fig 10.6 Sensei Masaki Maehara, c 1992, in the basketball court at TRC where we trained for years. Note the manji on the poster.

Fig 10.7 The poster for Tolwort dojo, featuring Sensei Maehara, c. 1995.

Fig 10.8 Sensei Masaki Maehara, wearing his hoi, *with Blaise Howard (L) and John Comber?*

Fig 10.9 With Kevin Wheelan I attempt a public deminstration of an "embu".

A Path of 21 Ms

When I met Catherine in October 1987, I had just proudly passed green belt, the 2nd grading up. (White -> yellow -> green > blue -> brown -> black belt). The dance studio of TRC became something of a sweaty second home, and (when exercising) I still tend to count in Japanese nowadays as a legacy of his phase.

One of the characteristic features of all training sessions of both the goho martial arts I have followed has been counting out loud in Japanese, as an accompaniment to minutes of punches or kicks. It becomes very much like a mantra (see 'M is for Meditation'). Phonetically they sound like this:

Chi -ni – san – shi -go – ruc – sitch – hatch – coo – joo (=1 2 3 4 5 6 7 8 9 10)

This sequence has been burned in by 28 years of repetitive training to the point where each time I do warm up exercises I count in Japanese. I have a totally informal limb stretch, which I used to do on Bookham Common each morning on the commute into work and which I now do in my *furi tame* spot by the pond, most mornings unless severely inclement. I do 10 kicks with one leg, counting chi – ni – san-shi – go etc, then swing that leg in as big an arc as I can, 20 times. Again I chi – ni – san etc twice, then repeat the other leg. Then 10 chin ups. Again I chi – ni – san etc.

The other lifelong habit I picked up in kempo, carried on in my aikido, is the greeting called a rei, putting your fingertips together with your thumbs together in front of your nose. It looks a lot like you are praying, but the intention is deeply different. This is a sign of respect, and is seen by the Japanese as equivalent to bowing. There is one difference which is that bowing denotes deference – you bow deeper to someone above you in the hierarchy. When you rei someone it is on the basis of equality, with both users' hand actions approximately level. At the same time you recite the Japanese phrase "Onegai shimasu" (pronounced "Onneyguy shimass"). This roughly translates as "please teach me". When you have finished you say "Arigato gozaimasta" (pronounced "Arrygarto gozaymastah"). To be especially polite or respectful say "domo arigato gozaimasta". When Sensei Maehara 7th Dan instructed a beginner who had just walked in off the street, they would rei to each other on the same level, denoting respect and equality, and say "Onegai shimasu" to each other. Very much the same thing happens in aikido dojos for the same reason. I have taken to doing exactly this with landscapes. Before walking up onto the Cairngorm plateau in Scotland, I looked the massif full on, did a rei, and said (in my head) 'Onegai shimasu'. Before setting off on a long run I have a ritual involving (1) activating the running App on my phone (2) Rei to the sun (3) Rei to the image in my head of my target location, eg

Leith Hill tower. I am sure that dozens of walkers think I am a devout Christian since I appear to be praying when I get to Leith Hill tower. No, that's not a at all Christian, more animist! I am saying thank you to the hill, doing a rei to the hill saying internally "Domo Arigato gozaimasta". "Thank you for teaching me".

Shorinji Kempo is rather little known in the UK, at least compared to aikido or karate (though both of these systems turn out to be so fissiparous that most schools within both these systems probably contain no more actively training students than kempo at a national level), and certainly it is minor in Europe when compared to its status in Japan, where it has a large headquarters and an official recognition as a religion. It achieves this as being a branch of Zen Buddhism, called Kongozen Buddhism, which I gather means 'Diamond Zen'. Happily for my peace of mind, Zen Buddhism is atheist, though it did emphasise meditation both in the classes and at home. Most monotheists have problems getting their heads around how Zen Buddhism can be a religion but atheist, but theists would think that, wouldn't they? This is paraphrasing massively, but my understanding is the Buddha, Siddhartha Gautama, didn't actually deny the existence of Gods, saying instead they would be irrelevant. Something to the effect that "You don't need Gods to do this, and anyway even if there were a God it would be impossible for them to keep you constantly happy". The golden principles of Buddhism state that (1) All life is desire, (2) all desire is suffering, so (3) all life Is suffering, and (4) the only solution is to let go of the search for gratification. This corresponds surprisingly well with what neurophysiologists call "The Shifting Baseline Effect", a general desensitisation to recurring stimuli (of whatever sort) occurring in humans as well as the sea slug *Aplysia* in which it was first described, and probably everything else with a CNS as well. This is why neurophysiologists attempting to study human consciousness find it more useful to talk to Buddhists than to monotheists.

Back to Shorinji Kempo. BTW The Wikipedia description is pretty good last time I checked. There are a small number of unexpected outcomes from its status as a religion. At the most trivial level, it means that I can honestly say that I have the robes of a Buddhist priest hanging in my wardrobe. This is the *hoi*, a ceremonial black outer jacket worn by senior instructors at major events and is regarded as equivalent to the robes of a Buddhist priest. It may be seen worn by Sensei Maehara in the poster and the 3-man demonstration (below). Why they come with such a bizarre belt I doubt I will ever know, but it looks remarkably like an undercooked sausage but 2m long with a tassel at each end. One is entitled to wear a *hoi* at an event once one has graded to Shodan – first Dan black belt. So when I passed shodan in 1992 I was entitled to wear a *hoi*, so bought a *hoi* plus its bizarre sausage-like belt, and it has hung in my wardrobe ever since. As it happened, I have never actually needed to wear it, though with hindsight there were a few demonstrations I helped with where we would all have been entitled to wear our *hois*. In practice only the most senior instructors did, a uniform emphasising the gap between us mere 2nd dan kenshi and the >4th dan instructors.

A second unexpected outcome of kempo being awarded religious status is that it conducts weddings. Not often, certainly not as a regular feature of training sessions, but Maehara Sensei was regarded by the Japanese as a priest who could conduct a wedding, invariably for students training within kempo at a high level. So I have records from the wedding of the shodan kenshi Gerry Tasker to his Asian wife Suranti, officiated by Sensei Maehara. As far as the UK state is concerned, Gerry's wedding was in a registry office with a party afterwards – as far as Gerry and Suranti are concerned, the real wedding was conducted by Maehara Sensei with some legal admin sorted out beforehand. Take your pick. In theory, wearing my *hoi*, I would be entitled to do the same, though neither have I the first intention of doing anything of the sort, nor would a mere 2nd Dan normally do such a symbolically important job.

A third odd outcome of Shorinji Kempo's quasi-religious status is that its founder sought and used Buddhist icons for his new system, and found an ancient symbol representing the yin/yang dichotomy, an ancient symbol of good luck used in early Buddhism. The symbol is the manji, and for something like four decades all kempo symbols featured a manji, recognised as a symbol of peace and good luck in Buddhism. What could possibly go wrong? Unfortunately, Doshin So was not the first person to spot how this particular symbol had a raw power to the human mind, plus potential for artistic embellishment, and the graphic

Fig 10.10 Sensei Maehara officiating the wedding of Gerry Tasker with Suranti.

Fig 10.11 The old Shorjini Kempo logo with its omote manji.

Fig 10.12 The new Shorjini Kempo logo, with no manji.

designer who picked up the yin manji and relaunched it as his own personal brand was called Adolf Hitler, from which we get the current understanding of the swastika. The word swastika is supposed to come from the Sanskrit meaning "conducive to well being". You can see behind Maehara Sensei a poster on the TRC wall with a swastika at the top. It has to be said this is not a good look in a post-WW2 world, though I do think that Doshi So was rather unlucky rather than provocative. For a start, look at the direction of rotation – it is the opposite to the Nazi insignia. I gather that the 'clockwise rotation' as seen in kempo, the omote manji, is associated with 'yang', the softer female element, while the anticlockwise version favoured by Adolf Hitler corresponds to 'yin', the hard male element. I am not sure that any of this has any actual meaning at all and would not believe a word of it apart from one important point: When you see a swastika on a kempo poster it does NOT mean the system advocates Nazism, at all. Anyway, sometime around 1996 someone had a quiet word with the kempo hierarchy and said that they had to rebrand away from a swastika to get anywhere in the West, and duly they came up with an inoffensive replacement (see image).

Things can go wrong in sessions. I trained a lot with a chap called Steve Hill. Once, about brown belt, he gave me a nose bleed. My fault for not blocking. We trained each Tuesday and Friday, we took (and passed) second Dan together in 2003. Then on 20 November 2007 I was training with Steve, doing 'randori' (punching and kicking), and I remember that Steve let his guard down unexpectedly, so I got a kick in. It was quite hard, we stopped, then Steve said he felt like his chest was squeezing. I should have spotted sooner, but was just worried about what I had done or damage I had caused, so we told Steve to sit down for a few minutes. He said he wanted to drive straight home but we persuaded him to stop a few minutes. Then he went off, and a bit later a TRC staff member told us "there's one of yours lying in the car park". As soon as they said this, I knew what had happened from first aid courses, and that it was probably too late. Steve's chest pains were a heart attack, he had dropped his guard allowing my kick in only because his body suddenly realised it was about to die. He probably died in the TRC car park, though the ambulance gave him enough zaps to get some hints of restarting his heart. I gathered later that he had high levels of cholesterol, was a heart attack waiting to happen. I should have picked up when he talked of a chest squeeze (classic first aid course stuff), maybe 999 earlier would have saved him. On the plus side, if any can be found, we stopped Steve driving home. He could have died driving in the outside lane of the A3 and taken someone else with him.

There is a curious interlock between Tolworth Shorinji Kempo and my subsequent family life. This goes back to beery evenings with kempo kenshi around 1987, when I must have grumbled to William O'Brien about not getting a girlfriend. Given I had a permanent job, a two-bedroom house, a scholarship to Oxford and a PhD this seemed like an incomprehensible oversight by the female half of the species. Maybe the 2m python living behind the sofa and the wardrobe full of *Cannabis* plants didn't help my chances as much as I imagined. William definitely said something over beer one club pizza session about my general appearance resembling a scarecrow called Worzel Gummidge. Oddly, some years later, my then wife Catherine made exactly the same analogy to exactly the same scarecrow. I don't even think it was the same old coat second time. Then one Saturday in June 1987 William got an ex-girlfriend of his to come over with a mission – to get me dressed. So I went to William's bijou house near Guildford, met him with his then girlfriend Eve and previous girlfriend Cathy DP (no connection to my subsequent wife Anne Catherine Neubert), who was then the chief clothes buyer for the fashion chain Dorothy Perkins. They booked me in to some posh hairdresser then toured various clothes shops: Cathy DP said "buy this" and I did. The before and after pictures are below. And the connection to the rest of my life? Guess what clothes I was wearing to the party where I met Catherine Neubert? It has to be said that a success rate of 0 went to 100% the evening I wore clothes selected by that woman . . . as a cynical statistician I observe it could be a random event. As an experimental designer I know that it could be confidence in my appearance rather than the appearance itself. Humf, or maybe William did make a difference after all.

That shopping expedition clearly made a powerful, if transient, effect on my clothing habits. Over 30 years later an ex-colleague from CERL (Dr Emma Wilson) recalled the change in my appearance the following Monday:

"The Keith comment [. . . about how unfamiliar I looked when wearing a suit . . .] made me chuckle and reminded me of the Monday when you appeared in a new jumper and trousers without holes and the right size – [snip]. We weren't sure it was an improvement as we liked our 'old Peter'!"

It has to be said that I didn't warm to Eve at all. She met William at an NLP course, and basically she was better at hypnosis than him. She came over as a perfectionist and controlling. She married William, followed by a very expensive divorce (which reputedly went to the House of Lords, though I cannot verify this). She tried to run Tolworth Shorinji Kempo admin like it was her own company/business, which didn't work out well. One evening in the Tolworth bar she turned up after Kempo, and I turned round to greet her. What I intended to say was "Hello Eve, how lovely to see you again". What actually came out of my mouth was a big beery belch, and she never acknowledged my existence again. Thereby improving my life! It's not often I'm proud of my catastrophic social faux pas, but that one was a positive experience.

I learned a lot from Kempo, not just about fighting. A lot about self-confidence and about trusting people. One of the key ideas behind kempo was encouraging self-control and independence. The Dokun, a creed, was said each session, and had the opening lines "Rely on yourself and not on others. No-one is as reliable as you own well disciplined self", which sounds right to me but, with hindsight, is not far from the US gun lobby. (A key difference is that if you lose self-control in a punch-up you might splat someone's nose, lose control with an automatic weapon and dozens of innocent people get killed plus even more have their

Fig 10.13 Before the makeover, June 1987.

Fig 10.14 And after . . . Eve with dark hair on the left of the scan, Cathy DP on the right.

lives ruined. I am deeply opposed to letting anyone play with guns without a compellingly good reason. You have deer or boar to control? Fine, you need a rifle. You want to own a lethal weapon for fun? Naff off.)

One other odd little skill – or is it a mindset? – is what kempo taught as 'happomoku'. I gather this comes from 'hachi moku' or eight-direction sight, and simply means using your peripheral vision to pick up what is going on all at the same time across your whole visual field. If someone gets out (say) a knife, your visual attention immediately tends to lock onto the knife to the exclusion of all else, so if he knows what he's doing he'll wave the knife high up above eye level, then get an easy but debilitating kick in low down that you don't even see coming because your attention was elsewhere. In a fight you should aim to use your all-round vision to keep on top of the whole situation, and to do this you do only look at their eyes; the rest of their body you monitor using your happomoku. It's as much about feeling their intention as you can get in a wholly visual model. Or, as I said when teaching beginners, "What is faster – moving your gaze and refocussing your eyes, or keeping your eyes still but moving your awareness?" (The answer should be that moving your awareness is faster.) Likewise when driving a car, look ahead and monitor everything else by happomoku. When getting chess pieces out of their box, I don't need to look at each one, just feel it (for the shape) then let it graze the edge of my visual field to pick up its colour.

You discover this way the uncomfortable psychological truth that your peripheral vision has remarkably poor colour perception, with the colour you think you perceive actually being pasted in by your nervous system based on what was there last time your fovea scanned it. This can be shown by a mind blowing experimental set up. Someone created a system that tracked a subject's gaze, and used this to control the colour on screens all around their field of vision. The experimenter set it up so peripheral screens were always one colour, let's say blue, but this changed to a new colour, maybe red, just in the split seconds that the subject looked at them directly. Then you get the subject to look forward, ask them what colour the peripheral screens are, and they tell you they see them as the colour they are NOT! They actually SEE red even though this is not what their eyes are picking up. Note that this really IS what they 'see' because your experience of 'seeing' is the internal experience of the visual image, not the optical setup outside your retinas. Most of your visual perception most of the time turns out to be a palimpsest of multiple neuronal modules pasted together into a nearly seamless whole. Occasionally experiences with Psilocybe alkaloids can give you some hints of insight into some of these pathways, when some of the feedback processing slips.

I got black belt, 1st Dan, in Shorinji Kempo September 1992, about the time that Catherine became pregnant with Louise. By 1993 our house, 1 Chester Close = 1CC, smelled of milk and resounded to squeaks and squeals, so two evenings a week with blokes and beer became as much a psychological lifeline as they has been when home was cold and empty! Black belt means (1) you mainly train less experienced kenshi, (2) the techniques you have to learn are harder and more painful than before. The second dan syllabus had more than 40 techniques to learn – just getting the names (all Japanese obviously) was a challenge, let alone making them work. I'd maybe train three-four in an evening, so it took years to get ready for 2nd Dan. Ten years in fact – I got 2nd Dan in 2003. No new belt, just a certificate and the nice thought that "I'm 2ND dan black belt".

I have to say that my kempo career rather lost direction after this – the remaining techniques became more difficult, more subtle (eg they don't work unless done perfectly) and more painful (when they are done perfectly). Drifting, I saw aikido advertised in Dorking Halls, and signed up for sessions with Nicola Endicott. These were very different, using balance and posture, not pain. Even now in a serious punch up I would revert to type and switch to Kempo, whose locks hurt and whose kicks and punches really mean business. In day-to-day life, especially when running, it is the aikido model I follow since this involves focussing on your 'Tannen' (Centre of Gravity – see above) and responding harmoniously to the body positions of people around you. My wife observed that the first time in my life that I showed any hint of competence at dancing in parties was after years of aikido, getting me used to awareness of people's body positions.

One key point emphasised in Kempo is '*atemi wasa*' – before doing some fancy wrist technique you distract attention by flicking them in the eyes or kicking their crotch. John Comber put it with characteristic bluntness in the TRC bar on evening: "In the street kempo works and aikido doesn't because we hit them first." I did hear from an aikido 3rd Dan, Steve Austwick, that there are forms of aikido that emphasise atemi as a precursor to technique, but this is generally seen as blocking energy and reducing your ability to feel their intentions.

In fact the two systems – kempo and aikido – complemented quite well, and I could run them side by side for a few years. I found it worked well for me – less well for the rest of my family. It was 21 June 2014, on midsummer's day the year Mum died, that I had a bad fall while jogging in Logmore Lane (Westcott), badly tearing a ligament in my right shoulder. (This shows as a strange mobile lump in my shoulder up each time I swim – I could never justify the months out implied by having shoulder surgery so it never got fixed.) This ended all training for months, and afterwards I returned to aikido (which has gentle pins) but never dared the return to kempo since the *gatame wasa* (= pins) use so much force on the shoulder that I am sure it would snap my remaining tendon. So that was that for kempo. I still hear from kenshi from time to time, it kept me fit from 1986 to 2014, gave me a lot of experiences, and teaching practice. Once about 2017 when I found a local ne'er-do-well trying to break into cars in the Whitelands college car park, I took his photo, he said he'd take my camera off me. So I put in in my pocket, looked him hard in the eye and switched to a fighting stance. He backed off, and has not been seen in college since. Had he been foolish enough to come within touching distance, I'd have dusted off a 2nd Dan catch-counterpunch-throw routine. Pure kempo legacy.

> *A facebook chat that is relevant here, from June 2020. The subject of unexpectedly broken ribs came up:*
>
> **Peter Shaw**
>
> BTW I got married in 1992 with a broken rib after a martial arts demonstration in front of a few hundred people got a bit heated. So we got married with me trying not to breathe too deeply. Then a little bit later it happened again. Catherine was very pregnant and her Mum and Dad had come over from France awaiting the birth, so when I said we needed to go to hospital her parents smiled benignly. No, not that, her pillock of a husband had injured himself again. Twit.

Aikido came twice in my life, and second time I graded to 1st kyu (one below black belt). In another life I am sure that I could have put the effort in to go to training camps and sessions at the main Shisekan aikido dojo in East London. I had other things in my life and nothing to prove – one black belt is enough for most people, though a second would have been cool. The first time was about 1985, some rather informal sessions during my PhD in York, mediated by a philosophy student called Phil Hunt, friend of Deb and Mark. The main things I got out of this training in York was a respect for aikido wrist locks, and a nagging suspicion that the muggers on the Wythenshawe estate did not punch you in the same slow predictable way that we learnt in the York University aikido dojo! Second time round was about 2008, the Shisekan dojo in Westcott, Dorking, run by Sensei Nicola Endicott, 3rd Dan.

Fig 10.15 Nicola Endicott in the Westcott aikido dojo.

I had 2nd Dan in kempo but had lost my way with the system since I did not see personal advancement in mastering the kempo 3rd dan syllabus. I tried some aikido sessions with Sensei Nicola Endicott, and found them utterly different to kempo, or anything else I had met. Nicola emphasised body posture and using the body's centre way above techniques, let alone names, let alone inflicting pain. Given that Sensei Nicola was shorter than me, it never ceased to impress me how I could come in with a fairly serious punch and somehow end up on the floor 2m away without any obvious force, let alone pain. Kempo would achieve the same result by blocking the punch, counter-punching them hard enough to distract them, then getting a hard wrist lock on before throwing. It was after starting here that I stopped slouching and finally paid attention to the angle of my spine! (Away from aikido, Nicola practises shiatzu and has a degree in mathematics. Plus a child.)

So when a shoulder injury ended my kempo career in 2014, I was lucky enough that I could carry on with aikido, since Nicola taught the gentlest of shoulder pins that posed little serious risk. The equivalent lock in kempo involves a 6'2" ex-army chap putting his full weight on your shoulder, which is just not a viable risk with a torn ligament. I kept up with aikido training until my tumour surgery in 2019 effectively ruined my balance and ended weekly training sessions of any sort. Before this, I persuaded my wife Catherine to come to aikido. Catherine had seen blokes kicking each other in kempo and wasn't silly enough to go near it, but I thought that she could benefit from Nicola's teachings, and am pleased to say it worked out. It probably helped that Nicola was her height as well as her gender! Catherine attended for several years, graded to 3rd Kyu, with gradings involving her throwing multiple attackers by 'receiving' their punches and flowing with their energy. We have several friends around Dorking met via aikido, including Nicola and her family whom we often see out and about around Dorking. From my point of view, positive aikido legacies include my quasi-daily stretching regime, my visualisation of my tannen chakra (see above), and a curious all-body warm up exercise called *furi tame* in Japanese ('shaking the soul') that involves shaking your hands in front of your tannen. This is actually quite a good warm up that I have utterly failed to explain – let's try again. I take a large polished stone about 500g (I use a 500g iridescent lump of labradorite), and hold it in both hands just in front of my navel (hence, CoG). I then shake my entire body up and down to drive a resonance between my CoG (bobbing up and down) and the *furi tame* stone (also bobbing up and down in synchrony). Keep this up for several minutes. When the resonance works all your limbs are shaking together and it really gets the circulation going. Looks really odd to the uninitiated though! For the "Covid spring" of lockdown in 2020 I started each day with a few minutes of *furi tame* in sunlight by my pond. I have a special stone-paved area in a patch by the pond that I use for the purpose since it catches the morning sun.

One of the many differences between kempo and Shisekan aikido is the latter's emphasis on sword work. Only senior instructors such as Paul Smith (5th Dan) demonstrated with a live blade. We used a wooden training sword – a bokkun) or a softer version with a leather skin, to avoid accidents. When used in expert hands the movements of a katana (Japanese killing sword) are utterly beautiful. Given that I have manged to bash someone on the head with a soft training sword by accident, and at least once someone else got their thumb hit painfully hard by a bokkun, then you simply cannot allow most kenshi to train with a live blade. We'd lose too many students to deep flesh wounds. Nicola once said that it is very bad etiquette to cut someone's finger off during a sword demonstration. Yes, bad on quite a few other levels too I'd say, but I've probably spent too long on H&S committees. At a philosophical level this use of swords needs some justification, since it clearly ceases to be anything to do with self-defence in modern Western society. In Edo-era Japan it might have been OK for samurai to carry a katana on their belt and to practise skills like getting a sword out of your belt, swinging it through a man's neck then back into its scabbard in one smooth motion. In 21st century UK it is not! People have been prosecuted for having a Swiss army penknife in the glove locker of their car in order to spread butter on sandwiches, so merely carrying a live blade for a demonstration in a public place needs to be thought about carefully. The justification is partly historical, reflecting aikido's samurai roots, but is more because there are deep similarities in the way you handle a sword and the techniques of aikido. Often a throw is described as "the same action as cutting with a sword". To handle a sword well you need good posture and correct use of your 'centre' (see CoG), and the bare-handed techniques of aikido often prove to be deeply connected to sword forms. The underlying body action of *Shiho nage* (roughly, a technique for throwing them backwards using a wrist lock, though this doesn't really do justice to the elegance of the move) turns out to be remarkably similar to a sword form. The same thing was said of some techniques in the kempo nidan syllabus – throw them by imagining their arm is your sword.

CHAPTER 11

M is for Marathons

Running

Overview

It's not the getting there or the speed that matter, it's the experience of being here now.

So when I was in Manchester or Oxford I went out for walks. Sometimes tree climbs! Never runs. I do have one good memory of the feeling of running around the (extensive) playing fields of Sandilands primary school – I must have been about nine then. What mattered in football is acceleration and speed, which I was never any good at, so I thought I was no good at running. It was in York in 1984 that Suzanne got me jogging. We went for short jogs of a few kilometres around the local fields – an area called the 'Outgang' in Heslington was our favourite route. After she left, I carried on jogging the same sort of routes, for the physical feel-good and workout.

It has to be said that after I moved to the SE in October 1985, my jogging just stopped. I went for walks, long walks, up Leith Hill or around the weald. I think the restart was when I was in Barley Mow Court 1986-1992, as I had a standard evening run past Brockham and back past the Dolphin in Betchworth – about 5Km on country lanes. No runs from 1CC, and it was thanks to Louise's A level revision that I got back into jogging. She went out running, I came on some runs to keep her company, and realised how much I liked doing so. There was a period about 2010 when I started trying to get up the local challenge – Leith Hill – the highest point in the south-east. It took me several goes, as much to test out my own limits as because I really was pushing my limits. I got to the Tillingbourne waterfall, then Broadmoor, then upwards and eventually the tower at 290m. This was about the time that Elinor Neubert died, October 2012, though I don't have a date recorded for the day I first made it.

By about 2015 I was running from 4LW to Leith Hill Tower each Saturday, and realised that I was quite a decent runner, and wondered about doing a marathon. It turns out to be surprisingly hard to find a marathon that doesn't require a huge charitable donation – about £3000 for the London marathon stuck in my gullet. Happily, I was able to run the Dorking marathon – Denbies have wine as well as water supplies (nice!) but this did involve running up and down the chalk face four times (not so nice). But I could finish a marathon, and enjoyed running on paths that were familiar from my weekend runs.

By luck I got a place in the Berlin marathon in September 2018, and completed the course in 4 hours 26 minutes. Like I've always known, I'm not fast.

At no stage have I been bothered about comparing to other people, or even my own times. It's between me and the land. Specifically it's about me and The Hill, the greensand prominence that is Leith Hill and over to Holmbury and Pitch Hill. This is as much like Scotland as you'll ever get in the south-east – pine trees, heather and bilberry on acid sandy soil with crossbills and roe deer. I just feel like I belong there, and running there isn't work, it's relaxation. The worst thing about being hospitalised for nearly a month in 2019 (and that is a long list!) was the pain in my legs – I really, really needed the exercise and they really hurt, leading me to have to do kicking and stretching exercises, to the annoyance of ward staff who liked their patients to lie still.

At one stage I found myself discussing this with someone who is almost certainly a better runner than myself, who was unable to understand why I was

Fig 11.1 End of the Berlin Marathon Sep 2018

Fig 11.2 The Denbies marathon 2019

not fussed about my timing. He always tried to push himself to beat his previous times, and said I was being very Zen. It's true I have the robes of a Zen Buddhist priest in my wardrobe, but even so this little aside got me thinking. Specifically, it gave me a vision of a model to reconcile different approaches, which I liked because it popped up as a picture in my head that combined statistical modelling (using a negative exponential curve) with evolutionary neuropsychology to come up with a result that looks like Buddhism. This popped into my mind while running through the woods near Saint Maximin one dawn, July 2021. (There is a specific flattish stretch after coming down from the helipad on Mont Aurelienne that I really like and where I seem often to get sudden visual insights such as this.)

This is explained in an email I attach below, to my cosmic twin Sally Thorogood in the aftermath of some unimportant football match. England vs Italy as it happens.

Dear Sally

Many thanks for the 60th birthday wishes.

With regards to the recent football game – wipe the emotions, look them in the eye and they evaporate. Quite a few people seem to be surprisingly bothered by the outcome of an unimportant interaction between 11 neo-chimpanzees that they don't know and another 11 neo-chimpanzees they don't know on the grounds that the first half have the same passport as them.

Or, to be pedantic, the same nationality. I am not English, and no-one has an English passport! My father was adamant that he was not English, he was 100% Scots. Mum was half Welsh, so I am ¼ English, ¼ Welsh, and ½ Scots Then I got a French passport, and since I refuse to let my percentages add up to >100%, I am 50% French, 25% Scots, 12.5% English and 12.5% Welsh. None of the above. I like you, like everyone else am 100% *Homo sapiens* and nothing else. As soon as we start dividing on the grounds of mind-viruses like nationality or beliefs (or skin colour or whatever) you get painful pointless damaging splits like partitions and Brexit. Ireland and India show how such divisions lead to mass killings, for no good reason beyond Pleistocene tribalism.

To put it another way
STLOT*

> I remain haunted by what passed for sport at Manchester Grammar School, which involved the master choosing two of the alpha male boys as captains, who then they took it in turn to choose 1 person at a time until the whole class was allocated. I was always among the last, along with the short fat ones. It took me till I won a university squash tournament, ran several marathons and got 2nd dan black belt to understand that I am actually perfectly fit. The problem wasn't with my body, the problem was that "sporty" meant "giving a damn about teams and about the team winning". The Zen Buddhism of Shorinji Kempo suits me far better, and has no notion of winning or losing, just of experience. I met a lovely local chap in Dorking called Leslie who was interested but puzzled when I explained that I run up the highest hill in SE weekly for enjoyment, but pay no attention to my time (except for not being late for lunch . . .) or how my speed relates to other people's time or my previous times. Why care? What matters is the experience of being there. In France I get up at dawn to jog in the Provence hills, to be there to see the sun rise over the Alps. Sod the time, sod my speed, the only time issue is being back in time to make Catherine her breakfast!
>
> So my cosmic twin, remember the 5 magic letters that ensure mental health: STLOT
>
> All the best for your 60th year, and best wishes to John
>
> *STLOT = Sod The Lot Of Them!

This got me thinking about whether team games are uniquely bad for equanimity, and proving to myself that they are not (it's just that I'm unusually hopeless at coordinating with teams, not being telepathic). I came up with a simple elegant proof of this (while running on the Aurelienne 13/7/21, just like I said I would to Sally), establishing that in most humans any attempt to get satisfaction from beating personal records is doomed to end in multiple negatives and potentially an overall negative lifetime experience, by fusing a simple asymptotic exponential model that includes stochastic noise with some basic Pleistocene psychology. (In the process I got a result that looks suspiciously close to a core teaching of Buddhism.)

So let's assume that you start off some new sport in which the aim is to get some objective measure of performance. What, and how it is measured or won, are immaterial secondary details. Solitary or team, the proof in 'untouched, All that matters in this proof' is that higher values of 'performance' are better. If your index is 'Time taken to complete some course', where low values are better, either work on the reciprocal (=speed) or tweak the model to make decrease with time – the result is equivalent and the proof unaffected. As you start off, practise at it, work at it and get better, your performance goes up, quickly at first then ever more slowly, up to a limit. The limit will be absolute and set by your body / DNA sequence; don't kid yourself otherwise. This limit is known as an asymptote, and anyone with a bit of maths will tell you that an asymptote is a value that you get closer and closer to but never quite reach. As you practise, your performance will approach an asymptote, as a result of the general rule that 'To get better at something, do it more often'. On top of this will be day-to-day variation, known by modellers as statistical noise. It will always be there, and might be in the milliseconds (if you're good and running a short distance) or in tens of minutes (eg my long-distance runs). Any model that includes this statistical noise as an explicit term is called a stochastic model.

I show a simple example of this in the graph below, which shows the true underlying trend of improvement as a continuous line, and each measurement of it as a grey dot. Between each grey dot and the 'true' line is a black arrow – this represents how far out from ideal your actual result was. These deviations from the fitted model are always called 'residuals' in statistical models, and show exactly how far away from reality your model is. (Or, maybe better, how far away from ideal each actual result was.) These residuals have one very important property: they must sum to zero.

So let's look at your experience as a human when you look back at your performance by comparing each day's result with what has gone before. You see an underlying improvement and you see statistical noise. It is in the nature of exponential functions that they decay rapidly, but the variance of the residuals stays roughly constant, so quickly almost all the pattern you see in your results is day-to-day statistical noise. The size of the black arrows at the right hand side of the graph becomes far larger than the difference between the predicted values, as shown by the smooth line. In simple terms, although you are getting slightly better, you must expect good days and bad days. Since they sum to zero, expect as many negatives as positives.

Now let's explore your emotional response to these 'good' and 'bad' results. (I dislike the loaded terms, so maybe 'positive residuals' and 'negative residuals' is better if harder to understand. *Whether they are 'good', 'bad' or 'just a result' is entirely your subjective evaluation post-hoc.) This is where things get messy because the emotional response function is not rational, but comes out of

$$Y_i = A *(1-\exp(B*X_i)) + e_i$$

Y_i = the ith actual measured value when X is X_i

A is the asymptote.

B is the "exponential coefficient", an index of how quickly the curve bends over, and is <0

e_i is the ith residual, the difference between the ith value and what it "should have been".

A hypothetical example of a stochastic model of an exponential approach to an asymptote. Each grey dot is an actual measured value, the line shows the underlying improvement in performance The key point concerns the black arrows, called residuals. These must sum to zero, and quickly become far larger than the change due to the true underlying trend.

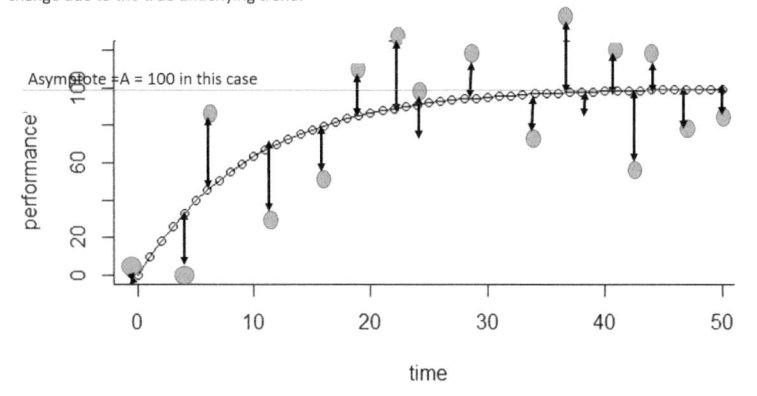

This will approach the asymptote, and (as it happens) the shortfall will decay over time with a half life of $\ln(1/2)/B$

Fig 11.3 This personal-improvement curve was modelled by a simple exponential approach to an assymptote.

somewhere in your CNS. I think it's the hypothalamus, but again that's a twiddly secondary detail. If you could engineer this response, you would probably aim for simple equality. I cannot engineer my emotional responses, nor do most people. The usual human response is to be risk-averse, to be more worried about negative results than positive. At a population level, when asked about financial investment options, people habitually choose safety over rapid growth. Personality has a strong genetic component, and in the African Pleistocene Darwinian evolution would be brutally selective against ignoring risks. No point winning a race if you race into a lion, or simply get scratched and it becomes infected. There are almost no outcomes where 'winning' will be heavily selected for, except becoming alpha male in charge of a harem. There are LOTS of outcomes where Darwinian selection will remove you totally for a negative outcome – think of snakes, lions, spiders, septicaemia, and any human with any knife, just for a start. So we should expect to be evolved to evaluate failure very negatively.

So most people most of the time will feel worse about a negative than a positive residual. Effectively the downward-pointing arrows are selectively multiplied in

---

As an unimportant and Nerdy aside – you can demonstrate to yourself this property of residuals summing to zero with simplest stochastic model

$Y_i = A + e_i$

This says that all the values are the same, the population average value, just with statistical noise.

Y_i = the ith actual value

A is the mean or average of the distribution.

e_i is the ith residual, the difference between the ith value and what it 'should have been'.

Now make up a set of N (N>1) numbers, whatever and however – a spreadsheet is easiest but use your fingers or an abacus if you prefer. The first number on your list is Y1, the second is Y2 etc. Now get the average of these by adding them up and dividing by N. Now calculate the difference between each number and the average – this is e_i the ith residual – and keep the sign! If Y_i is greater than the mean, e_i is positive, if Y_i is less than the mean e_i is negative. (If Y_i is exactly equal to the mean e_i =0, the arrow has zero length.) Now add these residuals up and I guarantee that they will add up to zero. This is both a statement of the mathematically bleedin' obvious, and a vital assumption in all statistical modelling. (This is why statisticians worry about the squares of these residual values, which generally do not add to zero and which give us variance etc. For another day . . .)

length in your perception. Hmm – but we know that they originally summed to zero, then the negative values get magnified, so the expected sum will be negative. In other words, most humans most of the time looking at their performance over time can be expected to feel a net negativity, a net unhappiness. This is pretty much encoded in the maths and the neurophysiology. How to get around it? The only way is to stop the negativity, which would be lovely but is not under conscious control. Or let go entirely, multiply both sides by zero, and stop seeing the residuals as 'good' or 'bad'. Just look at them as a result which is and exists as it is. Yes, you lose the burst of hormones from winning, but on average you will be happier this way. NOT stopping doing any exercise (there is lots of evidence that it is good for your mind and body), just stopping worrying about performance details.

And the link to Buddhist theory? A core Buddhist teaching, originating from the original Buddha Siddhartha Gautama, goes as follows:

All life is desire
All desire is suffering
Therefore all life is suffering
The only way to lose the suffering is to let go of the desire.

This syllogism always seemed needless gloomy to me – you get happy when a desire is fulfilled, don't you? In this particular interpretation, any desire to beat your/others' performance will inevitably lead to an expected negative feeling on long term average, by the proof above. The only way to lose that expected negative feeling is to multiply it by zero – let go, do not evaluate it as 'good' or 'bad', just observe it as is. It might tell you something about your body that is actually worth knowing, like a sudden drop in performance as a coronary artery gets clogged, but don't feel bad about it (just get checked out medically if needed!). What you SHOULD be revelling in is the experience of being alive, of being there and doing the run. That matters, and will always give you a good result. I see the absolute experience of being on a run as a bit like the squared value of a residual – always positive!

CHAPTER 12

M is for Meditation and Mushrooms

Inner visions: Personal development – meditation and mushrooms

This chapter is all about pictures that I see inside my head. I maybe should have added a section on geometry/mathematics as well, because (as far as I can tell) I use the same visual neuronal circuits to visualise a geometric proof, or to visualise the path through a field of equations, as I do to visualise a jogging route through remote woodland. Each time I think about differential calculus I see a picture of a vanishingly tiny right-angled triangle touching a smooth mathematical curve; each time I think of the question of 'debrouissaillage' around our place in Provence I see a picture in my head of the Euclidean geometry that evolves out of the Napoleonic rules on land clearance. (See the chapter on Provence for more on this.) Somehow I don't think that a chapter unravelling the basic philosophy of differential calculus will interest as many readers as one about seeing a spray of multicoloured flatpack flamingos. There is one key difference – the pictures I see when thinking about mathematics are under my conscious control, I can move the lines around at will and transfer the image to paper (/a whiteboard etc) as needed, to help explain them, lock them into my memories etc. Try visualising the linear function $Y = A + B*X$ in a standard XY plane – when $A = 0$, play with B and the line rotates around the origin (0.0). Play with A and the line rises up or down, but keeps the same gradient. I find that visions that come spontaneously are not like this – they come and go unbidden and uncontrollable, and are utterly outside my artistic ability to transcribe into any permanent medium. Pity. Some of the Psilocybe visions could probably be turned into amazing computer graphics if I knew how to generate dancing sheets of colour, though even then they'd just be 2D representations while a few of the images inside my head were 3D, with real depth. I sometimes muse about the neuronal equivalent of a video camera, but (even if possible) the replay would be such a scary and dangerous reprogramming of your visual cortex I doubt you'd be allowed to sell it. No computer file will ever recreate the experience of watching a flower bud opening in 3D, deep inside your skull (then waving its petals at you, like a sea creature).

So I leave the mathematical images to other chapters, but seek to give an insight into two of the more important – but publicly invisible – sets of experiences in my life associated with inner visions. These differ profoundly in all other details: meditation is a life-long daily feature of my normal life. "It's time for dodo," says Catherine most afternoons about 4pm, "dodo" here being the French baby-word meaning to fall asleep. I do explain that the important bit comes first while I'm still awake. Mushroom visions are quite the opposite – a rare special event, typically in late autumn as the Psilocybes are fresh because the alkaloids are unstable and decay to zilch by next summer. Some years, too many years, none at all.

Part 1: Meditation

One of the most important books in my life turned out to be something I borrowed from Wythenshawe library in 1978, by Lawrence LeShan, called 'How to meditate'. It is not an obvious life changer, and I had no big ambitions for it when I borrowed it. (I bought a copy many years later – it will turn up when you empty out the spare room.) What I liked about it was that it was a straightforward 'how to do' manual without any big fancy claims, still less any of the religious overtones that tend to associate themselves with schools of meditation. As a direct result I can more-or-less switch off my mind (. . . then tend to doze off) most afternoons, and if you could count patterns of word activity in my CNS the neurons associated with 'Om Nama Shivaya' would show massive overstimulation. (AFAIK we cannot do this.) This started as an interest in psychedelic pseudo-mysticism in my rebellious teens (having always rather regretted missing the true 1960s LSD revolution by an accident of birth date), and turned into a fundamental part of my self-management, a sort of mental version of having a daily shower.

To set a bit of background, meditation is not praying – though praying certainly has many features of meditation and I would suggest that most (if not all all) the alleged psychological benefits of prayer are in fact those of meditation. You are not trying to communicate with any other entities, just taking control of your mind. So try siting still for a short period, tell your muscles to be still, and your body obeys your mind – you sit still. Not always – there is a medical term 'extra-pyramidal symptoms' that I call "the twitches" when in fact your muscles don't obey you but shiver uncontrollably. This is a symptom of some anti-depressants (eg paroxetine), and a good reason to avoid them or stop taking them. I have met this once after ODing on an alleged sleeping tablet called Sominex that did nothing of the sort but made me hallucinate and twitch. That is by-the-by; generally your muscles obey you. Now in the same period tell your mind to be empty – and I guarantee you will fail. Daydreams will come and go, you will start imaginary conversations, run over recent events or things that bother you. Normal? Yes. But if you imagine you are in charge of your life and body and mind, try pointing out to yourself "Hang on a b***** minute – who is in charge here? It's my mind, so I tell it to be quiet and it doesn't even try to obey me". In fact, merely thinking this is in itself a failure, since it means that your mind is not blank. LeShan observes that a common cause of failure in experienced meditators is the thought "Yes, I am succeeding – got there". Which is by definition itself a failure. "Here I am – wasn't I?"

So, meditation is about taking control of your mind, your thought processes, of yourself at the deepest level available to the conscious mind. I won't claim it gives you access to autonomic processes (gut peristalsis, sexual responses etc) though some people probably do, but I do claim that it gives you an insight into the 'background chatter' of your conscious mind. Eastern teachers talk of the mind as being like a room full of monkeys, and while you shouldn't push the analogy too far you get the basic idea. Noah Hariri (21 lessons for the 21st century) observed how shocked he was that he could not focus his own mind on his own breathing despite being a clearly clever and successful chap, and how a week's retreat focussing on breathing changed his entire outlook on his mind.

I had much the same experience – it's my mind., my mind is me, so why does my self-control utterly fail on such a simple task as stillness? The neurophysiological answer about activity in networks doesn't really help for various reasons, internal and external. So meditation is the path to stillness, and with it comes remarkable subjective benefits (IMHO). From here on I must pass on other people's teaching as much as my experience, since unlike maths there are no proofs and unlike most biology we don't have much hard evidence to go on.

LeShan talked of two genetic classes of meditation, 'Structured meditation' and 'unstructured meditation'. The distinction is easy – structured meditation is a mental algorithm, you focus on some defined activity and in working at this focus you are meditating. Unstructured meditation is much more about letting your mid drift and observing the drift as a passive observer. Much more recently the phrase 'Mindfulness' has come into public awareness, publicised as a path to mental health, advocated by celebrities such as Ruby Wax. The word Mindfulness does not seem to occur in LeShan's book but all the descriptions I have met suggest strongly that Mindfulness a-la Ruby Wax is effectively a form of 'Unstructured meditation' à-la LeShan. You observe your mind and its drifting.

I have tried both, and recommend that you explore both to find what works for you. It is quite clear which school of meditation works for me, but everyone is different and I am persistently astonished at the extent to which other people's nervous systems work differently to mine! I will explain my experiences and understanding, but you must seek your own path.

I am a devotee of structured meditation, specifically the use of a mantra. The idea is remarkably simple – you have a phrase that you repeat in your head, so that ANYTHING else going on in your conscious mind is an error to be corrected. This is much like a computer executing the same line of code endlessly, and doesn't sound much like personal development. (When we get self-aware computers their internal focus will of course be more perfect than any mammalian wetware can ever be). I had a diving instructor Peter White who clearly thought I was delusional to imagine this mantra-based procedure gave any benefit, though I tried the analogy of doing weights in a gym. The action of doing the same weights again and again is beneficial not because the weight needs moving but because you built up the muscles (and the nervous pathways) by repetition. Ditto mantras, except instead of muscles it is mental focus. Maybe I should have just said "it works for me, has become an important daily part of my life and that should be good enough".

It certainly didn't help that Peter White was well-informed enough to spot (correctly) that this mantra-based system is effectively identical to the basic teachings of 'Transcendental Meditation' (TM), as taught by the Maharishi Mahesh yogi (https://en.wikipedia.org/wiki/Maharishi_Mahesh_Yogi) and he recounted the well-known anecdote about the monetarisation of mantras, as proof of the fraudulence of the system. These points are serious and need addressing, though (IMHO) quite miss the neurophysiological/developmental points of the exercise.

First the Yogi. The Maharishi probably got too much exposure too early via The Beatles, followed by international fame and serious money. This would be enough to inflate anyone's ambitions, and with hindsight his 'TM Empire' (my phrase, not his) certainly expanded unsustainably fast and made indefensible claims. The weirdest one was about 'yogic flying' (they don't fly, they bounce on their knees in a lotus position), but wild claims that critical numbers of meditators can reduce crime etc don't look defensible either. Set against this, the money didn't seem to go to his head nearly as badly as [by way of example] Bhagwan Rajneesh (or, probably, >90% of the males of our species given comparable promotion to super-rich alpha male status). Compared to what he could have done he seems to have been pretty moderate! I don't think that the behaviour of one guru is much of a basis for assessing the worth of a neurophysiological exercise – check the evidence, not the people. (One good tip given by LeShan is about deciding whether to have a personal guru. His advice is "Never mind how elegant his turban is or how well he sits in a lotus position – ask how he gets on with his wife".)

Then there is the story about the personalised mantras. Supposedly, the Maharishi told people that he would give them a personal mantra that only they would know or use, chosen specially to match your personality, that they must not tell anyone else what it was or share it in any way. So of course The Beatles signed up, got a mantra each, and promptly swapped notes to find that they had all been given the same mantra. (I think it was the word 'purple', though this detail is tangential.) LeShan says that in fact the choice of mantra is quite immaterial, and that you can make your own perfectly well with a telephone directory to generate random syllables. This assertion is testable given a brain-scanning tool to examine the meditating mind, and is probably right. The mantra is just a mental target, not instruction code. If this is the case, selling personalised mantras is a misleading scam but the technique itself is not invalidated. (To play Devil's advocate, if every mantra works equally well for everyone then it would be entirely true to say that that "this mantra will work well for you", though not "I chose it specially for you").

I know that I explored several different mantras before settling down on one, including a random syllable combination from a phone directory. I know that I mentioned my mantra 'Om nama shivaya' to friends in Oxford in 1980, and one person said that this was good because it had been used so long by so many people. I was deeply cynical as I didn't (/don't) believe in telepathy. Someone else pointed out that there was no need to invoke spooky spiritualism to explain why some mantras survive well, as there is a simpler explanation (a neo-Darwinian meme evolution model as I would now see it). Some patterns of sound just happen to work well with typical *Homo sapiens* neuronal processing systems, so these will tend to get used again and passed on to students. The meme that works best gets copied most, as I would now see it. This appealing simple model fits my experience well. I remember clearly explaining to a student called Chris in York in 1983 that I liked 'Om Nama Shivaya' because I could see it as a triangle. This is still, exactly, my daily experience with the same mantra. I suspect that tens of thousands of other people have the same experience, though have no way of establishing this. (There is a nice project for someone!)

How, you may ask, does a manta become a triangle? Easy – first split it into syllables. It is an auditory process at its root anyway. So we have one syllable – OM, then two syllables NA MA then three syllables SHI VAY YAH. Second you phase-link these to your breathing, so you are focussing on your breathing. Many schools of meditation (including mindfulness) emphasise as focussing on breathing being really important for self-awareness. The Japanese teach "To control the mind, control the breathing" in order to stay calm and focussed in martial arts. I operate '1 breath = 1 word', but maybe a more serious teacher might suggest "1 breath = 1 syllable". It works for me anyway. Thirdly you see the syllables as a triangle:

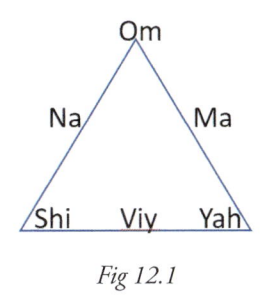

Fig 12.1

Then you keep on doing this. This is where the concept of 'Mayko' comes in, again I lift the word from LeShan, but the basic idea is simple. Your mind does not take readily to focussing on one thing, whether it is a sound or an internal image or anything else. Your consciousness is like a room full of monkeys, as they teach. So distractions arise, unavoidably and inevitably. These are the 'mayko', and are typically daydreams, or worries of the day, or random memories, or almost anything else that breaks the continuity. I have seen a few good internal visions while meditating, though nothing like what a big dose of Psilocybe mushrooms can do. Le Shan observes that such apparently transcendental experiences are quite common, and should not be sought after nor regarded as a result, they are just a distraction. Equally don't get cross (that is itself a break in focus). Like taking a small child for a walk and they run off distracted by a tree or a flower, take the approach of saying "That's fine, honey, now let's get back on track". All that matters is the mantra, the internal representation of the sound and its image. Go back again and again, nothing else matters. Not even think about thinking about it, just being there.

For how long? I find that after a while I just know when I've done enough. The focus juice has (metaphorically) run out. About 20 minutes I think, but refuse to set a timer switch or alarm, just keep going as needed. Then LeShan recommends as an important point that you end with a few minutes of 'just being' – lying there but NOT meditating. Yoga teaches relaxation at the end of a session. I highly recommend that during meditation you have a pillow under your knees – this reduces stress in the spine. Oddly similar advice came from an acid head in Oxford (Jules W. about how to optimise meditation) and from the radiotherapy unit at the Marsden (to keep relaxed during the deeply unpleasant experience of having your face strapped into place with a tight mask), that having a pillow under the knees is a good thing to do. Then after meditation is over, I move the pillow from under my knees to under my head. OK I then tend to doze off, but that is part of it for me. I think that the rest of the family just think I doze off and am making up the meditation bit, as this is the phase that they tend to see. As my daughter Louise put it "you were meditating loudly, Dad" – in other words snoring! At least once while getting over radiotherapy I had a proper meditate, then put my head on the pillow, and a moment later my wife came in asking if I knew what time it was. It turned out that after I'd finished meditating, she had a student come to the house for French tuition, had given him an hour's lesson, said goodbye and cooked dinner. I must have dozed off properly. I know that experienced meditators don't encourage sleeping, and I suspect that their use of the lotus position is precisely to stop this. John Comber at Kempo tried meditation, and when I explained about having a pillow under my knees asked, "don't you fall asleep?". Yes, it's not a problem IMHO, better seen as a life-enhancing feature.

Part 2: Magic Mushrooms

One of the more surprising discoveries of the 20th Century was that some reasonably common and widespread mushrooms contain unusual molecules that interfere with the operations of the human central nervous system, in ways that only affect the higher levels of consciousness without any significant toxicity to organs that matter and with no clear evidence of long lasting effects of any sort, let alone damage. (This is not true if you get the ID wrong and eat a *Galerina* instead – look out for cinnamon brown gills and avoid them like the plague. *Psilocybe*s all have purple brown gills and spore prints at maturity, though immature *P. cyanescens* gills are rather pale grey.) Knowledge of these mushrooms was introduced to modern Western society by Gordon Wasson, a banker who used his wealth to explore magic mushroom cults in Mexico, and came back with stories of amazing visions from relatively small amounts of rather low-key mushrooms in the genus *Psilocybe*.

The text is well known, but stands repeating to give an idea of the intensity. I think he must have had a good big dose!

BTW The Aztec name for these mushrooms is Teonanacatl = Gods' flesh. I think it is just one of those random linguistic coincidences that "Teo" means God in two such unconnected language families as Aztec and Indo-European.

> Gordon Wasson's first encounter with *Psilocybe mexicana*:
>
> *the visions came whether our eyes were opened or closed. They emerged from the center of the field of vision, opening up as they came, now rushing, now slowly, at the pace that our will chose. They were in vivid color, always harmonious. They began with art motifs, angular such as might decorate carpets or textiles or wallpaper or the drawing board of an architect. Then they evolved into palaces with courts, arcades, gardens–resplendent palaces all laid over with semiprecious stones. Then I saw a mythological beast drawing a regal chariot. Later it was though the walls of our house had dissolved, and my spirit had flown forth, and I was suspended in mid-air viewing landscapes of mountains, with camel caravans advancing slowly across the slopes, the mountains rising tier above tier to the very heavens.*

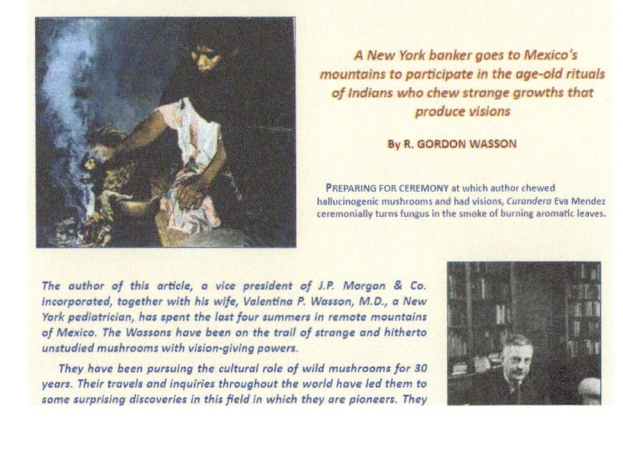

Fig 12.2 The original account of Gordon Wasson's magic mushroom experience, in Time Magazine, 1957.

These little brown decomposers full of tryptamine alkaloids are nothing to do with the red capped mycorrhizal fungus of birch trees fly agaric *Amanita muscaria*, also known to produce visions. The molecules are different and altogether more dangerous in *Amanita muscaria* – my advice is firmly to stick to *Psilocybe*! As far as I know, no-one has ever suffered dangerous toxicity from any *Psilocybe* (despite some heroic efforts . . .) but *Amanita muscaria* contains atropine and ibotenic acid (both toxic) and routinely makes users sick – with at least one documented human death; admittedly he ate 26 caps of *Amanita muscaria*, so was really asking for it. Before moving on to *Psilocybe*, the fly agaric deserves passing mention. It seems adequately well documented that reindeer herders in Siberia got high off the molecule muscimol,

Fig 12.3 Amanita muscaria – *suggested to be the ancient psychedelic behind the Vedic ghitas*

which is found in *Amanita muscaria*, and that they removed the toxic molecules by feeding the mushrooms to reindeer, who excreted the muscimol unchanged, so they drank the reindeer urine. Like I said, stick to Psilocybe. There are curious historical links here, mainly speculative. Firstly, please forget any connection to Father Christmas. You can make a lovely story about magic reindeer, flying on magic mushrooms, with the mushroom commemorated in Father Christmas' red and white coat. Lovely but utter historical garbage, that crumbles when any detail gets examined. Just by way of example, Saint Nicolas came in a green coat until Victorian times. Of much more historical interest is the possible connection to the roots of Hinduism, via the early Gitas, which refer to a divine potion called Soma that caused transformations and visions. Gordon Wasson was sure that this came from a folk memory of *Amanita muscaria*, suggesting that India was colonised by Siberians who brought the folk memory but no ability to recreate the magic potion since it is not a tropical species. He wrote a classic old book advocating this idea 'Soma divine mushroom of immortality' (reprinted in 2021 with added text by a Sanskrit scholar). This just might be accurate, may be rubbish, will probably remain as a 'never know'. A key problem is that although the Gitas praise Soma in detail, they do not say how to make it. In fact, I can't get any sense out of any of the stories.

There are some tangential references that suggest soma was recycled via urine. If this were established that would nail the fly agaric connection since no other drug has ever been processed this way. I met an internet connection called Mike Crowley who wrote an essay called 'The God who drank Urine', making exactly this point. Actually, *Amanita muscaria* does grow under pine trees in the Himalayan foothills. There is a human story that can be tested by genetic profiling, which is that Hindu India has always been riven by the caste system, with the highest caste being the Brahmins. The model that links these to *Amanita muscaria* is that idea that the original Brahmins were the Siberian shamans who brought knowledge of soma, and who avoided interbreeding with local tribes by enforcing a caste system. Testable and just might be right.

Back to *Psilocybe*. (As a useless aside the name comes from Psilos cybos = bald head in ancient Greek, referring to the detachable pellicle on the cap). These are all decomposers. In the UK we have a well-known native species in the genus, the 'liberty cap' *Psilocybe semilanceata*. Its name comes from a perceived similarity in its nipple-topped cap to the hats worn by revolutionaries in the 1789 French revolution. You need to eat at least 10 to get any effect as they are small, and I think 30 is a useful minimum. It is a typical species of Pennine hill grassland on acid soils. This is widespread in acid grassland and I cannot believe the European witches did not know about it. Presumably the Christian church stamped on the cult. I suspect that one day it will be transferred to a sister genus since its ecology is so different to other *Psilocybes*, having a perennial mycelium in stable grassland that will fruit in the same spot year after year for decades, if not more. I found one patch of *P. semilanceata* in Chorlton Meadows which fruited in the same exact spot in 1978 and 2012. There is a mycelium on Coldharbour cricket pitch, just inside the gateway in the SE corner, that had *Psilocybes* in 1987 and again in the same spot 2022 (just sadly few in both years). Almost all the other *Psilocybes* are transient species of evanescent habitats like dung or sawdust. *P. semilanceata* was the magic mushroom of my adolescence, as is probably true for millions of people in northern Europe. It grew each autumn in Wythenshawe Park, Tatton Park, all over the Pennine hill meadows. I remain blown away by a discovery I made in September 1985, just before leaving York with my PhD, where I took a friend David Gibeaut out to Farndale in the North York Moors looking for mushrooms, and by luck we found a valley that was just heaving with *P. semilanceata*. I have never seen so many, picking many hundreds in a few hours. More than a decade later I found myself back in York on a NERC committee, so took the afternoon off to revisit 'my' mushroom meadow and collect a few more hundred. (Yes, they were still there in abundance. Saw a late ring ousel, too.) The first time I got tripped out (and correspondingly freaked out) was one afternoon in 39FD in November 1978, two days before my Oxford entrance exam. Treating *P. semilanceata* as little brown pills, I'd previously at weekly intervals done five (just a little buzz), done 10 (a buzz), and done 20 (fun), so did 25. That was scary, with the classic 'symptoms' like altered colours and time dilation. The birch tree at the bottom of the garden had a giant snake wrapped around it at one stage. With hindsight this could all have been fine, but I was a schoolboy living at home trying to 'act normal', worried about an upcoming exam, with mother and sister looking on having no idea at all what was going on in my head. (Useful survival tip – when one is tripping people cannot spot it, unlike being drunk or stoned which are immediately obvious to onlookers. Just act confidently normal and sail on through, you'll be fine.) The experience was not pleasant, entirely because of the lack of control. As an adult on my own in my own home I'd have been fine – but I would also have planned ahead what to do. Tim Leary talked about 'Set and Setting' – basically plan your psychedelic trips in advance and make sure you are somewhere you feel comfortable, and all should be well.

Psilocybin was at the core of the only randomised controlled trial in theology. This was run by Tim Leary, self-styled LSD guru, and Thomas Pahnke, who collaborated with a medic to give 20 seminary students a pill, either psilocybin or a placebo, then left then in a religious setting to pray. This was Pahnke's famous 'Good Friday' experiment. A late review by Rick Doblin is here: Pahnke's "Good Friday Experiment" – Follow-up (druglibrary.org).

I should add the Rick Doblin is well known for his activity in the Multidisciplinary Association for Psychedelic Studies (MAPS), and I met him at a MAPS stone-in at some huge old farmhouse in Sussex one evening about 2012. He admired my giant chess set (after asking ". . . and are the pieces REALLY that big, or is it just me?" – yes they were giant pieces) and expressed worry that I might not be exposing my children sufficiently to the culture around psychedelic drugs. That's the spirit!

All but one of the treated group in the Good Friday experiment reported a divine and religious experience, while one of the control group did. The difference is statistically significant (I estimated chi squared =5.4 1df $P<0.05$). I have used this experiment as an introduction to randomised designs, and had a student say that the experiment was utterly unethical. (She was right that no modern ethics committee would sign this off, especially as the doctor alleged to be overseeing the H&S publicly denied all knowledge of the experiment, when the university started giving Tim Leary a hard time.) I also think this single experiment shows a reasonably convincing link between the 'tripped out' and 'transcendent' mind states, associated with reduced ACC activity. I also use this in lectures on experimental design as an example of a silly unexpected outcome that show the need for always having a control group. ("Odd events can happen – A man has survived falling from a plane onto a mountainside, a subject has had a spontaneous religious experience in a control group in an experimental setting . . .")

At a molecular level the effect seems to be that psilocybin reduces activity in two regions, the prefrontal cortex and anterior cingulate cortex, via binding to a post-synaptic serotonin receptor in the 5HT1A family. It seems that normally these areas act as overseers or filters for a lot of our conscious thoughts. The huge feeling of stimulation you can get is not actual stimulation but the removal of impediments. A not-very accurate analogy here is with a fictional office in Slough, featuring in the sitcom 'The Office', with an especially annoying, interfering and generally waste-of-space boss called David Brent. Imagine this boss is your Anterior Cingulate Nucleus. (This is deeply unfair on your ACN, but bear with me.) Now imagine the same office environment with the boss shut down for the day so everyone just gets on with doing what they are good at, happily, without any time-wasting hassle. This is the core of David Nutt's results of fMRI on psilocybin.

Recent brain imaging work by Professor David Nutt and Robin Carhart-Harris (two of my all-time heroes) has shown than psilocybin (acting on HT2A receptors) acts to reduce activity in a few central regions thought to be associated with coordination (the anterior cingulate cortex and medial prefrontal cortex): see http://www.pnas.org/content/109/6/2138.short and Muthukumaraswamy et al (2013).

BTW psilocybin seems to have genuine activity against depression, based on good randomized trials. I have not met David Nutt. I have once attended a talk by Robin Carhart-Harris at one of our lunchtime research seminars in Whitelands College, Roehampton about 2018, and subsequently sent him a seedling peyote cactus I had grown. I do not know how this little cactus has got on – it could easily outlive both of us, or if Robin ever watered it during winter it may have rotted away (see below).

Although I am always pleased to find *Psilocybe semilanceata*, it is really scarce in the hot, dry south-east of the UK. It is a species of Atlantic grassland on acid soils, common in Wales, Ireland and the Pennines. The species that has transformed my life, at least as far as psychedelic mushrooms is concerned, is the wavy capped magic mushroom *Psilocybe cyanescens*. First the name – cyanescens means 'going blue', and it diagnostically goes blue whenever tissue is damaged or if the mushroom is handled. This bluing is strongly indicative of psilocybin, though no one seems to know why. One of my lifetime achievements is to have exchanged emails with Alexander Shulgin, in which I asked him about the biochemistry of the bluing reaction and he said we don't know. Alexander Shulgin is up there in my pantheon along with Richard Feynman, David Attenborough and Richard Dawkins. He was a chemist who wrote books about the synthesis of new psychedelic molecules. If you have not read the personal bits in 'PIHKAL' you really should. Utterly mind-blowing before even touching the molecules. (PIHKAL = Phenyl Ethylamines I Have Known And Loved – molecules related to mescaline, including MDMA = 'ecstasy'). His other book is TIKHAL – Tryptamines I Have Known And Loved, describing the molecular family of Psilocybin and its analogues.

Date sent: Tue, 21 Apr 1998 19:20:46 -0700 (PDT)
From: "Alexander T. Shulgin"
To: chezshaw@pop3.mail.demon.net, p.shaw@roehampton.ac.uk, peters@roehampton.ac.uk, shaw@chezshaw.demon.co.uk
Subject: random dominoes

Hello Peter:

   Thank you so much for your mailing of a few days ago.

   First, yes, your donation to the defense was indeed received, and Ann had sent out a thank-you for it. Perhaps the address was messed up -- sorry -- but you were part of an extraordinary generosity that substantially offset both the fine and the legal fees associated with this shameful act on the part of our Government here. The issue is officially closed and, apart from some rather childish hassling by the DEA, there is nothing happening at the official level. The appearance of TIHKAL was seen by them as a second insult, and we are waiting to see if there will be any expression of their increased anger.

   Thanks so much for your contributions to my ramblings on the three letter acronym coincidences to drugs -- the 157 value will insist that I think about this for a while. I am not quite sure how many different TMA's and DOM's exist. If they are considered in sequence it seems that 26^3 or 17576 sounds right. But if sequence is not looked at (I cut the names into three unarranged snips of paper and mail them to you in a single envelop) then the number of different envelop contents you could have seems to be $26 + 26 \times 25 + 26 \times 25 \times 24$ or 16275. And although it is a different number, it is so close to being the same, it sounds wrong. I can clearly see that if there is an undo frequency of certain letters, there is a delightful uncertainty in the results. But now I am now spinning both numbers and hyphens into the code name so the task becomes even stranger.

   Thanks for your kind offer to meet us when or if we come into Gatwick airport. At the moment I can't foresee it, but it is gracious of you to extend the offer!

Sasha

● Why did Shulgin become known as the godfather of ecstasy?

Alexander Shulgin in his lab in 2001. Photograph: Scott Houston/Sygma/Corbis

Alexander "Sasha" Shulgin, who has died aged 88, was a pioneering and fearless scientist, but his chosen discipline - the design and synthesis of

Fig 12.4 Sasha Shulgin in his laboratory.

Fig 12.5 The Psilocybin molecule: 5 phospho-N,N dimethyl tryptamine. See https://www.ncbi.nlm.nih.gov/pmc/articles/PMC3277566/ for MRI work on its mode of action.

I have multiple stories about *Psilocybe cyanescens*, some best left untold. This mushroom more-or-less got me my citation classic paper, an article with Geoff Kibby in 'Field Mycology' about the unusual mixes of non-native fungi that appear on ornamental woodchips in gardens. The citation is: Shaw, PJA & Kibby G. (2001). Aliens in the flowerbeds: the fungal biodiversity of ornamental woodchips. *Field Mycology* 2, 6-11. In this we observe that such woodchip communities are marked by two non-native fungi, of which one is *Psilocybe cyanescens*. Geoff assures me that this is the most downloaded article from his web page. (The other typical woodchip fungus is the 'redleg roundhead' which I think of as *Stropharia aurantiaca* but is called *Leratiomyces ceres* now, an Australian species with no psychoactivity.) It is truly remarkable that we are still not really sure exactly where either of these fungi live in the wild! *Psilocybe cyanescens* may well come from the Pacific NW forests of the USA where something very similar grows and is psychoactive. *P cyanescens* was first discovered and described from woodchip beds in Kew Gardens in 1945 by a researcher called Elise Wakefield, and we need DNA profiling to establish where this lineage comes from. I fancy it evolved to live on the heaps of woodchips left by beavers, again with no evidence at all. Whatever, it hitched a lift into Kew with some foreign soil about 1910 and has been there ever since.

To use these, or any *Psilocybe*, you can simply eat them but they are a bit harsh on the tummy. I have once had a bad gastric experience with fresh *semilanceata* which I attribute to additional traces of fresh rabbit poo (which would have been killed had I boiled them). Not dangerous but a bit sore, so most people make *Psilocybes* into a tea. I highly recommend this route as being safe, comfortable and effective. Alkaloids extract best in acid, so lower the pH. Here is how: get >3g dried *Psilocybe*, put them in a pint glass with about 2cm depth of diet coke (or water with lemon juice or vinegar, or anything else to reduce pH <4 that you can safely drink). Put the glass in a microwave and belt it on high until the liquid boils Then stop, shake them down if stuck to the side, boil it for another 30 seconds, and filter into a clean glass. Repeat once to avoid wasting any alkaloids, then keep the boiled fruitbodies safe until the morning (. . . just in case the ID was wrong. I always do this and have not yet needed to). Combine the two liquid extracts and swallow immediately as the molecules are unstable even in ionic form (as the low pH environment mandates). Even keeping them by the bed overnight will lose activity. Do not schedule any work, driving or other interactions of any serious sort for at least nine hours (or beware mind bending scenarios as you have to pretend all is normal while colours morph and strange patterns appear in kitchen surfaces. BTDT).

Psilocybe cyanescens is reasonably tractable to outdoor culture (unlike *P. semilanceata*) and does not need sterile facilities. You DO need a lot of fresh clean new woodchips, then introduce spawn (ideally with spore-shedding mushrooms) to the woodchips and wait a year. This fungus goes through woodchips like a slow motion fire, and will eat away a big pile in a couple of years. In its first year it can have really big mass fruitings, with hundreds or thousands of fruitbodies, with the rule of thumb that 10 fruitbodies pack the same punch as a standard tab of LSD. Next year maybe a few come back up, maybe nothing ever again. I got a small paper out of following up this time dynamic, based on a roundabout in Leatherhead that was covered in woodchips and interesting fungi. The next year, just a few fruitbodies, then nothing more. See Shaw, Butlin & Kibby (2004). These are a short-lived phenomenon, but with a good track record of establishing given clean new wood chips. I found *P. cyanescens* in Wisley Gardens (yes, I spent days walking round Wisley Gardens, looking at pretty flowers and hallucinogenic fungi and called it research) and the grounds of Froebel College. Legend has it that *P. cyanescens* mycelium was given out by groupies at Grateful Dead concerts, a story with a ring of truth though I've not documented it. There is no doubt that the Grateful Dead did their best to promote and venerate psychedelics generally, and that this fungus is readily transplanted.

I wish to pass on some good advice from an expert. A real taxonomic expert, who knew his mushrooms. It surprised me, but is worth passing on. Having explained how he'd tried some of my *Psilocybes* and was blown away to be still hallucinating the next morning, he said, "If you are going to do *Psilocybe*, do a LOT of them". Since the usual advice with drugs is to start off at low doses and step up this rather surprised me, but in fact he was right if what you want is visions. If you fiddle around with low doses, you get somewhat stoned, nothing special. Somewhere upwards of 3g there is an apparent switch in the response and you get real, proper amazing visions, which is either utterly wonderful or very scary depending on set and setting. One of my students (whose dissertation kicked off this research) had "a friend who tried cyanescens" (yeah right) who reported that they completely lost touch with reality and started seeing multicoloured Roman legionaries everywhere. To give some ideas of what cyanescens can do, I can try to describe a tiny proportion of what I have seen. I would really like an internal camera to replay the images, but that's not going to happen ever. So try these anecdotes: a pink demon poking his head out of a hole in my visual field and sticking his tongue out at me, two golden beings of light pouring gold coins into a gold whirlpool, curtains of light that clone themselves constantly like paisley patterns being painted onto space by an invisible paintbrush, a book whose pages riffle spontaneously and are all moving images into other worlds, an infinite recursion of mirrored cubes with a woman's face in each one. I've been out in the woods and seen swarms of snowflakes, each one with a seductive woman's eye looking at me. Imagine a deck of cards collapsing, except that as each card falls it is a garishly coloured flatpack flamingo. A flowing carpet of luminous plasticine that sets hard then bursts to reveal dozens of tiny sunlit smiley faces. I giggled for weeks at seeing a teddy bear piloting an open-top plane full of toys – so sweet! The space between my ears briefly became a deep blue swimming pool awash with mermaids. Seeing a hauntingly beautiful silhouette world of fairytale castles, outlined in glowing neon lines, all in a purple twilight. A landscape covered in the complex knot-garden patterns of parterres (see the gardens of the chateau of Landery) but the shapes defining the patterns were not bushes, they were hundreds of copies of the smiling face of Sean the sheep! (see Wallace & Gromit – "A Close Shave"). I find that this effect of massed smiling faces popping up into my visual field (like seeds sprinkled and germinating as you watch) is a repeated and wonderful experience. Again, like the flying teddy bear, I found myself giggling for days afterwards at the silly cuteness of this inner vision of massed smiling sheep. I have a nasty feeling that if I told the university counsellors that I was laughing at an explosion of invisible cartoon sheep they would try to get me sectioned. We never really thought on the same wavelength.

Here is a good psychedelic game to try, that only works between about one and four hours after a significant *Psilocybe* dose: Briefly look at some bright light source (NOT the sun! Try a bedroom desk lamp) to get an after-image in your retinas. Now put your head somewhere dark, eg under the duvet, and watch those

A Path of 21 Ms

retinal images. They will spawn new images that themselves spawn new images, a bit like the process of diffusion-limited aggregation (by which crystals accumulate in spiky masses). One swipe of a desk lamp across my retinas turned into an amazingly beautiful view of flying through the empty streets of some mythical city as the after-image faded under my duvet!

I've been walking round gardens with a friend when we both felt the ground rumbling, only it wasn't an earthquake, it was just the shrooms. Visions are never guaranteed. Wasson noted his mushroom guide Maria Sabrina screamed at the mushroom spirits when the visions stopped mid-session for no apparent reason. Ritual seems to help psychedelic experiences, maybe because they remove the uncertainty of decision making. My version of the ritual is to get up before dawn, extract the alkaloids plus have a small breakfast – then back to bed to watch the dawn light creeping in. This is where and when the visions come. Bob Wallace (co-founder of Microsoft and keen psychedelic pioneer) observed that the visions are better if you are actively looking into a blindfold, maybe because this gets the optical pattern-recognition circuits activated but swamped by random noise? Anyway, he knew what he was doing and he made a bit of money selling a thing called a 'mindfold', which is a specially comfortable blindfold to gaze into while tripping. I recommend the idea, but there are free and easy alternatives in every home. I also really enjoy feeling tightly wrapped up, probably as a pre-birth neurological echo. Anyway, once daylight has come and visions settle down, I put on running stuff and go outside for a 15K run up Leith Hill in the dawn sunlight. Utterly magical, and I am sure it boosts serotonin etc. There is one point in this ritual that the visions verge on being reliable (. . . but still no promises . . .). At the start of a run I leave the house, stand in the sunlight, shut my eyes and do a 'Rei' to the sun and then to my target (eg Leith Hill Tower) which I visualise. This is a Japanese sign of respect, and is equivalent to bowing but without subservience. You hold your hands so each finger is touching its counterpart (looks like Christian prayer) and nod towards the partner, who does the same back. Straight out of Japanese martial arts. So I come out of the house about two hours after a chunky dose of Psilocybe, shut my eyes and Rei to the sun, and reliably see amazing visions, doubtless as my optical circuits adapt to the higher light levels. My internal image becomes sort-of pixelated, but not really since a pixel is by definition just one colour but in this case each 'pixel' is a separate screen, all playing an identical image. Once it was the gold mask of Tutankhamun (or rather hundreds of such identical masks swarming round a big central one, as if the sun God Ra). Once it was dozens of identical sandy puppies all smiling at me, which all morphed into lion cubs. Once a hemispherical wall of identical rectangular kaleidoscopes. The red and yellow of a jester's garb, condensed as ropes of light that form a network across my visual field – then I open my eyes and it's a standard overcast Tuesday morning, nothing special – I shut my eyes and again see the network of red and yellow bands of light, now flickering and bulging with hundreds of tiny faces, red and yellow silhouettes. Any neighbours looking on would have seen nothing and wondered what I was laughing at. In the 'M is for Marathon' chapter I suggest that I don't want you sitting on your bottom on the sofa watching a video of my runs, I want you to put on some old running shoes and get out in the woods. Ditto mushroom visions, but do check the gills and spore prints if it's a wild harvest.

Anyway, over the course of my life I have 'done' the following psychedelic mushrooms: All are species of Psilocybe, unless otherwise stated.

- *Copelandia cyanescens* – unusual, tiny bluing pin-heads, but actually really good. Cultivated only.
- *Panaeolus* spp – This genus is close to *Psilocybe*, and all over Africa a *Panaeolus* (*P. tropicalis*) grows on animal dung and is highly psychoactive. It is almost certain that some of your ancestors got spaced out on *Panaeolus tropicalis* in the Pleistocene, though there seems to be no cultural legacy of this now. One of the commonest UK lawn fungi is *Panaeolus foenisecii* – the haymakers' mushroom or brown mottle gill, now transferred to *Panaeolina*. There are stories of young kids eating this on their back lawn and being hospitalised with trippy symptoms (BTW all magic mushrooms seem much more unpleasant for kids than adults). I once knocked back 35 of this species and got NOTHING AT ALL, not even any interference with sleep. Utterly inert. I have also found *Panaeolus sphinctrinus* and *P. ater* in the UK that are meant to be active, but didn't dare (*sphinctrinus* contains atropine). A recent review found useful amounts of Psilocybin in *Panaeolus subbalteatus*, which sometimes grows as a weed in commercial mushroom beds.

Fig 12.6 Panaeolina foenisecii *the haymaker's mushroom. Common in lawns, but apparently largely inactive.*

A Path of 21 Ms

Psilocybes:

- *P. cubensis*. This is the easiest species to grow (spores onto nutrient agar, then brown rice, then 'case' it with sterile soil), and certainly contains alkaloids, but I have never thought much of the visions it generates. Or rather doesn't generate. This is the main magic mushroom on sale in Amsterdam, but would not be my first choice.
- *P. cyanescens* – a woodchip species that can be cultivated given enough fresh woodchips. This is the best species, with better visions than any other. Or more scary extreme experiences, depending on your experience – this is a species to cultivate, venerate and handle with respect. I am doing what I can to give it a helping hand locally.
- *P. mexicana* – supplied commercially as 'truffles' (sclerotia). I rate this one highly, as did Gordon Wasson.
- *P. semilanceata* – the only species growing wild around Manchester in my childhood so an old friend. Scarce in the hot, dry south-east, but may be found in small numbers on Leith Hill, eg Coldharbour cricket pitch. This is the magic mushroom that my head of department used to illustrate my retirement presentation!

This is the place to mention two other naturally occurring psychedelics, mescaline and DMT.

Fig 12.7 Psilocybe cubensis *growing in a jam jar of brown rice. The psychedelic species most common cultivated and sold.*

Fig 12.8 Psilocybe cyanescens. *The wavy capped magic mushroom, on woodchips in Inholms Clay Pit Oct 2016. Note blue stains.*

Fig 12.9 Psilocybe semilanceata, *in a Pennine hill meadow.*

DMT is the active molecule in ayauasca, occurs naturally in our brains all the time at low levels, and makes us see images of fantasy beings, 'DMT elves'. We are wired up to be able to undergo transcendent experiences. Although doubtless over-simplified, we seem to have a 'God-module' in our brain. This is a demonstrable feature of the human central nervous system (CNS), and can be demonstrated using a simple amine that occurs naturally (albeit at very low levels) in mammalian CNS. The amine is Dimethyl tryptamine.

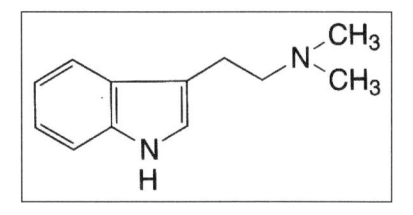

Fig 12.10 The DMT molecule.

This compound induces visions (often of non-earthly beings) when transfused into any normal healthy adult, along with a profound sense of having a transcendent experience. Richard Straussman has written a book called *DMT: Spirit molecule* – documenting the stunning and profound experiences induced by this drug. DMT is the psycho-active ingredient in the sacred tea Ayahuscha (pronounced ayawashka), which is accepted as a branch of the Christian church in South America. Ayahuashca users had respectable lives and full intellectual faculties – comparable or superior to controls. (The tea also contains a second compound that inhibits mono-amine oxidase in the gut: harmaline is usually used.) Since DMT is a Class A hallucinogen, I take great amusement in thinking that prohibitionists, like the rest of us, go around violating the control of drugs act merely by thinking :=)

I have not done DMT in any form and I harbour a lingering grudge against prohibition generally that I will probably die without having seen DMT visions. Never mind having seen the pyramids, Machu Picchu or Angkor Wat, I want to see DMT elves inside my head. It's really not easy to make DIY Ayahuscha. DMT comes from an amazon tree *Psychotria viridis* that won't grow in the UK and whose seeds won't germinate. DMT also occurs in some acacias, and I have got a fishy smell off the roots of acacia seedlings once suggesting amines but (1) it's a small tree that can't grow outside, (2) you need enough roots or bark to fill a cup, (3) you also need a monoamine oxidase inhibitor (MAOi) to stop the DMT being broken down in your gut. These can be dangerous especially if you eat cheese afterwards, and you need a different plant extracted in a different way. So the most plausible recipe involves about 20g acacia bark (DMT) and 5g of harmaline seeds *Perganum harmala* (MOAi), the latter plant having red seeds allegedly used to stain Persian carpets hence flying carpets. (With about the same reliability as linking Father Christmas to *Amanita muscaria*.) I have not heard of anyone actually making this work.

A Path of 21 Ms

Then we have the mescaline cacti. I love mescaline cacti, grow loads, have successfully got mescaline experiences, own enough mescaline cacti for a dozen full belt trips, have hallucinated all night by accident once, and take it from me as the voice of guidance and experience: STICK TO PSILOCYBE! A colleague had a father who was an organic chemist in California who managed to isolate pure mescaline from some *Trichocereus* and reported a really good experience. Yes, maybe, but the purification is not at all easy and otherwise you will be made sick by other alkaloids in the cactus. Not dangerous sick, no need for medical help, just feeling horrible and nauseous sick for hours. It will pass, but much more slowly than psilocybin. Psilocybin feels like an eternity while time slows down, but actually washes through quickly and without six hours most people are pretty much back down. With mescaline it can be 15 hours, which is truly scary if you didn't expect it.

Mescaline (3,4,5 Tri-methoxy phenyl ethyl amine) has been called the Grandfather of psychedelics, and it was exploring analogues of this molecule that led Alexander Shulgin to discover MDMA (ecstasy) along 2CB and many other wonderful molecules described in his book PIHKAL.

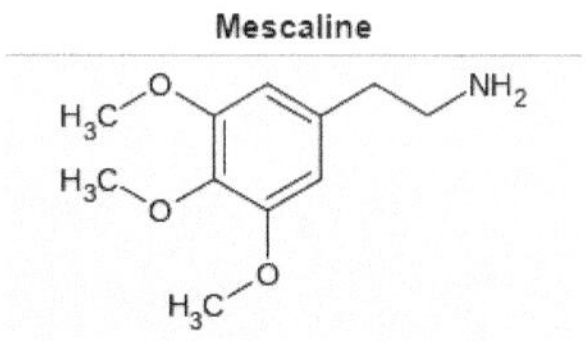

Fig 12.11 The mescaline molecule.

The extraction relies on the amphoteric behaviours of alkaloids – they are ionic molecules in acid so dissolve in low pH water, but become hydrophobic organic molecules in alkali so then dissolve in hexane (etc). To extract mescaline, or other alkaloids, you need to expose a mashed extract of the cactus to both solvents in a specific order, using the pH shift to change their molecular behaviour.

1. Make the plant extract acid – vinegar is fine – and use hexane (etc) to remove oily molecules. This is usually done by 'boiling under reflux', with a special spherical glass jar (that has a tap on the bottom) holding a 50/50 mix of hexane and water. The two layers will not mix.
2. Now add cactus extract to the aqueous layer and leave the mix to boil on a gentle heat, collecting all the vapours that come off and collecting them to return them to the mix – this is what 'reflux' means in this context. After a while – hours – discard the organic solvent by opening a special tap at the

bottom of the reflux jar, and closing the tap when the oil/water boundary approaches it. (This removes all the turpenes and other toxic oily organic molecules.)
3. Now add KOH or another strong alkali to the aqueous layer (+ I used red cabbage juice as an edible pH indicator) to convert the alkaloid molecules to hydrophobic state, shake it like mad, add fresh hexane and repeat the boiling under reflux. If you do it right, the alkaloids end up in the hexane layer, which you remove and evaporate. The crystals remaining should be fairly pure mescaline.

This is not nearly as easy as it sounds, and because it involves leaving a source of heat for a long time under a sealed unit full of a highly flammable solvent it has immense potential for catastrophic fire. I never got this to work in my garage, though as I said organic chemists are used to the reflux setup and can make it work.

The definitive famous mescaline cactus is peyote *Lophophora williamsii* (+ other similar species, *L. echinata* for example, and they all interbreed). I love peyote cacti and have a couple about as old as I am. I love their flowering habits, the way they don't prickle me unlike most cacti, adore their shapes and growth forms. Some are slow motion balloons swelling a few mm per year, others spiral on the timescale of decades. I do NOT grow them to eat. Not, as you will have gathered, out of puritanism – if peyote grew fast and didn't make you sick I'd be doing mescaline far more regularly. In fact, they are among the slowest growing plants on the world, with my oldest clump a plant I bought in Yorkshire in 1985 at about 20 years old. It is barely 20cm across and 5cm high, as almost as old as me. They do only two things fast.

1. Bend their anthers: When the flowers open, tickle them and you will see anthers bending over amazingly fast. This is called thigmotaxis, first described by Charles Darwin in *Opuntia* cacti.
2. Rot: If they get too wet (especially in winter) they will rot, VERY QUICKLY. By the time you notice they look a bit saggy it's too late, they're dead. Peyote cacti must be kept utterly dry September – February, and never allowed to get wet. About 1984 a senior cactus grower in the York cactus society looked me sternly in the face, bushed out his beard and said firmly "NOT A DROP. No water at all for peyote over winter, or you will lose them". He was right.

So you have the slowest growing of plants, and when you eat peyote you consume more molecules that make you sick than you do of mescaline. BTDT – you eat

A Path of 21 Ms

peyote buttons representing decades of growth, to make yourself feel sick for hours, and just get a bit spaced out. Unless you really seek the yaqui experience, don't bother. Better is to use *Trichocereus* spp, which grow much faster than peyote, branch easily (so can be harvested), have as much mescaline as peyote but less of the bad alkaloids. *Trichocerus pachanoi* = San Pedro is best known, and I have a fine specimen in my conservatory which has flowered. I haven't dared taste this one even when I pruned it, remembering what happened when I ate some *Trichocerus peruvianus* var matucana, a similar-looking plant sent to me by a native American peyote spiritual guide in Texas as being a particularly mescaline rich clone. I grow that clone now in St Maximin, Provence at the bottom of the garden by the sundial. Back about 1997 I ate about two inches of that same *T. mexicana* plant back late afternoon one half term to seek any mescaline effect, and somehow later on happened to find myself in a Dorking funfair that evening where they had a centrifugal wheel where people were lifted high in the air inside a giant spinning wheel – I remember it looked just like human wallpaper inside the spinning cylinder, very odd. Then home to sleep – or not, as it turned out. In fact, the experience was just starting, not ending as it would have been with mushrooms, and for the rest of the night it was like someone was pouring multicoloured oil paint on my visual cortex. Forget sleep, it took me days to get back into a normal sleep cycle. Not recommended – stick to *Psilocybe*!

Fig 12.12 My Trichocereus pachnoi *in flower, in the conservatory of 4LW. This has a powerful sweet fragrance at night.*

Fig 12.13 My oldest peyote, in full flower.

These plants have been and are used in the New World, with Mexican tribal cultures that had the same word for 'peyote' as for 'medicine'. In Peru we saw adverts for tourist retreats to 'do' *Trichocereus pachanoi* – san pedro, or excursions to see petroglyphs of San Pedro that pre-date the Spanish. So far so well documented. But be cautious! A few authentic children of the 1960s will spot the names 'Psilocybe' and 'peyote' and recall the writings of Carlos Castenada, an anthropologist who claimed to have entered psychedelic teachings of a yaqui wise man Don Juan in Mexico who (allegedly) gave him *Psilocybe*, peyote and *Datura*, using the visions for spiritual development. I read the books and maybe even half believed them (perhaps an embarrassing confession with hindsight, though I was not alone). I knew there was a contradiction, and in fact the pharmacology reveals the whole thing was an utter hoax. Carlos Castenada reported smoking *Psilocybe* mushrooms, immediately showing the falsity of the story. The psilocybin molecule is not volatile but is very heat-unstable. No one ever smokes magic mushrooms as it would not work – you would end up with a nasty cough, no mushrooms and no effects. Boil the mushrooms in diet coke for an acid extract. Carlos Castenada did not mention being horribly sick off peyote, like everyone is. He claimed to get good effects reliably off *Datura* – when a common bad effect is an unexpected early death, and survivors report nightmares not transcendence. By all means read the Castenada books as 1960s cultural fiction, but no more. Do not smoke mushrooms (. . . or anything else come to that – human lungs are just not evolved for drug exchange . . .), keep peyote to tickle their flowers, and never ever consume *Datura*.

CHAPTER 13

M is for Machete!

Inholms Clay Pit

One of the local features of the Holmwood Park estate is a forbidding-looking concrete tunnel under Inholms Lane, connecting the estate with a dug-out basin called Inholms Clay Pit (ICP). As time has gone on this has become an increasingly important part of my life. ICP conveniently combines two of my long-term interests in one attractive package within easy walking distance of my house! (In case you're interested, the interests are 1: birdwatching/natural history, and 2: the management of brownfield sites for biodiversity. I've been a birdwatcher since age 10, and much later got employed by the CEGB to advise on their fly ash and gypsum dumps.) I wrote a little article about my relationship with ICP for the Surrey Wildlife Trust magazine in 2015, reproduced below, which makes the point that the main woodland block is the same age as me!

To understand this site, we have to review its history. The core of the story is that the local weald clay happens to be ideal for firing into bricks. I was told you need a mix of yellow and blue clay, and we have both (yellow over blue). Dorking blue clay fires into especially hard bricks, once specified for building prisons (too hard to drill) and a real problem for householders to drill holes for curtains or bookshelves. So for a century, Dorking was synonymous with bricks. The dinosaur *Baryonyx* was discovered in a brick works south of Dorking (Skipjacks in 1983), and AFAIK there is no reason to think that this clay differed from ICP –130 MYBP fluvial deposits. There are probably other Mesozoic fossils waiting to be found in the weald clay, though having spent ages on exposed clay in ICP and finding zilch, I have to say that that the clay is not very rich, not compared to Yorkshire cliffs, Kimmeridge etc. Skipjacks is said to have crocodile teeth and an iguanodon. ICP has not given up one fossil! I have a smooth spherical dense stone that I like to fancy is a gastrolith from a Mesozoic giant, and – you never know – it just might be but I can't prove it.

Me and my clay pit – a short article in the Surrey Wildlife Trust magazine in 2015

By a sequence of events that don't concern us here, I now live next to, and am warden of, the Surrey Wildlife Trust reserve called Inholms Clay Pit. The name isn't terribly inspiring, indeed my wife used to think that it really was just a hole in the ground lined with sticky clay (based on the state of my clothes after working there), and was pleasantly surprised when she came in spring and saw that it was in fact a sunny bowl of flower-rich grassland and woodland. For me this reserve is a nexus, a focal point for multiple strands of my life, all connected in different ways with my lifelong love of nature.

To explain this needs a little site history. Inholms Clay Pit is a young site, having been standard arable farmland until about 1959. About 1959 Dorking brickworks expanded their operations under Inholms Lane and started digging out clay to make bricks. Having taken clay out they stopped digging and moved westwards, leaving bare land to its own devices. I like to think that the birch woodland by the entrance dates to about 1961, making the site's woodland exactly the same age as me. The site was abandoned when it ran out of accessible clay about 1979 (the year I left home), and has been recolonizing ever since.

In the 1980s I researched the colonisation of ex-industrial sites, which often have spectacular explosions of orchids. About the same time that my experiments at Tilbury power station were growing the largest colony of Early Marsh Orchids in Essex, spotted orchids were expanding in Inholms Clay Pit. Fifteen years of data showed me that the way to manage a brownfield site for conservation is to keep imposing disturbances. It felt like the completion of a circle when 'my' local nature reserve turned out to be an orchid-rich ex-industrial orchid site. Becoming accepted as a voluntary warden for the site was a lifetime ambition come true, and allows me to put theory into practice.

So now, each visit makes me think of my life trajectory – the woods are my body's age, while the orchids show how nature softens human dereliction with splashes of beauty. The mini-cliffs (dug for bees) are academic theory made solid by SWT diggers! Finally, the ancient hedgelines hide much older ghosts. The bluebells and anemones that flower here tell of the wildwood, cut down about 1610 for fields. These plants have the same genomes, are the same individuals, as flowered there when Henry VIII ruled. These woodland flowers, the ancient woodland indicators, outlive any orchids or birch, and as they brighten each spring, speak of the transience of our lives.

Peter Shaw 2015

Fig 13.2 The entrance tunnel to ICP, looking south from Holmwood Park, Feb 2020. The vertical distance from the track to Inholms Lane (c. 7m) shows the depth of clay removed by the old brickworks.

Fig 13.3 The old brickworks c. 1935, looking east. We only see 2 chimneys – the 3rd (steel) chimney was added 1955. Inholms Lane runs across the upper right hand corner.

There seems to have been a brickworks off Chart Lane (near the Royal Oak) in late Victorian times, presumably scraping off the local clay soil. According to Dorking museum, the first brick kilns were at Stubbs Farm, between North Holmwood and Blackbrook, c 1870. It employed >60 people by 1920. Around 1930 a new brick kiln was built, roughly by what is now Shellwood drive/Abinger Close. This – Dorking Brickworks (making bricks stamped Dorking Brickworks Company) – was a major local employer. Clay was dug by hand – Fig 13.3 shows men digging clay while standing on terraces around the site. In it you can see Inholms Lane, the wheat field that will become ICP, and some mature oak trees which are still in place.

Note in these photos how the land that is now our housing estate is dug-out clay. About 1950 the site was largely dug out. If you look up from the estate to Inholms Lane you see that the lane is c. 4m higher than your feet – and that shows you the original soil level. Inholms Lane is dated to about 1600 and hasn't changed much, so its 'hogsback' shape shows how much clay was dug out to make bricks. So DBC had the choice of getting more clay, or shutting down. They got permission to go under Inholms Lane to extract clay from what was then a wheat field, hence the concrete tunnel under the lane. The planning permission was submitted in 1958 and granted the next year. They put a narrow gauge railway to carry the clay to the kilns – the rails have gone but at one old cart has turned up in the clay along with its hopper, as a memento. I have no photos of this phase, but (running a bat walk) have met someone who remembers seeing men working on the railway, one autumn when blackberrying on Inholms Lane. I met one chap who had played on the claypit as a child – remembering a steep wall of mud, of which no trace remains now. I have one aerial photograph of the site in 1970, showing almost the whole claypit as bare scraped clay, but with two zones scrubbing up to young woodland. (Unsurprisingly these are the oldest woodlands on site nowadays, on the left of the entrance as you enter, also along the southern/eastern boundary.)

One legacy of this phase are council signs saying 'Quarry working' along Inholms Lane. Two still present in 2020, though oddly one was removed a few years before. Maybe in a very belated clean up?

I have made a DIY slope angle meter (based on a school protractor and a spirit level) to quantify the steepness of the clay slopes, and put these alongside old maps/photos to estimate dates to the various banks hidden in woodland and secondary scrub. Although the results are not yet published there seems to be a tendency for the older excavations to be steeper. Most of the pre-Abervan slopes were >30 degrees, while all the post-Abervan slopes were gentler, mainly <20 degrees. Some of the pre-WW2 slopes in the Holmwood park woods are >50 degrees, scary when wet in winter. ICP was thus formed by digging out a farmer's field, and the farmer's family still remembers this. (They are the Barkers – who were led to expect that the land would be returned to agriculture. Around 2010 Mr Barker still regarded the existence of the nature reserve, as an act of betrayal by MVDC. I include his explanation and map in the claypit archives. (Indeed, all the records in the council archive talked of the land returning to agriculture, even defining the seed mix to be used. I have not found any documentation about its transfer to a nature reserve, nor yet of the gifting of Holmwood Park woods to the Woodland Trust.) Around 1980 the site closed as it had been dug out – the operation started at the east of the site and moved west. When the western slope got too close to the cricket pitch, they had to stop, and DBC had to close. DBC left quite a reasonable archive of old photographs, and finally closed in 1981. The brownfield site left was a dangerous children's play site – at least one child died playing there. Housing beckoned, and I saw a photo of newly built houses by the entrance tunnel dated Xmas 1986. I have no photos of the claypit itself though, just the brickyard.

ICP was owned by MVDC, who linked up with Surrey Wildlife Trust (SWT) in 2007. The formal agreement was in 2009, for 10 years, to manage the site. I happened to come along the day in September 2007 that Stephen Glasspool led a tour of the site, with butterfly expert Gale Jeffcote. I enthused about creating insect cliffs, and got accepted as an honorary voluntary warden. No actual contract, but Stephen Glasspool got me an SWT sweatshirt and on the SWT voluntary wardens mailing list.

What was left behind when the site closed in 1981 was classic brownfield – bare land with infertile soil. The main brickyard, with the three chimneys and the kiln (and a lost lake) became the Holmwood Park housing estate, with many CERL staff moving into their new houses here in the late 1980s. By chance, I shared an office in CERL with Louise Stubberfield (latterly a headmistress in Tunbridge), who then lived in the Holmwood Park estate, opposite what is now the bus stop by Westlees Close.

I have spent a while trying to reconcile old photos with current site maps, and have a fairly good idea where the brickworks were in relation to the current Holmwood Park estate. This is shown below, but there is no trace left on the ground AFAIK. I suspect there will be hints of fuel or brick dust somewhere buried if you dig up the correct bits of someone's garden! Note that the lake south of the kilns – known as Durrell's Lake – is utterly gone. It had no connection to

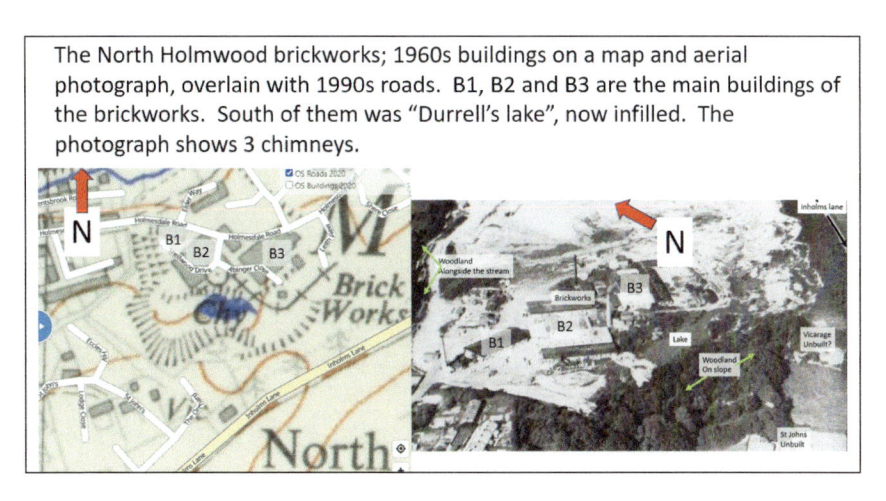

The North Holmwood brickworks; 1960s buildings on a map and aerial photograph, overlain with 1990s roads. B1, B2 and B3 are the main buildings of the brickworks. South of them was "Durrell's lake", now infilled. The photograph shows 3 chimneys.

Fig 13.4 An overlay of old and new maps of the estate. There seem to be no traces of the works now left on the ground.

A Path of 21 Ms

Fig 13.5 The deep liquid mud that once greeted visitors to the claypit.

Fig 13.6 The same view a few months later, with a new hardcore surface.

Fig 13.7 My son Alexander in a cold snap, standing on water upwellings, here seen as pillows of ice.

268

the new lake between Holmwood Park and the brook. There are still water-filled ditches and ponds in that region of Holmwood Park showing impeded drainage, and some of the houses are built on whatever was thrown into Durrell's Lake to fill it in.

The clay pit itself was variously planned to become farmland, an all-weather running track, and (by default I think) a nature reserve. I first explored the site in 1999 when we moved in – the wild wetness reminded me of Lyme Park in Cheshire, though with hindsight they are so different that the analogy really does not stand up. Anyway, I popped in, had a bash at filling in the entrance mud with anything I could find. It wasn't till about 2007 that a gravel entrance was put down – this made a huge difference. The local weald clay becomes 'bottomless mud' that swallows wellingtons, and takes a remarkable amount of hardcore to infill.

Once the site had proper access and a sort of status, things took shape better. Previously some clearance work had been done on site by two men who lived nearby, Alan Holloway (who worked for SWT at Nower Wood) and a big bearded local chap called Peter Page. I think that they created the network of woodland paths, though they didn't come along with Stephen Glasspool in 2007 and weren't seen much since then. As a sort of handover, I did a morning's clearing work with them one day January 2008, learning a bit of site history.

There is another link between Peter Page and the brickworks, because of his local roots. I found out about it via one of my sources of information about the brickworks, who was a local man called Brian Chandler of 40 Chart Downs, whom I had the honour to visit and interview in 2008, aged about 88. He died shortly afterwards. Brian worked in the Dorking brickyard before WW2, when he was paid to carry bricks around. He was paid 'piece rate' 3D = 3 old pence = 1.3 new pence per 1000 bricks moved. Brian Chandler worked alongside Peter Page's father. Peter Page died in a retirement home in Dorking April 2021.

My most visible contribution to the site was getting SWT to carve out two south-facing cliffs for bees, wasps etc to nest in. This is mainstream theory for invertebrate conservation, but seemed a novelty to SWT, and I have seen many hymenoptera (plus parasitic bee flies) there in sunny weather. I still want a proper hymenoptera survey. I know we had the long horned bee *Eucera longicornis* (which has huge antennae), which is scarce. When a SWT botanist Giles Groome visited in April 2021 he commented that this wasp cliff was self-maintaining far better than most of the examples he had seen. There have been quite a few similar insect cliffs that quickly cease to be bare soil but weed-covered urban

A Path of 21 Ms

> ### Inholms lane clay pit: The insect cliff
>
> During November 2007 heavy machinery dug out a novel feature for the site, an insect cliff (high up on the south facing slope, at the west end of the site). This is to recreate the hot bare conditions needed by solitary hymenoptera.
>
> When the quarry was young the bare clay surfaces were used by bees in the genera *Andrena, Lasioglossum, Nomada* and *Sphecodes* (the latter 2 being parasitic cuckoo bees), but as the vegetation has grown so has the bare ground been lost.
>
> New cliff, c. 1m high Sep 2007
>
> Dec 2012
>
> The cliff has aged nicely; I was worried it would be overgrown but dogs and kids and erosion have kept it unstable, fresh and packed with hymenoptera (+bee fly parasites), and spiders.

Fig 13.8 A slide from my lecture on brownfield sites.

commons. I have seen this myself in Richmond Park (try finding the 'bare soil' near Pen Ponds – long vanished!) and the Lee Valley. The Inholms 2007 insect cliff seems to self-maintain as bare soil, which I suspect is the action of dozens of naughty boys having fires/drinks/spliffs/N_2O there and making a mess of climbing up onto the path behind the cliff. This casual vandalism is exactly when the site needs to conserve its biological interest! In a similar vein I have heard a solitary-wasp specialist saying his best friend was the BMX mountain bike, for all the bare soil it creates. I'm not sure about that yet, but I am pleased about this insect cliff.

Since then I have spent hours going round the entire site with a GPS, mapping habitats. My son recalls me sending him into thick spiky blackthorn scrub with a GPS when he was much smaller than me, because he could get into small spiky spaces under blackthorn! The habitat map I came up with resembles that in the original management plan, but with more detail. I use grid cells of 10m × 10m, which is the limit of standard GPS resolution. These are entered onto a dedicated sheet with grid references. Fig 13.9 is an example, showing the distribution of Bluebells in the claypit in April 2020.

BTW If you look hard at Fig 13.9 you can see a single dot on the far right hand side (east) of the site. This is not rapid invasion, but where a different old hedgeline touches the boundary.

This in turn gets entered into a dedicated GIS that I wrote, just for the site. It works like a charm, was originally written to import data from the management

Peter Shaw

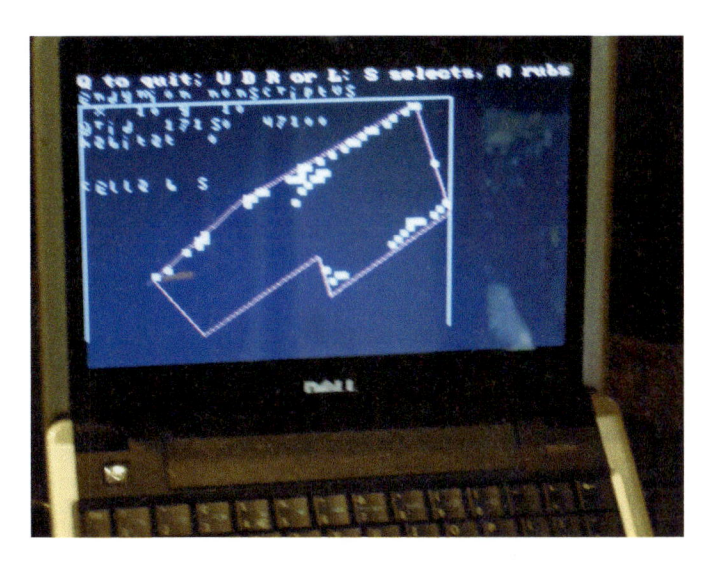

Fig 13.9 The distribution of bluebells in 2020, on a dedicated VISTA machine running my home-grown GIS. Note how bluebells are strongly edge associated and show old hedgelines. There is a clear invasion starting downslope of the main colony. In 2021 I found another medieval bluebell clump, in the bottom L (SW) corner, which turned out also to have an ancient woodland fungus Clitocybe geotropa *that I had overlooked for 20 years!*

plan (which used a different, coarser grid system). The downside of an otherwise excellent system is that I wrote it in DOS BASIC, which is a simple language that came with good graphics capability. Sadly, it requires features in Windows that were supported in 3.1 up to Vista, but then stopped. I lost years of data and of coding when Vista was withdrawn. People say "run a virtual DOS machine", but when you do this the graphics interface is not supported so the whole thing fails. I could, probably, re-write the whole package in R, but the core of my GIS is that it uses the arrow keys to select grid squares – this in turn relies on the "INKEYS$" function to monitor which key has been pressed. This returns a character corresponding to whatever key is being pushed, so I can identify when an arrow key is touched and move the cursor up/down/L/R as needed. DOS BASIC appears to be unique in having this function, which is the one thing between me and rewriting the GIS. So instead I had to buy an old DOS PC, solely to run my GIS. I have big archives of plant distribution each year, and hundreds of lines of code, which only run on old machines. Humf. The code is, of course, archived. It assumes that all data sit on a memory stick in a drive called: /BASIC/dataYYYY where YYYY is the year, Thus the plant data for 2020 are in the folder: /BASIC/data2020, and (eg) its bluebell data would be in the file ENDYNO20.TXT (=Endymion non-scriptus 2020).

To a first approximation, Inholms Clay Pit is open grassland (maintained by annual mowing), transitioning to secondary to willow/birch woodland. The oldest such woodland is by the entrance, the youngest is at the west end by the cricket pitch. This is an inevitable consequence of the way that clay was dug out. The oldest area, area 1 (dark green on the map below) is the blocks of willow/birch carr near the entrance, with masses of bramble underneath. Not much oak, despite what the books predict. It amuses me to observe that this soil would have been abandoned by the brickworks a few years after 1955, so that I can speculate that the woodland is 1961 vintage, just the same age as me! It's probably a year or two out but about plausible. Maybe in consequence, I do all I can to get this block of woodland left firmly alone. This included blocking off a path that cut through the middle of it, to reduce edge effects and disturbance. (The is a point about TQ 17430 47130 where three paths meet – Alan Holloway called this Clapham Junction, as there was a fourth path going off due east into the willows, which I blocked off. The email below explains the logic behind this in more depth.

The east-facing slope at the western end (habitat 6, salmon pink on map) has always been ecologically youngest, just bare clay for years. It still has lots of

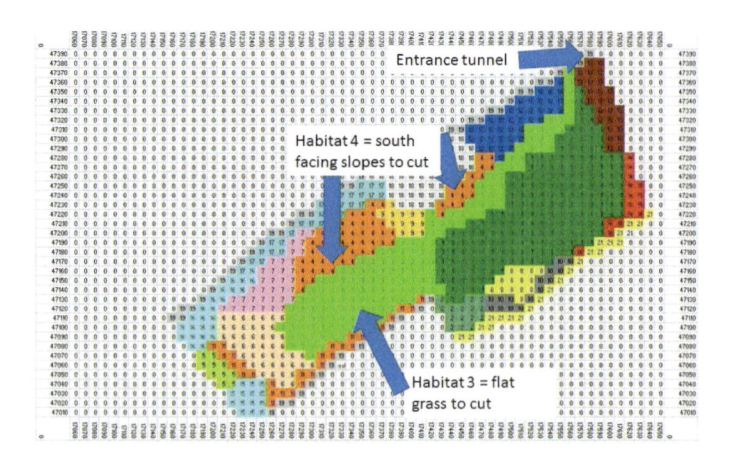

Fig 13.10 The ICP Habitat map. The dark green is habitat 1, the 1971 woodland.

Email sent to Sean Harrison of MVDC 14 May 2020 In response to a plan sent by MVDC that came from SWT, for consultation. It is useful because it sets out the philosophical justification underlying what is effectively benign neglect of the oldest woodland block.

Dear Sean

Many thanks for this query.

I was NOT consulted about this SWT woodland management plan, and have gone out of my way to say to everyone who will listen that the block of woodland near the entrance – habitat 1 on my habitat map – should be left alone to undergo whatever successional trajectory is "natural" given the absence of megafauna. I seem to recall a similar query about the time the site was transferred back last year, and I did what I could to quash the idea then. It's not that I am against woodland management at all – the entire strip along Inholms Lane would benefit from regular clearing and coppicing IMHO – it is that that whole philosophical rationale of the site management should be about creating maximum successional diversity, showing the development from bare clay back to oak woodland, and in order to have as wide a range of successional stages as possible you need to have an undisturbed "control" area, as old as possible. That would be habitat 1. It is also the best area on site for dead wood fungi – check Brian Spooner's list. It will of course also save money, time and effort that would otherwise be expended to dispose of all the cut birch/willow.

I have a database of clearance sites at Inholms going back to Peter Page and Alan Holloway's work about 2000, and can say with some authority that what you get at Inholms by cutting back the birch and willow is scrubby birch/willow coppice of no particular conservation interest. Quite good for blackcaps but not a whole lot else, not worth the effort for any species I can think of. The main interest of block 1 is not its plant species per se but the inaccessibility, which benefits deer and woodcock for a start. Opening it up would ruin this. I made a special point of blocking off a path into this woodland especially to keep the centre isolated for exactly this reason. In my PDF I talk about a multiway junction called Clapham Junction which has 3 paths radiating off it but used to have 4 paths, until I blocked one off to keep the woodland quiet.

> Does this help? If MVDC have resources spare to pour into woodland management at Inholms I'd point you to the pond area (done for a while), the orchard (a perennial sink for effort) and the boundary strip along Inholms Lane (untouched since the 1950s but with a hazel hedge that would like to see the sun again). Please leave woodland block 1 alone!
>
> I hope that this helps
>
> Kind regards
>
> Peter

lichens (*Cladonia portentosa* I am told), and a rare liverwort *Lophozia excisa* (ID by Howard Wallis 2009). It also has upwellings, areas where ground water wells up out of the clay. I think these come from porous shale strata, one stratum about 2m below the original soil surface. I am especially fond of a patch of upwellings TQ1725147070, to the south side of the middle of the slope. This is because one of the upwellings here often blows bubbles! When rainwater percolates through the clay beds after a dry spell what comes out is orange and frothy. I assume these are clay nanoparticles with some microbial biofilm. When we visited Geyser in Iceland, we did see the great geyser do its thing but I was more taken by one called 'littligeyser'. Both for its charming Icelandic name, and because littligeyser was very regular, putting on a display every few minutes. So I have taken to calling the little bubble-blowing mud hole below the cricket pitch 'Littligeyser'. It blows orange bubbles for me about October, as the water levels rise in the soil. The same spot in seriously sharp frosts (<-5C) yields ice crystals like 10cm needles, as the water rises from the warm earth and freezes on exposure to the air. This uproots any young plants, and leaves these upwelling patches bare years after the rest of the bare soil has vegetated over.

In the long term my main contribution to the site may not be the two insect cliffs (though they are a distinctive and important feature) but the oak benches SWT installed May 2009 with new MVDC money. One of these, the closest to the entrance, is only there because I suggested it. Sit on this bench and look west, you see Redlands Wood /Leith Hill, plus another bench (the one on the east-facing viewpoint). So the two benches cover the length of the site. I was sufficiently pleased with this 2to create a memorial stone. I can't carve stone, but punched holes in a sheet of copper saying:

1 May 2009 SWT

to commemorate the day we (Stephen Glasspool, myself + one other SWT worker) set the benches up. The copper sheet was glued to a lump of sandstone, into which I also attached an anchor and a chain. It's not a big stone, but impossible to carry off without a lot of digging. This bench does need its sight line clearing, but has several nice features. The path to it goes on into the main primrose colony, there is an easy oak you can climb there, it shows us the old soil level. Maybe a bit paranoid, but I built up the dead wood behind the bench so no-one can sneak up behind you un-noticed.

Ten years later the management reverted to MVDC, with Stephen Glasspool replaced by Sean Harrison (formerly warden of Sheepleas SWT reserve 1992-2010). Happily, everyone seemed content that I carry on being warden, the custodian of data sets, bat boxes, and beer cans.

Fig 13.11 The Primrose bank to the east of the entrance tunnel. This slope goes back to 1960.

Ecological succession

There is a standard principle that applies to all brownfield sites, which is the need to consider ecological succession. Most areas will have started off as (near) sterile soil, that starts to grow 'weeds', thence on to grassland and woodland. This is inevitable, but the interest is to see what species occur in what order. Often

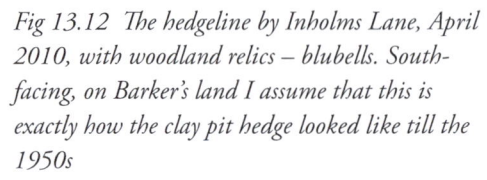

Fig 13.12 The hedgeline by Inholms Lane, April 2010, with woodland relics – blubells. South-facing, on Barker's land I assume that this is exactly how the clay pit hedge looked like till the 1950s

Fig 13.13 Common spotted orchids and ragged robin at western end of Inholms c. 2012

the scarcest species are found in the youngest stages, as secondary woodland is common but bare infertile soil is rare in modern UJK.

In ICP the early stages were little studied, but we have records of the small blue butterfly (very local and scarce), feeding on kidney vetch, a colonist of bare soil that disappeared from site before I came along in 1999. Various solitary bees and wasps used the bare clay too – *Nomada* and *Sphecodes* were mentioned – but it wasn't properly surveyed. The orchid populations show a similar, less extreme pattern, with many hundreds of flower spikes of the common spotted orchid around 2010, but fading as succession moves on to shadier woodland. (This is utterly typical, seen on many alkaline brownfield sites, notably PFA.)

Orchids on brownfield sites are famous for exploding in numbers on young sites, and equally notorious for disappearing as the succession moves on. Sure enough, about the time MVDC took the sites back from SWT the orchid population crashed. The images show visually how *Dactylorhiza fuchsii* used to be widespread then rapidly became hard to find in 2020.

The email (text box) to Sean Harrison explains and sets this into context. In summary – that's just what orchids do.

Brownfield sites have poor, infertile soil. This, paradoxically, is GOOD for biodiversity – you get far more species of plants and far more nectar-bearing

Fri 19 June 2020

Dear Sean

I think that you may be interested to know that there has recently been a sharp decline in the spotted orchids in Inholms clay pit. Being an ex-industrial site it was always good for them but ecological succession moves on and orchids fade away. As an executive summary of what I say below, the take home message is "don't worry, that's what you expect, it's their nature".

The attached PDF shows the decline in 10m square quadrats from 2018 to this year. I was not really up to data collection in 2019, sorry. Anyway, the decline has been stark. One could waspishly observe that this catastrophic decline coincided with the transfer to MVDC but that would be utterly unfair! Orchids on ex-industrial sites have a proven habit of causing political embarrassment by having the cheek to die off at some in-opportune moment. Examples include Meaford power station in Staffordshire, who threw open their vast orchid-covered pfa lagoons for public admiration about 1986, the year some blight fungus got in and wiped the whole orchid population out. The Lee Valley Park Authority set up special barges to visit their orchid colonies in "orchid wood" northmet pit (from northmet power station pfa). This was of course the year the Lee Valley orchids died off en masse, resulting in the Lee Valley Park Authority shipping barges of tipsy east Londoners to boring orchid-free swamps.

It's a successional site and *Dactylorhiza* is an early successional species – you need to be aware in case people spot and start complaining. Actually the main topic of conversation I get in the claypit is about lockdown litter, but you never know what daft ideas lurk out there. BTW Also not many starfruit visible yet, but maybe it's early yet.

On Friday, 19 June 2020, 21:25:06 BST, Harrison, Sean <sean.harrison@molevalley.gov.uk> wrote:

Thanks Peter,

I am aware of the transient nature of orchids. As manager of the Sheepleas, famed for its diverse orchid species, I continually had to bat off suggestions that work undertaken at one part of the site was responsible for the declines in (pick a species) of orchids at another part.

Brilliant though, for keeping me updated about Inholms.

All the very best

Sean

A Path of 21 Ms

flowers on infertile soil, and sure enough the claypit grasslands are a riot of colour in summer, yellow with meadow vetchling Lathyrus pratensis, purple with tufted vetch *Vicia cracca*, red with clover and the hemiparasite Red Bartsia *Bartsia odontites* (this latter promotes plant diversity by suppressing grasses). We have literally clouds of butterflies – meadow browns and marbles whites – in summer, and at least four species of bee including common carder bees. Given the national decline in flower-rich meadows, this makes it a significant local resource.

Another general principle on brownfield sites is less obvious, but came to light at Tilbury power station during long-running trials on PFA (Shaw P.J.A. 2009. Soil and fertiliser amendments and edge effects on the floral succession of Pulverised Fuel Ash (PFA). *Restoration Ecology* 17: 68-77.). This is that the 'youngest' community hangs on near the middle of the site while the 'old' community creeps into the site across external boundaries. Sure enough, although ICP is a brownfield site with bare soil and early successional communities, it also has species typical of ancient woodland – along its external boundaries. Mainly along Inholms Lane, which is known to have been carved from woodland about AD1600. The hazel boundary hedge is now classic old woodland, and in several locations along this boundary you have lovely displays of bluebells and wood

Fig 13.14 The largest wood anemone clump, by Inholms Lane, flowering every year around the start of April. This clone was certainly there in 1999, and I speculate that the original seed germination event could have been in medieval times, predating Inholms Lane, perhaps from a wild boar rooting the soil. (Pure, evidence-free speculation of course.)

Fig 13.15 The primrose on the right has pale purple flowers that denote garden Primula DNA. I have a policy to transplant these.

anemones, both classic indicators of ancient oak woodland. My interpretation is that these plants were present in the soil before Barkers' ancestors carved out the fields and the lane in 1600, and hung on in the boundary hedge of the wheat field. There are also a few bluebells (plus dogs mercury and *Adoxa moschatelina* and Wood melick grass *Melica uniflora* – also indicators) in the southern boundary hedge, presumably by the same mechanism. (There is also one clump of wood anemone by the path on the southern boundary, but I put it there.) Also acting as indicators of old woodland are greater stitchwort *Stellaria holostea* and the fungus funnel cap *Clitocybe geotropa*. A very similar community hangs on in the thick hazel hedge between Inholms land and Barkers field (east of ICP), with plenty of bluebells and one clump of Anemone. I counted woody species in the hedge and got about 4spp per 25m – by Hoopers law this makes the hedge line c. 400 years old, daring it to about 1600 (cross-checking with the enclosure date of 1610).

Fig 13.16 A classic Inholms summer view – a marbled white butterfly on a spotted orchid

Then there is the interesting ethical paradox thrown up by the claypit primroses. I am sure that the primroses here have local genomes going back centuries if not longer. They are recognised as good ancient woodland indicators (ASNWIs in the jargon). Brian Chandler shortly before he died talked of there always being lots of primroses on the banks around Inholms. The claypit has some really nice dense displays of primroses in late March, especially the west-facing back by the entrance tunnel. All the classic primrose yellow, lovely harbingers of warmer weather. Well, actually, not all yellow. There is clear evidence of what geneticists call 'introgression' from the DNA of garden Primulas. This shows up as primroses which are pink or purple. I have long had a policy of digging these garden-DNA plants up and relocating them in the public woodlands on the Holmwood Park estate, where their clearly garden-escape nature looks more natural. This is a simple idea, at its core the same logic as used by international conservation organisations (including the RSPB) to justify exterminating the ruddy duck *Oxynura jamaicensis* (before its DNA contaminates the endangered white headed duck *Oxynura leucocephala* in Spain). But I do worry that this question balloons out ethically on close examination. Consider this horticultural guidance: "Use only native plants, no non-natives should be allowed". The policy of Surrey Wildlife Trust maybe? No at all. I gather from Ian Rotherham that these were among the instructions given to government gardeners under the third Reich of Adolf Hitler. Does it matter to the bees or the leaf-miners what colour the flowers are? (Maybe the bees, probably not.) Will there be any other genes from garden escapes? Yes, thousands, but most will be invisible without a full genome profile. So why move the purple ones? Purely cosmetic I am sorry to say, a symbolic gesture towards the maintenance of the facade of genetic purity. Anyone involved in conservation genetics will tell you that purity is a problem to be solved, not a goal to be sought after. The extent of the paradox is given by the observation that the act of digging up wild primroses in a nature reserve is simultaneously a violation of the Wildlife and Countryside Act, and obeying it (by removing an invasive alien). So yes, I keep the primrose banks yellow, but with a distinct twinge of conscience that someone somewhere might accuse me of irrational Primula racism! In fact I have made a policy decision to keep one small colony of the pink cultivars, in dense scrub under the big boundary oak, utterly out of sight. There were eight pink/purple plants growing alongside 20 yellow wild-types. It is slightly odd the garden DNA flew so far – at least a kilometre. I find it curious that they are all the same colour. This pinky/purple is the universal colour for these escapes: despite the huge range of colours in garden Primulas, only this colour gets out, though in varying degrees of intensity. When I told MVDC they made a historical quip about giving yellow flowers "Lebensraum".

Inholms in the snow

Although snow is uncommon in Dorking it certainly happens, and when it comes the clay pit has its character transformed. I make a point of visiting it each snowfall to catch the atmosphere. For a start you can track animal activity in the woods, see where the deer go to the ditch to drink, check badger activity follow a fox's meanderings, put up a woodcock in the snowy carr. I live in hope of finding a big cat pawprint, but none so far. (It seems entirely clear that there have been big cats feeding themselves on wild deer in the UK, though what species, how many, whether they ever bred and whether any still survive are all utterly unclear. Big cats only live about 10 years and are very prone to genetic problems in small populations, so I cannot imagine a long-term population surviving.) Secondly the site becomes a real community asset. People dig out old toboggans and kiddy sledges and have great fun on the slopes. I like win-win solutions (they are stable to enforce and everyone is happy) and this is a win-win. People play with their

Fig 13.17 January 2021, looking south down the main slope. The ponds are there, bottom left, but invisible in the snow

kids (of all ages), keeping themselves fit, getting a good impression of a local nature reserve, and helping maintain successional diversity by scraping the soil in their sliding. What's not to like? (OK, since you ask, what is not to like is the collection of small bits of litter, gloves etc that vanish into the snow but resurface after it thaws. A standard grumble of mine.) There is one odd and interesting effect seen only in really cold weather, < -5°C. The upwellings of water that typify the site freeze on contact with air, producing either pillows of ice or beds of needle-like crystals (depending on the upwelling).

Ancient woodland indicator plants

Due to the geometry of the site, the residual ancient woodland community hangs on along the edges of the site, mainly along the northern boundary with Inholms Lane, also along the southern ditch. I got feedback from a local who told me "You are wrong, there is no ancient woodland on site". Except the hedgeline, which holds bluebells, dogs mercury and wood anemones as ghosts of the post-ice age wild wood that was assarted in 1610. It seems almost inevitable that these bluebells, wood anemones and dogs mercury will creep on down the slope into the rest of the site – but that I won't live long enough to see this happen much. There are some self-sown bluebells coming up well downslope of the main colonies, but as of 2020 no wood anemone has yet tiptoed over the edge. Research elsewhere in the UK has the ancient woodland plants colonising about 1m per decade, though I guess a steep slope will speed the process. A PhD I examined (Adrian Vickers, Sheffield Hallam University Dec 2001) used fancy mathematical modelling on distributions of ancient woodland indicator plants and still came up with a figure of about 1m per decade = 10m per century for bluebells. Given they've taken about 70 years to cross a distance a bit over 5m these figures seem to fit. (I really should get a good figure for the width of this flat shelf along Inholms Lane, but it's about 7m.)

Because of the rather binary nature of the site's soil history (either soil is generated by post-war heavy industry, or has been sitting there untouched since early farming), some organisms act as indicators of the old soil which are not of more general applicability. Thus, locally the wild cherry the gean *Prunus avium* is a reliable indicator of old woodland, and shows where the iron waste got dumped when the brickyard shut down! At least one fungus appears to be a good ancient woodland indicator, the Trooping Funnel Cap *Clitocybe geotropa*. There is a report of this fungus growing in a 600m diameter circle in a wood in France, estimated at 800 years old. I have four patches, all growing in bluebell zones of the boundary hedge, and unavoidably looking like a woodland relic. I have checked the local woods extensively, and only find this *Clitocybe* in these ancient fragments. (Not true for similar *Clitocybe nebularis* the clouded agaric, which grows in circles on compost in the middle of the site.) The email below sets out how in 2021 I was guided by a cherry tree to explore one particular section of hedge on an inaccessible spot on the southern boundary, and found a new patch of an ancient woodland indicator!

> Dear All 7 Nov 2021
>
> This email is just an FYI, to show how long it can take to get to know a site properly. I have been poking around in Inholms Clay Pit for 20 years and been warden since 2007 and it's only a few hectares I thought I knew the place! Not quite – Yesterday I discovered a hitherto overlooked patch of an ancient woodland indicator!
>
> The indicator species in question is a fungus called the trooping funnel cap, *Clitocybe geotropa*. It is a big easy to see mushroom, trooping in lines through old woodland. It comes with stories of forming huge (>600m) ancient (>800 years) rings in mainland European woods, and around the Holmwoods its distribution is exactly that of an ASNWI, being found in the same patches of boundary strip where bluebells and wood anemones persist alongside dogs mercury. The woodland soil here was protected from the excavators's diggers by the boundary hedge.

> I knew of two clumps of this fungus in ICP at TQ17317 47240 (on the bend in Inholms Lane) and TQ17620 47202 under blackthorn on southern boundary – both are just where I found them in 2011. This April I discovered a hitherto overlooked patch of bluebells on the southern boundary (tipped off by a big old gean, a wild cherry tree, which turns out to be a good local marker for prolonged neglect), and just yesterday I had a serious rummage under this cherry – to find a new patch of *Clitocybe geotropa*, almost exactly where the bluebells persist. This "new" patch is at TQ17329 47065, 5th fencepost west of the field corner, and has only grown about 1m out away from the fenceline in by Inholms Lane at TQ17515 47340, again in a bluebell patch but grown out about 9m from the hedgeline in c. 50 years. Even so, this is far slower than the figures I have seen quoted for a French clone, where a 600m diameter circle was interpreted as 800 years old. If the French clone grew at the speeds I am seeing in the claypit, 600m would take us to more like 2000 years! I get the impression that each clone has its own personality, its own shape (ratio on height/width, depth of umbo etc), as you'd expect for genetically isolated clones, so extrapolating thus to a different woodland is at best speculative.
>
> As a tangential aside, the only place in the north Holmwood area where *Clitocybe geotropa* grows AWAY from a hedgeline is in the "special" ANSWI section of the Holmwood Park woods, where there are two troops of this fungus by the bluebell/anemone zone, protected by the vicarage garden (?), showing this to be a special patch of soil worthy of special care. Woodland Trust please note.
>
> Best
>
> Peter Shaw
> Warden, Inholms Clay Pit LNR

I can see a dark scenario whereby bluebells don't get to take over the wooded slopes. If our food supply chains are disrupted and the good folk of Holmwood Park find themselves in a 'dig for victory' situation, I am sure that the claypit will become a giant allotment and the woodland cleared for food crops. This won't end well – ICP has bottom quality soil (literally) and top quality herbivores. BTDT.

Humans and litter

On the subject of humans and dark scenarios . . . there is no doubt that my main job at ICP has been as collector of drinkers' litter. There was an especially bad phase in 2010, with youths coming in off Chart Downs to be noisy and messy in the clay pit, which came to an abrupt end when the police stepped in on 10 July.

There was another especial problem in the sunny weather of the Covid-19 lockdown in April/May 2020, with far more people using the site than normal (good) leaving far more litter then normal (bad).

This was a country-wide phenomenon, and my experience at Inholms was mild compared to the experiences of popular beach spots.

Fig 13.18 Dorking advertiser 15 July 2010 'Alcohol was seized off a group of rowdy youths at the weekend. Police received several reports from neighbours of ongoing disturbances around the clay pit area. Special constable Martin David attended Holmbury Drive on 10 July. The youths were dealt with and a large quantity of alcohol was seized.'

Dogs

I have a lecture about nature reserves, in which I grumble that everything that dogs do in nature reserves is undesirable. I was lucky enough to be invited back to give it as a guest lecture on 7 March 2023, when it was recorded and made available to any contact I chose. So I sent it out to every warden or site manager I knew. In 2023 it was online at: https://roehampton.cloud.panopto.eu/Panopto/Pages/Viewer.aspx?id=5036833d-2ac5-4cb6-9684-afbe00ca84c.

Systematically, every well-established/retired manager who saw this talk came back to me to agree about how much of a nuisance dogs are. Several people separately have said that they should be banned from reserves entirely. This little story below gives you some idea of how some dogs (indirectly, some owners) can be an unmitigated nuisance, following a not-quite incident in the claypit in 2019.

A few years ago I was sent an email from an irate local warning me of a dog napper on the loose – a strange looking man in black who went off with someone's dog. Maybe we should call the police? The email was actually entitled "Strange man in black". Happily the prized pooch got away unscathed. Unfortunately I knew all about the story. The alleged dognapper in question was me, black and muddy on the way back from a long jog. It is true that the dog parted from the blue rinse lady who was alleged to be in charge of it. The reason was that the bloody thing was chasing after me in order to have fun chewing my leg, and the reason the dog napper legged it was that I was running away as fast as I could to try to escape from the little so and so. I had to climb up a steep muddy bank to get away, and by then we were so far from the owner and the dog was so badly behaved that it took a while to find its way back. Pity it didn't come after me as I was waiting at the top of the slope with a stick and would have knocked it back down the bank with a loud yelp. So my reply was rather terse, with a request to convey the idea that dogs should be under control in nature reserves. I have a publication about how dogs damage heathland by fertilising the soil (Shaw, Lankey & Hollingham 1996) – and was miffed that someone else published the same thing in 2022 and got interviewed on Radio 4 for his amazing discovery.

The Orchard

The site has an orchard, in the land adjacent to the Sports & Social club. The trees – mainly apple, pears and a cherry, were initially paid for and planted by members of the S&SC around Feb 2011. This patch of soil is old wheatfield topsoil, never scraped off, so should be well supplied with NPK. (In 2010ish this land was covered in hogweed *Heracleum sphondylium*, but it's not been seen there for years. Succession is like that.)

I added a few young apple trees in Feb 2020 – Winter Gem and Core Blimey. It has been hard work carrying water / NPK in bottles on my back to these two young trees in the dry spell of 2020 – reminiscent of the French film Jean de Florette if you know that. (If you don't know the film, it is black and white about a Provence occupied only by peasants, and centres on water rights in a dry hillside in Provence, predicated on the highly implausible idea that a malign neighbour can totally stop water flow from an artesian well by sticking a bit of wood in it. As if . . .)

The trouble with a rich fertile soil is that weeds grow fast too – in this case brambles and blackthorn, both fast, tough, spiky and fond of NPK. SWT let this area slip, I let them get away with it, and the blackthorn scrub is here to stay. The last thing SWT did was plant a hedge across the skyline of the orchard, to demarcate the orchard zone. It was designed by an SWT ranger called Lucy Bryce so I think of it as Lucy's hedge. During Covid/retirement lockdown winter 20/21 I popped along to this overgrown orchard most afternoons to hack back

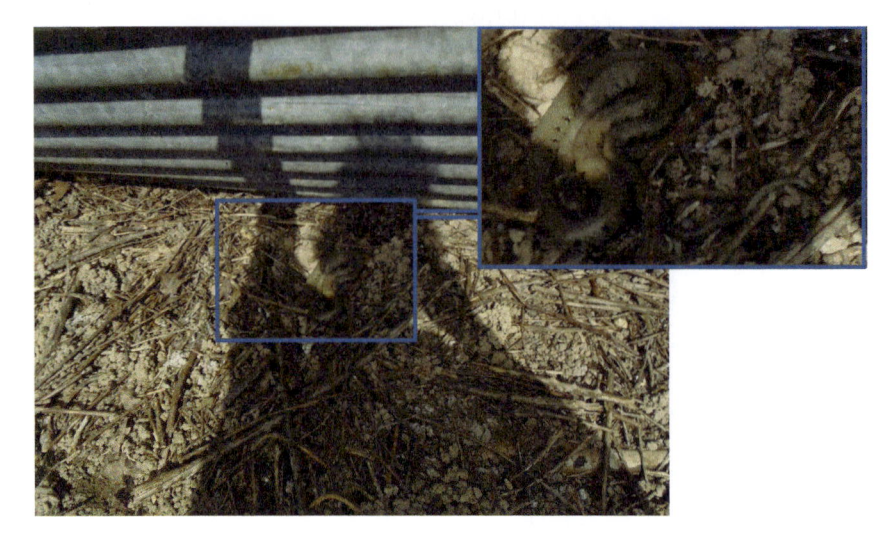

Fig 13.19 This iron sheet was the roof from a DIY hut that appeared in the woods, which I retasked as a reptile sheet in the orchard. Look what was hiding underneath it – a grass snake April 2020.

a few more square metres of blackthorn. The water-on-stone approach, which actually works remarkably well given tenacity. Let's see if I can manage to keep it clipped each year! In the NE corner of this orchard is a sheet of corrugated iron. It came from a hut kids erected in the woods years ago, which I demolished, and repurposed the roof as a reptile shelter.

This is where grass snakes *Natrix natrix* bask, sometime also common lizard *Zootoca vivipara* (the only place in the area I know where either are in any way reliable). My record is four snakes in a tangle together here, though singles are much commoner Sometimes also a vole nest – an unwise choice by the voles I feel.

About 2012 I drew up a sort of map of the orchard listing which apple tree is where, based on labels from planting. By 2020, when a combination of sick leave and Covid-19 kept me off work for most of the year, several trees had died and the labels had all fallen off. Obvious – I use a GPS to map what is where, along with the nice new hedge left as a legacy by SWT. So I went back with my favourite GPS, wrote down the coordinates of each tree, and plotted them out. Embarrassingly, the pattern was totally different to my earlier map, with some trees clearly not in the correct relative positions. The hedge wiggled around by a few metres too. For once this wasn't my ineptitude but a technical limitation in the basic GPS system, which has about 10m random noise added as Pentagon policy. For mapping habitats that's not too bad (though some years the wood anemones are recorded as growing IN Inholms Lane!) but for mapping trees on a scale of 1-2m it's useless. Worse than useless in fact as each number is credible, and over time the average error settles down to zero, so the numbers are worth paying attention to, just not actually believing. Rather in despair I decided to set up a pentagon-proof GPS system in the orchard with a compass, tape measure and labelled bamboo canes. This sounds really simple, primary school stuff – how hard can it be to set up canes exactly N-S or E-W from each other at 5m intervals? The answer, at least in spiky blackthorn scrub that incessantly tangles measuring tapes and where the hedgelines run about 20 degrees to N-S, turns out to be 'remarkably hard'. The key problem is that you cannot use GPS for the last few metres, but have no real choice when first setting the points up. Then, of course, you turn out to need more bamboo canes than expected and you forget to bring some labels along. You should see that all the (eg) the TQ17200 stakes should be in a N-S line (these are the stakes TQ17200 47XXX). Then you check your labels and find that there are three such in a straight line but the fourth is TQ17205 . . . so something is wrong! Likewise, the EW lines should have the same Y coordinate. Iterative as well as spiky.

North and south of the orchard are huge poplars, white poplar and balsam poplar. (These smell amazing as the buds burst each May.) These were planted all around the quarry N and W edges as screening, probably going back to the 1950s. There is a conspicuous gap in this ring of poplars where the orchard now is. This was probably not due to the brickwork managers' planning. Local legend has that poplars were planted all across the line of sight of the S&SC, and one day a clandestine tree-cutting operation was launched by S&SC members to preserve their lovely view of Reigate Hill. It's hard to argue that this was anything other than beneficial to the site.

Pond life

One more notable feature of Inholms is its ponds. These are relatively new, dug out as part pf the 'million ponds' project in 2012. An initial four were excavated, and while one dried up, one did so well that a Pondlife grant got us more dug in October2017, as well as a dog-excluding fence. A pondlife grant paid for some willow removal too, though volunteers helped too.

Why were 'Pondlife' so keen? Certainly when they checked the water chemistry it was admirably infertile, with minimal NPK. This keeps the water clear, and on

A Path of 21 Ms

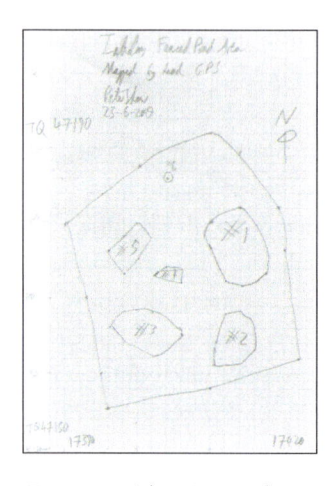

Fig 13.20 The ICP ponds. Before this mapping exercise I was fairly sure that the pond fencing was square. Shows how you can't rely on instinct! The scale is given as metres on X and Y axes.

Fig 13.21 Starfruit at Inholms 20 July 2019.

the whole these ponds are beautifully clear. This clarity has helped the establishment of a very rare plant, starfruit, *Damasonium alisma*. This is one of those iconic plants that botanists talk about in hushed tones as a famously fussy rare native. Not to be confused with the (tasteless, bland) supermarket fruit, this is a tiny freshwater lily (. . . well, monocotyledon anyway) which has tiny inconspicuous white flowers followed by seed heads shaped like a medieval caltrops.

Starfruit is associated with pond edges, and the old story is it likes cows to disturb the mud. I'd never seen it until it appeared in the claypit pond in 2014. Dennis Skinner (not the MP of the same name) made the introduction with the help of the SWT warden Steve Glasspool. It was wholly justifiable genetically since the seeds came from Headley Heath, Heath House pond, so is local genotype. I gather that the plant reappeared there at Heath House pond in 2019 after digging work – doubtless dormant seeds became exposed.

Anyway it's a nice feature, but a bit of a prima donna. As well as starfruit, Dennis introduced another rare pond plant, a fern called Pillwort *Pillularia*. I would not know it's a fern, only the way its leaves uncurl like fern croziers would you know. (I think you need to put the pills under a microscope, when they prove to be sporangia.) Anyway, pillwort is less visually impressive than starfruit but much tougher, coming back each year in larger, thicker mats. Starfruit by contrast seems to explode on bare submerged mud but vanishes the year after as Pillwort moves in. I am sure we will lose it unless I can emulate a herd of cows somehow and churn up the pillwort. Starfruit dominated pond 1 for a couple of years then faded out, moving into the newer ponds 2 and 5.

In 2021, starfruit all but covered pond 5, having all but vanished from the other ponds. There appears to be no more Pillularia in 2021. It may re-appear as water levels fall.

Away from plants the ponds have good spawnings of frogs and toads, and I have recorded smooth newts *Triturus vulgaris* there on several occasions. Definite palmate newts in June 2021 as well (no mistaking that tail filament). I have a record of great created newts *Triturus cristatus* – GCNs in the jargon – too, but this is the standard 'must find' species people like to claim, and frankly I don't believe it. A former EGS lecturer Jonathan Horner claimed a sighting of GCN on campus, in Froebel campus lake. I came back to work after kempo one night with a torch specially to find newts, and yup I just found bog-standard *T vulgaris*. Likewise, no proof of GCN at Inholms, though they do like brownfield sites.

Similarly Inholms claypit has a record of adder, and again I don't believe it. Adders are easier to ID than newts, but my notes record the ID was made by "mad Jeremy", someone I had the dubious pleasure of meeting via Dorking Dive Club. Jeremy was known for his love of buried treasure, and is on record for going into a dive shop in Ewell and asking if they sold maps of the Caribbean showing lost pirates' treasure. The lady there giggled about it for years afterwards, and considered laying in an eye patch and some old maps in case he came back. I'd have prepared a special chart for him showing Blackbeard's main loot stash was left in shallow water just outside Guantanamo Bay, in the hope he'd end up in an orange jump suit. We were quietly warned that when diving with him, always take a handful of old coins and scatter them secretly on the seabed under Jeremy's nose when the air gets low as Jeremy didn't like ending a dive without finding treasure to take home. So Jeremy's adder record is another unicorn! I had a second record of adders from a dog walker, but when I followed the story up they turned out to be grass snakes. Adders are really rare nowadays, as I once explained to a local dog walker:

> "I think it is worth quietly putting out the observation that local reports of adders have tended to morph into grass snakes or slow worms on closer inspection. Just to set it in context, adders are typically species of open heathy ground as they like sunshine, Leith Hill has them, is ideal for them, but maybe because of all the pheasants they are very rare. I have seen one once, a baby trapped in a cycle rut that I rescued. Nicky Scott was National Trust warden for Leith Hill for over a year and never saw a single adder. So yes I would dearly love to get adders locally, turn over sheets of iron in the hope of seeing one, follow up all stories of them. But locally, adders are like local great crested newts, angels and unicorns in their tendency to evaporate on inspection :=)"

Future aims and plans

Should anyone ask me about the future of the Inholms site as a whole, my number one observation is the importance of continuing management, especially mowing the grassland (which will otherwise revert to oak scrub in a couple of years). Mowing is vital to maintain the site's suitability for butterflies, notably the marbled whites. Or heavy grazing, but the dogs make that a problem. I would also suggest leaving the main block of woodland firmly alone to demonstrate the local successional sequence. This means not cutting things back in area 1 (dark green on the habitat map – where the deer hide) more than needed, though there will be endless dangerous snags above paths that must be made safe. This wood is the same age as me, so I feel protective of it. My biggest omission in ICP data is that I have never done a proper floral survey in this woodland. It's mainly birch and willow, and ought to be heading to oak if it had read the books. In fact, it seems to be heading for hawthorn/ash dominance, though maybe oak will emerge later. I like to show visitors the sheer number of dead trunks leaning at all angles, and observe that this is how woodlands are 'meant' to be. This is open to philosophical queries (meant to be by whom? What about mammoths? Etc) but the general principle that your woodland generates lots of flopping rotting small stems is valid. Excellent for wood decay fungi too. A microfungi course at Juniper Hall (run by Brian Spooner) visited ICP in 2016 to collect fungi of standing dead wood, and we added about 100 species to the site list. Piles of woodchips in the muddy paths sprouted good fungi including *Hohenbuellia* and *Psilocybe cyanescens*.

And what would I really like for the site's future? With a nod to my PhD supervisor restoring orchids at Wharram Quarry, I would suggest using a JCB to scrape a large area of soil away to expose bare clay subsoil. This is the whole point of the site's ecological interest! Then re-introduce kidney vetch for the small blues. Really and truthfully, I'd like to see it hosting megafauna to recreate Pleistocene woodland, with beavers damming the ditch and bison churning up the soil. Passing visits by lynx to keep deer under control. I'm also realistic enough to know it won't happen! You can't mix European bison and dog walkers. Given that Mr Barker doesn't like the reserve at all and didn't like an MSc student sampling soil from his fields, I can't see him welcoming lynx sampling his sheep. Beavers would also really annoy him by flooding his horse fields with muddy water, and there probably isn't enough depth of water for them (. . . yet . . .), but as part of a larger return to Surrey I could imagine European beavers moving in and coppicing the birches very happily. Pleistocene fantasies aside, the main thing to keep the site

Fig 13.22 The Willow snow effect, June 2021.

diverse is to maintain a mosaic of different successional ages, which in turn needs endless (though not necessarily annual) heavy mechanical disturbance. Annually you must mow the grass hard on the sunny slopes for the butterflies (or the oak scrub, planted by jays, will take over within a year) and keep the orchard in as good a state as possible to keep up community relationships! Someone should monitor the ancient woodland indicator plants (and fungi) as they creep back out of the old hedge line along Inholms Lane, southward down the slope into the 1950s woodland. I predict they will start to approach the lower woodland edge somewhere around 2040-50, starting with a thin scattering of bluebells. Wood anemones are slower, maybe not getting there until the 22nd Century. I have no idea about the funnel cap *Clitocybe nebularis*, but expect its spores should allow fast dispersal. Literally, time will tell.

The site would be improved as a community resource if we could put a circular all-weather walkway around the base, as has been done on Holmwood Common. I confess to having initially been unkeen on the Holmwood Common hard surfaced path as the common was revoltingly muddy all winter, and this new dry path would increase footfall. In fact, it has benefited both the humans (with a nice safe easy path) and the wildlife (most humans stay on the path, thereby leaving 95% of the land area totally alone). Similarly, the Inholms paths are liquid mud for three months at a time, and this could be fixed with about 1km of geotextile and hardcore.

One final, very long term plan. There is a stream path forming naturally, running diagonally across the site. This clearly cannot have existed until the site was abandoned, and seems to have taken about 50 years to start to cut its own path. As of 2021 the stream was clearly visible as deep (>10cm) flowing water in the willow coppice and the uncut birch wood, and will continue to deepen into a proper stream over the decades. The fact I cut a channel with a spade to help drain the path makes me think of it as my own personal geomorphological feature! Peter Page once told me that the stream ran into the wood and disappeared down a hole – strange, but true. I followed the stream and indeed it disappeared down a hole, a land drain. About 2008 I poured some (home-made from MGS) fluorescein down this hole and the stream outflow in the bottom SE corner went green. So the stream seems to have partially blocked its land drain and carved itself a new path, probably just above its subterranean flow path. It is also forming surprisingly deep pools in the willow coppice between the fenced-off pond area and the old woodland, and will become a stream bed soon. I have thoroughly enjoyed hacking out a path alongside this proto-stream with my favourite machete, and expect that in the long run it will become a natural feature of the site with its own streamside walkway. Open up boggy areas for woodcock and mandarin ducks? I am not at all clear how this neostream should be incorporated into the wider path network, and suggest it stay informal for as long as possible. It will be a useful access path for my much-needed floral surveys in that woodland, which is otherwise rather inaccessible. Where the neostream crosses a path is always a quagmire (three such spots), all fixable with plastic piping.

One final entertaining detail. When the willows shed seed (May) they make so much that it looks like a fine mist, a special-effect gone too far, and eerie mistiness over the soil. Harmless, a sea of DNA!

CHAPTER 14

M is for 'Mediterranean'

Provence

Preface

I have spent a lot of time in Provence, and hope to continue to do so for as long as my health holds out. It is a stereotype of the well-off Briton having a villa in Provence, but in as much as beauty can be objectified, Provence has a lot of truly beautiful places blessed by glorious weather. It's also very French. My first encounter with Provence was a family holiday in August 1975. We stayed in Cap d'Ail, just west of Monaco, and I learned to snorkel. The sea was warm (at least compared to Wales), clear and full of life. We drove inland to the Gorges du Verdon, and marvelled at the canyons with crag martins. I saw a flamingo fly east along the coast – assumed a zoo escape but actually it was almost certainly wild! There are thousands in the Camargue and they are very mobile birds that could easily fly to Cyprus (where I have also seen them). Being so close to Monaco we did of course visit, and I still remember marvelling at the cacti on cliffs in the botanic garden.

Much later, 31-10-1987, I met Catherine Neubert, whose parents had just bought a place in Provence, in the village of Maubec, which in due course we stayed in many times, and grew to love. All six owners eventually agreed that, with the inevitable declines that come with ages around 80, that house had to be sold. It was finally sold in 2006. We maintained a contact in Provence in the shape of Catherine's youngest sister, (Dr) Sophie Roynette, who lives in Calas, near Marignane. In 2012 our summer holiday was a rented villa near Maubec, allowing us to revisit old haunts.

After the death of my mother in 2014 a significant amount of money was liberated. I faced a fairly profound question of what to do with it. How to buy happiness? Cars don't do it for me, nor expensive wines (sorry, everyone!), and my favourite holiday is one where I go sleep in my own bed, wake up in my own bed, run in my local woods and eat a home-cooked dinner. Maybe because of this, I did have extremely happy memories of our times in Maubec. This was – potentially – recreateable, after a fashion, so I diverted my cash to my 'villa fund', which in due course became the money spent on 867 les Batailloles. Shortly after this the pound crashed (Brexit was seen as a disaster chez Shaw) and the effective value of the house shot up in £ value by more than 40%, easily swamping all the management costs it generated. Like Maubec it has given us a lovely base in a lovely part of Provence with some built-in social life. Unlike Maubec we live there alone, but have total liberty to repaint or redesign, giving me a gardening project for the rest of my life.

Provence part 1: Maubec and the Magnanerie

Jean and Elinor Neubert bought their old house in Maubec in 1985, in a joint purchase with two other families, the Caldiers, Jean and (Ja)-Caline, and the Otts (Jean and Claire-Lise). All knew each other by Huguenot connections and family planning (the two being closely linked in Catholic France). It was run as a legal entity with three families sharing joint rights. Jean Caldier had been a tax inspector and Jean Neubert trained as an accountant, so the paperwork was always in order. All three families had children about the same age, and everyone got on well.

Before enlarging on Maubec, I wish to make specific mention of Jean Ott. Jean Ott was the architect who re-designed the Neuberts' house in Rue Rakoczi, Yerres, and made a humdrum if decent bungalow into a really interesting and

Fig 14.1 Here is a Jean Ott watercolour of the cliffs above Maubec, now on display in 867 LB, showing the broken beak that gave Maubec its name.

practical multi-level family house. He was also an artist as a hobby, and left us a legacy of some lovely watercolours, which can be seen in St Maximin, Dorking and Sophie's house in Calas.

The house was, and is, known just as 'La Magnanerie' – no house number or unique postcode. This means 'The silkworm factory', which is (1) interesting in itself, (2) explains the various odd indents in the wall, where cocoons were placed, (3) gives a lovely Huguenot connection since silk weavers were predominantly Huguenot. Some of the old mulberry trees in London are supposedly associated with Huguenot exiles fleeing Catholic persecution. (As a linguistic aside, these Huguenots seeking refuge were called 'refugees', a word that subsequently evolved into more general usage.)

Over the archway of La Magnanerie was carved '1775', presumably the date of construction, making it pre-revolution. This archway was blocked with a hefty wooden gateway, and led to a courtyard onto which each household had an entrance and the rest of the world was shut out. When the Magnanerie gate was shut, its courtyard felt a really safe place.

The whole village of Maubec was overshadowed – literally – by the limestone mass of the Petit Luberon. One set of cliffs near Oppede is supposed to resemble

Fig 14.3 Magnanerie signpost.

Fig 14.2 Magnanerie courtyard, Maubec.

Fig 14.4 Magnanerie gateway, with the 1775 logo

Fig 14.5 The Magnanerie in the snow

a broken beak, hence the Provencal Maubec = broken beak. Maybe! The town is old enough to have a decent little castle on the high point of limestone ridge, and there was certainly extensive Roman settlement all round the area.

Based in Maubec we explored classic sites like the Fontaine de Vaucluse (best flow in winter but lovely and shady in summer), or the Calanques near Cassis (think limestone Mediterranean fjords), the Camargue and the Alpilles. I still think that the Calanques are amazingly lovely – blue sea, green trees and white stone. The downside is that when you most want to visit them in hot, dry weather the Powers-That-Be habitually shut them due to fire risk. I really get cross when the state forbids you doing something fun because you are taking too much risk, though the excuse given is that fire risk correlates with human usage. Having seen how many idiots chuck away cigarette ends in the garrigue, I have to admit some logic there.

If the setup had a downside, it was that we had to make do with a free-standing swimming pool rather than one sunk into the soil. It's a tough life but we coped somehow. Often we'd have communal aperitifs under the shade of big cypresses in the front garden, or maybe in the courtyard to shelter from wind. (This was my first encounter with the pseudo-Mexican beer "Desperados", a long-standing and happy relationship.) Other meals other times were taken under the awning outside our kitchen, or at a round stone table behind the house.

The garden was rather minimal, as expected from a long-deserted old pile. A few trees in the front, Iris along the side and dry lawn at the back. Elinor Neubert persuaded an olive tree, a *Lantana* and a *Campsis* (*Bignonia*) to survive, but really it was hard as plants get 12+ weeks baked at 40C with no water at all, then frozen to -10C in wet winters. Plenty of plants take either, but few take both. I cut the hedge, and amazingly for a conifer hedge it regrew. (With hindsight that was beginner's luck.)

Like many old heaps of Provencal stone, Maubec had scorpions. *Euscorpio flavicaudis*, the provencal scorpion has a brown body, yellow legs and a sting said to be like a wasp. They are a bit off-putting in the shower plughole, and we took to having a torch to check the floor on the way to the loo overnight. I spent time at night looking for scorpions in the old barn at the back of the house, without much luck. We also had a 10-minute walk to the Luberon or 30 minutes to the charming ruins of Oppede le vieux, where the castle was ruinous and open to the public.

Each time we stayed in Maubec, I'd try to expand my knowledge of the paths up / on the Petit Luberon. They were few but steep up the sides, then numerous and treacherous up on top. Treacherous as some were hunters' paths that stopped in a spiky nowhere, and once I really had to follow cairns down to get off the hill before darkness. Another time I made the mistake of trying to get down a cliff, but got stuck 10m up a real limestone cliff in the middle of nowhere with no phone. Luckily I traversed across to where an oak tree touched the cliff, then climbed down the oak shaken but unharmed. On top of the Luberon was a different biotope, subalpine warblers and a blue flower on leafless stems *Aphyllanthes monspeliensis*. White limestone, baking sun, back home for tea, or a beer, in the shade.

Although a considerable drive, we could get to Arles, thence the Camargue. At the park Ornithologique near St Marie de la Mer you can easily get to 20m from hundreds of free wild flamingos, along with white stork and various egrets. Amazing place! Every salt pan has black winged stilts, with white horses and black bulls setting the atmosphere. More nerdy birdwatching can be found in La Crau, some semidesert steppe near the Camargue, but east of the Rhone (where I saw a Little bustard).

The magnanerie had piping issues, as might be expected in a pre-revolutionary farmhouse. The toilets emptied into a septic tank. Or rather, they did when things went well, and the annual visit of the 'Pompe a Merde' removed all blockages. This was not always the case – at least twice I had to bleach the downstairs shower after a nasty rising of dirty water following a mysterious blockage somewhere.

A Path of 21 Ms

We stayed in the Magnanerie before kids, and all family members brought all their small people on holiday to Maubec, so it was a good opportunity for family mixing and getting to know cousins. Our son Alexander says that one of his earliest memories is making a den in a giant reed (*Arundo donax* I think) in a quarry down the road from Maubec. We took the kids to play in ochre at Roussillon, where the cliffs are powdered rust that never washes out of clothes!

Properties pass on, parents grow old for the half day drive from Paris, so the Magnanerie was sold in 2006. We pop back regularly to have a look – the new owners removed the shade-giving cypresses (I don't approve) and sunk a proper pool in the back garden, but otherwise the place has kept its character. The principle it embodied, of retreating to Provence when possible, inspired my purchase in St. Maximin nine years later. As a minor but remarkable aside, the reason we pop back regularly is that we know the next-door neighbour Jean-Luc Rey who went to college with Catherine in Paris about 1980. Translator college is female-dominated, and he was one of the few males in a year group of women. Jean Luc had two children who played with ours about 1998-2005ish. It always feels like a time slip to see the standard children photos in Jean Luc's house because they are (for me) faces from a previous life. He is a real local – father from Maubec, mother from Coustellet (next village north), cousins all over Maubec. As we walked round the village in 2020, he said things like "that vineyard belongs to my cousin" etc. He literally lives next door to the Magnanerie.

Fig 14.6 Reed den, Alex and Louise Shaw c.2001

While Jean and Elinor owned the Magnanerie we often stopped off in their house in Yerres on the drive back to the UK, and this is where I met Jean's brother Paul Neubert. So I will introduce Paul Neubert here.

The only time I actually met Paul Neubert was in Yerres in August 1989, on our way back from Maubec. Paul was undoubtedly a character who stuck in mind, clearly talented and an ex-pilot. On this memorable evening Paul had a temporary business problem, based on a bulk order of combs. Quite why he had a bulk order of combs remains slightly mysterious, something to do with a promotional company. Anyway, he had a contract to take some pure white plastic combs and paint the tips of its teeth with a bright yellow paint. So he subcontracted to job to some visually impaired people who duly dipped the combs into a thick yellow paint. Being visually impaired they failed to see that the paint glued the tips together, making the comb utterly useless. So, as Paul explained to us as we stared at the black binbags of combs scattered all over Elinor's living room, "we take ze clippers and clip ze teeth like Zees and zees and zees . . ." (he clipped all 20 yellow teeth on a white comb) "zen we take a file like zees, and file each tooth like zees" (he filed away at each tooth with a small hand file) ". . . and zen she is all good." Sure enough, having clipped all the teeth and filed all the teeth he was holding a perfectly useable comb, though the exercise took several minutes and looked fiddly. There seemed to be rather a lot, so I had to enquire "Tu en a combiens?" (how many?) I fancy that a pained expression flashed over his face – " One hundred and twenty thousand," he said. I did a quick calculation of how long that would take, and collapsed in giggles. I don't think I have laughed so much in my life. Of course he never got the job finished and we still have a few of these white combs, that turned up when we cleared the house in Yerres for sale. What really impressed me was the array of help he had roped in to tackle his impossible task. Next to Paul on Elinor's sofa was his current girlfriend, ex-girlfriend and ex-wife, all sitting side by side clipping and filing at combs, all surrounded by bags overflowing with useless combs. Quite why no-one told him exactly where to stick his combs remains a mystery to me. I know in general outline where I'd have told him to put them, though whether it would have been anatomically plausible is another question.

I have to observe that this typified Paul – hilarious, excellent company, clearly good at persuading people, but you did raise an eyebrow at his choices. The only reason he needed this daft comb contract is that he turned down a perfectly good job for life as an airline pilot, as he refused to "drive buses" and in the delusional

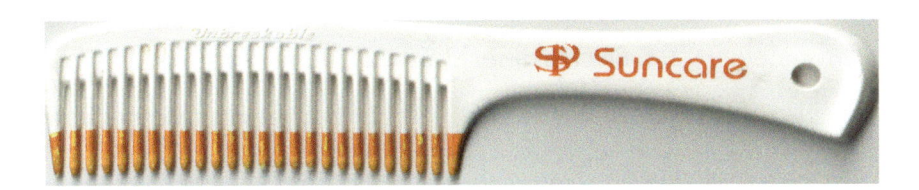

Fig 14.7 One of Paul Neubert's 120,000 combs

belief that he was a talented businessman. He was certainly good at persuading people, but also very good at spending money (before earning it). Having given up a well-paid job as a pilot, he bought and drove around in a gold coloured Mercedes instead of re-investing the money. Because of this his widow Trudy still had to work (as a music teacher) into her 80s because Paul left debts not money and she faced being homeless (the French traditionally rent rather than buy houses). I should add that Trudy Neubert was Paul's second wife, mother of Frank Neubert but not of Thierry Neubert (whose mother was called Lydia, and also got left with huge debts when Paul left her). Trudy and her brother Gabi were Jews in Budapest during WW2 and were lucky to survive. She was told to wait in a room for a train to the camps – but simply ran away and survived. Her brother spent time in a Nazi detention camp, got typhus, but managed to escape despite a high fever, walked home and survived, much later swimming in the Mediterranean each day well into his 80s.

Although I must express some reservations about Paul Neubert's value system, I have to note that on the positive side he initiated the family habit of publishing an autobiography. His DIY autobiography is called 'Ma Vie D'Aventures' ('My life of adventures'), to which his calm and responsible brother Jean published a riposte autobiography called 'Une Vie Paisible' ('A peaceful life'). So the mere fact you are reading this is a more-or-less direct tribute to Paul Neubert's idea of writing bits of his life down for family records. I refer you to Paul's book for his account of his life in his words. This includes memories of being in Vietnam when it was a French problem rather than an American problem. He once landed a bishop somewhere under live fire, pushed this bishop onto the tarmac under live fire and flew off again. He stole a plane from some opium dealers and flew it along an international boundary to avoid being shot down. The best I can come up with is losing a few dope plants in a churchyard in Oxford, which doesn't really come into the same league. Paul also taught US bomber pilots how to fly B52s. As Catherine and I walked around the ruined temples at Mi Sun – each 5m crater was one bomb from a B52 used to flush the Vietcong out of their ancient and beautiful temples – I kept saying "Keep quiet about Uncle Paul".

Provence part 2: Saint Maximin la Sainte Baume ('St Max')

By early 2015, 39FD was sold and the money from Elizabeth Shaw's estate was all in (this took months longer than it should have because a key policy had been forgotten about when the legal firm got bought out). We were in the once-in-a-lifetime position of going villa shopping. It had to be in France, ideally near one of

Fig 14.8 Views of 867 Les Batailloles.

Catherine's sisters. Since Juliette lived in flat sprawling suburbs near Paris, while Sophie lived in Provence near Mont Saint Victoire, the choice was easy! Catherine and Louise led an initial expedition in February 2015 to Provence, to visit the village of Jouques, to find that the estate agent's photos had been over-flattering (astonishing), and the infinity pool was more like the standalone pool in Maubec. Shocking!! So Catherine and I came over in April 2015, and tried estate agents in St Maximin. Why St Max? All the other villages in the area were of the 'two restaurants, both shut' variety, while you could buy food and beer in St Max any time, plus it had estate agents and supermarkets.

Pretty much the first house we got taken to was 867 Les Batailloles, shown round by the owner Marcel Zagari, a painter and decorator newly divorced from Anne Zagari, but still living at home with son Lauren and new (much younger) woman Oana. The house was then 37 years old, so built 1978, and its front garden filled with soil scraped from the local quarry while around it were the oaks of the local garrigue. I think at least some oaks were cut to stumps then regrew, thus we have multi-stemmed trees much older than the width of the existing trunks would suggest. One cluster of twigs by the pool turned out (in 2021) to be a full-sized stump that pre-dated the pool and took me two days to dig out.

To cut out irrelevancies about houses we saw and didn't like – this is the one we ended up buying. The view of snow on the distant sub-alps helped to sell the place, but it really ticked all our boxes.

Six weeks later, after the cash transfer had been made, the house became ours in a legal paperfest in the lawyers' office opposite the pre du foire, St Max. There

Fig 14.9 The welcoming party 19 June 2015
L-R: Vincent Gentile, Marcel Zagari, Oana, Tom, Louise, Lucy Gentile.

were dark mutterings about the town hall forgetting something crucial till the last minute, the lawyer was checking his investments on the Bali stock exchange during the paper signing, I had to write contractual stuff in French just like a school exercise, but it all worked out and we moved in that same day. Catherine needed an emergency run to Ikea for basics like plates and cutlery, helped by Louise and her (then) new boyfriend Tom (and husband-to-be). Tom grew hugely in my estimation that day, as I loathe Ikea and he seemed to get on shopping and car loading just fine. The next-door neighbours Vincent and Valerie Gentile gave us a welcoming barbecue, at which Tom just drank whisky as he didn't speak a word of French.

After that, we had a second home! Mainly for summer holidays, plus as much time as possible the rest of the year. We call it "St Max", or (in this document) 867LB.

Like Maubec, the house has piping issues. I thought – since we ARE connected to mains sewerage – that nothing could go wrong. How naïve. First a plumber advised me to use expanding polyurethane foam to stop a nasty smell from the pipes. It stopped the smell, but also stopped the toilets working. (I had to dig out the whole blasted pipe, as dusk fell in October 2015, while Sophie and her friends were on the motorway on the way over.) Secondly, a lump of calcium carbonate ('calcaire') blocked our drains totally. A man drilled a hole in the outlet pipe, and the ensuing fountain in the flower bed was one of the happiest things I have seen since it meant not more flooding in the studio. I live in dread of a major leak in the garden as there seems to be no way of isolating those pipes, stupidly. (Also, no loft, hence no loft insulation hence cold in winter.). About the only upside from some new houses being built nearby in 2020 was that we stopped getting blasts of really foul smells after heavy rain – I am sure we had been the highest point in the St Maximin sewage system so when the pipes flooded the gases floated upwards. Fingers crossed that one has been fixed.

On 2 September 2020 the gardener who created the site, Frank Bagnol, happened to revisit, so I have an update on the piping. I was sitting by the pool in my dressing gown having a cup of tea and pain-au-chocolate for breakfast when an unfamiliar bloke turned up and said bonjour. Having got over the shock (he came through the neighbour's gate) I was delighted, and we spent much of the day digging up defunct water pipes. For a start we found the supply to the main garden, which had been worrying me for years. It turned out to be under the car port, hidden with no indication it was there and with the only support for the weight of a car being a rotten sheet of thin plywood. So we cut that and plugged it, and whatever happens the former lawn watering system will no longer be able to leak. The same water supply also had a branch to the (filled in) pond, also now cut. The pond supply box was a masterpiece, not just fed by a water pipe that could not be turned off but with several separate 240volt supply cables dangling loose in the soil, one for the water pump (unused since I bought the house) and one for a lamp I have never even seen. I paid a man to isolate the supply, so hopefully will never have to worry about it again.

Having retired on 31 July 2020, I expect to spend quite a bit of time keeping this garden in order. There is a neglected area behind the pool that could become a nice ornamental patch with comfy seating, and the oak woodland patch of the 'Sainte Baume' has a perfect shady spot for a stone table. I have rigged up a hammock, and then a load of old climbing rope (about to chucked out by Eric and Sophie Roynette) which I used to create easy climbing routes in the oaks. I quip that this is to help me find my inner chimpanzee – certainly I do feel happy swinging about in trees. Even so this can only ever be my second home – my first home is Dorking where the kids grew up, the photos and family archives are kept and the nature reserve is next door, where the doctors have my medical records, speak my language, and I can run in the woods at any time of year without risk of being burnt alive or shot in mistake for a wild boar.

It was events of August 2021 that made me look hard and anew at some aspects of the garden and landscape. The core problem is wildfire. In the suburbs of Manchester, on a university campus, in a Dorking housing estate, this is simply not an issue. Even when one is stupid enough to put live embers on the compost heap and set fire to the hedge (oops sorry, Louise – it was 48 hours after the BBQ) the blaze hardly got 2m along the conifer hedge before being extinguished, and never endangered the wider locality. In Provence in a mistral that same initiation would have started a fire that could destroy dozens of houses and thousands of hectares of woodland. People routinely die in large Provencal fires, and anyone starting one is looking at a serious court case. The trouble is that the garrigue vegetation is naturally fire-prone. It's evolution in action – pines especially have cones that resist fire well and open after fire to start a new pine forest in the ashes of the old. Oddly the local oak, evergreen oak Quercus ilex (chene vert) is almost as serious a fire hazard as pines because – being evergreen – it self-shades badly and accumulates great thicknesses of dead dry twigs up in the air ready to burn. Then we have the 'cad', *Juniperus oxycedrus*, a spiky evergreen that is covered in flammable oils. A local said "Le cad, il brule comme l'essence" (*Juniperus oxycedrus* burns like petrol). The wild land that touches our southern boundary is a mixture of all three of the pyromaniac scrub species, and has not been managed for many decades. It has interesting lines of stones suggesting old agriculture, but probably abandoned after WW2. If someone lit this, it would burn to the ground. It was several events in summer 2021 that brought this home, literally. About the same time as we got back to France for my 60th birthday there were two relevant events. Probably coincidential, but who knows? First there was a huge wildfire inland from Saint Tropez, destroying 8000ha in the Massif des Maures and killing two people. Secondly, the Mairie de Saint Maximin sent us a letter about our duties to control fire.

This mayoral letter was a great deal more worrying than it sounds, since it told us for the first time that it is the responsibility of the householder to control scrub near their house, even if the land is not theirs. (This is only true if the land is defined as 'non-constructible', which was the case here.) We had problems believing that it was our responsibility to manage someone else's land, and started asking questions. Our lovely intelligent and well-connected next-door neighbours the Gentiles knew nothing about this and said they planned to do nothing. We called a man out from the Mairie, who said the rules were complex so he would come back with his boss. Sue enough next day two blokes and Madame la patron (the boss) came along, and Madame la patron said that the rule was that it was each householder's responsibility to clear a circle radius 50m around their house. We had first to get formal permission from the landowner, so had to get their address from the Mairie. And that she lived nearby and that the law was clearly stupid and that she had no intention of obeying it herself.

To say that Mairie did not facilitate this exercise is to be kind. We emailed the Mairie asking for our neighbour's address, twice, and got no reply. So we went to visit the 'Urbanism' section of the Mairie, in a different building from the main town hall a short walk away. The sign on the door said it was open from 2 – 5 pm, but at 1415 hrs the door was firmly locked shut, just with a notice saying they open at 2pm (15 minutes ago). So we walked across to the main Mairie, and a helpful bloke behind the reception desk heard our story, laughed and said something to the effect of "no-one worries about that silly rule" before sending us to a secretary upstairs. The secretary made a few phone calls and found someone alive in the Urbanism building who would let us in, so we went back there, rang the bell and got let in, by one rather harassed woman who seemed friendly but overwhelmed with doing the work of the whole department by herself. She denied ever receiving any emails, and when shown proof of the email on our mobile phone, she admitted it looked like an email but that it had not arrived. Probably in a spam filter along with hundreds of other important emails. Then she established where we live, who owned the land near us, and gave us their names and addresses. The wrong name as it happens – the chap had been dead for five years, but his son picked up the letter.

Looking at various web pages and asking Sophie and her friends, it seems that yes the liability is on the householder to keep land clear near their house, out to a radius of 50m. Where two such circles intersect, the land is the responsibility of the closest house, so you draw a dividing line at equal distance. It seems that almost everyone in the Var knew this and expected everyone to know this, except around Saint Maximin where even the best informed and most careful locals did not have the first clue. I drew up a map for our responsibility to find (1) I was clearly responsible for the land near my house. (2) I had two zones of overlap, and needed a detailed GPS-drawn map to decide where the boundaries of responsibility lay. (3) That the government advice was actually sensible and needed heeding. To deal with point 2, I drew up a little excel sheet that allowed you to enter the coordinates of two houses and get out predicted points on the line of separation. This is not as hard as it sounds with a little basic trigonometry and algebra. First you say house 1 is at X1, Y1 and house 2 is at X2, Y2. The exact midway point is at (X1+X2)/2, (Y1_Y2)/2, call this x_m, y_m. The line between the two houses has gradient (Y2-Y1) / (X2-X1). Call this gradient B1. You can express the line between the houses as Y=A1+B1*X where A1 = y_m-B1*x_m though actually only B1 matters. What you want is the line that passes through x_m, y_m but at 90 degrees to it – the perpendicular. This is the dividing line, you can show by simple Euclidean triangles that points on one side of the line must be closer to one house, points on the other are closer to the other. This perpendicular line has gradient B2 = -1/B1 (there is a simple proof of this O level result by considering the tangent of the line in a right angled triangle). So the line you want is defined by Y=A2+B2*X, where you know B2 as =1/B1 and since it must pass through x_m, y_m then A2 = y_m – B2* x_m. Now you know the equation of the line you can predict values of Y given X, or vice versa. GCSE stuff. I used this to add the straight lines on the map.

The government advice that shook me is hardly remarkable, more a simple statement of the bleedin' obvious. They suggested that you should not keep flammable material next to the house, so I had a bit of a fresh look. And realised to my horror that the setup left me was somewhere between a stupid risk and a death trap. The central heating was powered by 1500L tank of fuel oil, under the terrace outside the kitchen. The whole area smelled faintly of fuel. Marcel Zagari kept his firewood there, and I remember estimating in the first winter that the stockpile would last till 2019. That seemed a long way, but I have observed repeatedly that – with patience – the future has a habit of coming along anyway. I was almost right – by the end of 2019 I had just one of Zagari's logs left.

What I realised in August 2021 was that I HAD accumulated my own stuff under there, including a stash of my own firewood drying out, plus some other fire-starters like old cardboard boxes, and 20 years accumulation of oak leaves. So I briefly explored the scenario that fire swept the hillside. The wooden cabin would be torched – dry pinewood surrounded and touched by green oaks connected to the scrubland. This would ignite my pile of oak twigs and cardboard boxes under the terrace. Next to a plastic tub holding >1000 litres fuel oil. The question would not be whether the house would be destroyed, the question would be whether we would be killed by following government advice (which is to stay IN the house during a fire, presumably on the basis that you will not be stupid enough to be sitting on a massive oil explosion, will you?). Get a move-on, Shaw, fix that! So I emptied out the lot next day, to realise that it was just luck that had prevented a disaster. First I moved out all the firewood – good start. Then looked harder at the fuel tank. The (plastic) fuel tank was sunk into the bedrock, and there was a gap about 60cm wide between it and the stone. Over the years this gap had filled up with dry leaves, dry paper, dry cardboard and dry kindling. The whole thing was packed into place on a large bed of oil-soaked rags. Next to it Zagari had stored five wooden door panels, just for improved ignition. I don't think you could improve on it if you wanted to write a parody, a litany of H&S stupidities. We bought a leaf vacuum and emptied the area, me swearing more and more and each new horror came to light. Once fully cleaned out, the space around the fuel tank was filled in with soil, and with breezeblocks piled up around it as a heat-proof wall. With that and a load more clearance, the house might survive a fire. Given that this is a fire-adapted ecosystem in a runaway greenhouse scenario, the question is not "Whether" there will be a next fire but "When". Now to convince the neighbours . . .

While enjoyable, the ownership certainly comes with some pressures, especially when mixed with an international pandemic. The email below explains how December 2021 didn't go quite as planned.

From: Peter Shaw <pja_shaw@yahoo.com>
Sent: Thursday, December 23, 2021 9:12:37 PM
To: Peter Shaw <pja_shaw@yahoo.com>
Subject: Why the Shaws are back early

Dear All

This email is to be sent out quite widely by bcc to a broad spectrum of my email addresses. Some of you actually need to know that Peter and Catherine Shaw are back in Dorking today 23 Dec 2012, as you were keeping an eye on the house in various ways. Rather more of you will have a direct interest in our whereabouts. Some of you don't have any need to know this at all, but might find the saga to give you some passing amusement – it may make you feel a bit better about sitting safely at home in a dull quiet bit of the UK! To cut a very long story short, the executive summary is "we're back in Dorking from France, Happy Xmas to all". The rest is background FYI.

So the plan was that Catherine and I would pop over to our place in France to sit out Xmas and the shortest coldest days in Provence. We envisaged a family Xmas eating home cooked food by a nice fire in a warm comfortable house, maybe having a nice warm shower before snoozing off happily in nice warm beds. We got out to Provence OK a bit over a week ago, albeit after some hours on various government web pages uploading passport numbers and details of negative covid tests which had to be done just in the nick of time.

The house in France is about 30 years old, just old enough that things are starting to pack up. We knew that some b****** had smashed a door to get in during September (immense thanks to all who helped fix this), so had an engineer from a door company turn up the next day to give us a quote for whole new set of super tough doors and windows. To be installed soon I hope.

We knew the boiler had unaccountably stopped behaving, but it's usually just a circuit breaker getting twitchy, so had another engineer out to fix it. We also knew that the old cooker was a bit temperamental and prone to blacking out the house, so decided to get a nice new replacement as well as an upgrade to the power supply (which turned out to be limited to 6KW – roughly two heaters and a kettle). We knew that the covid situation was going exponential again, but since HMG's policy had been to encourage Downing Street Xmas parties it didn't seem a lot to hope the kids might be allowed to pop over.

The best laid plans of mice and men gang oft awry, as I think Robbie Burns put it. First the boiler engineer discovered that the problem was a bit deeper than I had hoped. The power supply had not failed this time (gosh), but sometime during the autumn Provence had experienced a whopper of a thunder storm, whose lightning bolts had been so big that their EMPs* induced massive voltages in exposed wires all over the place, burning out unhardened wiring and circuit boards. Boilers stopped working all over Provence (we were assured). Our circuit board had not been EMP-hardened, and duly burned out. The engineer explained that this design had stopped being made about 30 years ago, could not be fixed or bought, and without it the boiler was a dead lump of steel. (A 1.8m high by 50cm by 50cm lump of steel in fact – slightly undermining someone's clever suggestion of buying one in England and shipping it over in the car boot). Without the boiler we had no heat in the radiators, nor any hot water. It is really surprising how cold Provence gets on clear nights, and we found ourselves wearing lots of thick layers, adding thick socks to go to bed, and generally reminding me of frigid family holidays in North Wales in an unheated farmhouse. Showers were just above freezing, but happily we had a huge steel pot that would boil water (in about an hour per bath on the old cooker!). So you risk hideous injury by carrying a gallon of boiling water to the bath, chucking it in with a magnificent cloud of steam, then run cold water in until no longer scalding (this bit leads to burned toes). It quickly goes cold, but the knack is to ask someone to come in with a newly boiled kettle 5 minutes after you get in, and (if pour carefully and accurately) this extends the bearable ablution window by a good 5 minutes. Not ideal with 6 people, two of them honoured guests. Again, reminiscent of family experiences in an unheated North Wales farmhouse at Easter.

The boiler man went on to explain that – on the interests of national CO_2 targets, all new boilers had to be heat pumps, so we would not be allowed to get one to finish the year's supply of oil sitting in the tank, but had instead to get a heat pump. There were no heat pumps available to fit until March. Oh yes even when available, the best heat pump would not be able to cope until the house was better insulated, so we had to get some insulation engineers out to explain what a big job it was going to be to attach insulation to our ceiling. And that they would have to make a hole in the roof to get in to insulate the loft. Humf. It's experiences like this that turn the public against "green energy".

Then the cooker engineers came along with the new cooker I had paid for, which has exactly the same external dimensions as before (I checked), and took out the old one. They then started explaining something rather excitedly, which turned out to have two components. 1: the new one was the same size on top but half a cm fatter underneath so didn't fit. Normalement someone would saw away the mounting space (solid tiles obviously), BUT . . . 2: the electrical supply it was inadequate, a fire risk, illegal to fit and illegal to put the old one back. So they gave us a gallic shrug, walked off with the old cooker (which HAD worked passably well, but couldn't any more) and told us to get an electrician to change all the wiring. Then presumably get a mason to cut a bigger hole, then they might finish their job. Thereby meaning I had paid them to replace a functional cooker with a non-functional one – thanks a bundle. Another great job done.

Then it became clear that the covid regulations were getting so tight that our children's partners probably couldn't come out, or if they did couldn't get back. Maybe unfair to invite them?

So we were faced with no heat, hot water, no cooking facilities and probably no guests . . . You know what? We have a nice warm home in Dorking with a shower and a cooker, just a few hours' drive away from all relevant family members. The decision seemed forced, and we have come back to Dorking. Sad but I think inevitable – all the arrows were pointing in the same direction.

Was this an easy process? Guess! It was more cognitively complex than most of the PhD interviews I have conducted. Before returning to the UK, one has to upload a special "passenger locator" form to a government web page within 48 hours of planned arrival in the UK, which includes a reference number for the 2 day PCR tests you must have paid for before starting the exercise. The algorithm checks that it really is <48 hours, so if you are honest and say mid-afternoon when typing in the early afternoon it spits the form back at you. So having waded through this form, paid for the PCR, saved the details, the web page gives you a PDF that must be printed out and uploaded to the Eurotunnel page. I generated the PDF, saved it in my chosen path (a special "boarding passes" directory in a special folder), and noticed it had lost Catherine's details. Then I tried to upload it, and got a cheery message that it failed validation, but might be OK with a manual check on a paper copy. Yes we have a printer out there as well as an internet router and spare PCs, so I printed this PDF. (How would a little old lady cope on a hotel holiday?) Did it print? Did it heck, for some reason I have never met before, none of the text printed out, just putting the government logo on each sheet of A4, making its reuse impossible. I started by getting screendumps of each half page and printing each screendump as a separate jpg but the silly coloured fonts didn't work well. Thankfully Catherine's sister Sophie lived nearby and has a PhD in physics, so we emailed it to her and she generated a hard copy (though missing Catherine's details for reasons I still don't understand).

A day later we arrived in the Paris suburbs, to stay with sister Juliette. I did get a strange feeling as we turned right off the main road when I always thought it was left, buy hey I'm not a local. A little while later, utterly lost, I rather lost patience, mea culpa, and suggested that we put the address into Google maps. The French state has not caught up with postcodes, but I could search the google database for the street name. Yes, Google maps on my phone found a Rue Jaque Cartier about 4 minutes away, and I navigated us there successfully. Was it the correct Rue Jaques Cartier? No, there turned out to be at least two . . . (This is why you need postcodes.) Eventually we parked next to the town hall and waited to be rescued.

The next day we had to get pharmacy to certify us a negative lateral flow test before being allowed home. So we got up early, got the pre-booked Paris pharmacist to tickle our noses, and they said that normalement we'd have the paper copy of our certificates in half an hour. Half an hour later Catherine went in, and I waited outside. This pharmacist was between us and the Eurotunnel booking, after a long drive to Calais. So I waited, and waited, and waited. Guess what? They had a computer fault. It was nearly an hour before someone kicked the power supply or reloaded the system or whatever it took. By time the print out actually came I'd gone off to find the maps that had fallen out of my pocket (did I find them? No of course not), and Catherine couldn't find me, so she called my phone which had just experienced a system fault and died. I came back to the car to fiddle with my phone's power supply, to find Catherine (good), but that she had lost her phone (bad). We had to wait till my phone had charged, got itself together, and tell me that due to a system fault it needed to reload and ask me whether would I like to reset all my data (NO! DON'T!!). Eventually it rebooted, and I was able to call her phone, which had fallen down the back of the seat. Phew . . . We drove to Calais, got to the Eurotunnel check-in, and the chap behind the desk said he couldn't find the passenger locator form that I painfully uploaded 48 hours before. It's what I dread most "Le ordinateur dit 'non'". So he phoned someone, chatted cheerfully with them, and they obviously told him to look in the correct place because was there AOK when he actually looked. After 10 minutes of worry during which time I was facing an indeterminate future in some guest house in Calais over Xmas, and a queue of tense cross Brits built up behind us. Eventually the passenger locator form turned up just where I had put it (he never asked for the paper copy of course, or spotted that Catherine's details were missing), and we were let through. Then the French border chap looked hard at his computer and our UK passports, and pointed to a date stamp while waving his fingers excitedly. It turns out that we had outstayed our allowed time in France (90 days in 180) and he might hold onto our passports to enforce the subsequent fine. Pas de problem – we are dual national, and when he saw we were actually French he became charm embodied, returning passports with a smile. A cheery "Good Afternoon" to the UK guard (no administrative problems – gosh!) and got actually on board the train. Oh yes a minor tweak is that they don't allow you out of the car in the Eurotunnel now (first time ever – they always did before). So to change drivers we had to invent a new physical exercise – Eurotunnel yoga, in which the passenger prostrates themselves across the back seat luggage in a position I quipped as "salute to the suitcase", while the driver does a 2-chair leg stretch without sitting on the pointy bit of the handbrake. I never thought I'd be glad to see the M25! Could we go straight home? No, we had to go first to the pharmacy to collect our 2 day PCR test kit before they shut for Xmas, getting there with several minutes to spare. Once home, we still were not home and dry (as it were . . .). To catch the last posting before Xmas we had to swab our tonsils and post the sealed Covid-swab tubes off to the dedicated lab before sitting down with a cup of tea.

So, thankfully, we're home. So far so good – not even any dead mice (yet anyway.)

As a reflection, the administration of the Covid regulations was so complex that it would have looked rather implausible in a 1950s Isaac Asimov sci-fi story. People would have laughed at the mind bending complexity, then said something like "Come on, we can split the atom but this complexity really is a bit far fetched". The process involved 3 wifi-enabled internet routers, 2 laptops, 2 printers and 2 internet-enabled smart phones. We had to create, download, store, forward and re-upload a PDF file. I am quite sure my late-lamented parents (bright forward thinkers in their day) would have been unable to visualise the IT architecture, let alone navigate it. How on earth a normal tourist is ever meant to make it work is beyond me – I wonder whether it is designed to be so hard as to stop people going abroad on holiday. More likely the people behind its design were so embedded in an internet culture that the idea of NOT having internet access would be outside their world view, as incomprehensible as not having a credit card (which, BTW, was a mandatory condition). Or presumably as not having spare cash or an IQ above 100. There seem to me to be some issues of exclusion here, but maybe I am being a naïve idealist again?

Kind regards

Peter Shaw 23 Dec 2021
Warden, Inholms Clay Pit LNR

*EMP = Electromagnetic Pulse. This is basically a radio wave with enough energy to induce measurable voltages in exposed copper cables. In York University in the early 1980s, each terminal was connected to a central server by unshielded copper cables hundreds of metres long, and each time there was a thunderstorm the voltages induced by the lightning were enough to burn out a few chips in a few monitors. At the start of a nuclear exchange, expect that the first thing to happen will be a megaton-range exo-atmospheric blast that creates a huge EMP that burns out every unshielded chip in the underlying countries, unless the circuits are EMP hardened. This is why military aircraft have EMP-hardened circuits. It is easy to EMP a circuit – you wrap in in aluminium foil, and the faraday cage effect protects the contents. I keep my memory sticks in a steel box for this reason. Clearly our boiler designer 30 years ago never thought about this. (in a separate EMP incident, our router had been burned out by a thunderstorm EMP a few years ago, and we were assured that this router design burned out all over Provence.) To be fair no-one in our banking system seems to worry about EMPs either. It's not just a lightning and nuclear blast do this – the sun can as well. Look up the Carrington Event of 1859 – if that solar flare happened tomorrow most of our computers and microchips would burn out and never work again. https://www.nationalgeographic.com/science/article/110302-solar-flares-sun-storms-earth-danger-carrington-event-science

Dear Anne
 Thanks for these kind wishes. We are now safely back home, hoping it's all over for this xmas. Hoping yours went well.
 . . . and, given all the events described below, when I saw some sickly sweet advert for some programme themed around "the best Christmas ever" I wanted to get my hands on whoever said that to explain a few things . . .
 See you in January in the lab

Peter Shaw

On Saturday, 25 December 2021, 20:01:19 GMT, Anne Robertson <a.robertson@roehampton.ac.uk> wrote:

Crikey Peter -never a dull moment! I hope the casualty survived.

Best wishes
anne

Anne Robertson
Professor of Ecology

> **From:** Peter Shaw <pja_shaw@yahoo.com>
> **Sent:** 25 December 2021 10:07
> **To:** [snip]
> **Subject:** Re: Why the Shaws are back early
>
> Dear Anne
>
> Thanks for the wishes. Despite your kind hope, this Xmas has not quite gone to plan so far. No sleigh bells last night. Last night, Christmas Eve, we were sitting down quietly about 2130 thinking "phew made it", when there was a weird big huge deep banging noise, more of a dull thud amplified. A firework maybe? Something in the loft?? We looked around a bit, no sign. Then Catherine looked out of the window to see headlamps in a pile of timber where our cherry tree should be. A chap had a heart attack at the wheel and ploughed down the hill into our front garden. He would have demolished the front of the house had the tree not stopped him. I did CPR straight out of university first aid courses for 5 minutes, and think that he may have survived. This was the third time I have pulled someone from a car crash. The first time they were on fire, the second time they were soaked in blood, this third time he was effectively dead. (The floppy inert lump of a dead body is remarkably hard to handle – I used a judo hip throw to move him.) The lamppost and tree are gone, having saved our house from demolition. As an aside, the Range Rover snapped a mature cherry tree and a lamp post, but its bonnet was hardly dented. I don't know if this is good design, or terrifying for what it would do when it hit someone. Should have been designed with a crumple zone.
>
> Best
> Peter

Brexit and this house are of course the reason I applied for French citizenship, getting my second nationality in December 2019 and a French passport shortly afterwards. The ceremony was in the Embassy in Kensington, a memorable experience in which we drank champagne and sang the Marseillaise under a photo of Emmanuel Macron. To get this I had previously to prove my ability to speak French, which was altogether more challenging. The test was held in the HQ of the Alliance Francaise in London (not in the embassy nor anywhere near it), and involved a comprehension test just like the sort of thing I had to do at school from 1972-1976. Among other things we listened to stories in French and answered questions about them. One was a fictitious interview with a fictional French pop star, followed by questions like "why did he choose that Caribbean island to set up his recording studio". As one of the blokes on the same course grumbled, "that was a real b******". I also had to chat in French with two pretty young women about pretending to want to join a French astronomical society, which was more familiar – very much like a soiree chez Sophie Roynette (but without the wine). I talked about binoculars, telescopes and the total eclipse we saw in Brittany 1999. The building this was held in used to be the HQ of the French government-in-exile in WW2 and was full of WW2 memorabilia, including some grim accounts of what the Nazis did to resistance leaders. It happened to be the end of Eid, and it seemed like many of the London Middle Eastern community lived nearby and were out in the sun celebrating, so the local park (St James) was full of Muslims in colourful headscarves enjoying ice cream and sweet drinks. The culture clash of modern UK Islam with WW2 France was stark and odd feeling, an island of the sort of stuff my parents grew up under in a sea of neo-Arabic, and since my cultural leanings are hard 21st century Anglophone science leavened with a touch of 1960s psychedelic liberalism, I didn't really feel I belonged in either. Anyway I got a B2, which is fluent enough for a passport, but not to claim that I'm a native speaker.

In the embassy I was only four months post-operative and had some facial asymmetry if you look hard. No-one seemed to notice apart from me, or if they did were too polite to comment.

Fig 14.10 I gain French nationality. In the embassy, with my certificate December 2019.

CHAPTER 15

M is for Meltdown!

EGIFF

The rest of this publication has been wholly retrospective, setting out my personal history in the hope that someone in the future may pay some passing attention to my life (if only to shake their heads in disbelief). This final chapter is utterly different, a prediction of a dystopian future based on some simple mathematical analyses of publicly available data about Planet Earth. Whatever the future thinks of me, I hope that someone will take the time to put my numerical predictions (especially of CO_2, global temperature and Arctic ice cover) against what actually happened. I think that my predictions deviate from the current scientific consensus after about 2100, and actually very much hope that I am wrong! You will see why. This version of the future looks so destructive of so many things that make life worth living that I want it to be wrong. The trouble is that the mathematics look inexorable. I explore this with a short work of fiction, whose details will undoubtedly not come to pass! Its lifestyle predictions, however, may focus a few minds on what is coming as the Arctic permafrost thaws out, and the timescales that humanity needs to engage with.

In doing this I am, at best, putting down a bid to go down in history as a scientific Cassandra. Not that this does much good – Garry Kasparov told us exactly what Putin was like in his terrifying book 'Winter is coming', and has been proved alarmingly right, for all the difference it seems to have made. The trouble is that I see things that most people don't. (And don't see things that normal people do see, like styles of clothing!) The story that haunts me, the 'Phew, we didn't deserve to get away with that gamble' story, concerns an old chestnut tree in Whitelands College. It was tall, wide, old, and just next to our shiny new student accommodation block, which it towered over. Too close for safety in fact – had it all gone wrong, I fear the council may have had some liability for giving permission for the development so close to such a dangerous tree. It's not till you encounter bits of falling tree that you understand how awfully heavy they are, as well as awfully high up and awfully hard. BTDT – handle with caution! But I kept noticing big crops of mushrooms around this old chestnut each autumn, and I knew my mushrooms well enough to know it was the honey fungus *Armillaria mellea*. This is a complex of multiple lineages, some proven tree killers, the rest just active decayers of dead timber. It is notorious for being a warning that a tree is dying, liable to fall, so therefore dangerous. Every tree surgeon knows honey fungus (and fears it, for what it means). Worse, after a few years the Armillaria started to decline but a new fungus appeared alongside it, *Meripilus giganteus*. This is a parasite on the honey fungus, and shows that the decay process is approaching its end. It was the mushroom community screaming "This tree is going to fall over". I had the dubious honour of sitting on some college Health and Safety committee at the time, and made a point of telling them about the danger posed by the tree. I think I even got it put on some agenda as an A.o.B., but no action came. One day the college principal (who sat on the same H&S committee) suggested that we game-play what would happen in a genuine emergency, maybe a terrorist attack, and asked the committee for suggestions of scenarios to consider. I told them to consider what would happen if the big old chestnut were blown over by a westerly gale, because I knew it was dangerous. "The mushrooms told me," I explained. Maybe word had got out about me and *Psilocybe* mushrooms, because they smiled, then carried on as though I had said nothing. Presumably they had decided I stood under the tree in a stoned but transcendent state and received mystical visions from the tree telling me of imminent catastrophe.

Of course, the main gale-force winds here almost always come from the west. If that tree had been blown over it would probably have fallen east, smashing the building. Then, fortunately, shortly afterwards, on a still calm windless night in April 2010, the chestnut fell over with no provocation whatsoever. It fell towards the west, causing no property damage, but shattering a large mature oak which it landed on. When I told the tree surgeon (who tidied up the mess) about my mushroom story, his comments were unprintable. Paraphrasing and removing the expletives, he said that they had planned to send men up that tree to trim it, but would never have considered doing something so risky if they had known what I told them about the mushrooms. (Shortly afterwards the university took on a professional arboriculturist, Mark Clews, who knew his trees and his mushrooms, and I think all should be safe in his hands.) The failure of management to take my warnings seriously had not just risked students' lives (which I think to be

Fig 15.1 The Whitelands chestnut 2010, fallen away from the student lodgings. Now imagine what it would have done if it had fallen the other way.

unforgiveable), but tree surgeons' lives too. I still feel a sense of failure that no-one listened to me, that we got away without killing 20 students by sheer good luck.

Cassandra was a character in Greek mythology cursed by the God Apollo always to speak the truth, but never to be believed. I know the feeling. So it is that when I started playing with public data relating to the greenhouse effect and saw something scary in the r2 values, I have tried telling people: "There is a real problem coming our way – the exponential coefficients told me so." So people smile, ignore me, and carry on unchanged. Presumably they see me as getting some kind of mystical kick out of my computer coding? Maybe reading this story might get a few people to realise that maths, like mushrooms, can give useful predictions about what is coming up. There is a reason that the kids in my story keep asking the adults "Did no-one see it coming?".

In June 2022, BBC Radio 4 ran a short series about climatic tipping points. (See https://www.bbc.co.uk/programmes/m00180cc/episodes/guide) The first episode opens with the presenter Justin Rowlatt saying "if you are listening to this on a podcast in the year 2122, I just want to say that I am sorry. Our generation messed up". He saw the sort of things coming down the track that I tell of. About the same time (6 April 2022) a NASA data analyst Peter Kalmus took to direct action, chaining himself to a branch of the Chase Manhattan bank, to try to get his climate protest noticed. Another 1200 scientists and analysts took part in action that day for the same reason. I have once written a book on multivariate analysis, and am so bothered by the trends in the data that I have been moved to write a children's story in the hope of jolting people's awareness. When scientists and data analysts start going wobbly, humanity should get scared as a species because we see the patterns in the data while they are just details withhin computer outputs, long before they become a howling reality that destroys lives and societies.

Prelude – The Exponential Growth in Forcing Function.

At the core of this story is the mathematics of exponential growth. This is the doubling-doubling again mathematics that underlies doors slamming in the wind, population explosions (eg rabbits in Australia), epidemic explosions (eg the rapidly evolving variants of Covid-19 during 2021/2022), and nuclear explosions. I would love to claim that it was my discovery that global carbon dioxide (henceforth CO_2) is growing exponentially, and indeed I did discover this in 2021 using public data from NOAA, but in fact someone else got there first, publishing this disturbing factoid in 2009 (Hoffman et al 2009). In fact when I contacted NOAA, Pieter Tans pointed out that my estimate of the doubling time (c. 120 years) was too optimistic – if you plot $\log(CO_2-280)$ against time it is almost perfectly linear, showing it to be exponential. Why 280? This is the pre-industrial level. The doubling time on this model is 31 years. Frankly, on a planetary scale a doubling time of 31 years would be effectively instantaneous, too fast to show up in the fossil record except as a sudden switch, just like we see at the Permo-triassic boundary (251MYBP) or the Palaeocene-Eocene (55mybp). Why this has not been emphasised is beyond me, it is the most important and scary thing I have uncovered.

I have probably spent more time chewing over exponential CO_2 models than is really necessary. They all agree to within a few ppm over the kind of timescales I can realistically expect to see, and anyway the only difference of substance will be in the lower cells in an excel spreadsheet. I can confirm that this '280 ppm offset' model has a much shorter doubling time, 31 years against 120 for the 'zero offset'. The figure of 280 is of course the pre-industrial level of CO_2. The more I try to justify this based on the underlying physical processes, the less I can see how it works. The CO_2 present before we kicked off the industrial revolution – why is that a static pool, not growing like the newer molecules? How does a peat bog know about 280 ppm? At a philosophical level, I cannot see how Planet Earth can 'know' that 280 is a special figure. I have explored various combinations of offset and date range to see how changing the offset changes the overall fit. It is true that the r2 value is very slightly higher for the 280 ppm offset than for zero offset, but a different index of goodness of fit (Aikike's Information Criterion – AIC) consistently finds that the best model has zero offset. Also, there is a linear decrease in doubling time with increasing offset, which looks worryingly like a simple mathematical artefact to me.

A Path of 21 Ms

For readers in the 21st century, the question of whether or not to include an offset (280 ppm) in the equation is a minor nerdy aside. The difference between these models blossoms out a century later, where the much shorter doubling time of the 280ppm offset model leads to all-out oxidation of the planetary soil carbon within a few generations, while the more leisurely zero offset model suggests a doubling time around 120 years, allowing us time to take stock. It is almost certainly optimistic and naïve to hope that the net outcome of lots of human decisions and natural decay processes can be predicted reliably with one simple equation with just one key parameter. Call me an idealist, but I do like to try! Perhaps typically for a scientist, even for a fictional short story, when I make predictions about the CO_2 levels, marine pH etc experienced by children in 2160, I like to have some confidence in the model I use.

The problem can be seen by looking at the basic graph of $\log(CO_2)$ against time (Fig 15.2). If the process were a nice simple exponential this graph would be a straight line. Gordon Moore gave us a nice example of this. But this graph is not straight – the line is bending upwards! This means that it is faster than a simple exponential, a new experience for me.

If I have done any original analyses here at all, it is to write R code to extract doubling times from sub-windows in the data, to check how stable the doubling

Fig 15.2 A graph of atmospheric CO_2 after a logarithmic transformation. This appears to show that the growth is faster than an exponential model, because the points curve upwards away from the fitted straight line.

Fig 15.3 Extrapolating the two competing exponential models forward. Note how both fit current data almost perfectly, but disagree wildly about the rate at which the function takes off.

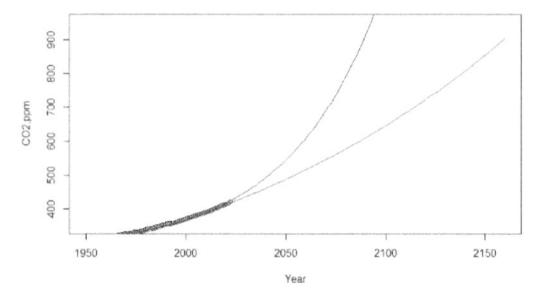

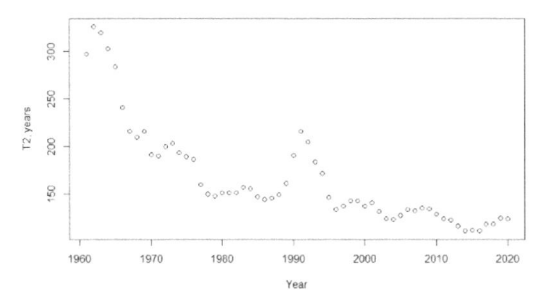

Fig 15.4 The estimated CO_2 doubling time for a range of values of a shifting seven year window. Note how the Pinatubo eruption (1991), which caused planetary cooling, shows as a blip.

time estimates are. Taking a sliding seven-year window we can get multiple estimates for planetary CO_2 doubling time for each year from 1963 to 2020 (Fig 15.4)

Note that in this case the Y variable means a doubling time – low values are more scary because they mean faster growth. Something happened in 1991 causing the exponential growth to slow. That something was almost certainly Pinatubo, a volcano that cooled the planet by about 0.4C for two years. So, I think, cooling the planet slows the greenhouse. As a logical corollary of this, warming the planet will certainly not help! Because of this, my subsequent model only use data after 1993, when when the Pinatubo effect faded and the doubling times stabilised (to 124 years). Let's see if they stay stable – I have my doubts. Here is why:

> It was the Pinatubo blip that gave me a deep new insight into this process. I mention it here and leave it to history to assess whether Planet Earth actually agrees with my equations in years to come! So there are actually four little observations that don't quite fit the "pure exponential" model of CO_2 growth. (1) The short but clear blip – reduction in the rate of CO_2 growth – in a short period following Pinatubo in 1991 [fig 15:4], which should not have happened if the growth parameters were global constants just displaying year-on-year random variation. (2) The log-tranformed graph still curves upwards [fig 15: 2] even though it should be a straight line. (3) The model fit improves if we use log(CO2-280) rather than log(CO2), as noted above. Pure exponential curves do not do not behave this way. (4) The exponential parameter correlates positively with temperature – or if you prefer, the doubling time reduces as temperature increases. Again, this should not have happened if the growth parameters were global constants just displaying year-on-year random variation. (As an aside, this correlation is significant for all indices of planetary temperature, but is strongest and

most significant if we correlate the parameter with the temperature just of the seas.)

So I tried making a model in which CO_2 grows exponentially, but the exponential coefficient is linearly related to temperature, using parameters calculated from the data. I call this the accelerated model – not just exponential growth, but faster than exponential. This is done step-by-step: For each year, its initial CO_2 determines global temperature, then this temperature determines doubling time, then doubling time determines CO_2 growth hence CO_2 at the start of next year. Worryingly, this model fitted the data very well. It curves upwards after log transformation just like the real data, and just like the real data its fit is improved with an offset. (I have graphed how the r2 value alters with the value of the offset both for real data and for the accelerated model, and the response looks very similar, peaking at 250ppm in both cases.) The high sea temperatures in 2023 will provide a good test of this model, though the data will not be available to process properly until the 2026 data come available (since we need the seven-year window 2020-2026 to estimate the rate of growth in 2023). I predict a bit of a jump in 2023, maybe 3ppm, in response to these warm seas, and paradoxically expect people to talk about an unexpected acceleration. Let's hope I'm wrong.

When we look at the two models side by side, we can see that the shorter doubling time of the blue model really takes off about 2100. By 2160, the blue model hits 3000ppm, which is probably impossibly high unless we degas sea water. The Red model predicts a much more reasonable 900 ppm.

The difference between these two competing models is tiny in our lifetimes, but makes a very big difference after about 2100, when the short doubling time of the 280ppm model takes off dramatically. Only time will tell, but my instinct is that the true doubling time will be closer to the more relaxed model implicit in the zero offset model. As a hostage to fortune, I include a table in the paper output, predicting the atmospheric CO_2, and associated environmental parameters. On my hard drives I leave two different versions of this predictive spreadsheet, one as published (the 280 ppm offset model) and the other the zero offset model. Someone should compare them in the future. The answer should be fairly clear by 2100!

Why should planetary CO_2 behave like a door slamming in the wind? The simplest, most reassuring answer is that maybe CO_2 is simply mirroring the exponential growth in our international economy and human population.

All we have to do is stop humans burning fossil carbon and having so many babies, and the planet can stabilise. Easy! But there is another much more scary interpretation, which fits better with geological records. Another reason to expect ongoing exponential growth in CO_2 is that our planet has enormous reserves of fossil carbon in the Arctic soils, c, 1500 Gigatons of carbon stored as peat, which are protected from oxidation by waterlogging and cold. Although hard to believe, this store of carbon is considerably larger than the amount of carbon in ALL Earth's biomass plus ALL the atmosphere combined. As the Arctic warms up due to CO_2, permafrost vanishes and fires break out, releasing more CO_2. Hence more warming, more CO_2, just like a door slamming in the wind. Once this process starts to bite, it will carry on until the planet has run out of 'labile soil carbon'. By which time the Arctic carbon will be in the atmosphere as CO_2, warming the planet. Or worse, partly also as CH_4 warming the planet.

So I set up a simple spreadsheet to project exponential growth in CO_2 at this rate into the future. No exponential function can carry on forever; it stops when its resource base is exhausted. In this case the CO_2 pool is topped up by two inputs: human combustion (of coal, oil etc), and natural oxidation (peat oxidation, burning forests etc). I don't know when we will stop burning coal and oil but can say that once the Arctic warms up, most of its peat will oxidise away. So we can project exponential growth in CO_2 until (at least) the Arctic soil carbon has gone, then ask what the atmosphere looks like after that.

I then used this model of CO_2 to predict the global temperature based on a simple linear extrapolation from existing data. There has been a nice simple linear relationship between CO_2 and the planetary mean temperature since at least the 1950s, so I use this to predict what global temperatures might be expected given the continuing growth in CO_2. Atmospheric experts will point out that I am ignoring methane CH_4 – guilty as charged. Methane is a potent greenhouse gas and there are huge, alarming reserves of it in the Arctic muds and clathrates. We think it was a similar methane feedback that gave us the exponential growth in temperatures that triggered the massive Permo-Triassic extinction event. The trouble is that methane emissions are hard to model, very non-linear. If it gases off slowly it gets oxidised to CO_2 in the soil. If it all gases off quickly the methanotrophs are overwhelmed and you could have a HUGE warming spike. In the end I simply ignore this and say "this model is overly cautious – in reality things will be considerably hotter due to the CH_4 forcing". Bear that in mind!

Table 1 – predicted decadal environmental data up to 2160

Year	CO_2, ppmv	T anomaly, deg C	Arctic ice minimum. Mega-KM2	Sea pH	Sea level, mm (0 in AD2000)
2020	413.1	0.6	3.86	8.05	64
2030	436.8	0.8	2.72	8.03	100
2040	461.9	1.0	1.51	8.02	136
2050	488.4	1.2	0.22	8.00	172
2060	516.5	1.4	0.00	7.98	208
2070	546.2	1.6	0.00	7.96	244
2080	577.6	1.7	0.00	7.94	280
2090	610.8	1.9	0.00	7.93	316
2100	645.9	2.1	0.00	7.91	352
2110	683.0	2.3	0.00	7.89	388
2120	722.3	2.5	0.00	7.87	424
2130	763.8	2.7	0.00	7.86	460
2140	807.7	2.9	0.00	7.84	496
2150	854.1	3.1	0.00	7.82	532
2160	903.2	3.3	0.00	7.80	568

When we plot the global temperature anomaly against annual mean CO_2 (from Mauna Lua), we get a nice straight line.

There is a linear relationship between CO_2 and the annual Arctic ice minimum. Not surprisingly, the relationship is also linear with temperature, with more CO_2 and higher temperatures giving less ice. Slightly surprisingly the correlation (as measured by r2) is slightly better for CO_2 than for temperature, though the effect is small and may disappear with more data. It is convenient to use CO_2 as the proxy throughout this modelling exercise. As a first approximation, the minimum

Fig 15.5 The relationship between Log(CO_2) and planetary temperature since 1950. The Y axis is the temperature anomaly, so 0 = pre-industrial baseline (not global freezing).

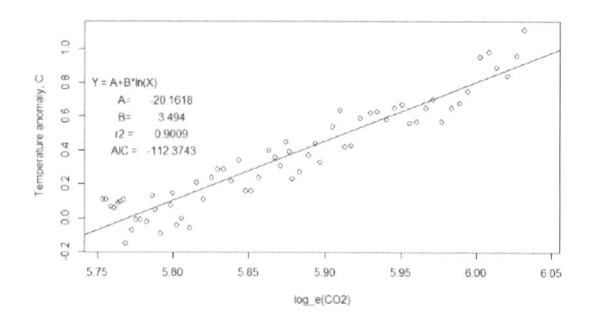

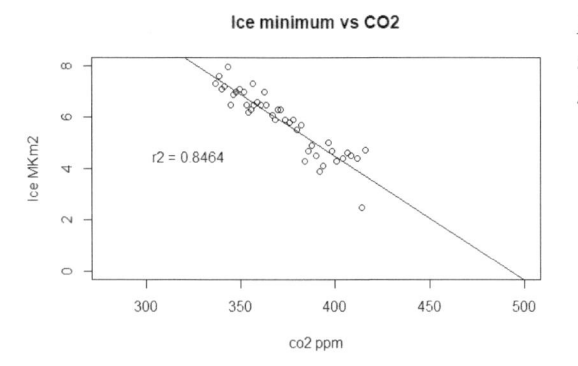

Fig 15.6 The linear relationship between arctic ice and CO_2.

Arctic ice cover falls to zero at just under 500ppm CO_2. I get this as expected to first happen about the year 2050. This is just annual minimum – while the total disappearance of the ice cap even at the end of winter is credible and fits fossil data, I haven't explored data about ice maxima.

There are two more environmental properties that are clearly influenced by increasing CO_2. One is the acidity of surface water, including sea water and rain water. The other is sea level rise. Of these, I have good data on marine pH and am confident to predict its behaviour. I have some curious data about sea level rise, but am not confident to predict it. I have no data at all on rainfall pH, except that I am sure it will decline as CO_2 rises. Limestone will erode slightly faster (though not in the same league as when boosted with sulphur dioxide – see the comments on Sheffield gravestones in the 'Roehampton' chapter.)

Marine pH has been accurately measured for decades, should be expected to fall as CO_2 rises, and indeed can be seen to fall. I remain appalled and shocked that we have succeeded in affecting the acidity of something so vast (and mildly alkaline) as our oceans, but the data above are clear. There is a steady and

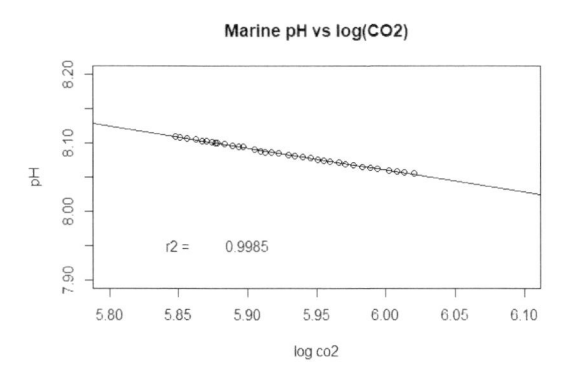

Fig 15.7 Marine pH vs $ln(CO_2)$.

inexorable decline in oceanic pH as CO_2 rises, which will affect the ability of calcifying invertebrates (corals etc) to immobilise CO_2 as calcium carbonate. Another feedback loop fighting against us. Warmer, more acidic seas absorb less CO_2.

A final question, one that probably gets asked more than any other, is about the sea level rise as the greenhouse effect takes off. This should not be any more difficult than the other parameters – we plug the data into a linear model and see what pops out. In fact, the results are so bizarre that I am simply going to avoid the question. This uncertainty has multiple facets. Firstly, there is a philosophical question of how we measure the sea level. This should be easy – you get the distance from the sea surface to the centre of the earth. In fact, we cannot do this, and instead use the land surface. This is immediately a problem, as some land is still rebounding from the weight of ice that melted 10,000 years ago. This 'isostatic uplift' is why we have dry beaches in northern Scotland far inland from the sea. Other bits of land are sinking. Weirder still is 'fore bulge collapse' – the pull by the gravitational attraction of ice sheets. It has been estimated that if the whole Greenland ice sheet melted, the sea around Scotland would FALL because its level is lifted up by gravitation attraction to the Greenland ice. The worst trouble seems to come out of using a geological time series. My analyses give answers that clearly do not fit!

We have some reasonable estimates of sea level going back about 2e4 years, to the depths of the last ice age when the sea was very much lower than today. Thus:

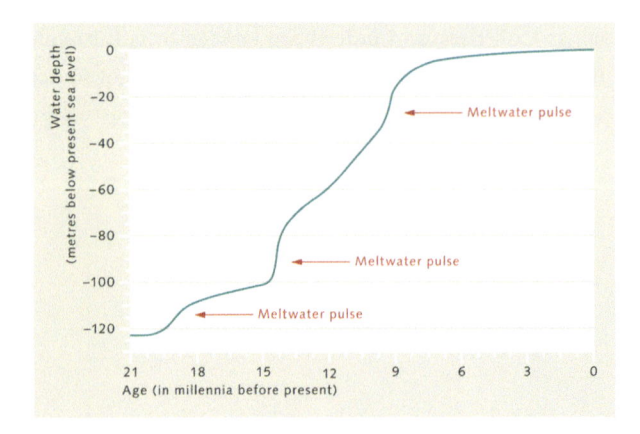

Fig 15.8 Estimates of sea level during the Pleistocene.

Or see this image at https://en.wikipedia.org/wiki/Sea_level_rise#/media/File:Post-Glacial_Sea_Level.png.

I have spent quite a while quantifying this time series with a ruler and protractor, measuring Y values and slope angles (since tan(angle) is the slope, the rate of change). The first thing to observe is that there was a definite trend for less CO_2 to correspond to lower sea levels. (The colder the planet, the more water is locked up in ice.) Secondly, that the rise after the end of the ice sheets was not smooth but irregular. The CO_2 record also shows irregular rapid changes – the obvious question is the extent that they line up with changes in sea level. And the answer is "not very well". Less obvious is to repeat the linear regression using the CO_2 from 500 years ago, then for the CO_2 from 1000 years ago, etc, to see which offset gave the best fit. If both trends were smooth we could not estimate lags, but in fact both the CO_2 profile and the sea level profile have steep bits and shallow bits. It is not difficult – in theory – to estimate goodness of fit for different delays, to make a first stab at getting a time lag between CO_2 and sea level rise. I did this, and found that the best fit was a model in which sea level rise matched CO_2 2500 years before. Yes, a 2.5 millennia delay. This is compatible with estimates I have seen that the big ice caps should last a couple of thousand years. So if we put in this 2500 year time lag we get a good linear relationship, except for the most recent 2000 years when sea level has stayed remarkably stable. If we use these most-recent ice age results to ask where our sea level SHOULD be, the numbers come out as just silly. They are so much higher than what we actually see, I am forced to conclude that either (1) planetary dynamics have fundamentally changed in the last 2000 years, or (2) we have a huge sea-level rise locked into the system, but its inertia is so long and slow that the dramatic change is not yet detectable. I suspect the latter to be true, and that we are locked into an unavoidable rise of at least 50m in the next 2000 years. If this is the case, then predicting sea level rise in the near future (say 2100) is outside the scope of this simple linear analysis since the levels will be defined by year-on-year dynamics rather than equilibrium values.

Note that the gradient is almost identical in these two models, about 1.47m per ppm. This is remarkably large. We are observing sea level rise of around 3mm per year, against a CO_2 rise of around 4 ppm per year. From the regression parameters from these Pleistocene data we should be seeing sea level rise of c. 6000mm, per year. This is clearly wrong, it is c. 1500 times higher than we observe (my worst ever estimate!). My interpretation, for what it is worth, is simply the thermal inertia of huge ice sheets is so vast that we are simply not seeing the equilibrium value. It seems established that ice sheets are excellent indicators of average temperature, so over the last 20 millennia the slow changes in CO_2 show up as even slower changes in land ice. On our puny human timescales, we cannot hope to see these glacial changes. Glaciers are undoubtedly melting worldwide, but the system is nowhere near its equilibrium. To give some idea of the predicted sea level today from this simple linear model, the prediction comes out at 223m (!) for 420 ppm. There is not enough ice on land to achieve this – I gather that 70m rise is about the limit, which we hit at 315ppm way back in 1959. This extrapolation suggests that the terrestrial ice sheets were irretrievably doomed about the time I was born, it's just that no-one had noticed. Another runaway process that stops because it runs out of resource. So the question of predicting sea level rise is not about historical precedent, when Earth could respond on a timescale of 2500 years, but about the dynamics of heat penetrating into terrestrial ice. Too complex, sorry, I'm not going there. All I will say about average sea level is that it will continue going up steadily for the foreseeable future, and that many coastal towns are ultimately doomed. Just keep adding 3.6mm per year for the rest of your civilisation and you'll be about right, at least until you get to the upper limit of the sea's reach, around 70m. So I have stuck a really silly, simple fix into my predictive spreadsheet, without pretending that this will be definitive. I simply have an annual sea level rise, that copies previous values unless updated. It's about 3.6mm per year and will only increase slowly. I keep a running total – pathetically simple, but good enough to suggest that – for the next couple of hundred years – it's not the sea level rise that's scary so much as the temperatures. By the time that the Arctic soil carbon is mainly oxidised (c. 2160, the timescale of this novella), the sea will have risen by less than one metre. The ultimate rise to 70m looks inexorable, but will take at least a thousand years. Civilisation will have other more pressing concerns in this phase than losing low-lying bits of coastal cities, like food supplies, mega-floods and lethal heat spikes. We would really need a benign world government to oversee the mess, but probably won't get one given how often human male leaders prove to prefer their domination of a wasteland over a functional state being controlled by someone else.

It has been interesting to put my simple linear predictions next to those made in the linked novel 'The Ministry For the Future' (Kim Stanley Robinson 2021), which states that CO_2 should be 470 ppm by 2034 (I estimate we get there about 2045) and Arctic ice disappears about the same time (I predict 2050). The book opens with a disturbing but plausible account of a 20 megadeath event from a heat cell in India, referring to 'wet bulb' temperatures of 35C being deadly. This is not just the absolute temperature, but the temperature mixed with high humidity that stops us from cooling down by sweating, and makes the point that people (and other animals – almost all other animals) die in large numbers well below

Peter Shaw

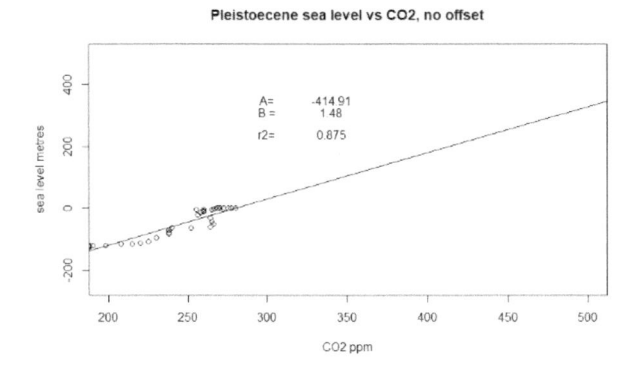

Pleistocene sea level vs CO2, no offset

A = -414.91
B = 1.48
r2 = 0.875

Fig 15.9 Sea level vs CO_2 with no offset – note how stupidly high the sea level should now be.

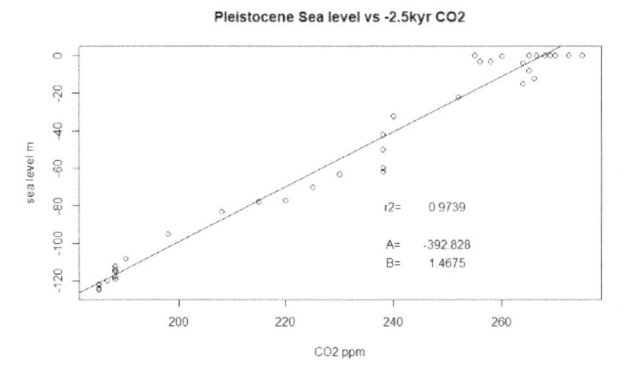

Pleistocene Sea level vs -2.5kyr CO2

r2 = 0.9739
A = -392.828
B = 1.4675

Fig 15.10 As Fig. 15.9, but with a 2500 year offset. Still the gradient is far steeper than it should be based on observed current data, c. 1467mm rise per ppm CO_2.

50C if humidity is high. I am assuming that the sort of lethal heatwave described here will become routine for much of the inhabited regions of the Earth's surface once CO_2 exceeds 800 ppm. In the book an eco-terrorist group tries to take out people they see as responsible for the megadeaths, while the Indian government flies hundreds of sorties to dump sulphur dioxide into the upper atmosphere to buy a few years' respite, aiming to emulate the effect of Pinatubo (1991) whose dust and sulphate aerosols cooled the planet by a degree or two for a few years.

We can use some simple linear calculations to relate carbon oxidation to atmospheric CO_2. The calculations below use a strange technical term – the 'Mole'. This is nothing to do with furry little insectivores that spoil your lawn, but is a chemist's term describing a large number. Specifically a mole of any molecule is 6E23 copies of that molecule (Avogadro's number), which happens to be the number of atoms of H1 hydrogen in 1g of hydrogen gas. It is also the number of atoms of C12 in 12g of carbon, of O16 atoms in 16g of oxygen, etc. It is a handy convenient way to convert masses to number of atoms, and is familiar to anyone with a qualification in chemistry. Another standard shorthand that needs explaining – the engineering hierarchy. Kilo, Mega, Giga, Tera, Peta in this case. Kilo = 1E3 = 1000. 1Kg is 1000 g, 1Km = 1000m etc. Mega = 1E6 = 1 million. A megaton of carbon = 1 million tons of carbon (which would be held in 44/12 million tons of CO_2). Giga = 1E9 = 1000,000, 000. Tera = 1E12 = 1000,000,000,000 = a million million. Peta = 1E15, Exa = 1E18. I once had a tutee who complained that these fancy scientific terms were created to confuse and deter people, and I made a point of explaining that this belief is utterly wrong. These scaling terms are used to keep life simple and to avoid confusion, allowing us to use the same units (like grams or metres) for tiny, tiny values like the size of an atom, or huge numbers like the weight of our atmosphere. I get cross at hearing newsreaders (etc) talking of (eg) "a hundred thousand billion tonnes" – useless. Call it 1E14, 100 teratonnes, then we can do the calculations easily. I HATE people using terms like a "quadrillion", or even "billion" – these are ambiguous. To avoid ambiguity, always specify the actual order of magnitude. Throughout this text I use "tonne" as the metric ton = 1000Kg = 1 Megagram. If you value your sanity, never bother doing calculations in imperial units. Just to remind you, an Imperial (Henry 8th) ton is 20 'hundredweights', based on a 'stone' of 14 pounds of 16 ounces. I once had some US students on an exchange who only thought in imperial units and protested that with "lookup tables" they were easy to handle. So I set them a challenge in front of the whole class. You have a cubic mile of water, I have a cubic kilometre of water. You work out its volume in pints and its mass in pounds, using your favourite pocket calculator. While trying to do that (and failing), I did the calculations by hand on the board in front of the whole class in a few seconds and showed them the metric answer is "volume = $1E9m^3$ = 1E12 litres = 1E12 Kg = 1E15g". At least one satellite has been lost because some US citizens prefer imperial units, at which obduracy I can only shake my head in disbelief.

First a little chemical background: A key conceptual detail that non-chemists may not know is that (to a first approximation) 1 mole of any gas occupies the same volume as 1 mole of any other gas, even though the weights of different molecules differ based on their atomic composition. (Roughly 1 mole of gas occupies 24 L at standard temperature and pressure, increasing with temperature and decreasing with pressure.) Atmospheric concentrations of CO_2 are always quoted in ppmv (parts per million by volume), which is calculated by volume, not by mass, so when estimating ppms we need to be careful to convert everything from grams into moles for comparability. Luckily for ease of calculation, 1 mole of carbon generates 1 mole of CO_2. The atmosphere is roughly 80% nitrogen (molar mass = 28) and 20% oxygen (molar mass = 32), so the average weight of

1 mole of atmosphere is c. 28.97 g. The molar masses of carbon and oxygen are 12 and 16, so 1 mole of CO_2 weighs 44g, of which 12/44 = 27.3% is carbon.

At time of writing the atmosphere is estimated to weigh c. 5.4E21 g, hence 1.77E20 moles gas. [We do not need this result, but as a confirmatory calculation, since CO_2 is 420 ppmv, this corresponds to 1.77E20*420/1000000 moles CO_2. Hence the atmosphere holds 7.45E16 moles CO_2 = c. 8.94E17 g carbon or 3.28E18 g CO_2.] So adding 1Gt Carbon to the atmosphere adds 1E9 tons C = 1E15 g = 1E15/12 moles carbon = 8.3E13 moles C, giving us 8.3E13 moles CO_2. This raises the atmospheric CO_2 composition by a factor of 8.3e13/1.77E20 = 4.7E-7, or (multiplying by 1E6 to convert to ppm) 0.47 ppm.

Result: oxidising 1 gigaton of carbon raises atmospheric CO_2 by c. 0.47 ppm.

How much carbon are we adding to the atmosphere each year? This figure has a surprising amount of uncertainty, but is estimated as roughly 10.9 GT carbon (or 40 GT CO_2). This suggests that CO_2 should be rising by 10.9*0.47 = 5.12 ppm. In fact, the figure is rather lower, about 2.2 ppm per year. The difference is important, and does not show an error in the calculations, it shows that Planet Earth is removing over half our CO_2 emissions.

The removal comes from uptake into biomass and dissolution into the sea. Far from being reassuring, this is actually scary because the uptake mechanisms can be expected to weaken as the planet warms up. Can we expect it to continue at this level? No, assuredly not, for at least two interlinked reasons. Firstly, if we continue to clear forest and peat bogs, as the climate runs away, we can be sure that the biosphere will not absorb as much CO_2 as it has so far. The Amazon is drying and burning, Arctic peat is drying and burning, Bornean peat forests are drying and burning. Secondly, as the oceans become warmer and more acidic, they are utterly guaranteed to absorb less CO_2 than before by basic physical chemistry. Like when you boil a kettle, long before it boils it hisses as dissolved gases come out of solution – warm water holds less dissolved gas than cold water. Simple equilibrium chemistry also says that as the pH falls less CO_2 will dissolve to form carbonic acid. So, we could reduce our emission drastically and still see CO_2 soar out of control once Planet Earth stops acting as our unpaid carbon bin. I do not know how to model this feedback, and suspect that no-one is quite sure. This alone is enough to predict an exponential growth in CO_2 as the atmosphere warms.

So if we lose all the 1650 GT Arctic soil carbon, ignoring all the fossil fuels burned in that period and ignoring the carbon released by the burning forests, we might expect atmospheric CO_2 to rise by c. 1650*0.47 = 705 ppm, though if Earth continues to remove half of this we could get off with a mere 350 ppm. That's added to whatever was there before, and ignores any heating effect from methane (which could itself be catastrophic – ask the Permian reptiles!). Given that we are starting at 420ppm the Arctic is just beginning to oxidise, and we look likely to lose the Amazon, I can't see how we can expect to avoid seeing 800 ppm CO_2. That's before any additional fossil carbon and ignoring the methane warming, which is c. 25 times CO_2. I have found an estimate that Arctic methane stores are c. 1400 GT methane, which if simply oxidised to CO_2 will alone increase CO_2 by 656 ppm. On the scary, worst-case scenario that this methane gasses out unoxidized, its heating effect might look like 25*656 ppm of CO_2, or roughly 16400 ppm CO_2, which is frankly off scale. Taking a simple linear extrapolation from our historical data predicts that global temperature anomaly for this atmosphere would be about 153 degrees Celsius. I am sure that this linear calculation figure cannot be right, but was astonished at a prediction of surface water boiling somewhere. (The first time I got this alarming result I was reminded of a line from the protest song 'Downpressor Man' by Peter Tosh. "Downpressor man – where you going to run to? You can run to the sea but the sea will be boiling . . .".) Any chemist would tell me to use a logarithmic regression, which gives a much more reasonable prediction for the anomaly of about 13.7 degrees, which looks like the sort of figures coming out of the Palaeocene/Eocene and Permo-Triassic boundaries. Multicellular life damn nearly went extinct at the P/T due to heat and lack of oxygen (but no actual boiling water as far as we know). That time it took about a million years for the climate to settle down. The Palaeocene recovery started at about 160 Kyrs according to McInerney & Wing (2011). So if we do lose control of the atmosphere, our descendants will be living with the consequences for the indefinite future.

These disturbing calculations raise the question of HOW humans might live in such a runaway-GHE world. I absolutely do not believe Greta Thunberg when she says we will go extinct, as humans are clever enough to adapt to a huge variety of circumstances. By contrast I think that the late James Lovelock got it right ('The Revenge of Gaia') in saying that we will need to move to high latitudes to escape the unbearable heat. There will be two zones that should remain habitable under the most extreme circumstances – around the Arctic sea, and on the Antarctic landmass. We can look to previous hot periods to see how the climate here might behave. For the Arctic sea, we know that (after the Palaeocene boundary event) it was once a green soup, full of a tropical freshwater fern called *Azolla*. Presumably living on the warm fresh water from melted glaciers, floating above the denser cold salt water. Look up 'The Arctic Azolla event'. Incredibly, there are dense beds of fossil fern leaves under the (doomed) Arctic ice floes, with fossils of crocodiles. We also find fossil evidence that some dinosaurs passed the winter at the South Pole, showing it never went much below zero in their days. (As a tangential aside, marsupials evolved in South America and only got to Australia by walking across the Antarctic landmass in the Eocene warmth). For much of our land surface, once CO_2 goes above 1000 ppm the sporadic temperature extremes would seem to rule out what we consider to be normal life. Temperatures above 50°C tend to kill people, above 55°C is I gather lethal even when standing in a shower, so we can easily see a scenario where large areas of currently populous landmasses become uninhabitable. Presumably we would follow the traditional model, whereby the rich evacuate and the poor die of heatstroke?

Then there is the question of food supply chains. As far as I know no-one has ever grown crops on the Antarctic landmass, nor much inside the Arctic circle (though there are geothermal bananas grown in glasshouses in Iceland!) This may have to change. The calculation which I most hope proves to be wrong concerns food supply chains. We generally have enough food for 7E9 or so humans, by using really quite large areas of the Earth's surface. Something like 40% of all the energy capture by plants on the planet goes to feeding humans (look up 'Human Appropriated Net Primary Production' or HANPP), and this depends on cultivars that have evolved to match their soils and weather. If the climate runs away into meltdown as CO_2 goes exponential, most of the major breadbaskets can be expected to become desert, and the farmable zones will inevitably move polewards. Quite apart from the soils being poor and the lightless winters being cruel, this will leave less land available than before to cultivate, as well as this land being unsuitable for cultivation. The fertility can be fixed, given fertiliser, agricultural science and a few centuries. The reduced land area cannot. Together, I made a back of the envelope guestimate that we can expect to lose about 90% of our crop production, before (hopefully) science and soil management sort out high latitude productivity. I am not clear where the cultivatable zones will be at 1000 ppm CO_2, maybe the glacial outflows from the Antarctic mainland will feed fertile alpine meadows – but it seems unlikely. To be honest, 90% looks a bit optimistic. Roughly 10 to the power 10 people (1E10 if you prefer) facing a 90% reduction in food supply? That looks like 9 gigadeaths to me. Like I said, I hope I'm wrong. In 2023 the Bulletin of Atomic Scientists reported that there was surprise and concern at a new model of a nuclear war that predicted 5 gigadeaths, with most of these deaths rising from starvation as the food chains collapsed. Having studied the K/T boundary, and given our long range food chains, I am surprised that anyone is surprised at these figures.

So I wanted to finish with a little section that explores what life might look like if CO_2 continues to grow exponentially. People will continue to exist, and continue to have children. Where do they live, what will they tell their children, and what information do you safeguard? What constants will be taught in all schools for the rest of civilisation? I make a few suggestions, in the expectation that most will turn out to be wrong!

Prelude – The Exponential Growth in Forcing Function

The fundamental problem came down to two words defining an abstruse mathematical concept: 'Exponential Growth'. This is usually cast in the form of off-putting sets of mathematical symbols, equations along the lines of:

$$Y = A * \exp(B*t)$$

Where Y is the thing you are interested in, t is time (measured in whatever units you prefer), A and B are just numbers that make the answers correct. A and B might variously be called 'constants', 'parameters' or 'fudge factors' according to your whim, and are usually fitted to data by least-squares algorithms that date back to Carl Gauss early in the 19th century. The interesting term is the 'exp()' bit, which means 'calculate the exponential of', and involves raising the number e to that power. Raising the number 2 to the power 5 is a headache for most people (it is actually 2*2*2*2*2 = 32), raising any number to a non-integer power is beyond most people, and e is a non-integer that goes on for ever but starts as 2.718281828459036 . . . (This natural number was discovered – or was it invented? – by Bernouilli and turns out to be magically useful in almost any equation that involves differential calculus). At this point it would be quite reasonable to give up in despair, but fortunately there are easy ways round this. The calculations are done by computers with surprising ease, you don't actually have to use e at all, and all exponential functions have the same important property, simple to state and easy to understand. They have a doubling time (if B>0) or a half-life (if B<0). It would be quite valid to say that a half-life is just a doubling time, but going backwards in time. Half lives are familiar in the context of radioactive decay, and look like this:

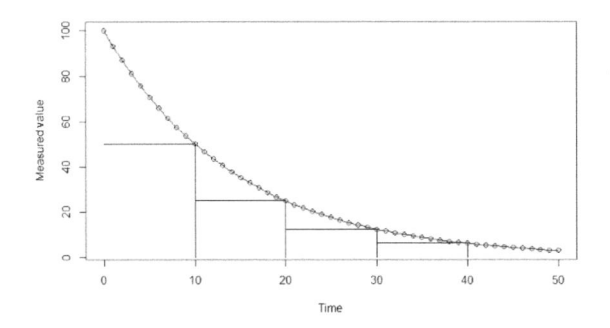

*Fig 15.11
A demonstration of
exponential decay.*

Doubling times are slightly less familiar, but make sense in terms of a disease outbreak or other population growth, and look like this:

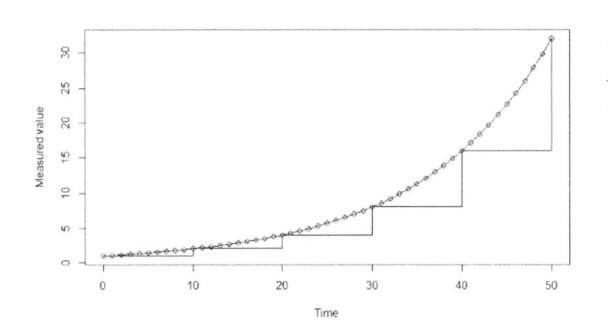

*Fig 15.12
A demonstration of
exponential growth.*

You can see that the two curves are the same, just flipped round. Exponential growth is the property that the thing you are interested in doubles in a set time interval, then doubles again in the same time interval, and again and again . . . The point is that this process takes off spectacularly quickly once it gets going. The classic story to illustrate this is almost certainly fictional, and concerns grains of rice on a chessboard. The king, for whom the game of chess was invented, was so pleased that he asked the inventor what reward he wanted for the new game, and the inventor asked for some grains of rice. Specifically, one grain of rice on the first square of the chessboard. Then two on the next square. Then four on the next, and eight on the next and so forth, doubling each time. This is a simple exponential growth with a 'doubling time' of one square. There are 64 squares on a chessboard, so the king thought a few grains of rice a trifling fee but wasn't much good at maths so asked his court advisors what was actually needed. The actual answer is about $1.844 * 10^{19}$ (or 1.844E19), which would come in at about 18 thousand million metric tons (at 1mg per grain). On learning this the king had the inventor executed for his cheek. Apocryphal from start to finish but makes the point that doubling times should not be trifled with. When a new coronavirus jumped species into *Homo sapiens* in 2019 it proved alarmingly infectious, plus dangerous to the elderly. The UK Prime Minister 'Boris' Johnson was personally warned about its lethality, and the potential effects of exponential growth by the world Ebola expert (and my school friend) Dr Ian Cropley in January 2020, and laughed it off as a mathematical scare story. Then people saw what happened in the Italian hospital system when numbers of the dying elderly doubled every few days, and doubled and doubled again. Traumatised nurses and overflowing graveyards. Crematoria literally had meltdowns from incessant over-demand, and Johnson (not known for his puritanical views) ended up shutting down pubs and airports before nearly dying himself from the virus. Had the growth been linear, things might have been different, but exponential growth just gets out of control.

Economists have long understood the mathematics of exponential growth, and generally like it since with a bit of patience it allows you to turn a small amount of money into a very large amount of money. "The magic of compound interest" they say, the idea being that if dividends are re-invested to pay more dividends they make more dividends, and the pot grows exponentially. Many governments for many years have relied on this logic to wash away national debts. Conversely, if you have a debt to a money lender that grows exponentially it quickly becomes crippling, paying him vastly more than the sum originally borrowed but with no prospect of ever being free of the debt. (This is why usury was so frowned upon by many religions and legislatures, though it has re-appeared in the form of the euphemistically called 'payday lenders'.) Standard economic growth is, in fact, an example of exponential growth. An economy or investment that grows at 2% per annum is in fact doubling every 35 years. (Try it – ask your computer what 1.02 to the power of 35 is). This is also why economists are so fixated on endless growth – they see the economy as an exponential model. And why people who understand Earth systems are so worried about the endless search for exponential economic growth.

In 1965 Gordon Moore, an engineer involved in designing silicon microcircuits, observed that the number of processors that could be packed into a given space doubled every two years, and realised that this implied exponential growth. See: https://www.intel.com/content/www/us/en/silicon-innovations/moores-law-technology.html.

This prediction became known as 'Moore's Law', and seemed outlandish. He predicted that we might have a computer in every household. This seemed laughable, and the article was nearly lost for ever. (The last ever copy turned up in someone's loft decades later.) At the time computers were the size of a large car and needed air conditioned rooms. One serious statistician had recently suggested that one or two computers would suffice for all the calculations likely to be performed in the UK (Swann, 1953). As it happened, the exponential growth in transistor power was sustained and Moore's vision was utterly vindicated.

Outside of pandemics and financial calculations, exponential growth is rarely met in day-to-day life. Much commoner is exponential decay: just by way of example, the temperature of a forgotten cup of coffee falls away to room temperature with an exponential decay, with a half-life around five minutes. This half-life depends on the details of the cup, though (curiously) not on the temperature of the room or the coffee. Proving this is where the number 'e' comes in, and is for another day. The reason you rarely meet exponential growth is simple: it explodes then burns out. No real-world system can ever grow exponentially for long because it will inevitably use up its resources. Diseases run out of hosts to infect, bacteria in a test tube or yeast in a fermenting jar exhaust their food supply. When mice populations explode, you know the numbers must crash when the food is gone. The neutron flux inside an atomic bomb grow exponentially, until either most of the fissile atoms have been split or the assembly expands so much as to be sub-critical – in this case the doubling time is measured in nanoseconds, and the explosion is spectacular. Sooner or later Moore's law will bump into the constraints of quantum mechanics and slow down.

At first sight, Planet Earth should be incapable of doing anything approximating exponential growth. It has been spinning round the sun for 4.6 Gigayears, slowly settling down as its radio-isotopes decay, gently losing some hydrogen and helium into space as it sucks in new mass from meteors. The only hints that it can do anything fast come from the fossil record, mute evidence of our planet from unimaginably long ago. We have known from the early days of geology that the fossils of shelly animals can change surprisingly abruptly between apparently closely adjacent strata. This finding has been repeatedly confirmed, not just for marine shells but equally for bony vertebrates and land plants, marine micro-algae and just about anything else whose remains we can identify. These became known as 'Mass Extinction Events', henceforth MEEs. These fossil boundaries proved to be very useful for geologists since they allow rapid identification of the age of stones based on their fossils. One easy example – lots of trilobites – arthropods with three body regions – in marine shales up to the end of what we now call the Permian, not a hint of a trilobite anywhere ever since. Giant bones of giant reptiles ('dinosaurs') in the Jurassic and Cretaceous but none after a sharp boundary, the K/T boundary, followed by a spike of ferns that the appearance of large mammals. For a century no-one knew what to make of these abrupt changes, and to be honest a lot of the ideas about them look frankly laughable with our position of hindsight and isotopic data. One especially daft idea that amused me was that dinosaurs died of constipation after flowering plants appeared. Given that nothing in the fossil record agreed in any way with the claims made in the Old Testament, a lot of people preferred not to think about such heretical fantasies.

The really important understandings about Planet Earth's past history came with the discovery of isotopes, and their study in geological strata. First came the discovery of radioactive isotopes, whose decay was defined by a half-life. Unsurprisingly, old stones contain little or no short-lived isotopes, as they all decayed long ago. But they still contain traces of isotopes whose half-lives are measured in gigayears, since the age of Planet Earth is measured in gigayears, and the stardust from which earth coalesced presumably once held atoms of every possible isotope that could be forged in a dying star. One useful such isotope is potassium 40, an atom which behaves exactly like any other potassium atom (and is whizzing in and out of your nerve cells and muscles as you read this). But which decays to argon 40 (Ar^{40}) with a half-life of about 1.29 gigayears. Argon 40 is a gas, famously inert, like all its family (the 'noble gases') refusing to take part in any chemical reactions. So when rocks are melted in a volcano, any argon that might have built up since the dawn of the solar system just boils away like air forms bubbles in a kettle as water gets near boiling. Then the lava cools down again, the potassium 40 atoms carry on decaying slowly, and the new argon atoms are stuck inside the rock matrix, unable to escape. So when geologists find old lava and find it contains argon 40, they know it must have been formed since the lava set. Measure how much potassium 40 remains in the stone and that gives you an objective age for the stone. This sort of clock is how we know that earth is about 4.6 gigayears old, and that most stones on most continents have ages measured in the hundreds of millions of years. This alone proves conclusively that the account of creation given in Genesis is utterly fallacious, since it requires Earth to have been created in its modern form about 4000BC. Not just inaccurate, wrong by a factor of nearly a million and omitting key points about multiple changes in just about everything measurable (as I habitually point out to believers of all Abrahamic creeds).

These isotopic dates give us objective dates for the big mass extinction events. Three are worth picking up on as they will be referred to again. The biggest of them, the grand-daddy of mass extinction events, was the Permo/Triassic boundary at 251 MYBP, the P/T MEE, taking out the trilobites (and almost everything else). Another well-known event was the K/T boundary at 65 MYBP, that famously took out the dinosaurs and ammonites. (Pedants can observe that one lineage of dinosaurs lived on – the feathered ones we now call birds.) Finally in this grim roll call comes a much less well-known event, the Palaeocene/Eocene Thermal Maximum at 55MYBP – the PETM. This gave us the dawn of modern mammals.

There were other MEEs, in fact one for each geological era, but only these have given us clear evidence of their causation that seems relevant to us today. Hopefully as future geologists gather more data from these boundary strata, we may understand them better.

A second line of isotopic evidence came with the realisation that most elements have multiple stable isotopes. These have identical chemical properties and do not decay radioactively, so are very hard to tell apart and at first sight seem to convey no useful information. Even if you can tell an atom of carbon 12 from an atom of carbon 13, they incorporate into any biomolecule in exactly the same way so seem to tell the same story. In fact, they do differ in one important respect – they weigh a little bit differently. This was first realised during the Manhattan project, when we needed to separate atoms of Uranium 235 (U^{235}) from atoms of Uranium 238 (U^{238}). It was done by firing a beam of uranium atoms at high speed through a magnetic field, which deflected them, and the lighter U^{235} atoms were deflected more so could be collected relatively easily. The magnitude of this operation was mind-blowing: at one stage the entire silver bullion deposits in Fort Knox were removed and melted down to make the magnets needed for the Hiroshima bomb. Nowadays Uranium enrichment uses centrifuges, but the basic idea of separating atoms by weight still applies.

The relevance of this is that biochemical processes are quite complex atomic operations relying on random diffusion of molecules, and heavier molecules diffuse just a bit more slowly. So over thousands of processing cycles, the ratio of heavy and light isotopes in chemicals drift apart slightly in many biological reactions, also in things like the evaporation of water. For example, heavy isotopes tend to accumulate in carnivores just as pesticides do. A top carnivore turns out to have slightly higher ratios of C^{13} to C^{12} and N^{15} to N^{14} than does a herbivore. A few monocotyledonous plants (like sweetcorn) called C4 plants have a distinct $C^{13}:C^{12}$ ratio, so much so that a hair or tooth of a citizen of the USA (brought up on sweetcorn, corn-fed pigs and corn syrup) can be told apart from most other humans just by their carbon isotope profile. This way we also know that your remote ancestors the Neanderthals were top carnivores on a par with wolves, while their contemporaries the cave bears were almost vegetarian. [As an aside, before raising an eyebrow at my assertion that Neanderthals were your ancestors, get your genome checked. Most humans have about 2% Neanderthal in their genome, showing that clandestine matings were going on in our earliest days as humans.]

How do stable isotopes help explain MEEs? They supply two new lines of evidence. Firstly, we can reconstruct average global temperatures from the amount of the heavy oxygen isotope Oxygen 18, which means that water molecules need more energy to evaporate. More O^{18} means hotter. Secondly, one particular biological reaction with a marked isotopic signal is the microbial production of Methane CH_4. Microbial methane shows a strong elevation in the lighter isotope C^{12}.

When scientists looked at the isotopic signals in ancient stones, things generally looked similar to nowadays, but there were some odd patterns around some MEE boundaries. In particular, the P/T boundary was marked by a lot of O^{18} and of C^{12}. The world got a lot hotter, and acquired a vast amount of C^{12} very quickly. The only way we have thought of to explain this is called a 'methane catastrophe'. It involves the observation that microbial methane does not always gas off from its anaerobic sediments, but can stay put in a strange white, waxy ice-like form ('burning ice') called a clathrate. The gas does not actually dissolve in water any more than oil does, but stays locked inside ice as long as conditions stay cold and pressures stay high. Arctic drilling engineers know about this material and fear it as it can bubble then burn, or explode, if disturbed. And bubble it will if it gets warmed up. And once in the atmosphere it exerts a remarkable heating effect, at least 20* that of CO_2. The actual ratio rather depends on the technical details of the question, since methane decays quickly in air, so its calculated heating effect against CO_2 is a different number if calculated over a one-year time scale, a ten-year time scale or a 100-year time scale. The figure of 25 times is often used. So the methane catastrophe scenario for the P/T boundary is that a lot of methane clathrates built up in cold sediments, then a warming event tipped some over the edge and they de-gassed, releasing a warming pulse of methane. This made the planet warmer, releasing more methane. This continued until most of the available methane was in the atmosphere, making things very hot. This feedback process would be an example of an exponential growth, and like all exponential growths it exploded until it used up its resource. The result was a warming pulse like nothing seen before or since. The seas became too hot to hold much dissolved oxygen – we have traces of anaerobic bacteria in what should have been open ocean. Pretty much all large land animals vanished, and the only animal form still alive today that sailed through this boundary is a brachiopod (lamp shell) called *Lingula* that specialises in living in anoxic mud. This was the biggest killing in Earth's history. What was the heating trigger for this catastrophe? The best evidence points to volcanoes. For the previous few million years Earth had experienced vast volcanic eruptions pouring out huge amounts of CO_2, known to warm the planet. The outpourings covered most of what is now Siberia in molten lava – the 'Siberian Trappes'. Quite why a long gradual build-up snapped into such a sharp event is not understood.

No such CO_2 pulse was associated with the K/T boundary, instead lots of evidence points to the impact of a large asteroid. Roughly a 15km diameter boulder falling out of the sky at the speed of a rifle bullet. There was a lot of volcanic activity shortly afterwards, maybe a coincidence or maybe the impact damaged the Earth's crust. But the more recent PETM (55MYBP) also showed isotopic evidence of a methane pulse and intense warming, with a brief intensely warm period and acid seas associated with a huge injection of carbon 12 into the atmosphere. This was not such a mass killing, but marked the end of the 'early mammals', to be replaced by the modern mammals pretty much as we see today.

So it looks as though Planet Earth can undergo exponential explosions it its atmospheric composition – not often, brief rare events, pulses associated with extreme warming and with a geological boundary.

This is a core premise behind this fiction, an attempt to use anecdote to bring to life geological pasts in our immediate future. For the last 10,000 years humanity has developed advanced civilisations based on roughly stable climates and habitable landscapes. The evidence of geology shows clearly that this should not be assumed to be some God-given right, more a lucky happenstance.

The concern is that something similar may be underway now, in your lifetime. From the viewpoint of geologists, mass extinction events are thin lines, immeasurably fast compared to the aeons that precede them and follow them, followed by a rapid recovery. Yes, an asteroid strike is a brief immediate event, but runaway changes in the atmosphere might take a few hundred years to develop, followed by a recovery measured in the hundreds of thousands of years. Modern humans have only been around for about 300,000 years, so to us such a 'brief, fast' geological event would look like a slow unfolding of a catastrophic new world.

A few more vital background details to set the context:

Alexandra Elbakyan was the courageous brain behind the sci hub project, having got very fed up as a student at important research papers being hidden behind a paywall. She has her own Wikipedia page at https://en.wikipedia.org/wiki/Alexandra_Elbakyan, and is known as science's pirate queen. Her website jumps between jurisdictions and appears to contain most of the published scientific knowledge of humanity, for free.

The Arkive database was an attempt to document as many macroscopic life forms as feasible, while possible. It was online for free for years, we used it for student projects. In 2022 its Wikipedia entry noted it had been taken offline "The complete Arkive collection of over 100,000 images and videos is now being stored securely offline in perpetuity for future generations." [See https://www.wildscreen.org/arkive-closure/ and https://en.wikipedia.org/wiki/ARKive] From my point of view it was available and is no longer. Like the engineers in France who 'fixed' our cooker by taking it away, the 'fix' made a perfectly good situation untenable. Thanks a bundle.

The great library of Alexandria was an attempt in Roman times to hold all published knowledge. For a while that was probably the case. Its manuscripts were not well protected, and suffered from age and fires, being partly burned in some civil war. There is a legend that it was finally destroyed at the behest of some Islamic sultan who said something to the effect that "if it is already in the Koran it has been said, and if it has not been said in the Koran it is not worth saying, so destroy them". This is certainly false; I suspect crusader-age black propaganda. Rather by contrast, the Islamic scholars copied many classical texts, and it is thanks to them that we have the originals of works like Pliny or Virgil. None of the original parchments have survived, but Islamic transcriptions of them have, or have been recopied. It was apparently Christian zealots who burned what few books were left. I suppose that the British Library or the Library of Congress would claim to be modern equivalents.

EMP = Electromagnetic Pulse. This idea is used as a warning about our vulnerability from total reliance on computers for data processing. Yes, they are far better than anything else, but they are also prone to dying terminally without warning or possibility of recovery. An EMP is basically a radio wave with enough energy to induce large voltages in exposed copper cables. In York University in the early 1980s, each terminal was connected to a central server by unshielded copper cables hundreds of metres long, and each time there was a thunderstorm the voltages induced in these cables by the lightning EMPs were enough to burn out a few chips in a few monitors. The warfare version involves detonating a nuclear device about 10km outside the atmosphere. This briefly creates a line of plasma between the fireball and the atmosphere, which conducts electricity and acts as a huge antenna transmitting enormous amounts of energy as radio waves. (This effect does not happen in deep space – a whopper of a nuclear explosion outside our solar system would probably leave us unaffected.) At the start of a nuclear exchange, you should expect that the first thing to happen will be a series of megaton-range exo-atmospheric blasts that creates huge EMPs that burn out every unshielded chip in the underlying countries, unless the circuits are EMP hardened. This is why military aircraft have EMP-hardened circuits. It is easy to EMP a circuit – you wrap it in aluminium foil, and the Faraday cage effect protects the contents. I keep my memory sticks in a steel box for this reason. Our boiler designer 30 years ago never thought about this, and the boiler was burned out by a thunderstorm in 2021. To be fair, no-one in our banking system worries about it either. It's not just a lightning and nuclear blast can do this – the sun can as well. Look up the Carrington Event of 1859 – if that solar flare happened tomorrow, most of our computers and microchips would burn out and never work again. Then look up the bizarrely named 'Starfish Prime' test, to see how the US military burned out streetlights in Hawaii with a nuclear bomb hundreds of miles away. Then worry about your PC backups.

Hippies and Hawkwind

There is a curious if tenuous link between the hippy visionaries I mention (Hawkwind and Tim Blake) and my younger days. There really were a lot of people who thought we were headed for a new age, with space-age science under-writing a spiritual lifestyle featuring a lot of psychedelic drugs. Hawkwind were a rock band who formed in 1971, explicitly merging space science with pseudo-medieval mystical imagery. They are the only band to have a rock song about Albert Einstein's "Twins paradox" (whereby time appears to slow down if you move near the speed of light). A space traveller laments that when he gets home back to earth, a fit young man, the young girl he left behind on earth that he loves will be long dead.

"I would like you to have been deep frozen too, waiting still as fresh in your flesh for my return to earth.

But your father refused to sign the forms to freeze you.

Let's see – you'd be about 60 now, and long dead by the time I return to earth."

(Hawkwind – "Spirit of the age" on the album "Quark, strangeness and charm".) The theme of space aliens overseeing planet earth is explicit in Tim Blake's songs (Eg "Lighthouse") and Jefferson Airplane ("Have you seen the saucers?") Well worth a listen).

Tim Blake came (briefly) to Hawkwind from the legendary weird 70s band Planet Gong, with Dave Allen and Gilly Smith. They also invented a weird pseudo-world, but theirs was populated with PHPs (Pot Head Pixies) who flew around in flying teapots. (Find the album "Flying teapot" if you want to see them.) The combination of near-science and mystical other worlds is not that far off from Scientology, which is effectively a mind virus created by a sci-fi author that got loose in the community. Luckily, neither Hawkwind nor Gong nor their fans took themselves particularly seriously, and since the band members and the fans were perennially too stoned to focus beyond the next spliff there was never much danger of the idea going viral, but I suspect there may be a PhD in studying the analogies for someone!

Oh yes the link to my life: when Tim Blake played with Hawkwind, they played Oxford in November 1979, and I saw them as a new 1st year student, stoned of course, with the hippy chick who first taught me about weed. Yes they played "Lighthouse", I can just about remember seeing Tim Blake in his shiny suit getting his synthesisers to burble away. The concert is immortalised in the "live'79" album.

It is worth trying to find the original "Hawkwind Log" (1971), a booklet that accompanied the album "in search of space". The weird combination of space-age science with hippy mysticism is epitomised by the first thing you see here – a pseudo-female android using the language of a motivational trainer to get you to say the word "Om".

On the subject of Islamic sultans, **Genghis Khan**'s Y chromosome gets a mention. The original Genghis Khan was a Mongolian warlord who managed to unify the Mongol hordes into a global force, by a combination of utter ruthlessness, good tactics, and a policy that people he conquered were given a choice to merge with him and offer absolute loyalty, or die on the spot with their families. [Shakar brought the Zulu tribe to great power by following almost exactly the same playbook.] His blitzkrieg war machine ransacked towns from Poland to India and China. It seems well established that he had a firm policy that whenever his men ransacked a town, they were allowed to do much as they wanted, except that the loveliest women were to be kept unharmed and brought to Genghis Khan for his personal pleasure. Loyal soldiers who disobeyed this edict were killed on the spot. Not surprisingly, this created a lot of babies who went on to claim Genghis Khan as their father. An entire tribe in Pakistan have long claimed to be founded by children of the Khan, and (uniquely for that region) they have the correct Y chromosome in abundance. Recently we think we have identified his Y chromosome, a variant of the haplotype C-M217. This is found in 8% of the men alive on the planet today, making Genghis Khan the most genetically successful man we know of. (See also the charmingly named 'Ismael the bloodthirsty' of Morocco, who probably comes second and generated an Ignoble prize for the researchers who explored whether his claim to >800 babies was credible.) We may never be sure, because (like the prophet Muhammed), Genghis Khan's grave is unmarked. His funeral cortege killed anyone they encountered, to prevent people from knowing where they had been. Although Genghis Khan is popularly associated with boiling enemies alive, this may be a transfer from his arch-enemy Jamukha, who is recorded as having had an array of 70 giant cauldrons set up, to slowly boil alive generals from an opposing army. (When Europeans tried this, they found the prolonged slow painfulness of the spectacle intolerable to watch.) Genghis Khan does, however, seem to have dipped someone in a bath of molten silver, and it wasn't out of kindness!

Mount Mutnovsky – a geothermal region in Kamchatka, with pools of boiling mud etc.

Omar's stories

The account of a schoolboy adding up the numbers 1 to 100 in his head, writing it down on his slate, then throwing it at the exasperated master did happen, when the young Karl Gauss was at primary school. Karl Gauss was probably the greatest mathematician in history, though I think Ramanujan would have given him stiff competition if he hadn't died too young (illness from an avoidable childhood infection).

The rate of change of a function $Y=A*X^B$, its gradient or 'differential', is $dY/dX = A*B*X^{(B-1)}$, so no simple polynomial can be its own differential. The exponential function is indeed its own differential, and achieves this seemingly impossible feat by being an infinite series, where each term becomes the next term along after differentiation. You see a picture in your mind of an infinite conveyor belt loaded with the successive terms, and each time you calculate the differential the conveyor belt moves one place to the left. Here N! means N factorial, $2*3*4*5 \ldots *N$. Hence $3!=6$, $4! = 24$, $5! = 120$, etc.

$$\text{Exp}(x) = \quad 1 + X + X^2/2 + X^3/6 + X^4/24 \ldots + X^N/N!$$
$$\downarrow \quad \downarrow \quad \downarrow \quad \downarrow \quad \downarrow \quad \downarrow$$
$$d/dX \text{ of exp}(x) = 0 + 1 + X + X^2/2 + X^3/6 \ldots X^{n-1}/(N-1)!$$

these are the same – QED

A curious thing about this infinite series is that it looks remarkably like the infinite series for the sine of an angle and the cosine of an angle. In fact, if you pretend that the number 'i' – the square root of minus 1 – is a meaningful concept, you plug one of these 'complex numbers' into an exponential series, and out pops an answer consisting of the cosine of the angle (the real number) plus a complex number which is the sine of the angle.

A Path of 21 Ms

This realisation led the great mathematician Euler to formulate what I think is my favourite equation:

Exp(i*π) = -1

It works because pi radians means 180 degrees means that the sine term (multiplied by i) is zero, so you only get the real term. Omar discovering this for himself as a schoolboy would put him in the global mathematical elite for our species. [My friend in York, Romano Baino, liked this equation so much that he used it as his email signature!]

Ramanujan

I mention the Indian genius Ramanujan as an inspiration for Omar. He was a poor clerk in India, self-taught in mathematics from an ad-hoc collection of books he managed to find lying around. He undoubtedly was at the top of our global elites, ended up impressing the UK's top man on number theory, Hardy, in Cambridge.

Most people found his work incomprehensible, and even good mathematicians get their minds blown by his equations describing (for example) infinite series of recursive functions that popped out of his mind without proof. The world's finest living mathematical minds have gone through his notebooks, finding deep results and new fields on every page.

Fig 15.13 Srinivasa Ramanujan.

$$\sqrt{1+2\sqrt{1+3\sqrt{1+\cdots}}}.$$

Fig 15.14 An example of the sort of equation that (self-taught) Srinivasa Ramanujan derived and intuitively understood.

The Riemann Zeta function conjecture

This has been described as one of the most important outstanding maths problems. It states that all the non-trivial solutions to a particular infinitely long equation involving all the prime numbers take the form of a complex number whose real part is 0.5, a+bi where a = 0.5 and b can be any value. We have used computers to find many solutions, and they all take this form. Dozens of mathematical proofs start by saying "Assuming that the Riemann conjecture is true . . .". It surely is true, but proving this has defeated the best minds, so far.

On with the speculation

Welcome to the Anthropocene. The year is 2160, and the pH of the sea has fallen to 7.8, its lowest value for 55 million years. Carbon dioxide is also at a record high, 900 ppm, and has only stopped its rapid rise because there is little organic sediment left to oxidise. The Arctic ice and permafrost have gone, along with the vast peat deposits that they shielded. The massive, kilometre-deep ice covering the Antarctic survives merely by its immense thermal inertia, melting in huge floods each austral summer. The hippies of 200 years ago were almost right when they sang of a coming new age, of the need to come together, the need for peace and love. Hairy, well-meaning iconoclasts, they spurned conformity and all organised religion, venerating *Cannabis* and finding neo-transcendence in psychedelics, modulating activity in their cingulate cortices with LSD or psilocybin rather than by decades of prayer, though it wasn't till David Nutt's neuro-imaging work 30 years later that the results were shown to be similar. (To this day true believers do not accept this result.) In the words of some hippy icons: "In visions of Acid we through delusion, a great revolution, we knew we were right" (Hawkwind – Days of the Underground), "It's the New Age, Harmony, Science and Love – Living and loving inside the New Age – It's better for you" (Tim Blake, song for a New Age). Sure enough, a new world has come to pass, and it can even include *Psilocybe* mushrooms if you live in the correct states in Antarctica and your psychiatrists prescribes them. *Cannabis* plants still grow well under lights, and help lots of people stay sane during the long lightless winters. But peace and love – dream on! When your parents fled gigadeaths as the continents emptied out and food chains stopped functioning, being nice to people became more difficult. Ironically, the communities where authorities still talk most about peace and love are the religious enclaves around the Arctic Sea, where the evidence consistently shows that deviations from accepted modes of thought are met with baying mobs and cruel punishments. Religions never cared much about evidence, so each one maintained it was the true path to peace and love as they tortured unbelievers for the alleged good of their alleged souls.

Every family that made it to safety had horror stories of their exodus experience. The old analogy used to be with the last helicopter out of Saigon in 1968, in a pointless minor turf war, almost forgotten except in some famous old folk songs. A mere tiny vignette, handfuls of people and hardly any deaths. Kabul airport August 2021 was a bit closer, with hundreds of desperate people climbing onto the outside of transport planes like peasants on the fabled Mexican buses. (They all fell off to their death, of course.) Still just one city, still only triple digit deaths. Everyone there knew where they wanted to go to be safe, it just involved getting a lift. There was even food and accommodation available at the other end, maybe even people who remembered you. Now try scaling that experience up to evacuating a continent, with no-one clear where was safe, where the future might be found. Stay in your traditional homeland and expect to die of heatstroke. Go far away to the polar cool, and maybe you have a chance to live. The civil, well-behaved folks stayed obediently in queues, then died there along with their families. When you are that desperate you fight and if needed you kill, or be killed. The ones who made it to safety in the new lands at the poles combined luck with aggressive ruthlessness, and those that went on to raise children made sure to pass on some stories. (Usually omitting the worst details, except perhaps in confessionals with their counsellors. A surprising number of PTSD cases turned out to be guilt at a clandestine killing somewhere in some port or airport.)

Previously your ancestors might walk barefoot in a forest to look up at the trees, smell the pine oils as the terpenes volatilise, and know that their experience was just like their ancestors had been experiencing since time immemorial, walking on the soil of their nation, their homeland. Since about 10,000 years to be picky, less for immigrants in the Americas, but it felt like forever. Walking barefoot was actually a bad idea because of the likelihood of standing on a spiky plant, and they would check a weather forecast for the probability of heavy rain. Now you could revisit your parental homeland if you chose, in a convoy of air-conditioned vehicles. You would not want to walk barefoot on the bare rock in most cases because it would be hot enough to hurt, and if the air had a distinct odour, it would be of old fires. You certainly checked the weather forecast to get a probability, but in order to see how likely it was that the temperature would exceed the lethal threshold of 55C. This is why vehicles had to go in convoy – after a spate of coachloads of tourists dying of heatstroke due to an electrical fault, the rule became that every vehicle had a backup, and in the event of a breakdown you aborted the journey to head for the nearest shelter. National identity – what does that mean when you dare not stand outside for part of the year? Lines on a map are useful for administrators, but that needs people living there to administer.

So your ancestors moved to places where you did dare to stand outside at (almost) any time of year, given suitable clothing. This started off as being the high latitude islands – places like New Zealand, Britain, Greenland, Japan. The trouble with being an island next to a hot sea is that you get very large amounts of rainfall. The British had long joked about their wet weather, but once CO_2 got above 600ppm the downpours stopped being a joke and became dangerous. Lethal floods in rich stable places like Germany and Japan in the 2020s started off as being a shock before being seen as straws in the wind. People started taking their carbon budgets more seriously, even taxing fossil emissions in the teeth of populist protest. By that time it was too late – Planet Earth had taken over the process, and twiddly human details like stopping flights or shutting coal-fired power stations barely scratched the surface of the global fluxes of carbon atoms. The Covid-19 pandemic almost shut down commuting and international flights, but barely registered on the CO_2 graphs. "Stop burning Putin's gas" they (almost) all said in 2022, and tried as hard as they could to cut back. "Freeze for Ukraine" became a curious political slogan to encourage turning down domestic thermostats. The CO_2 concentration kept on rising exponentially as though Earth had not so much as noticed the difference.

Charlotte Bay, Antarctica

Class 3B of the Charlotte Bay Secondary school, on the Antarctic peninsula, is preparing for an educational outing to a regional archaeological feature. In this case the Charlotte Bay Hut, where Wally Herbert waited for three months to be rescued as they had no suitable radios back in 1956. The story of his rescue by Shackleton after a three-month wait is repeated by the school as a lesson in the need to trust that the future will work out. At the time Antarctica was unknown and very cold, whereas now its bare rock is fully mapped and gives welcome refuge from the lethal continental heat spikes. Faith in the future working out is a valuable psychological resource, given how dramatically the good times of past societies crumbled in the global heat. To be honest there wasn't much to see at the Charlotte Bay historical site, the wood long decayed in the warm wet air (but replaced by newer planks to keep up appearances), but its context was important for the children's understanding, and anyway school trips are always a welcome change from daily teaching.

A little voice chirped up: "Did the old whalers keep camels, like you told us to look out for?" Alexandra Elbakyan shook her head. She had seen the old photos, lots of bearded men and snow, but no camels. Mainly dogs, no other domestic animals except a few unfortunate ponies with the Scott expedition. It was family legend that her father had planted the first trees in Antarctica, lines of downy birch *Betula pubescens*, now grown tall enough to give some shelter to the cultivated plots from the fierce winds. Once upon a time the only green on the surface of Antarctica came from moss mats, but once the climate heated up, conditions allowed some approximation to horticulture. The lack of light in winter was offset by the extra light in summer, and in fact the main limitation to crops became the soil. Or rather the complete lack of native soil, so it had to be imported by boat at great effort and expense from the nearby land masses. Even with tons of imported soil, the browsing was always tough and sparse, and it took several failed attempts at livestock farming before someone noticed that the combination of poor food, cold winters and high salt were like a home from home for the Bactrian camels of the Mongolian deserts. There were now more camels in Antarctica than in their homeland, but they were still irascible beasts that could kick and bite without provocation, best stayed well away from. Especially when you are small. (Similarly, there were by 2160 many more dromedary camels living feral on the coolest southern coastal parts of the Australian mainland than survived in their homeland of Arabia.)

Alexandra stuck her hand up – "Please, Miss, no they had dogs, didn't they? Not camels."

Miss Frazer saw an opportunity. "Almost, Alexandra, but not quite. Wally Herbert's team didn't have any animals with them, though other people did use dogs to pull sleighs across the ice cap." She hoped no-one would ask where the meat came from to feed the dogs, since the idea of killing household pets to feed others is a bit of a shock at such a tender age. She knew Alexandra as one of the brighter children, often coming up with surprisingly well-informed comments. Partly from her family background undoubtedly, but clearly talented and maybe hiding something special. "Alexandra – did your father have anything to do with the Charlotte Bay site?" she asked, knowing perfectly well that he did.

"Yes, Miss, he gave it soil," Alexandra replied, exactly on cue.

Alexandra's father was a soil importer, whose job involved heavy machinery depositing layers of imported soil in carefully planned strata and positions. One of those jobs that hardly existed on the old continents in the old world – soil appeared unbidden for free, created from the annual cycle of growth, death and decay of plants. Trees or grass worked fine, creating good soil in a century or less, but Antarctic moss mats on top of lifeless granite simply did not give a fertile soil (mosses decay poorly). So people followed the example of the former inhabitants of Malta in importing soil by ships. Some soil was mined in Tasmania, some came from South America (or its archipelago Tierra del Fuego), the rest from southern Africa. There was skill required to build up a useful soil profile, with low-grade heavy clay-rich subsoil laid down first on the bedrock, followed by just enough rich topsoil to support a crop (about 10cm). When you are transporting hundreds of tons of soil hundreds of kilometres without fossil fuels, soil becomes far too precious a resource to lay down thickly. Providing the climate continues to support grass and the Bactrian camels continue to tolerate the lifestyle and recycle the nutrients, the soil profile should become self-sustaining in a few centuries. Until then, any hope of feeding people on locally grown plants requires massive soil management.

A little note of family pride lit up her voice: "He also planted the first trees in Antarctica, on some south American soil he'd imported." In fact, admiring his woodland glade would be one of the features of the school trip, though up to about 100 years ago the hectare of scrubby willows would barely have rated a mention in anyone's woodland inventory anywhere. She wondered whether anyone would remember her in years to come, except maybe as having helped plant some baby Arctic trees in Charlotte Bay, alongside her dad.

Maybe someone could even use her trees to make the fabled wood derivative called paper, that had been so useful in so many ways to her ancestors, but needed so many big trees that just didn't grow wide enough on the bare rock of Antarctica. It also didn't store well in the warm wetness that dominated the Antarctic peninsula, going soft and mouldy. Schools still referred to educational blocks as 'books', but these were electronic displays. There were no libraries of physical books in the new land, just servers that acted as online sources to supply the files that downloaded as e-books.

"Please, Miss – when Wally Herbert lived here, did people see all this coming?" asked Alexandra in genuine puzzlement, as the school tour prepared for its visit to the remains of the old hut.

Miss Frazer sighed – she didn't like having to own up to the stupidity of her predecessors. "It depends what you mean by 'They' and 'This'," she replied, evasively.

Alexandra was not easily put off. "I mean the ice all melting, and the world being split into two."

It was part of growing up in 22nd century Antarctica that you understood that the human population was split, with one set living around the cool of the Antarctic, the others living in the habitable zone inside the Arctic Circle. Between them, the continental land masses were dangerous archaeological ghost worlds. Lethal temperature spikes regularly forced survivors underground, and any mechanical breakdown could lead to an unpleasant death with no rescue services. The geography of the two polar regions differed profoundly, leading two almost isolated populations. The Antarctic land mass held a wholly new community, assembled from a diverse mix of immigrants with no pre-existing natives or traditions. People came there from all over the planet, not just the southern hemisphere, because it was set up as a democratic republic with similar founding principles to the French Republic. Equality, one person one vote, no automatic hierarchies, and no state religion. By contrast the Arctic communities were condensed down subsets of existing states, retaining religious identities. As states collapsed, their religious identities magnified in importance, eventually boiling down to intolerant monocultures sharing an ice-free Arctic Sea. What used to be Canada was predominantly Christian, Protestants and Catholics in uneasy co-existence. The Orthodox church moved north to claim its zone, the north coast of Siberia. There was even a New Jerusalem by a red sea, the Jewish enclave overlooking the Arctic Sea. Red with the fern *Azolla* of course. Then there was the Islamic enclave, in what used to be Kamchatka. No-one seemed to know how this land transfer came to happen, with suspicions that remarkably large sums of money were involved. Reporters who asked too many questions about the deal systematically died young, coming over suddenly suicidal, unexpectedly hanging themselves without warning or goodbye notes. The surviving editors learned to steer clear of the topic – just quote the official explanation about a goodwill gesture. Suffice to say that there was one enclave, in what used to be called Kamchatka, where a version of Sharia law still ran, with catastrophic consequences for the few remaining non-Muslim original inhabitants (Russian/Chinese descent). Russian administrators involved in the transfer tended to retire early to palatial dachas with sea views over the Arctic, saying nothing.

A historical analogy might be with the city states of antiquity, and as before there was no love lost between isolated groups, despite the economic benefits from co-operating. The main reason that none of them had got round to launching a religious war against godless Antarctica (to spread whichever belief underwrote their constitution) was the sheer distance and time involved. As foreseen by Jefferson Airplane in their song 'Wooden Ships', post-apocalypse you revert to traditional windpower because that's what you have available. Communication was perfectly possible as the undersea cables remained in place, so internet, video and telephone communication between the Arctic and Antarctic communities was routine. The satellite links that used to give global coverage had been destroyed by the EMPs at the start of a relatively minor nuclear exchange. People had forgotten how vulnerable unshielded systems were, and most of the non-military satellites had been fried along with most of the computers in the banking system. ("Did no-one see this coming?" people asked when the scale of the disaster became obvious. Luckily, at least one engineer at Intel had seen it coming and had backed up a full chip-making resource in EMP-hardened containers. His paranoia allowed humans to continue making new computers after the first big nuclear EMP burnt all their chips out.) Also luckily, old fashioned copper cables are made of sterner stuff than semiconductors, and even though they briefly held fields around 1MV/m, the old copper links remained intact. Allowing communication, if not mutual understanding.

Miss Frazer sighed. Most aspects of being a teacher were interesting and enjoyable, but trying to explain the runaway greenhouse effect to children who knew nothing of atmospheric chemistry or human politics was always a challenge. "Our planet is experiencing the birth pangs of a new geological era. We have entered a new hot phase called the Anthropocene. It has happened before, in the Eocene and before that in the Permian. Yes, people saw it coming. There was even a famous book warning us called 'An Inconvenient Truth' by a presidential candidate. Not that it made much difference. President Carter was told of this as far back as in 1977. Not that it made much difference."

Alexa frowned. Sometimes grown-ups said things that didn't make sense, and this was another one. "How could they NOT pay attention when the President says something?" she asked.

Explaining the automatic unthinking loathing between Democrats and Republicans was above Miss Frazer's paygrade, so she pretended not to hear.

"My parents told me it was caused by Arctic bogs. Didn't people think to look at Arctic bogs?"

Again, given the choice between an honest review of how environmental policies had been navigated, and feigning deafness, Miss Frazer found that deafness proved the simplest solution. But Alexandra realised she was being fobbed off, and she had enough determination to make a mental note to look into this herself or with her parents.

New Riyadh

Omar Patel looked out of the classroom over the pinky fern growth on the waves of the Arctic Sea. He knew that he didn't fit in, but didn't know why not. The current phrasing in western psychological literature would be 'neuro-atypical'. He saw pictures inside his head, saw the world only by its visual portrayal. This worked very well for the science syllabus, especially the mathematics. It did not work at all for any other aspect of his life, especially not anything involving religion or people or human relationships. By seeing mathematical functions as simple pictures he breezed through the simple proofs underlying the school syllabus, leaving him under-stimulated and bored. Sadly, not only could no-one else in his school get into the same league as him, but no-one understood anything about the amazing imagery going on inside his head. He just kept coming top in class at maths, and bottom of pretty much everything else. The social hierarchy in his (all-male) classes involved a mixture of physical strength, propensity to violence, and social status of your father. Omar had none of these, and his father (technically a chemist) used his knowledge of chemistry to extract elements from landfill mining. Some of the richest deposits of some rare elements turned out to be the legacy of domestic waste heaps from the 20th and 21st centuries. Astonishing amounts of electrical goods had been just thrown out, all containing as a minimum some useful amounts of copper and nickel. An old mobile phone held some 40 elements, many unavailable in the new super-heated world. Literal gold dust came in the form of some old calculators. The Hewlett-Packard RPN calculators had metallic gold in their keypads, with one such find repaying days of work. (Of course, the main product mined from landfill were plastic wastes. Legally they should be reburied, but they lit easily and burned well so deposits of these were inevitably burned. Human settlements have always smelled of burning wood, now they also smell of burning plastic.) Landfill chemists were therefore important members of society, recycling atoms to enable technology to continue. They were also looked down on by the devout, rather like the Dajit (untouchables) had been in the Hindu caste system. Omar learned this the hard way, especially at the hands of the big, strong and psychopathic son of a Mufti. "Your dad does rubbish, talks about chemicals, is rubbish. So you must be rubbish too" became his standard greeting across the playground.

The mathematics lesson was normally something Omar normally looked forward to, but today it was about an ancient Greek called Euclid and seemed very dusty and old fashioned. Mr Khan's teaching style didn't help – handing down other people's ideas without inviting discussion. Some of Euclid's ideas seemed so obvious that he didn't see why they needed stating. "If A = B then B = A" for example. I could be playing with my console rather than being told this basic obvious stuff, he thought.

Then the teacher moved onto a weird step-by-step analysis of prime numbers, the building blocks of all integers. The logic followed was ancient, dating back to a Greek man called Euclid, long before Islam came into being. Omar stopped looking at the waves to think about the reasoning. What Euclid did was quite outside the sort of didactic logic the rest of their (explicitly Islamic) syllabus imposed. He proved something must be false by first exploring the belief that it was true. He proved that there could not possibly be a final biggest prime number, by assuming that such a number did exist. If this were true, you could write down a list of all the prime numbers. Maybe a long list but a finite list. Now you multiply them together to get an answer, then add one to it. Voila – a number that proves your belief to be false. Either it is prime itself, or (if it can be divided) there must be some other prime number you forgot. He tried a few simple examples to reassure himself. If the highest prime number were 7, the number 211 (= $2 \times 3 \times 5 \times 7 +1$) would be the counter proof (and indeed is prime though this takes a few calculations to be sure). "Can we use this sort of inverted logic in other cases?" Omar asked. Mr Khan frowned, sensing deep and dangerous waters if he gave the wrong answer. "Only in pure mathematics," he snapped back.

Omar persisted: "If the ancients were so clever, how come they ended up having to move out of their homelands?"

The teacher sighed. Teaching was generally a good vocation, but explaining how supposedly intelligent societies ignored evidence-based warnings was somewhat outside his remit. "You must not confuse the pre-Islamic ancient Greeks with the unbelievers and sinners who led the destruction of our holy earth," he said, not actually explaining anything. "Euclid and Pythagoras never used fuels dug out from the earth, never even saw any, so they could not possibly know what world they could cause. The old societies were sinful, and paid the penalty."

Omar had the sense to ask no more, but found himself wondering about the vast body of knowledge and proofs that must have been accumulated over human history, if something so mind-expanding was established so long ago. How much of it was still available? He knew that there were still old collections of books made of paper, though paper had become a rare and precious commodity since the main forest lands had burned. The fact that paper inevitably decayed in the permanent high humidity, and that (even kept dry) it tended to rot away to brown dust in a few decades, meant that around the Arctic Sea most 'books' were electronic screens. Outside the school system in any case they were mainly religious. A lot of questions seemed to go unasked or unanswered. Curious that our ancestors claimed to have walked men on the moon, and certainly learned how to turn sand into machines that could harvest sunlight and think faster than any human, but somehow no-one seemed to know about planetary history, or where animals fitted in. Strange that the creation of the world was described in accurate detail in the Old Testament but its transition to a meltdown world seemed a total surprise to humanity. He suspected that a lot of adults knew more than they were letting on, and wasn't far off the mark. A lot of adults knew that they didn't know, but they also knew that expressing doubt or asking the wrong questions meant ostracism, accusations of blasphemy so potentially death. You kept quiet and stayed safe in the comfort of ignorance. In the worst case you got sent to Mount Mutnovsky. This was a place of unspoken horror, where Genghis Khan 2 sent the people he most disliked.

Omar made a mental note to ask his parents . . . but wasn't sure what to ask.

Prudhoe Bay, York township, Alaska

It is mid-afternoon at the Prudhoe Bay primary school, on the north coast of Alaska. This settlement is proud of its roots in the USA, unlike the majority of the north coast which thinks of itself as Canada. The founders considered calling it New Miami, but even with runaway warming the ambience never matched the (now partly submerged) old Miami, so they opted for 'New New York'. That was so clearly inconvenient that it just became 'York', forgetting about the original Viking settlement of this name in northern England, whose cathedral and walls still projected from the Ouse floodplain. Elinor came from one of the founding families, fleeing Miami. Family tradition was that one heirloom painting, art from old Japan taking pride of place on the living room wall, came all the way from the old York (in England) well over 150 years ago. Elinor, like the rest of the class, newly settled at their old wooden desks, finds it hard to stay switched on during the long nights as mid-winter approaches. In summer you can hardly sleep due to constant light – in winter the problem is getting out of bed. This is the unavoidable consequence of the earth's orbit, but does mean that the school lights are on for all of the day in the winter months. She looked out over the sea, pink in the early-afternoon setting sun, the pink light picking out what looked like pink feather down floating on the waves. Welcome to the freshwater Arctic Sea. Just a surface layer of warm fresh water from melting ice caps (overlying the salt), but covered with a dense bloom of the floating fern *Azolla*. She tried to focus on the lesson. The teacher, Mr Jones, stood in front of a projection of tropical islands covered in green forest. "Today's geography lesson is about two islands in the Pacific Ocean, and how human use has changed them. Nauru and Easter Island."

"Is Easter Island in the Bible"? asked one little voice.

The school had a strongly biblical core to its curriculum, and they had already endured extensive instruction on why the Easter story was the most important in the Bible.

Mr Jones smiled indulgently. "No, it was only discovered in 1722. By a man from a tiny submerged zone in Europe called Netherlands. Its name came from the first people who discovered it – they arrived there on Easter day, so they called it

Easter Island. They found that the Polynesian natives who lived there had already carved giant stone statues. The natives were therefore called 'Easter Islanders'."

Elinor tried to absorb this, and saw a logical impossibility. "Please sir, if the natives were already carving statues then surely the netherworlders were the second people to find it, not the first?"

Mr Jones frowned, saw deep waters, and skirted the question. "Netherland not netherworld, and they were the first Christian explorers, representatives of civilisation. The Netherlands were a tiny state on the west of Asia, now lost to the seas, but they even had their own royal family, own coinage and a unique language. They sent out boats around the world, and even took over some big islands near Australia for a while."

The class were totally unimpressed with this display of historical erudition, and cared nothing about pre-meltdown colonial history. Sensibly, Mr Jones carried on.

"Let's look at Nauru first. This was, or in fact still is, a small island north of Australia in the Pacific." He got out a globe, still an indispensable aid to teaching geography. The globe could at first sight have been used in a school in the 1950s, since the shapes of the lands and seas were almost identical. Close comparison would show that the 2150 globe had had some low-lying areas replaced by sea. The western European coastline, and the deltas east of India were especially nibbled away by the rising seas. The difference of course was in the national boundaries. The 20th century globes were patchworks of different colours, each a different state. The 22nd century globe still has lines marking old country names, hypothetical lines on a mathematical space, but what people worried about more were two things. Firstly, the red zones. These were areas that were uninhabitable due to the frequency of lethal heat spikes, and they now covered most of the mid latitudes, like someone had daubed a red paintbrush along the planet's equator. Well, almost uninhabitable, though Mecca showed what could be done. When it became clear that visiting Mecca for the Haj (a duty of Islam) risked becoming involved in a horrible mass death after repeated experiences of what happens when temperatures spiked into the 60s (Celsius not Fahrenheit), a solution had to be found. The engineers of the day created the biggest insulated hangar in history, eclipsing even the Chernobyl sarcophagus, completely encasing the zones of pilgrimage. With good enough insulation and a generous supply of solar-power air conditioners, the space could be made safe and the Haj did indeed continue even though Mecca is shown as sitting well into the middle of the Asian red zone.

The other unfamiliar new features on Mr Jones' globe were the Arctic states, belligerent new city-states with no real history to fall back on and no clear idea of where their peoples are going. The north coast of Russia had four major conglomerations, self-defining by their religions. Going from west to east you had two Christian blocks (one an uneasy coalition of Catholics and Protestants, the other Orthodox) separated from each other by a small enclave from Israel (who really had moved into a New Jerusalem by a red sea), while the Islamic community settled in Kamchatka. The north coast of Canada still called itself Canada, though its enclaves tended to Christian fundamentalism despite the wordings of its various constitutions.

"So the islands of the Pacific ocean like Nauru here . . ." he pointed his index finger at a point a bit up and right of the livid scarlet block that was Australia . . . "used to be thought of as an ultimate paradise, with lovely weather all the time, nice seas and good food." ('and easy women' he thought, but had the sense to keep such thoughts to himself.) The people who lived on Nauru were dark skinned fishermen who kept little vegetable gardens in the native forest, to grow the plants to eat along with their fish. Simple but happy lives." Mr Jones fiddled with the keyboard, clicked on something, and the picture on the screen behind him changed to one of smiling Polynesian children playing in the surf. Warming to his theme, he glossed over a few niggly ecological details: "This lifestyle had been stable for hundreds of years. That is what we call 'Sustainable'." Sad to say, evidence shows that the Polynesians routinely exterminated everything edible on an island chain then moved on to somewhere new. (An entire group of flightless rails has all-but been wiped out this way, leaving one population on Henderson Island, where dense spiky scrub protected them from starving Polynesians.) Mr Jones didn't know that, and would have kept quiet if had known it.

"Then one day someone looked at the rocks on Nauru, the stone that the island was made from. It turned out to be made of top quality fertiliser. That is why the gardens grew so well there. So people discovered that they could dig up the stone with big machines, then sell it to farmers in Australia. The farmers were happy because their crops grew better. The Nauru fishermen were happy because they were getting enough money to feed themselves without fishing every day."

Elinor liked the idea that everyone was happy. Most of the stories adults told her were about people being unhappy, and this sounded more fun.

Mr Jones continued: "So people came in with more and bigger machines and took away more rock, and gave the people of Nauru more money. In fact, they had so much money that they didn't know what to do with it. The government built a road round the island going nowhere, then people spent lots of money on buying really fast cars to drive very quickly round this tiny island. Oddly, the people's health got worse not better, because they stopped exercising and started too much eating the food of the rich – unlimited cake. And their native forest was destroyed, to mine the stone. So the island ended up ruined, horrible to live on with no future, and the people were fat and sad with nowhere to go."

Mr Jones pushed another button, and a photograph came up of a white barren lifeless landscape, the Nauru landscape post-quarrying. "So this left the people less happy than before. They even tried getting more money out of the Australian government, even though it was money that had caused their problems."

Elinor frowned – maybe not such a happy story after all. "Please, sir, why didn't they see it coming and stop it?" After all, how can you possibly NOT be aware of a massive mining operation round your house?

Mr Jones sighed. Geography was fine but teaching psychology was really outside his job specification. "I think that the people who saw it coming were not listened to by the people making decisions," he replied truthfully but unhelpfully.

"So how long will they have to wait to get their island back?"

"Do you mean if the climate hadn't run out of control?" he asked, slightly stalling for time. "I think that would have been thousands of years. The stone accumulates very slowly."

Elinor tried to digest the idea. "So people made themselves unhappy by trying to make themselves happy by destroying their island for hundreds of years – is that right? That sounds silly. And how does the stone grow?"

Seeing a splendid diversion, Mr Jones pounced. "The stone is very interesting. It is produced by seabirds that catch fish out at sea then bring them back to be digested while on the nest. A conveyor belt carrying phosphate from the sea to be concentrated on land. When sitting on nests, birds just poop out what is left. This dried to a crumbly white stone, which is excellent fertiliser for plants because of its phosphate content."

The class responded as anticipated, with cries of "bird poo" and "yuck". Thereby missing the depth of understanding behind Elinor's question.

One more question – "Please, sir, does it still exist?"

Yes, he explained. Even after the inevitable 70m sea level rise, the highest point of Nauru will continue to stick out of the mid-Pacific, more of a hazard to shipping than a global morality tale. Not that anyone much bothered going there now, lacking as it does either archaeology or significant vegetation. In any case that was vaguely two millennia in the future.

Mr Jones moved on. Another click, another PowerPoint image projected, of huge scowling stone carved faces standing surrounded by waves. A green conical mountain in the background showed where the land was. "This is Easter Island. The stone heads were carved from the hard volcanic stone by the Polynesian settlers, and no-one really knows what they represented. When Rogeveen landed in 1722 he noted that there were stone statues, and that the island had trees. Fifty years later, when Europeans returned, the statues were overturned and there were no trees."

Previous students in previous classrooms elsewhere on the planet had found this concept difficult. Every other land mass had supported forests of trees for all of human history. In the 22nd century arctic, the idea of being treeless was normal, so no-one asked the obvious question: "You mean that someone chopped down the last tree? How could they?" He clicked again, and an old photograph appeared, showing bare grassy slopes with a bare hill in the background. There were a few white blobs in the distance, dwarfed by the landscape. "Can you see these white animals? Does anyone know what they are?" No-one replied. None of the children had met one in the wool, though most had seen pictures in story books and poetry anthologies. The poem 'Bah Bah black sheep' still got taught in primary schools, though made even less sense to them than it does to us.

"They are sheep, and were introduced by westerners from south America long after the phase of statue carving. They like open treeless landscapes, so adapted well to Easter Island after its trees had gone. People ate their meat and used their hair to make woollen clothes."

Elinor raised a quizzical hand. "You mean that there did used to be trees there, and didn't used to be sheep? Is that why they cut the trees down?"

Mr Jones picked up the question as a gift to his rhetorical flow. "The evidence from the landscape is quite clear: Easter Island was completely wooded with palm trees until humans settled it, about 1000 years ago. They needed the trees to make boats and to roll the huge stone heads into position. But they cut so many trees that there were none left. Then they stopped making statues and stopped making boats." He might have added that the trees were probably wiped out by the rats *Rattus exulans* which came in with the human settlers, though even if he had known that he'd have kept quiet, to keep this awkward complication out of the way.

"Did the Easter Islanders write anything down?" someone asked. Again, a welcome opportunity to change the subject away from awkward questions by demonstrating erudition. "Actually yes, sort-of. They came from an illiterate Polynesian culture, no-one in the Pacific islands wrote anything, until Europeans taught them. Except on Easter Island, where people carved a strange script called Rongo-rongo. We only have a few pieces left now, carved onto driftwood, and no-one can translate the mysterious symbols." He flashed up a picture of a strange piece of old wood, covered in stranger glyphs.

Fig 15.15 An Easter Island Rongo-rongo carving.

"No-one can read these now," the teacher intoned, expecting the question that duly came: "Please sir, what happened to the people who could read it?" Mr Jones knew enough of the background to know that the story does not make Europeans sound good. "There was a priest class on Easter Island, we think that they were called the Ariki class, and that they could read the glyphs. They were taken away in the 1840s by Spanish slavers to work in their guano mines. They were Catholics, so happy to take slaves." (Even now, Protestants didn't miss a chance to poison the well of Christian unity. Some families in York came from French-speaking stock Canadian families and still used the phrase "c'est la galère" – La Galère being a folk memory of French Catholics forcing French Protestants to work as galley-slaves rowing commercial boats across the Mediterranean, usually until they died.) This was the second mention of guano in a short period, so got a shocked laugh. "Ooh bird poo again. Yuck!" of course.

More profound was Elinor's observation: "You mean that all the knowledge of this lost language the rongo scripts, was lost because the priests were taken away in chains to dig bird poop?"

"Yes, Elinor, exactly that, and it looks like we will never now be able to translate those glyphs."

There were more details to fill in that got skipped – the role of diseases in eradicating a culture, the ransacking of statues, but even so the story stuck in Elinor's mind. Especially about how you can lose old texts forever.

"How did they go fishing with no trees? How did they get away?" someone else chipped in.

"They didn't, they were stuck there with no escape and very little food. There was a phase of intense warfare as people fought for food. This seems to be when the statues were toppled, probably as an act of tribal war. They even kept chickens in miniature stone castles to stop them from being stolen by starving neighbours. So can anyone see any similarities between these two islands?"

Elinor stuck a keen hand up. "Please, sir. Yes. In both cases humans settled a nice island and made it into a horrible place. That was very silly of them. Didn't anyone see it coming? Isn't that just what has now happened to the Earth? Aren't we living on a planet Nauru? What caused this?"

Mr Jones frowned, thought deeply for a moment, then nodded his head. "Yes, Elinor, you are quite correct. Disturbingly correct. Caused by generations of uncontrolled, sinful self-indulgence by your ancestors."

He paused, thought deeply for a while, then sighed. "Out of the mouths of babes and sucklings," he thought to himself. "At least tomorrow I'm teaching them Euclid's proof about the infinity of primes. That is very satisfying, and never creates such awkward questions."

Charlotte Bay, Antarctica

Alexandra Elbakyan preferred dealing with computers to humans, especially those of her own age. Computers did what they were told, and did what they should do. Unlike humans, who rarely made sense and often teased her. You saw pictures in your mind about how their logic should work, and that was how they worked. Computers never made jokes about body parts, or asked her about making babies (unlike adolescent boys, and more than a few adult men). She came from a family of computer coders, and was supposedly named after an ancestor in Kazakstan who did something involving scraping files off servers, whatever that meant. She even enjoyed writing computer code, simple old languages like PYTHON and BASIC, so was delighted when Miss Frazer asked her to help set up a computer resource to help her classmates. To be honest, Miss Frazer was no coder, and had been quite anxious when the headmaster suggested in a staff meeting that each class could create its own learning resources web page. It may be an old, 20th century technology, but the black and white absolutism of computer logic jarred with her more empathic approach to life. She could discuss syllabus contents with a class of young students or get governors to expand on their views about the school functions, but she couldn't discuss with an executable compiler what it was looking for in terms of output content. So Alexandra's input could take a real load off her, help the class, maybe teach her some computer tricks.

Miss Frazer was teaching traditional mathematics. "For today's lesson, we will study an ancient and famous result by a Greek called Euclid. Long before anyone had thought of computers, he proved that there must be an infinite number of prime integers." She went on to give exactly the same proof that schoolchildren still receive around the planet, that Omar had received in Kamchatka, that Elinor had received in Alaska.

When the bell rang for the end of class, she called Alexandra over for a special chat. This is usually an ominous thing for a teacher to say, but in this case the message was friendly and interesting. "Alexandra: We want to create a special computer hub, just for this class, about some of the subjects we have covered. Maybe things like our local school environment, our visit to the Herbert hut. The idea is to involve the class in creating and designing the web page – would you be interested in getting involved?"

Alexandra beamed – sounded like fun. "Yes, I'd like to. Can I add some of our science projects?" she asked earnestly.

New Riyadh, Kamchatka

Omar loved seeing pictures in his head. This was how he escaped the rather low quality of life on offer in the self-styled neo-Caliphate. Humans endlessly worried about things that didn't seem to matter, like clothes or adherence to meaningless rules. They expected him to read their thoughts, and know intuitively when to stay quiet, when not to draw attention to himself. Adults seemed obsessed with social stuff – hierarchies, family ties. Adolescent boys were far worse, endlessly teasing him about anything to do with sex, or enjoying teasing him just to annoy him. Computers just did what you told them, and by seeing the flow of their logic in your head you could predict their behaviour accurately. Even better, when they did something odd you could find the error in the code to explain it. When humans did something odd you kept your mouth shut or risked a beating.

Numbers embodied beauty, because they behaved with such crystallized perfection. When lying in bed waiting to fall asleep, Omar didn't count sheep (in fact he'd never seen a live sheep). He saw numbers in his head. Working out how high he could get the powers of two kept him amused (2,4, 8, 16, 32, 64 was easy, but around 16384 (the fourteenth power of two) he tended to get lost. Then there was the appealing simplicity of the number line. He saw the numbers from 1 to 100 laid out in order, and played with them, getting pleasure in finding patterns. An easy starter was adding up pairs of numbers. $1+2 = 3$. $3+4 = 7$. $5+6 = 11$. Each answer was four bigger than the previous one: 3, 7, 11 etc. So the next one should be 15. Sure enough, $7+8=15$. Briefly (following a particularly hard line theology lesson) he wondered whether Allah had imposed this rule. A little invocation of algebra gave him an insight here. Let's consider any consecutive list of four integers, starting at X. So he noted that adding the first two gave $X+X+1 = 2X+1$. Adding the second two gave $X+2+X+3 = 2X+5$. The difference between these was $0x+4 = 4$. So the question was not about any God imposing the rule, but that this rule was an unavoidable consequence of how things were. No God would ever be able to arrange things any other way.

Even more interesting was what he found when he folded the number line in two in his head, so the two ends touched. Now adding adjacent pairs behaved quite differently. The first such pair was $1+100 = 101$. The second such pair was $2+99 = 101$. The third such pair was $3+98 = 101$. Omar could see that this pattern was equally solid by a similar proof. Each pair was $X + (101-X) = 101$.

A Path of 21 Ms

Again, an unavoidable consequence of just how things were. So when he saw the folded number line, he saw two lines of numbers one above the other, 1 . . . 50 then underneath them 100 . . . 51. Under this a third line, the sums, all saying 101. So the line of sums was 50 long and each value was 101, so it must add up to 5050. A neat result that he committed to memory.

Mr Khan was having trouble keeping up with Omar. The mathematics syllabus was basic, teaching stuff needed for day-to-day life, geometry, engineering, and dominated by calculations. Given that most adults did most calculations on spreadsheets or calculators, this wasn't really needed, but was easy to teach and assess without raising any awkward philosophical questions. Omar sailed through the calculations faster than Mr Khan, and could see the logic underlying linear algebra so intuitively he couldn't always explain the key steps. It was so obvious that $(X+Y)*(X-Y) = X^2-Y^2$ that he just took it as an axiom.

"What is 19 squared, Omar?" Mr Khan asked.

"It must be 361 because 20 squared is 400, and 20 squared minus 19 squared must be (20-19)*(20+19)=39. Is that right, sir?"

"Omar, have you been reading lessons from other classes? Where did you get that result?"

To be honest, Mr Khan was rather scared of the situation, because he could see that Omar was genuinely talented, a more natural talent than he ever could be. That is not a comfortable situation for a teacher. Rather in despair, one day he decided to keep Omar quiet for a while. "Omar, I know you like doing calculations, so I want you to do something special. I want you to add up all the numbers from 1 to 100." Omar absorbed the request, and saw his old friend the folded number line in his head. The third line down must add up to 5050. So, Omar took his e-slate, and wrote on it the four digits 5 0 5 0. Maybe he should have been a bit more respectful in passing this back to Mr Khan, rather than throwing it onto his desk. This display of insolence could not go unchallenged. "Prove it! On the board, now."

So Omar wrote down his folded number line, and proved that the answer must be 5050.

"No, do it properly! 1+2+3 etc." Mr Khan had been so far outclassed that he failed to appreciate a rock solid proof under his nose.

So Omar duly wrote down a vertical list of numbers, starting at 1, and by it wrote the sum of that number plus the previous sum. Next to 1 he wrote 1. Next to 2 he wrote 3. Next to 3 came 6, and 4 paired to 10. This went on, and on. After the class reconvened after lunch, the list was complete, and next to 100 was the answer 5050. Mr Khan was presented with a second, rock solid proof, but still made a public fuss of checking the calculations (making a few mistakes of his own). After a while he gave up trying to find the fault. In fact, he'd checked the answer on a spreadsheet of his own so knew that Omar was right, though he had problems accepting it. "Are you telling me that you did all that in your head in that moment this morning?" he asked, in a mixture of awe and horror.

Omar saw an image of the three number lines, so logically replied, "Yes, sir, that's right. You told me to."

York Township, Prudhoe Bay, Alaska

Elinor knew she liked plants, and knew the names for everything her parents grew at home. There weren't many, as the high latitude sunlight and poor acid soils only suited a few tough species. Her mother specialised in new cultivars of Arctic lupins, putting on a display of pretty colours each summer. Naming the wild plants was harder, since no-one seemed to have produced a guide for the strange mixtures of southern weeds and garden escapes that now grew on untended land. She was particularly fond of the little pink pea-flowers and purple spotted leaves of a creeping wildflower that her mother thought to be a vetch. Whatever it was, it liked their path edges, and she liked seeing it there. "Aren't there any web pages that might tell me its name?" she asked, as her mother pulled up yet another handful of vetch, revealing some rather smothered lupins that Elinor had hoped would stay un-noticed.

Elinor's mother wanted to help, but it wasn't like the old days when you opened up a paper book full of pictures of plants that grew in your neighbourhood. Paper was too precious and short lived in the wet warmth, and public computer databases had largely been accidentally wiped. "You know that the nuclear pulses burned out most of the computer chips on the planet, so yes there were lots of good plant identification web pages, but these are mainly lost now. I think my father's ancestors kept a few backups that might help."

In the dusty boxes of family memorabilia were all sorts of things from previous lives in a previous world. Photos of Miami before the king tides took over. The crumbling remains of a few books, foolishly printed on acid paper and now barely openable. And some computer gadgets, of such antiquity that most were unreadable. A quaint old 20cm disk called a floppy, that (incredibly) only held 1.5 MB. A funny box labelled a zip drive, that needed a special mains power plug that no longer fitted anything. Some plug-and-go drives, wrapped in foil, that had not seen the light of day for as long as anyone could recall.

"Please can we have a look, Mummy?" Elinor implored, doing her best to tug her mother's sentiments.

"Why was this drive wrapped in silver foil?" Elinor asked, as the dusty treasures came to light. Her mother knew enough about physics and chemistry to answer this accurately. "Your grandfather was worried about all his data being burned out by an electrical pulse, and talked about putting his memory drives into a Faraday cage for safety. It is just kitchen foil, and it is aluminum foil not silver foil. Silver is a much more expensive element, and mildly toxic, so no-one wraps food in it. Anyway, he was right to see the burnout coming, because that is exactly what happened. The international banking system stopped working when all the chips burned out at the same moment. Maybe Grandpa's aluminum Faraday cage kept this one safe."

The old drive just had one lead, a short cable leading to a standard USB plug. No worries about the power supply anyway. They plugged it into a USB port on their main family computer, and (somewhat unexpectedly), a little light came on the drive, and a file explorer window popped up on screen. It worked! The file listing just showed one directory, called ARKIVE. She clicked on the directory, and started seeing images of animals and plants. Each associated with its own web page, each unfamiliar, a new image. Opening up the web pages she saw descriptions of where plants and animals used to be found, what they looked like and how they behaved. So many, so beautiful. How come no-one had shown her a quetzal or a kingfisher, a snow monkey or an okapi? Did people really used to share their land with elephants and hippopotamus? She had seen a picture of the head of a Eurasian badger on some brand logo, but had no idea what the rest of it looked like, let alone that there had been different looking ones in North America. Half an hour later she was still exploring the contents, making excited, happy, squeaky noises as each new wonder appeared. "Look at this tiger – so lovely. Are there any left, Mummy?" A few were so amazing that she thought everyone should have met them. She had of course seen pictures of the long-extinct African rhinoceroses, big hairless beasts of open plains, but she found that there had been a cute little woolly rhinoceros not long ago, living in dense forest. "Are there any of these left, Mummy?" became the question of the evening, and always got the same answer. "Sorry, no. Their forests burned, and the zoos were closed down for lack of food." In the case of the forest rhinoceros, one might have added that they never bred in zoos anyway so were doomed to follow their forest homes into oblivion. Elinor felt a profound stab of sadness at what was lost, what she would never experience. Things that people didn't know to value, until too late. She would never look up to see a giraffe's head looking down at her. Never swim with a dolphin, never see a whale as big as your boat, never see a mountain covered in blue-green pine trees. There used to be common birds that followed the seasons – swallows and golden plovers for spring, geese for winter. This didn't happen anymore, as the major wintering grounds were transformed from insect-rich woodland savannahs to baked bare rock and charcoal. A new population of migrant birds would evolve, but only when the climate allowed in about 100,000 years. "These images should be shared – can I show my school?" It was a big step up from a normal show-and-tell, but a sensible ambition.

"So this was a Tragopan, a sort of pheasant, that lived in the Himalayan forests." Elinor flashed up a superbly coloured pheasant for her classmates to admire. "And I even found some wild plants that grow around here" – one more click, and the far more sedate colours of a common vetch popped up. "This is the common vetch, vikkia sative." (She read *'Vicia sativa'*, but could not know it was pronounced vissya sat-eye-va). "It grows all over our garden, and is a legacy of farmland in the cooler days. There is a family story that I have a distant grandmother who worked on this plant in England, asking why it has purple spots."

Mr Jones frowned. Evolutionary biology sat uncomfortably with the school's religious ethos. "I am sure that The Almighty had his divine reasons for giving the vetch its spots, and it is not for us to query them. What did you say this was from?"

Elinor looked the picture of youthful innocence. "It was about the plants and animals that Noah saved in his ark, and that is why it is called Arkive," she explained, pushing the truth rather further than was really defensible.

It did the trick though, and Mr Jones relented. "Very impressive, Elinor. Would you like to make that available to the school through our 2B web server?" He could see a way to keep everyone busy and offload a technically difficult job onto younger shoulders. "Come and see me later and we can sort out what you need."

By the end of the class Elinor knew exactly what she needed. The biggest memory drive she could lay her hands on. "Please, sir, the pictures are quite big files, so I will need a big memory backup. Can I have five petabytes?"

Mr Jones had spent too much time learning biblical quotations to waste his time mastering the nerdy details of scientific names, and was not sure how much a petabyte was. His counting scheme went roughly "Kilo, Mega, a lot". Gigabytes, terabytes, petabytes, whatever. So he nodded, wrote it down and passed the request to the headmaster, who signed it off without even noticing. Soon Elinor had the kind of storage space that would have taken a supercomputer to handle in the previous millennium. Just as well: the Arkive database was huge. It took the best part of a weekend to transfer the files, but in the end everyone who could access the school server had open access to photos and documentation of pretty much every plant and animal that had been described. Vast numbers were small and obscure, for example ants, wasps, mites, grasses and orchids. Invariably these would not just be very tedious to look at, but no-one seemed to know anything interesting about them. Even so, there were so many ghosts of lost life forms, everyone who explored the files came away saddened at what had been and what they could never hope to see alive. Quickly everyone who met it on the school web server had a favourite species. Usually a bird or an animal. Elinor was hard pushed to name one favourite, there were so many. She was especially fond of the lost group of 'monkeys' from Madagascar called lemurs. (Yes, I know they're not monkeys, but the distinction will be entirely academic by 2160.) She loved watching the lemurs called sifakas as they danced along. Actually that's how they walk on a flat surface, but it looks like dancing. She loved hearing the sound of another lemur, the indri, as it sang to the dawn in the lost forests of Andisabe. She had just set up the school server as one of the most important biodiversity archives for the future of humanity. Its root URL title was 'Arkive'.

New Riyadh

Omar liked to hide inside his head by seeing pictures, especially when they led to a deeper understanding – proofs. Once he watched three classmates squabbling over how to divide a square lump of cake fairly between them. Of course the biggest boy just cut it unevenly and took the biggest piece for himself, but it got Omar thinking. Cutting a square into three has no natural elegant solution in the way that cutting it into four would do. You can cut a square into four with just two lines, and create four identical new squares. So Omar found himself seeing pictures where a big square cake gets cut up into four square cakes, each one quarter the area of its parent. Then you give one square to each of three people, and keep one square back. Then you cut this one square into four smaller ones, all identical. You can repeat this, giving one smaller square to each person, and keeping one back. Then cut this small square into four identical smaller ones, and give each person one. He could see that this way, everyone got a fair and equal portion. He could see that the residue declined quickly to such tiny values that they ceased to be worth worrying about. So he had divided a square cake into three equal portions by cutting it into squares! Each person gets the following portions of the cake: 1/4, 1/16, 1/64, etc. This is a fair and equal division, so everyone got 1/3. This is a rock-solid visual proof of a result that is otherwise far from obvious. So $1/4 + (1/4)^2 + (1/4)^3 + \ldots (1/4)^n = 1/3$.

In fact, a moment's visionary insight when he woke up in the night showed him that this result generalises. You cut a cake into X equal pieces, give all bar one away, then repeat. This allows an equal distribution of the cake between (X-1) people. Proving that

$$1/x + (1/x)^2 + (1/x)^3 + \ldots (1/x)^n = 1/(x-1) \text{ for any integer value of } x>1.$$

Mr Khan had found another plan to keep Omar busy. The boy really was too smart to give simple calculations to, and yesterday Omar had spotted an error in his linear equations on the board. Even Omar would take his time when facing down infinite calculations! So the next plan was to keep him busy with the simple question "What is a half plus a quarter plus an eighth plus a sixteenth plus a thirty-second etc? By hand please." He also knew the answer, having set up a spreadsheet that emulated the calculation. The answer came out about 0.99999, strangely close to 1.0.

"Omar – I have a special question for you," boomed Mr Khan. "I know you like calculations, and this should keep you busy. What do you get when you add one half plus one quarter plus one eighth etc?" That should keep him busy for the morning, he thought.

Omar saw a picture in his head of slices of cake, given to one person. The crumb left got smaller and smaller with each cut, so the difference between the answer and 1.0 must decline to nothing. "Please, sir, it is exactly 1.0 isn't it?"

Mr Khan gasped. "How did you do that?"

Charlotte Bay, Antarctica

Today's geography lesson had been about hydropower. Miss Frazer had been explaining some basics about how the energy of flowing water could be captured and turned into electricity. Much of their baseload energy supply came from the great Beardmore hydropower plant, harnessing the waterfall which formed where early explorers had climbed up onto the main Antarctic land mass. "The powerful river which turns our turbines comes from the melting ice sheets. The scientists think these will last about 2000 years, so this is a sustainable way to gather energy."

Alexandra's brow furrowed. "Please, Miss – did you say that melting ice is sustainable? Won't it melt away? That's not sustainable."

Miss Frazer sighed inwardly. Alexandra was right, again. "Well yes, but the melting is so far into the future that it won't bother us. That is almost as far into the future as Jesus and the Romans were in our past."

Alexandra had a flush of youthful idealism. "But it's still not sustainable, is it? One day the last of the ice will melt, there will be no more hydropower, and someone will say 'Didn't anyone see this coming?'. We know that the future is going to happen – is it nice of us to leave that for others to worry about?"

Miss Frazer sighed inwardly again. No, it wasn't sustainable, of course. The fact that none of them could hope to live long enough to run into this limitation did not undermine the logic of the argument. "I think that the way to look at it is that we have a massive resource giving us free energy, so it would be silly not to exploit it. It is not as if we cause any damage to anything or anyone by catching the Beardmore waterfall. It is a 2000-year gift to our people."

Anxious to distract attention, she moved on to the latest 'good idea' being foisted on the staff by the higher echelons of the educational establishment. At least it might keep Alexandra's awkward questions at bay!

"The headmaster has suggested that we create a form 2B web page, showing what we have seen and done. He also suggested that we try to contact children in schools in other countries, even around the Arctic. Alexandra has been kind enough to volunteer to help set this up. Alexandra – do you think you could create some files for this? Maybe something about our visit to the Herbert Hut? About the Beardmore hydropower scheme?"

Alexandra relished the responsibility and the challenge, and applied herself to creating a collection of pictures and descriptions of what they had seen. The visit to the Herbert Hut was easy, lots of photographs of classmates playing in the rain, of Miss Frazer pointing out features of the site. Some distant views of camels, and the intricately complex landscape engineering of the paddy field system, carrying the endless deluge of heavy rains around green lakes of life-giving crops. The Beardmore scheme was more of a challenge. Getting photographs of the generating machinery was easy enough, but she had more problems trying to explain the timescales. The only source for the claim that the scheme was good for thousands of years was what Miss Frazer had said in class. A good start, but somehow she knew that it needed more. The public information about the scheme didn't use the word 'Sustainable'. It said nothing about longevity at all. So how was one to know?

Alexandra decided to gather as much information as she could, using the opportunity as an excuse to tie in a lot of loose ends. Where did the camels fit in? What about sheep? How come everyone referred to birds flying – and indeed there were escaped domestic sparrows flying around the coastal settlements – while most of the birds she met were chickens or penguins, which didn't. Chickens ran away, penguins swam fast enough to eat fish, neither flew. Surely science could tell her all the answers? She decided to call her web pages her Science Hub, or Sci-Hub for short. There was so much more to load into it. Maybe other children could help her?

"I have received email contact from a school in the Arctic, called 'Prudhoe Bay'. They want to share images and stories of their children with our children. Here is the email address. Isn't it amazing that we can still communicate so easily over such a long distance using such old fashioned technology? Those copper wires are over 100 years old. They have a student who like you is interested in setting up a class story page – called Elinor." Alexandra saw an unfamiliar address – E. Pchar@Prudhoe.edu – and opened contact without great hope. In her experience most school children were interested in talking about sport, human naughty bits or just teasing her to make a statement, to put her down. Still, she opened contact.

"Dear Elinor. I am a pupil in the new lands of Antarctica, and I love animals, plants and science. I am hoping to set up a science web page on our school server, and was told you have similar plans."

Prudhoe Bay

Mr Jones called Elinor to his desk. No space for private offices in the new world. "Elinor, I know you are interested in the natural world. I have been asked to get students to liaise with students in other schools for some international collaboration. Not just in Alaska – anywhere, even Kamchatka or Antarctica. They will write in English, though it may not be their first language. Would you be interested in helping?"

Yes, she would be delighted.

Elinor saw an unfamiliar address – A.elbakyan@charlotte.ac.aq. She had an idea.

'Dear Alexandra' she typed. 'My school overlooks the Arctic Ocean, we have birds and flowers and a lovely school garden. I think that you may be interested in swapping stories and pictures. Please tell us about yourselves and your school. I have some wonderful pictures to show you.'

Charlotte Bay, Antarctica

Alexandra was delighted to receive a contact from a girl called Elinor somewhere in the north. Prudhoe Bay, where-ever that might be – somewhere in 'America' not 'Russia'. They chatted a bit, with Alexandra sending links to pictures of the school trip – classmates and a (distant) camel for example. "Do you know what this is?"

Elinor was briefly surprised – what a strange creature to meet on a school trip! She had seen pictures, but not the real thing. It took her extensive poking around on the ARKIVE database to come up with a full answer. "It's a camel. There are two sorts – have a look. One has one hump, the other has two. Both are still alive as farm animals. Do you want the files?"

Alexandra did want the files, very much. It took a surprising length of time to copy over the whole database – days; luckily no-one noticed that the school's new server was taking a week to fill up with petabytes. Eventually the Arkive database was safely backed up in Charlotte Bay. The contents were not just enormous but amazing – a horrific testament to what had been lost as the forests burned and the sea acidified. Alexandra introduced a new feature on the site – 'This week's extinct species'. Always choosing pretty ones – colourful flowers, smiling dolphins, huge herbivores. Owls were an especially rich vein to mine – the Amur fish owl was her favourite, a huge bird that used to walk on snow while stalking a migratory fish called the salmon. Not that anyone really believed that fish would come out of the sea into fresh water – this never happened in the new streams coming off the Antarctic ice sheet. Secretly a lot of adults thought something along the lines of "Wow! [Or less polite versions]. I never knew that." Publicly they told Alexandra what a good job she was doing for the school.

As well as the Arkive files, Elinor made a point of sending Alexandra what she had about Nauru and Easter Island. This was mainly the images of stone heads and bare island landscapes, plus the Rongo rongo carving. The stories hit Alexandra deeply – the idea that an entire script, a whole way of knowledge, could come into being, flower, then just vanish, leaving a few mysterious traces to puzzle future generations. Such a loss, and now utterly irretrievable. Send priests to their deaths to mine bird poo – how come no-one even seemed shocked by this awful waste? Alexandra put the story onto the school web page, under the heading 'Planet Nauru', along with pictures of lost species.

New Riyadh

Mr Khan had inherited some old computer kit, supposedly left behind in a college basement after the Islamic takeover. Weird old disks, unusable keyboards, plus some plug-and-go USB drives that somehow still worked and held lots of files. Clearly not koranic, apparently written in English, but in most cases they might as well have been in Hopi Indian for all the sense it made to him. Still, there may be something of value there. He knew just the person who might help. If it was rubbish, none of the staff would be any the wiser. If there was gold dust hidden in the mess, he could claim credit for its discovery. "Omar, please can you see me after class?" These words usually preceded deep trouble, so Omar was apprehensive. "Don't worry, I'm not cross with you this time, I have a small project that might interest you. Two in fact.

"Firstly, the school suggests that we share stories and pictures with other school children from other places. Do you know how to set up images on web pages?" Omar had been doing this from about the age of six, so nodded happily. "Good, I will ask that you help me set up a school page telling everyone about our lives here."

Omar frowned – if he told people what life was like he would be in trouble again.

"Secondly, I have some old computer kit that seems to have interesting files that need sorting out. They look to be up your street – perhaps you could have a look?" He could have said "I don't have a clue what they mean and need someone to explain them to me" but that would not fit his status or self-image.

Omar tried to look interested, expecting something religious or maybe old family photographs. "Yes of course, I would be pleased," he fibbed. So he went home with an old metal box full of older USB drives, and started to plug them in to the family PC.

Although clearly a computer database, someone had written explanatory labels in old fashioned pen on something durable, clearly not standard paper. One just said 'Alexandra Elbakyan Sci-Hub'. Whatever that meant. The other said 'New Scientist archive'. Ironic for something so old to call itself 'New'. He found himself thinking, 'No, Old Scientist archive!'

The first surprise was that the drives worked at all. Some very old kit refused to work due to moving parts that didn't move anymore (physical disks need motors and hate dust), or just got burned out by the nuclear EMPs. These drives had no moving parts to pack up, and had been shielded from EMPs by their steel box, so woke up as though nothing had happened.

A Path of 21 Ms

The second surprise was their contents. Files in an old format, labelled PDF. Long out of date, but he had found a converter in some utility files on his father's machine. A little installing and clicking later, Omar could start to the read the files. So many, so hard to follow.

Named like books, but with boring titles and many copies separated by years and volume numbers. Some looked like magazines – 'The Geological Journal', 'the Journal of Emergency Medicine', others frankly made no sense to him. 'Pedobiologia', 'Lloydia', and so many more. Inside each were lots of separate chapters, each with a different title, most of which made no sense at all. Looking harder, each chapter had the same basic layout: a title (which sometimes made sense), authors (so many strange names), an abstract (which started by making sense then became incomprehensible), Methods (incomprehensible), Results (incomprehensible but with graphs that he liked), Discussion (incomprehensible), Acknowledgements (polite and easy to understand but boring), then References (boring). They all had dates, all at least 150 years old. Some went back to the 1960s – 200 years old. Astonishing.

The other astonishing thing was the sheer size of the collection. An evening's worth of exploration barely scratched the surface. Omar had heard stories of old paper libraries where you could stand in a large room and see lines of books heading off into the distance as far as the eye could see – each book taking days to read and years to write. Mind-blowing amounts of condensed effort. This archive was equivalent, but digital.

One other feature that took a little exploring was a 'Search' function. You could type in a word, and get a list of results whose titles often included that word. Of course he typed in words that light up male brains: 'Sex' gave him such a huge list of baffling titles, none of them in any way interesting or naughty. 'Explosive' worked slightly better, actually listing a few titles about real explosives along with a lot of biological results that looks boring.

The New Scientist files were much more welcoming, though still weirdly all over the place and quite at odds with his religious schooling. At least they contained easy-to-read articles that generally made sense, and some were actually funny. There were a lot of articles called 'feedback' featuring people using elephants as a standard unit of weight, or people with silly names. A doctor of urine called Dr Weedon for example. They were easy to get lost in, absorbing. He spent an hour reading and re-reading an article 'The lost tribes of humanity', about how humans had been mating (whatever that meant) with people called Neanderthals a long time ago, and with someone called Denisova, a name that reminded him of one of the girls at primary school. None of this really fitted with what anyone had said to him so far. Puzzling.

Easier was following up the school's international contacts with other children in other countries. He sent a generic sort of "Hello this is my school" to the contacts he'd been given, without much enthusiasm that anyone interesting was out there. He felt isolated and alone in his own community, so expected the same with people from other worlds that he would never meet. Still, emails were easier than face-to-face talking, where people habitually took offence at tiny incomprehensible trivia. Indeed, most of the contacts never replied.

One schoolchild did email back, quickly. A schoolgirl called Alexandra Elbakyan in Antarctica replied next day, with a picture of her class by a rather desolate hut by a rather desolate bay by some nasty looking cliffs. They looked remarkably normal children, if much paler skinned than most of his classmates. From what teachers had said about the Antarctic unbelievers, he had expected something stranger. Plus she sent a photo of a strange big animal with brown curly hair and a hump on its back. "Do you know what this is?" she asked.

Omar had seen pictures of camels from old files, but they always lived in sandy places and had just one hump. "It looks like a strange sort of camel? Is that right?"

Omar decided to return the challenge. The New Scientist archive contained many images of strange creatures (along with lots of graphs, and photos of long-dead humans). One article referred to a close relative called chimpanzee, whoever that might be. "Do you know what a chimpanzee is?" he mailed out. The next day Alexandra had replied with a photograph of a black, hairy animal that looked half human, and said they used to live in Africa, ate fruit, and that their ancestors were close to human ancestors until about six million years ago. She added two more photos, one of a more stocky black-haired thing called a gorilla, and a red hairy thing called an orangutan. All lacked tails, ate fruit, used to climb trees when there were trees tall enough to take their weight, and all went extinct when the last zoos closed down. All were said to be close relatives of humans.

"How did you know that? No-one here in Kamchatka knows about them." (It would have been more accurate to say that no-one spoke about them, but in school you do not understand adults' tendency to prioritise social conformity over truth telling.)

Alexandra explained about the huge Arkive database sent from Canada, and explained how it greatly improved her school's web page update. She made a point of starting each week by checking her 'Extinct species of the week'. This week it was a cute little monkey from the former Amazon called the Emperor Tamarin, with an enormous moustache. Omar laughed, and copied the image. This remined Omar very much of his headmaster Mr Shaffiq – exactly the same size, shape and colour of moustache! [NB I do know that tamarins are not monkeys.

The distinction will be academic once the Amazon has burned.] It was perhaps unwise that Omar's first class web page included this picture, along with a line about how much this looked like a head-masterly little monkey. Less wise that no-one checked it before emails went to the parents or that the headmaster first saw it when it was proudly projected to the school assembly (to raucous laughter).

Of course, Omar wanted a copy of Arkive, to explore at leisure. "Can you mail me a copy?" he asked.

"With pleasure! It is very big though – petabytes. Will take days to transfer. Have you any interesting files to share?"

Omar thought about this, and realised that the names were telling him something. He needed a little extra kit.

"Mr Khan, I have found some interesting stuff for the class web page but I need more space on the server. How much can I have? A few petabytes should do," he asked innocently after class the next day. "And I opened those old drives, lots of stuff in an old format called PDF. It still opens easily enough, looks like old scientific stories. Lots of medical information." He decided that it would be safer to stay technical and medical than give any idea of the range of subjects covered.

Mr Khan grunted, not having any idea what PDF or petabyte meant.

So thanks to a puzzled IT technician and Moore's law, Omar got himself a multi-petabyte server, and set about downloading Alexandra's Arkive files.

Another day, another teacher, another class, another set of explanations that didn't seem to explain anything. The teacher was in full flow, as far as Omar could tell each time he tried to pay attention. "Nothing happens without a purpose. It is planned, if it happens it was meant to happen. You should look for signs of what the plan is." Quite how this was meant to illuminate a chemistry lesson was unclear. "The wisdom of the ancients included an idea called the Doctrine of Signatures. Plants were given a value to man in the Creation, and their value was indicated by signs. The lungwort looks like lung tissues and was used to cure lung diseases for example." Omar wondered whether it actually worked, but had more sense than to ask. "The willow tree grows by water, and it gave us the medicine called aspirin that cures the fevers that afflict men near water." Again – was it really that simple? Don't ask – thought crimes are dangerous.

But then a thought popped up that hit him hard. The name on Mr Khan's old USB drive – Alexandra Elbkyan Sci Hub. This sounded very like the girl in Antarctica who had sent him the pictures of animals. Maybe there was some guiding principle there after all.

He emailed her back that evening. "Did you say you wanted files for your school science hub? I have found some files that might interest you."

She did, very much. So the vast collection of scientific research clandestinely collated by her distant ancestor ended up on a school web server in Antarctica.

Charlotte Bay, Antarctica

The Sci-Hub transfer was even larger and longer than the Arkive database, with two sets of school technical support staff bemused at the size of files being transferred. In Kamchatka, no-one could quite work out why the school routers were so occupied for so long, while at the other end of the planet eyebrows were raised even further.

"Alexandra, I thought you were having me on when you talked about your disk drive needs. What on earth are you putting on the web pages??" asked one assistant in Charlotte Bay. Then he started reading some of the New Scientist archives, and got so fascinated that he forgot what he was meant to be doing that day. He had already got into minor trouble for spending an entire morning browsing extinct animals on the Arkive database instead of helping staff prepare their evaluation forms, gaining a reputation as a bit of a daydreamer.

Once finally downloaded, Alexandra had oversight of tens of thousands of millennial scientific research papers. She found it amusing just to dive into the Sci-hub database for a random name, just out of amazement at some of the strange and trivially incomprehensible things people had written about. Some of the titles were so utterly obscure they made her laugh at the thought that anyone spent time reading the work, let alone doing it, let alone writing about it. Just by way of passing examples: A paper by Parker-Rhodes in 1955 about mushrooms on lawns, called 'Fairy Ring kinetics'. He seems to have spent the Second World War following the exact position of every mushroom on his back lawn, then spent ten years analysing what he found. One paper called 'The Collembola of fly ash dumps in East London' by a chap called Shaw – whatever springtails were and whatever fly ash might have been. Astonishing that anyone did something so useless. She could understand what her father did – turning bare rock into living soil to grow food made sense. Counting mushrooms on lawns did not! (Or studying springtails on industrial waste sites, or so much else in there.)

York township

There is always trouble when the uncertain, evidence-based world of Science meets the dogmatic convictions of absolute faith. This is inevitable. Whatever you believe about reality, sooner or later something will come along that shows

A Path of 21 Ms

some part of your belief to be incorrect. Always has, always must, always will. So then you have the choice of saying "I was wrong, so now I am correcting my understanding in the light of the new evidence", or of shutting your eyes, ears and mind and deciding that reality must be wrong and anyone who says otherwise is your enemy. The first path is why scientific models are always open to improvement, scientists are required to be humble in the face of new evidence, and why science actually works when tested against reality. The second path is why the absolute faith of religious belief detests scientific thought, and why religions do not actually work when tested against objective evidence. (By way of anecdote, I have had Jehovah's Witnesses on my doorstep saying in disgust and contempt "I see that you think like a scientist" before marching off with their noses in the air. Yes, and I am proud of doing so and systematically exhorted all my students to do the same. All I did was to ask them what the Bible says about the age of planet earth.) Also why religions have a track record of intolerance leading to violence. Galileo was told to choose – either he must say that the universe was wrong about the universe, or he would be tortured by the Inquisition. "Show him the instruments of torture as if they are meant to be used" was the instruction given to his inquisitors.

So the religiously-dominated communities of the high Arctic were unimpressed by any part of the treasure trove of old research that they had happened upon. Elinor discovered this when her 'extinct animal of the week' was a dinosaur, the famous *Tyrannosaurus rex*. When the headmaster Mr Harris spotted this on the school web page he frowned, and decided that this game had gone far enough. He bypassed her form teacher and called her in directly: "Elinor, you should not be putting these mythical animals on our school pages. Monkeys and birds are fine, people saw them, we have old photographs and descriptions. But this animal has never been seen, its kind was never mentioned in the Bible, it is a false fable. You may as well put a unicorn or a dragon there."

Elinor stood her ground. "No, people have seen its bones, even its teeth. Lots of them. It's just that most of the dinosaurs went extinct before humans evolved. Long, long before, in a big explosion caused by a rock that fell from the sky."

Several things here lit up red warning lights in his head, starting with a small girl in his care contradicting him. Then there was the non-biblical explanation for an event that no-one had witnessed. And even those unbelievers who accepted that dinosaurs existed knew that they all died out before humans were created. "What on earth do you mean, 'MOST of the dinosaurs'," he queried, trying not to lose his temper in public. "The legend is that ALL the dinosaurs vanished."

Elinor had done her homework well. "No sir, one line of feathered dinosaurs survived to evolve into birds. The correct term is that the non-avian dinosaurs went extinct at the Katie boundary." (She meant the K/T boundary, but hadn't quite understood the letters. To be fair most adults and most biologists today don't know it means Keuper/Tertiary either. And it should be Keuper/Palaeogene, but that never caught on.) "It's on this database here." She showed him the drive holding the Arkive database.

"Elinor – what is on this computer disk directly contradicts what is written in the Bible. Birds were created as birds, like animals were created as animals, and Man was created as Man, the crown of creation. Our saviour Jesus never said otherwise, and he was the son of the creator of everything, so he must have known. Are you saying that Jesus lied to us? Or that he was ignorant of the creation? This is blasphemy, and it cannot be tolerated. I must save you from your stupidity, to give you a chance of eternal salvation." He took the computer drive from her, walked to the edge of the sea and threw it out as far as he could. Anyone with an ounce of compassion would have felt a twinge of remorse as she collapsed in tears – she really had been trying to help the school and meant no harm to anyone. But Mr Harris had Faith, and Faith meant more than evidence or understanding or human kindness. His faith meant that he had to destroy all traces of the blasphemy to protect her immortal soul for eternity, and his own while he was at it. Like the inquisition as they tortured and killed in 17th century Spain, like ISIS as they tortured and killed in 21st century Iraq, he knew that God was on his side.

Elinor was, of course, distraught. Her parents complained to the school, thereby earning a (dangerous) public reputation as atheists, but of course could do no more. There was one glimmer of hope. She had sent a copy by file transfer to Antarctica – were the files safe? Alexandra replied with a cute picture of a fish owl to cheer her up, giving reassurance that the Arkive files were safe. Alexandra also made a point of telling her parents, to get adult help to back the files up again on spare disks. One copy of a digital archive is simply not safe. Then to make her opinion clear, she sent Elinor a picture of *Psychrolutes marcidus* the deep sea blobfish (https://australian.museum/learn/animals/fishes/fathead-psychrolutes-aka-mr-blobby/), on the basis that way back in 2013 it had been voted the ugliest known life form. "Say this is a mrharris fish," she joked. So Elinor put up on the school page a note that this would be her final life form, and to thank the headmaster it would be the mrharris fish.

The likeness was striking – the same bald head, squat ugly nose and morose expression. Then she changed the password and returned to the rest of her life. It

Fig 15.16 The MrHarris fish Psychrolutes marcidus. © *Australian museum.*

Fig 15.17 An Emperor Tamarin, looking like the headmaster.

took Mr Harris days to realise he had been royally set up, by which time dozens of parents and staff had giggled at the photo, and taken a screenshot, copies of which re-appeared throughout the rest of his career (to his intense annoyance). Having saved about 10,000 animals and plants from being forgotten for the geological future, Elinor disappeared from the story. Almost, but not quite. She remained a botanist at heart, and went into the vital field of selective breeding for agronomy. Even the most narrow-minded creationists could not object to work improving food plants, and Elinor was able to breed a line of her mother's vetches with large and edible seed pods. Being a nitrogen fixer, these had a good protein content; being a weed they were tough and easy to grow. Year later she called the cultivar 'Easter Island', in memory of the island paradise that became a hell. For many generations after, people assumed that the Easter Island vetch was so called because you plant it at Easter and it grows on islands, only to go on to be corrected by someone with a bit more history. The Easter Island vetch's seeds ground down to a nutritious flour that became a high-protein pasta that became a mainstay of Arctic cooking for millennia afterwards, proving more useful as a crop than middle-eastern grasses like wheat which never really adapted to life near the Arctic Circle.

Omar's experience was similar, but worse. Legend was that Mr Khan had an ancestor, Abdul Khan, who created the first Islamic atomic bomb (in Pakistan 1998). The secret joke in the staff room was that he had inherited the explosive tendency without the corresponding brainpower. Trouble started shortly after the sci-hub transfer to Antarctica has been completed. Among the low hills of gravel that remained after the Siberian peat bogs had burned away, men found some huge bones, some leg bones as big as the men who found them. The great beast's skull had two huge teeth, and a hole in the middle of its forehead. This was a disturbing find, as it was clearly too real to ignore, but clearly not like anything anyone knew or had ever seen. A few well-read men noted it seemed to be the fabled cyclops of ancient Greece, a one-eyed monster that ate men. Others suggested an elephant, an extinct giant from Africa and India. The ivory tusks seemed right, stained dark brown with age and peat, but their shape seemed wrong for the elephant pictures available. [NB The cyclops myth came exactly this way – elephant skulls have a hole in the forehead where the nose goes in. The Mediterranean islands held dwarf elephants, extinct since the bronze age, whose skulls were found in classical times. These had of course been previously wiped out by human hunting pressure.] Mr Khan didn't like uncertainty, but had to admit this find was odd. Perhaps unwisely, he mentioned it in class. Omar actually paid attention (for once), and wondered whether anything in the New Scientist archive might help. That evening he tried searching the database for 'Siberian elephants', and hit gold. It was of course a mammoth; everything fitted. Siberia turned out to be well known for its mammoth remains, dating back to a legendary period when the land was partly covered in a strange solid cold form of water – ice. Nowadays in Kamchatka ice was only found inside electrical boxes like freezers, used for storing food away from the oppressive summer heat.

"Please, sir, I have found your elephant. It was a Siberian mammoth – here is a picture." He showed a photograph of what looked just like a small version of the elephants people wrote about in India, but with a long red hair. (It was the famous Yuka mammoth mummy.)

Mr Khan should have been delighted, but wasn't. He knew that elephants did not have red hair. This finding seemed to contradict the simple comforting world view of the Old Testament. "Omar – are you making fun of me? A hairy elephant is an abomination, an impossibility, like a hairy frog."

A more tactful student might have kept his mouth shut, or observed that this animal was accepted to have existed. Omar had some focussed intellectual talents, but tact was not one. He remembered something on the Arkive files Alexandra had sent him. "No sir, there was a hairy frog. It lived in Africa. I will find you a picture." [The hairy frog *Trichobatrachus robustus* has a fringe of fine skin projections for oxygen exchange on its thighs that do look just like hairs. Gerald Durrell caught some in Cameroon, noting that the local hunters laughed at him for seeking such a clearly impossible creature. It also has weird bony outgrowths on its feet that act like retractable claws.] Overnight Omar searched the Arkive database for pictures, and Sci Hub for anything else that might help his case. The next day he went up to Mr Khan, beaming with pleasure at his success.

"Here it is, sir, the African Hairy Frog. It had hairy sides and retractable claws like a cat. Here is an article all about it, on the old drive that you asked me to unpack."

Mr Khan might have been expected to be pleased. He actually went bright pink, assuming that Omar was making a fool of him in public. Angels and demons were fine of course, but hairy frogs and Siberian elephants belonged with mermaids and dragons in books of make-believe. "You should not lie to me, Omar, you will regret this," he snarled. "Bring me those old drives tomorrow and we will have a look."

So Omar showed Mr Khan what came up when he searched databases for hairy frogs. The Sci Hub database gave hundreds of links to publications with titles that more or less made sense. 'Concealed weapons: erectile claws in African frogs – Biology letters 2008' was understandable if weird, while 'Archaeobatrachian paraphyly and Pangaean diversification of crown-group frogs – Systematic Biology' was frankly unintelligible. The Arkive database gave a remarkable picture of what was clearly a frog which was clearly hairy. Mr Khan didn't know what to say, so he just got annoyed. "Is this what you have been finding on these old drives? I thought you said they were medical? These are incomprehensible and about frogs!"

"Yes, sir, a lot of them are medical. Not all of course. Try this." He called up the New Scientist archive for the article on 'The Lost Tribes of Humanity'. That was a bad mistake, precisely because it was well written and easy to understand.

Mr Khan started reading the old article by someone called Brahic way back in 2018, and began to change colour. The article talked about humans having sex with Neanderthals and Denisovans (whatever they were) on timescales of 70,000 or 500,000 years. This was not what the school taught children about human history, not at all. He flicked away to another random article in New Scientist – unfortunately choosing one with the innocent-sounding name of 'Inner Strength' by Nicola Jones from 2022, about training pelvic floor muscles. Its opening sentences blew his mind. "I am playing a video game on my phone. It is simple and unremarkable except for one thing: I am using my vagina as a game controller." He flushed pink, then white, as he struggled to avoid screaming. Eventually his thoughts focussed into words. "Omar – do you know how blasphemy is punished?" Omar did, but knew he was going to be told anyway. "Blasphemers die. We dip them into the boiling pools on Mount Mutnovsky." Everyone knew this. The dedicated cable loop – a modified ski lift – had been personally designed by the second Genghis Khan, following the notorious example of his famous namesake who (it was incorrectly rumoured) killed all the generals of a captured army in an array of 70 giant boiling pots. He had the name and the correct Y chromosome, so he was only keeping up a family tradition. How this linked to the New Scientist archive was not clear to Omar though.

"Omar – think. If this pornographic filth were to be true, every human would have ancestors who had carnal liaisons with non-humans, with animals." Omar knew this logic was sound. "And anyone who communicated with the One True God would know this. But nowhere in any holy book is this stated." Yes, presumably. Mr Khan continued, furious: "So if you were to say that this were true, not a stupid mythical story, all holy men must have ancestors who came from animals and who did not know about our creation. That would be blasphemy. You cannot be allowed to promulgate this. You and your family will be destroyed, deserve to be destroyed. Everyone who learns this would be haram. This is awful. It must be lost for ever." Mr Khan picked up the drives, took them outside to the edge of the sea and threw them in. Omar was aghast. "Now go away and never speak of this again."

Omar's parents were far less supportive than Elinor's had been, not understanding anything about data loss and being terrified of ostracism within their community. The Sci Hub files were lost, decades of scientific research might as well have never happened. Lost to all humanity for the rest of our species . . . Or maybe not just yet. He had sent the files to Alexandra in Antarctica. Had she still got them safe? The next day she confirmed that they had been backed up on her server.

Deeply relieved, the experience of loss made Omar think hard what he most valued in the data store. The lovely animal pictures certainly, but also some of the mathematics. The basic texts he had breezed through, but there had been some results by an Indian self-taught number theorist called Ramanujan that struck him forcibly. Omar found himself asking Alexandra by email for copies of any of the easier texts on mathematics, or especially anything featuring Ramanujan? (He was getting bored with the best his school could offer and needed stimulation.) Most humans either fail to understand these infinite recursions at all, and most of the few who do understand them find their intellectual limits to hit the buffers. Omar was different – he saw immediately where Ramanujan was coming from, the pictures Ramanujan must have seen in his mind to come up with those amazing results.

These events made Alexandra's machines the repository of last records on the planet of huge amounts of research – not just narrowly biological but physics, chemistry, mathematical, medical and more. Plus all the animals and plants surviving only as photographs on the Arkive database. Alexandra only vaguely understood the magnitude of the situation, but understood enough that she needed other backups, and asked her parents to help. They duly bought out a hardware shop of external drives, and made a backup of every single file onto new media, wrapped in foil and deposited in a dry vault. She then started looking harder at the kind of information. Most of the titles were simply meaningless, with words she had never met before (nor, in most cases, would her parents either). But the abstracts almost always made some kind of sense. She realised that this might be her opportunity to actually ask questions about the history of the runaway climatic shift, since the school seemed to want to say little about such a dramatic change in human history. She started exploring search terms, initially for fun. Then realised that something in this vast archive might help her understand the events leading to the world transition, the great heat. Searches on terms like 'runaway greenhouse effect' took her to some apparently irrelevant publications in geological journals, about the Permo-Triassic boundary and something called the Palaeocene thermal maximum, whatever that was.

New Riyadh

Mr Khan was introducing his class to the rudiments of calculus. Omar was, partially, almost paying attention, though to be honest daydreaming as well. "Today we will be calculating gradients of lines, first straight lines then curves. You already know this – if Y is a function of X, the gradient of the graph is the change in Y divided by the change in X. Let's start with an easy example." He drew X and Y axes on the board, and a right-angled triangle whose sides aligned with the axes; the horizontal side was labelled '5', the vertical side '12'. "Omar – if this triangle were a hill, what would its gradient be?"

Omar was puzzled at such a simple question. "Isn't that equal to change in Y divided by change in X = 12/5 = 2.4?" he asked, expecting some deep trick he'd overlooked. "And its hypotenuse is obviously 13," he added, accidentally ruining Mr Khan's plans to pad out five minutes of the class by revising Pythagoras.

"Yes, correct, and for any straight line like this, the gradient is simple to understand and calculate. But how about a curve?" Mr Khan drew in the parabolic curve of Y=X*X, which obviously did not have a constant gradient. "We can see that the gradient is never the same, it goes steeper as X gets bigger. There are no fixed triangles here, but we can ask what the gradient would be of a tiny little triangle at any point on the curve." He drew in a small right-angled triangle touching the curve at a roughly plausible angle.

Omar saw immediately how this worked. "Please, sir, can't you add just a little number onto X, then calculate the new Y, then find the change in Y divided by the change in X?"

Mr Khan had a frisson of apprehension – this was exactly right, a concept that had taken leading mathematicians generations to develop.

"So if we add a small amount to X, call it d, then ask for the change in X2 divided by d it comes out as roughly 2X. $((X+d)*(X+d)/ - X2)/d = 2X+d$, so as d gets smaller the value approaches 2X. Is that right, sir?"

Omar had just anticipated the rest of the lesson, indeed the rest of this part of the syllabus. Mr Khan tried not to show his shock. Push him to his limits to make him sweat, make it clear who is running this class. "Yes, Omar, that is right. How about extending that logic to the gradient of X cubed?"

Omar briefly saw a picture in his head of the expanding brackets around $(X+d)^3 - X^3$, and saw that the answer had to be $3X^2$. "It is 3 X squared of course."

The rest of the class were just left behind, and kept paying attention out of interest in the human tension rather than the pure maths. Mr Khan sighed, then made a mistake that showed how far he was out of his depth. "Yes, correct. In general, if $Y=A*X^B$, the gradient, the differential, is written as:

$$dY/dX = A*B*X^{(B-1)}."$$

This bit was correct, basic school calculus. Then he over-reached himself. "This shows that no equation can be its own differential." This bit was deeply false, though if he had said "no simple polynomial equation can be its own differential" he'd have been right.

Omar frowned – he could visualise in his head a graph whose gradient at any value of Y was equal to Y. It went up very quickly of course, but didn't seem impossible.

"So if I wanted an equation whose differential is Y=X, that equation would be $Y=X^2/2$, wouldn't it?" asked Omar.

"Yes, correct, Omar, well done. But in the differential you lost the term $X^2/2$, haven't you?" Mr Khan was clear on this simple point.

"So you add $X^3/6$, don't you? That differentiates to $Y=X^2/2$," Omar persisted.

"So where do you get the term $X^3/6$?" asked the master, now getting exasperated.

"By adding $X^4/24$ of course," Omar explained, puzzled by why this caused any problem.

"But Omar, think – this goes on for ever, so never ends. This is an example of Zeno's paradox, and shows your function is impossible." Mr Khan was utterly wrong, just as Zeno's paradox is utterly wrong.

Omar saw a picture in his head of infinite cake slices from one segment, and realised that he could easily create this function in a simple spreadsheet.

The next day Omar came in with a spreadsheet to show Mr Khan, summing the series $1+X+ X^2/2$ etc, and a few results showing that (1) the function was indeed its own differential, that its gradient equalled its Y value at all points, and (2) it appeared to correspond with raising the number 2.718 to a power. "Please, sir – I looked up Zeno's paradox and it is false. It proved that Achilles could not outrun a tortoise! Here is the function we talked about yesterday."

Mr Khan grunted, took the sheet away to look at in in peace in the staff room. A rather more mathematically literate man, the headmaster Mr Shaffiq, came over and had a look, then whistled. "You really give them hard homework – he has derived the exponential function from scratch. A few leaps of intuition there but well worth 8/10 I'd say."

Mr Khan tried to look like he understood, and rather failed.

"If I were you, I would get him onto the infinite series for sine and cosine – they are very similar, he would see the similarities."

Mr Khan smiled vaguely and nodded as though he understood, then dived for a notebook, and started scribbling something down before he forgot.

Antarctica

Alexandra knew that she was in an unusually privileged position to ask questions about what had happened to her world, and what might happen. The huge cache of old publications must hold some stories to explain, since the adults around her either could not or would not. It seemed like the planet had undergone a catastrophic transition from a benign world to a dangerous one, but the best anyone could tell her was "greenhouse effect". She knew greenhouses – her father grew young trees in them, and they didn't seem too bad. The phrases "Extinction event" and "Boundary event" came up, without really explaining anything.

The Arkive database was no help here – it just talked of "habitat loss", or sometimes over-hunting. The Sci-hub database was far more helpful, with its search function producing lots of results about event boundaries. Unfortunately she could not relate any of these papers to what she saw around her. A recurring pattern was for 'runaway greenhouse effect' and 'boundary event' to direct her to articles about two specific events, one called the Permo-Triassic and one called the Palaeocene/Eocene. She re and re-read some of these, but still didn't see how it all fitted together. Words she didn't know about things she didn't understand.

She wanted to find someone of her own age to help her see in her mind the explanations behind what had happened, and maybe where she fitted in. That boy in Kamchatka who sent her the whole archive – he would be the obvious starting point. So it was that Omar started getting papers back from Alexandra, about geological events and ecological collapse in remote islands. And a plea: "Dear Omar. Please can you explain these to me? Do they tell us what happened, what will happen?"

He breezed through the geological papers, got the underlying mathematical ideas, then tried to come up with simple mental pictures to explain the results to Alexandra. Here is his explanation:

"Those papers you sent me talk about events way back in the Earth's geological past, and disagree with the account of creation given in Genesis. The Permo-triassic boundary was the biggest mass killing in earth's history, until the Anthropocene anyway. The Palaeocene boundary was less severe. At both the Permo-triassic boundary and at the Palaeocene boundary the temperature of Planet Earth rose very quickly, giving a brief spike of unusually high global temperatures. It looks as though these temperature spikes come out of a feedback loop, so that more warmth makes more warming gases, makes more warmth makes more warming gases, etc. This is exactly what happened to our ancestors over the last 150 years, and again we got a sharp temperature spike.

"These temperature spikes fade with time. Although the recovery from these events was quick by geological standards, this is slow to humans. The Permo-triassic boundary took about one million years to settle down to a new normal. The Palaeocene boundary was shorter, taking about 100,000 years, with waves of heating and cooling.

"Here are a few pictures to explain those figures. This is how long you need to keep those scientific records safe." These graphs turned out to be Omar's last contribution to history, and certainly his most important.

The heat spike duration, if earth follows the palaeocene:

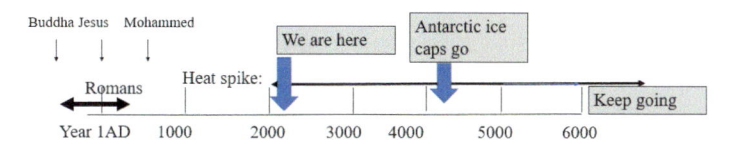

Fig 15.18 Omar's first diagram.

A Path of 21 Ms

The timescale of recovery if earth follows the palaeocene model, from Fig 2 of Mcinerney &Wing(2011): Note that the Permo-Triassic recovery took 10 times longer

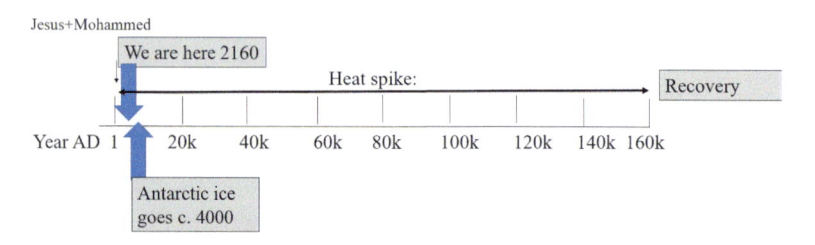

```
Jesus+Mohammed
         ┌──────────────┐
         │ We are here 2160 │
         └──────────────┘      Heat spike:                    ┌──────────┐
              ↓                                                │ Recovery │
    ├────────┼────────┼────────┼────────┼────────┼────────┼──└──────────┘
  Year AD 1  ↑  20k    40k     60k     80k    100k    120k   140k 160k
         ┌──────────────┐
         │ Antarctic ice │
         │ goes c. 4000  │
         └──────────────┘
```

Fig 15.19 Omar's second diagram.

Alexandra saw first a rather mathematical graph explaining how exponential growth behaves, then two images that blew her mind and changed her life. These simply showed how long Earth could be expected to stay in its new super-heated state, based on what happened in previous geological events. First was one she could relate to. It said: "The heat spike duration, if Earth follows the Palaeocene model". It used the Christian calendar with no 0 but 1AD (marking Jesus), Mohammed around 600, then intervals of 1000 years, with a big easy "you are here" at 2160. It showed the heat spike starting a bit after the year 2000, then just carrying on.

She wasn't sure she could get her head around a timescale of 1000 years – just ten years was hard enough as a teenager. The eternal ice caps of the high Antarctic, whose melting supplied sustainable power to her community – destined to vanish somewhere around 4200. Still the heat will be on. Move on – when does it end? The next graph was similar, but said: "The timescale of recovery if Earth follows the Palaeocene model: Note that the Permo-Triassic recovery took ten times longer". This graph was very compressed. It merged Jesus and Mohammed into the same pixel, only just before "you are here". The units were now 20,000 years. If we're lucky, it says, the heat spike should settle down a bit before 100,000 years, if Earth follows that Palaeocene model.

At that moment Alexandra had a vision of her place in history. She had to be the brief, temporary custodian of the most huge, amazing body of knowledge for the long-term future of the species and our understanding of everything. On Planet Nauru. The last custodian of the Easter Island scripts, literally and metaphorically. The birds and monkeys, whales and forests that would otherwise be forgotten for ever, like most life forms that ever existed. Their memory alone was vital to keep. Otherwise, like the Rongo rongo script on Easter Island, the knowledge would vanish for ever, lost to all future humans. But 100,000 years?! That far back in time she didn't think humans even had books. The New Scientist articles talked about hunters on the African Savannah, maybe not even burying their dead, let alone writing. That far into the future, how will people have changed? But one thing she wanted them to remember and thank her for was for the great digital library of Alexandra. Now, how on earth to keep it all safe? Safe not just for this week, not just for the next system upgrade, but for the distant future? Safe against EMPs and human bigotry. There's a lifetime ambition for anyone. Just the small problem of working out how . . .

New Rhidayha

Word went round the staffroom, of a call for students to be chosen for a new Madrassa. This was to teach jihad, with a view to missions such as punitive raids against the Jewish enclave. Everyone understood it would lead to suicide missions, literally and metaphorically. Military drones were just too good and too deadly. Most of the teachers had private doubts, but kept quiet. Mr Khan smiled deeply – he knew exactly whose eternal chances would be improved by youthful martyrdom.

Omar came into class the next day, his head buzzing with what he had been reading and exploring. "Please sir, I have found two amazing things last night. Firstly, if you pretend that the square root of minus 1 is a valid concept, I can prove that $\exp(i*pi) = -1$. This proves that $\log(-1)$ equals pi times the square root of minus one. Secondly, do you know about the Riemann Zeta function? People have had problems with it for centuries, but I've found a link to one of Ramanujan's ideas, and putting them together the number 0.5 just pops out. This solves a real old mystery. Can I show you the proof?" He got out a slate covered in frankly incomprehensible functions written in a very non-standard format.

Mr Khan decided he must be taking the mickey, again. No more you won't. "Omar, don't be silly. Everyone knows you can't have the logarithm of a negative number. Now, good news, I am delighted to say that you have been given a great honour. You are to start at the special new Madrassa, immediately. You will need to empty your desk, take your stuff home to your parents then report here tomorrow morning. Now go, and stop wasting your time with silly games, you need to make a mark in the real world." He handed over a card identifying Omar's new school, ominously featuring the word 'jihad'.

Postscript

Like I say, I hope I'm wrong. But the timescales of recovery written in the geological record stand, and should put us into awe of the issues we are leaving people to live with. We clearly should make proper long-term plans for how we safeguard scientific knowledge into the geological future. Along with finding ways to live without burning fossil carbon. Hypocrite – guilty as charged. It is effectively impossible to live a normal functional life off-grid or transport-free, though buying a villa in Provence was perhaps an extravagant choice. It has certainly transformed our lives, for the better. I guess anyone can say that to justify almost anything. What I must say is that I am passionately in favour of nuclear power, precisely because I am an ecologist. Every ecologist who opposes nuclear power is doing so on emotional grounds. Cite Chernobyl? Yes, do cite Chernobyl. It maybe killed 4000 people and created the best nature reserve in Ukraine. (Put that figure against gigadeaths from runaway overheating.) Don't believe me, check it. The hot zone is hot with wildlife, bears and eagles, wolves and feral horses. The problem for biodiversity is not radiation, it's humans. Where to put the waste? Put it in my nature reserve, I'd be honoured and delighted. Look at your objections, and try to put numbers on the actual issues, and you will find the numbers are only big enough to matter if you look selectively at them. My former boss the late Lord Walter Marshall of Goring (head, CEGB) said, "In 2020 the greens will be campaigning for nuclear power." I have immense respect for Lord Marshall, and he should have been right. If the rest of the species were as intelligent as he was, the greens WOULD now be clamouring for a massive switch to nuclear, maybe advocating research into thorium reactors too. The fact that they are not means that I refuse to vote for the Green Party because I AM an ecologist, because I want to protect the environment from what ACTUALLY matters, rather than worrying about irrational human paranoia. The choice appears to be nuclear power vs the Permo-Triassic.

It seems to be a sad, un-reported tendency for disagreements about energy/GHE policy to start off with dry discussions about numbers but somehow end up with deep, bitter, irreconcilable friendship-splitting disagreements. I have told someone that her objections to nuclear power were just emotional and therefore worthless. I have done what I can to advertise my concern about someone who is perfectly intelligent but somehow, incomprehensibly, a flat-out climate change denier, perhaps thereby blocking him from future employment contracts. I know of people in a social circle in France with whom I just have to agree to disagree about energy policy because the arguments get too loud and too bitter. I am afraid that this pattern will repeat itself at the species level, and all I can say is that I would always suggest following the numbers, because you will absolutely have to, sooner or later.

In the meantime, just by way of a thought-inducing geological quip, I came up with this slogan while out running in the woods. It implicitly advocates biomass storage as a form of carbon capture and removal: "The Anthropocene needs to re-enact the Carboniferous to avoid re-enacting the Permo-Triassic".

Peter Shaw
Dorking Surrey
November 2023

APPENDIX 1

My publications – books, papers and other outputs

Books

Shaw, PJA (2003). *Multivariate Statistics for the Environmental Sciences*. Hodder Arnold. ISBN 0-340-80763-6.

Comment: I am working on a second edition with Dr Edwin Pos of Utrecht, to update the maths and incorporate R code

Shaw, PJA (2000). *The Acid tests*. Innogy publications. ISBN: 0 9517172 5 1.

Refereed publications

Shaw P.J.A. & Usher M.B. (2024). Spider species and assemblages in forest plantations of various ages. Journal of Arachnology, in press.

Comment: an unexpected late paper analysing Michael Usher's spider data.

Barnett A., Stone, A., & **Shaw P.J.A.** Ronchi-Teles B., Santos-Barnett T., Pimenta N., Kinap N.M., Spironello W.R., Bitencourt A., Penhorwood G., Umeed R.N., Oliveira T.G., Bezerra B.M., Boyle S.A., Ross C., Wenzell J. (2023). When food fights back: Cebid primate strategies of larval paper wasp predation and the high energy yield of high risk foraging. *Austral Ecology* **48**: 719-742.

Comment: this late paper got me a namecheck on the back page of New Scientist 4 Feb 2023: "Can anyone beat this for a slow paper. 11 years and 15 journals?" Mark Abrahams emailed me, then got an out-of-office message from Roehampton, explaining that I had retired two years earlier.

Jaques R.G., Allison G., **Shaw P.**, Griffith G.W.& Scullion S. (2021). Earthworm-Collembola interactions affecting water-soluble nutrients, fauna and physiochemistry in a mesocosm manure-straw composting experiment. Waste management **154**: 57-66.

Collins, P.M, Green, J.A., Elliott, K.A., **Shaw, P.J.A.**, Chivers, L., Hatch, S.A., Halsey, L.G. (2020). Coping with the commute: behavioural responses to wind conditions in a foraging seabird. *Journal of Avian Biology* **51** (4). http://dx.doi.org/10.1111/jav.02057.

Betti, L., **Shaw P.** & Behrends V. (2020). Acceptance of biological evolution in first-year Life Sciences university students. Science & Education **29**: 395-409.

Faria, C.M.A., **Shaw P.** & Emerson, B.C. (2019). Evidence for the Pleistocene persistence of Collembola in Great Britain. *Journal of Biogeography* **46**: 1479-1493. DOI: 10.1111/jbi.13610

Shaw, P. & Trewhella S. (2019). Recent Unusual Collembola records: Entomobryomorpha and Poduromorpha. British Journal of Entomology and Natural History, **32**: 217-230.

Faria C.M.A., **Shaw P.** & Emerson B. (2019). Evidence for the Pleistocene persistence of Collembola in Great Britain. Journal of Biogeography **46**: 179-193. DOI: 10.1111/jbi.13610

Dunscombe, M., Robertson A., Peralta-Maraver I. & **Shaw P.** (2018). Community structure and functioning below the streambed across contrasting geologies. Science of the Total Environment **630**: 1028-1035.

Barnett A., Ronchi-Teles B., Silva W.S., Andrade R., Almeida T., Bezerra B.M., Gonçalves de Lima M, Spironello W.R.,, MacLarnon A., Ross C. & **Shaw P.J.A.** (2017). Covert Carnivory? A Seed-Predating Primate, the Golden-Backed Uacari, Shows Preferences for Insect-Infested Fruits. Journal of Zoological Research **1**: 16-31.

Standing V. & **Shaw P.J.A.** (2017). Edge effects in corticolous Collembola in Richmond Park. British Journal of Entomology and Natural History **30**: 157-169.

Pacioglu, O., Moldovan, O. T., **Shaw, P.** & Robertson, A. (2016). Response of invertebrates from the hyporheic zone of chalk rivers to eutrophication and land use In: Environmental Science & Pollution Research **23**: p. 4741-4741.

Collins, P. M., Halsey, L. G., Arnould, J. P. Y., **Shaw, P. J. A.**, Dodd, S., Green, J. A. (2016). Energetic consequences of time-activity budgets for a breeding seabird. Journal of Zoology 10.1111/jzo.12370

Crotty F.V., Fychan, R., Benefer, C.M., Allen, D., **Shaw P.** & Marley C.L. (2016). First documented pest outbreak of the herbivorous springtail *Sminthurus viridis* (Collembola) in Europe. Grass Forage Science **71**: 699–704. doi:10.1111/gfs.12235

Barnett A., Bezerra, B.M., Santos P.J.P, Spironello W.R., **Shaw P.J.A.**, MacLarnon, A. & Ross C. (2016). Foraging with Finesse: A hard-fruit-Eating Primate selects the Weakest Areas as Bite Sites. American Journal of Physical Anthropology **160**: 113-125.

Shaw P.J.A. (2015). How high do Collembola climb? Studies of vertical migration in arboreal Collembola. Soil Organisms **87**: 227-235.

Shaw P.J.A. & Benefer C. (2015). Development of a barcoding database for the UK Collembola: early results. Soil Organisms **87**: 197-202.

Shaw P.J.A. & Boardman P. (2015). The first occurrence of *Bilobella braunerae* Deharveng (Collembola: poduridae) in the UK. British Journal of Entomology and Natural History **28**: 165-167.

Shaw, P.J.A. (2015). Nature reserves, orchids and fly ash. *Urban Ecology Review* **5**: 89-90. Ed. Ian Rotherham

Collins, P., Green, J.A., Warwick-Evans V., Dodd S., **Shaw, P.J.A.**, Arnould J.Y.P & Halsey L. (2015). Interpreting behaviors from accelerometry: a method combining simplicity and objectivity. Ecology & Evolution 5.20: 4642-4654. doi: 10.1002/ece3.1660 http://onlinelibrary.wiley.com/doi/10.1002/ece3.1660/abstract

Groome G. & **Shaw P.J.A** (2015). Vegetation response to the reintroduction of cattle grazing on an English lowland valley mire and wet heath. Conservation Evidence **12**: 33-39.

Barnett A., Silva WS, **Shaw P.J.A** & Ramsay P. (2015). Inundation duration and vertical vegetation zonation: a preliminary description of the vegetation and structuring factors in Borokotóh (hummock igapó), an overlooked, high-diversity, Amazonian vegetation association. Nordic Journal of Botany **33**: 601-614.

Robertson A, Dineen G, Baker, R., Hancock B & **Shaw P.JA**. (2014). Microinvertebrate community colonisation and succession in a new urban river: lessons for river restoration. Fundamental and Applied Limnology **185**: 31-41.

Barnett A. & **Shaw P.J.A** (2014). More food or fewer predators? The benefits to birds of associating with a Neotropical primate varies with their foraging strategy. Journal of Zoology **294**: 224-233. doi:10.1111/jzo.12182

Ozanne C., Cabral C. & **Shaw P.J.A.** (2014). Variation in Indigenous Forest Resource Use in Central Guyana. PloS One DOI: 10.1371/journal.pone.0102952

Berbesque J.C., Marlowe F.W., **Shaw P.** & Thompson P. (2014). Hunter–gatherers have less famine than agriculturalists. Biology Letters **10**: 20130853.

Collins, P., Green, J., **Shaw, P.J.A.** & Halsey, L. (2014). 'Predation of Black-legged Kittiwake chicks *Rissa tridactyla* by a Peregrine Falcon *Falco peregrinus*: insights from time-lapse cameras'. Wilson Journal of Ornithology March 2014, 158-161. http://www.bioone.org/doi/abs/10.1676/13-141.1

Shaw, P.J.A, Faria C. & B. Emerson (2013). Updating taxonomic biogeography in the light of new methods – examples from Collembola. Soil Organisms **85**: 161-170.

Bhatti, I., Ozanne, C.M.P. & **Shaw P.J.A.** (2013). Parasitoids and parasitism rates of the horse chestnut leaf miner *Cameraria ohridella* Deschka and Dimic [Lepidoptera: Gracillariidae] across four sites in south-west London. Arboricultural Journal: The International Journal of Urban Forestry, http://dx.doi.org/10.1080/03071375.2013.813706

Shaw P.J.A. (2013). The use of inert pads to study the Collembola of suspended soils. Soil Organisms 85: 69-74. http://www.senckenberg.de/root/index.php?page_id=16668

Pacioglu, O., **Shaw P.** & A. Robertson (2012). Patch scale response of hyporheic invertebrates to fine sediment removal in two chalk rivers. – Fundamental and Applied Limnology **181**: 283–288.

Barnett A. **Shaw P.J.A.**, Sprinello A.R., Maclarnon A. & Ross C. (2012). Sleeping site selection by golden-backed uacaris, *Cacajao melanocephalus ouakary* (Pitheciidae), in Amazonian flooded forests. *Primates*. DOI 10.1007/s10329-012-0296-4.

Shaw P.J.A., Dunscombe M. & Robertson A. (2012). Collembola in the hyporheos of a karstic river: a new Collembolan community containing a new genus for the UK. *Soil Organisms* **83**: 507-514.

Shaw P.J.A. & Ozanne C.M.P. (2011). A calibration of the efficiency of Winkler funnels for extracting Collembola at different humidities. *Soil Organisms* **83**: 515-522.

Emerson B.C., Cicconardi F., Fanciulli P.P., **Shaw P.J.A.** (2011). Phylogeny, phylogeography, phylobetadiversity and the molecular analysis of community structure. *Philosophical Transactions of the Royal Society B*, 366, 2391-2402.

Shaw P.J.A. (2011). Management of brownfield sites for biodiversity *Aspects of Applied Biology* **108**: 179-192.

Shaw P.J.A. & Shackleton K. (2011). Carnivory in the Teasel *Dipsacus fullonum* – the effect of experimental feeding on growth and seed set. PLoS PLoS ONE **6**(3): e17935. doi:10.1371/journal.pone.0017935

McDermott M.J., Robertson A.L., **Shaw P.J.A** & Milner A.M. (2010) The hyporheic assemblage of a recently formed stream following deglaciation in Glacier Bay, Alaska. *Canadian Journal of Fisheries Aquatic Science* 67: 304-313.

Shaw P.J.A. (2009). Succession on the PFA/Gypsum Trial Mounds at Drax Power Station: The First Fifteen Years. *Journal of Practical Ecology and Conservation* **8**: 1–13. Ed. Ian Rotherham

Shaw P.J.A. (2009). Soil and fertiliser amendments and edge effects on the floral succession of Pulverised Fuel Ash (PFA). *Restoration Ecology* **17**: 68-77.

Shaw P.J.A. & Reeve N. (2008). Influence of a parking area on soils and vegetation in an urban nature reserve. *Urban Ecosystems* **11**: 107-120.

Pinhasi R., Evered V. & **Shaw P.J.A.** (2008). Evolutionary changes in the masticatory complex following transition to farming in the southern Levant. American Journal of Physical anthropology **135**: 136-148.

Shaw P.J.A., Ozanne C.M.P., Speight M. & Palmer I. (2007). Edge effects and arboreal Collembola in coniferous plantations. *Pedobiologia,* **51**: 287-293.

Cole, L., Bradford, M., **Shaw P.J.A.** & Bardgett R. (2006). The abundance, richness and functional role of soil meso- and macrofauna in temperate grassland – a case study. *Applied Soil Ecology* **33**: 186-198.

Pinhasi, R., **Shaw, P.J.A.** an White, B. & Ogden (2006). Morbidity, Rickets and long bone growth in post-medieval Britain – a cross population analysis. *Annals of Human Biology* **33**: 372-389

Pinhasi R., Teschler-Nicola M., Prossinger H. & **Shaw P.J.A.** (2006). Diachronic trends in dental dimensions of Late Pleistocene and Early Holocene European and Near Eastern Populations. BIENNIAL BOOKS OF EAA, 2006, Vol. 4.

Pinhasi R., Teschler-Nicola M., Knaus, A. & **Shaw P.J.A.** (2005). A cross-population analysis of the growth of long bones and the os coxae of three early medieval Austrian populations. *American Journal of Human Biology* **17**, 470-488.

Fitter A.H., Gilligan C.A., Hollingworth K., Kleczkowski A., Twyman R.M., Pitchford J.W. and the members of the NERC Soil Biodiversity Programme (2005) Biodiversity and ecosystem function in soil *Func. Ecol.* 19, 369-377. [Note that although I am not an explicit author, I was on the NERC programme and did contribute to the development of the manual for this software.]

Shaw P.J.A., Butlin J. & Kibby G. (2004). Fungi of ornamental woodchips in Surrey. Mycologist **18**: 12-16.

Shaw P.J.A., Kibby G. & Mayes J. (2003). Effects of thinning treatment on an ectomycorrhizal succession under Scots pine. *Mycological Research* **107**: 317-328.

Shaw P.J.A. (2003). Collembola of pulverised fuel ash sites in East London. *European Journal of Soil Biology* **39**: 1-8.

Brierley E.D.R., **Shaw P.J.A**. & Wood M. (2001). Nitrogen cycling and proton fluxes in an acid forest soil. *Plant & Soil* **229**: 83-96.

Brierley E.D.R., Wood M. & **Shaw P.J.A**. (2001). Influence of tree species and ground vegetation on nitrification in an acid forest soil. *Plant & Soil* **229**: 97-104.

Shaw, P.J.A. (1998). Morphometric analyses of mixed *Dactylorhiza* colonies (Orchidaceae) on industrial waste sites in England. *Botanical Journal of the Linnean Society* **128**: 385–401.

Shaw P.J.A. (1998). Conservation management of Industrial wastes. *Journal of Practical Ecology and Conservation* **2**(1): 13-17. Ed. Ian Rotherham

Shaw, P.J.A. (1997). Post-fire successions in Collembola on lowland heaths in the UK. *Pedobiologia* **41**: 40-47.

Shaw, P.J.A. & Usher, M.B. (1996). Edaphic Collembola of lodgepole pine *Pinus contorta* plantations in Cumbria, UK. *European Journal of Soil Biology* **32**: 89-97.

Shaw, P.J.A., Lankey, K. & Jourdan, A. (1996). Factors affecting yield of *Tuber melanosporum* in a *Quercus ilex* plantation in southern France. *Mycological Research* **100**: 1176-1178.

Shaw, P.J.A. (1996). Role Of Seedbank Substrates in the Revegetation of Fly Ash and Gypsum in the U.K. *Restoration Ecology* **4** (1): 61-69.

Shaw, P.J.A., Lankey, K. & Hollingham S.A. (1995). Impacts of trampling and dog fouling on vegetation and soil conditions on Headley Heath. *The London Naturalist* **74**: 77-82.

Shaw, P.J.A. & McLeod, A.R. (1995). The effects of SO_2 and O_3 on the foliar nutrition of Scots pine, Norway spruce and Sitka spruce in the Liphook open-air fumigation experiment. *Plant, Cell and Environment* **18**: 237-245.

Holland M.R., Mueller, P.W., Rutter, A.J., & **Shaw, P.J.A.** (1995). Growth of coniferous forest trees exposed to SO_2 and O_3 using an open air fumigation system. *Plant Cell and Environment* **18**: 227-236.

Shaw, P.J.A. (1995). Establishment of sand dune flora on power station wastes. *Land Contamination and Reclamation* **3**: 148-149.

Shaw, P.J.A. & Lankey, K. (1994). Studies on the Scots pine mycorrhizal fruitbody succession. *The Mycologist* **8**: 172-175.

Moffat, A.J. & **Shaw, P.J.A.** (1993). Establishment of trees on mixtures of pulverised fuel ash and gypsum. I. Tree performance. *Land Degradation and Rehabilitation* **4**: 87-97.

Shaw, P.J.A. & Moffat, A.J. (1993). Establishment of trees on mixtures of PFA and gypsum. Part II. Nutrition and trace elements. *Land degradation and rehabilitation* **4**: 123-129.

Shaw, P.J.A. and Johnston, J.P.N. (1993). Effects of SO_2 and O_3 on the chemistry and FDA activity of coniferous leaf litter in an open air fumigation experiment. *Soil Biology and Biochemistry* **25**: 897-908.

Shaw, P.J.A., Dighton, J.& Poskitt, J. (1993) Studies on the mycorrhizal community infecting trees in the Liphook forest fumigation experiment Agriculture Ecosystems and Environment **47**: 185-191.

Shaw, P.J.A., Holland, M.R., Darrell, N.M. & McLeod A.R. (1993). The occurrence of SO_2-related foliar symptoms on Scots pine (*Pinus sylvestris* L.) in an open air fumigation experiment. *New Phytologist* **123**: 143-152.

McLeod, A.R., **Shaw, P.J.A.** & Holland, M.R. (1992). The Liphook forest fumigation project: studies of sulphur dioxide and ozone effects on coniferous trees. *Forest Ecology and Management* **51**: 121-127.

Shaw, P.J.A., Dighton, J., Poskitt, J. and McLeod, A.R. (1992). The effects of sulphur dioxide and ozone on the mycorrhizas of Scots pine and Norway spruce in a field fumigation system. *Mycological Research* **96**: 785-791.

Shaw, P.J.A., Dightoon & Poskitt (1993). Studies on the mycorrhizal community toinfecting trees in the Liphook forest fumigation experiment. Agriculture Ecosystems & Environment **47**: 185-191.

Shaw, P.J.A. (1992). A preliminary study of successional changes in vegetation and soil development on unamended fly ash (PFA) in southern England. *Journal of Applied Ecology* **29**: 728-736.

Stubberfield, L.C.F. and **Shaw, P.J.A.** (1990). A comparison of tetrazolium reduction and FDA hydrolysis with other measures of microbial activity. *Journal of Microbiological Methods* **12**: 151-162.

McLeod, A.R., Holland, M.R., **Shaw, P.J.A.**, Sutherland, P.M., Darrall, N.M. and Skeffington, R.A. (1990). Enhancement of nitrogen deposition to forest trees exposed to SO2. *Nature* **347**: 277–279.

Shaw, P.J.A. (1988). A consistent hierarchy in the fungal feeding preferences of the Collembola *Onychiurus armatus*. *Pedobiologia* **31**: 179-187.

Book chapters

Shaw P.J.A. (2021). The ecology of post-industrial sites and the Oliver Gilbert legacy. In: Frontiers of Urban and Restoration Ecology, Ed. Ian Rotherham, pp 135-152.

Shaw, P.J.A. (1996). The influence of acid mist and ozone on the fluorescein di-acetate activity of leaf litter. In *Fungi and Environmental Change* (Eds J. Frankland and D. Gadd), Cambridge University Press, pp. 102-108.

Shaw, P.J.A. (1992). Fungi, fungivores and fungal food webs. In *The Fungal Community*, Vol. 2 (G.C. Carroll and D. Wicklow, Eds.), 295 – 310.

Shaw, P.J.A., Dighton, J. and Poskitt, J. (1992). Studies on the effects of SO2 and O3 on the mycorrhizal succession under Scots pine and Norway spruce as observed above and below ground. *Mycorrhizas in Ecosystems* (Eds. DJ Read, DH Lewis and IJ Alexander), pp. 208-213.

Shaw, P.J.A. (1988). The Liphook Forest Fumigation Experiment. In *Acid Rain and Britain's Natural Ecosystems* (Eds. M.R. Ashmore, J.N.B. Bell and C. Garrety) p. 127.

Shaw, P.J.A. (1985). Grazing preferences of *Onychiurus armatus* (Insecta: Collembola) for mycorrhizal and saprophytic fungi of pine plantations. In *Ecological Interactions in the Soil* (Special Publication of the British Ecological Society No. 4), (A.H. Fitter, D.J. Read & M.B. Usher, Eds.), 333-337.

Other publications

Shaw P.J.A. & Watson Featherstone A. (2020). Collembola (springtails) of the Dundreggan Conservation estate, Scotland. British Journal of Entomology and Natural History **33**: 121-132.

Ware, C., Lowe, M., Sivell, D., Cooper, L., Greaves, P., Root, T., **Shaw, P.**, Shubert, E., Spooner, B. & Strekopytov, S. (2017). Further developments of the flora and fauna of the wildlife garden at the Natural History Museum, London: part 2 – twenty one years of species recording. London Naturalist **96**: 126-181.

Shaw P.J.A. (2016). Woodland soils explained. Woodwise (Woodland Trust magazine) March 2016, 7-8.

Dallimore T. & **Shaw P.J.A.** (2013). Key to families of UK Collembola. AIDAP: FSC.

Shaw P.J.A., Dunscombe M. and Robertson A. (2010). *Hymenaphorura nova* Pomorski, 1990 (Collembola: Onychiuridae) in the hyporheos of a karstic river: a new species and genus for the UK in a novel habitat. *Entomologist's Journal and Record of Variation* **122**: 213-215

Shaw, P. (2010) UK Invasive fungi – benign additions to our fungal flora ECOS 31 (1) Ed. Ian Rotherham

Shaw P.J.A., Berg M.P. & Higgins J. (2003). *Orchesella quinquefasciata* (Bourlet, 1843) (Collembola: Entomobryidae) from chalk grassland in the south downs. *Entomologist's Record* **115**: 45-48.

Shaw, P.J.A. & Kibby G. (2001). Aliens in the flowerbeds: the fungal biodiversity of ornamental woodchips. *Field Mycology* **2**: 6-11.

Shaw P.J.A. & Buckhoree Z. (2001). Collembola (springtails) of Brockham lime kilns, Box Hill. *London Naturalist* **80**: 159-165.

Shaw, P.J.A. (1999). Studies on the vegetation succession at Brockham lime kilns, Box Hill. *London Naturalist* **78**: 87-92.

Shaw, P.J.A. (1995). Mycological societies of the world: L'association trufficulture du Canton de Lambesc et Environs. *The Mycologist* **9**: 115-116.

Shaw, P.J.A. & Halton W. (1998). Classic sites: Nob End, Bolton. *British Wildlife* **10**: 13-17.

Shaw, P.J.A. (1994). Orchid woods and floating islands – the ecology of fly ash. *British Wildlife* **5**: 149-157.

Shaw, P.J.A. (1992). The manipulation of the natural plant succession on PFA for conservation purposes. *Verwertung von Restoffen aus Kohlekraftwerken zur Bodenverbesserung und Pflanzenernahrung (Proceedings of the VGB conference on Utilization of Power Station Byproducts for soil Improvement and Plant Nutrition)*, Essen, October 1991, chapter 21. VGB Sondertagung.

Shaw P.J.A. (1986). The Liphook forest fumigation experiment description and project plan. CEGB Research report TPRD/L/2985/R86

Comment: this was easily my 'best seller' CEGB report since a copy was given to everyone involved in Liphook.

See Also http://www.newscientist.com/article/mg21929254.700-uks-industrial-badlands-are-surprise-ecology-hotspots.html about my PFA research.

Shaw P.J.A. (1992). A Preliminary survey of Gale Common. PPV 2661.001 National Power

Shaw P.J.A. (1988). Fluorescein diacetate hydrolysis a simple and sensitive method for measuring microbial activity. RD/L/3344/R88

Blank L.W., McLeod A.R., **Shaw P.J.A.** & Roberts T.M. (1988). ESTD/L/3331/R89 The Liphook forest fumigation project 2nd report: Pre-fumigation phase. Central Electricity Generating Board.

Blank L.W., McLeod A.R., **Shaw P.J.A.** & Roberts T.M. (1989). ESTD/L/0052/R89 The Liphook forest fumigation project 3rd report: first fumigation phase. Central Electricity Generating Board.

Shaw P.J.A. (1989). Fluorescein di-acetate hydrolysis as a measure of decomposer activity and its application to pollution studies. RD/L/3475/R89 Central Electricity Generating Board.

Shaw P.J.A. (1989). Comments on the Carmarthen bay power station site development environmental impact assessment. ESTD/L/ELS/026 c National Power

Shaw P.J.A. (1990). The Ecology and conservation potential of PFA and other alkaline wastes. Hatfield Polytechnic 30 May 1992. TPRD/L/ELS/0046/90 National Power

Shaw P.J.A. (1990). Workshop on invertebrate conservation Peterborough 12 December 1989. ESTD/L/ELS/0030/M90. National Power.

Shaw P.J.A. (1991). The production of sulphide-rich leachates from pfa /municipal waste codisposal site at Godstone, Surrey. TEC/L/0131/TAN91

Shaw P.J.A. (1989). Natural revegetation and soil development processes on pfa at the former rye house power station. Estd/l/0124/r89 National Power.

Shaw P.J.A. (1990). comments on the preliminary results of leachate analyses from the Drax gypsum/pfa mounds, ESTD/ELS/042/TAN90. National Power

Shaw P.J.A. Roberts T.M. & Johnson P. (1986). The disposal of bulk gypsum: a review of existing practices, their relevance to FGD gypsum and research into revegetation procedures. TPRD/L/LIS/115/M87 CEGB

Shaw P.J.A. (1991). Studies on the mycorrhizal fungi in the Liphook forest fumigation experiment. TEC/L/0460/R91

Shaw P.J.A., Simpson D. & Sutherland P.M. (1990) Studies on the west burton gypsum mound: phase1, chemical and hydrological measurement TEC/L/0025/r90

References mentioned in the text but for which I was not an author

Arrhenius, S. (1896). On the Influence of Carbonic Acid in the Air upon the Temperature of the Ground. Philosophical Magazine and Journal of Science Series 5, Volume 41, pp 237-276. https://www.rsc.org/images/Arrhenius1896_tcm18-173546.pdf

Comment – the original observation the CO_2 traps heat unusually effectively, predicting global warming as it accumulates. His estimates were made with a pencil and paper over many weeks, but still stand up today.

Einstein A., Podolsky B. and N. Rosen, (1935). Can quantum-mechanical description of physical reality be considered complete?, Physical Review, 47: 777–780. See also https://plato.stanford.edu/entries/qt-epr/

Comment – this is the classic "EPR" paper, which predicts entanglement in order to disprove the mathematics of the standard quantum physics model. Reality just shrugged, and obeyed the mathematics anyway, giving us some truly bizarre behaviours that seems to violate relativity.

Hoffman D.J., Butler J.H. & Tans P. (2009). A new look at carbon dioxide. Atmospheric Environment **43**: 2084-2086.

Comment – observes that CO2 is exponential with a doubling time of 31 years.

Lockley, R. (1980) *Orielton – the human and natural history of a Welsh manor.* Penguin, London.

Comment: We ran a field course based in Orielton manor (eg fig 7: 21), and many of the features mentioned here by Lockley were still visible. He mentions the Mackworth-Praed family, who went on to be my wife's landlord in 1987.

Lyall, S. (10 March 2007). "How the Young Poor Measure Poverty in Britain: Drink, Drugs and Their Time in Jail". The New York Times.

Comment: Lyall described the housing estates in Wythenshawe as representing an "extreme pocket of social deprivation and alienation".

McInerney F.A. & Wing S.L. (2011). The Paleocene-Eocene Thermal Maximum: A Perturbation of Carbon Cycle, Climate, and Biosphere with Implications for the Future. *Annual Review Earth Planetary Science* **39**: 489–516.

Comment – Gives the PETM background, and the timescales of recovery used by Omar to create his diagrams.

Muthukumaraswamy S.D., Carhart-Harris R.L., Moran R.J., et al., 2013, Broadband Cortical Desynchronization Underlies the Human Psychedelic State, *Journal of Neuroscience* **33:** 15171-15183

Comment – the paper showing that psychedelic effects arise from inhibition not stimulation.

Parker-Rhodes, A.F. (1955). Fairy ring kinetics. *Transactions of the British Mycological Society* 38: 59-72.

Comment: Alexandra was amused by the utter monumental pointlessness of this research, as an example of publications that look to be an incomprehensible waste of effort (along with Shaw's work on fly ash Collembola!)

Pattee, E. (2022). The 1977 White House climate memo that should have changed the world. *The Guardian* 14 June 2022, p, 1.

Comment – this reproduces the memo given to President Carter that refers to exponential CO_2 driving catastrophic damage to nation states and food supplies.

Rutherford A. & Fry H. (H) 2021. Rutherford and Fry's Complete Guide to Absolutely Everything (Abridged). Bantam Press. ISBN: 9781787632639

Shaw W.G. (1871). Memoirs of the Clan Shaw. Available at www.Hansebooka.com

Comment: As it says, an old history of the clan Shaw. I'm not sure that I am totally proud of all my ancestors' actions, but the 15th century had different value systems. Contains references to Invercauld.

Swann, B.B. (1953). Statistical computation and electronic machines. *The Incorporated Statistician* **4:** 81-91.

Comment – this eminent expert confidently predicted the UK would not need more than a handful of computing machines in the foreseeable future.

Wall T. (2014). *The Singular Stiperstones*. Publisher: TomWall. https://tomwall.co.uk/

Comment – Tom took me round the Stiperstones in June 2022

Wall T. (2019 a). *Rostherne Mere: Birds of mere and margin: One hundred and thirty years of observations*. Publisher: TomWall. https://tomwall.co.uk/

Comment – see my gap year, 1979. I worked there under Tom.

Wall T. (2019 b). *Rostherne Mere: Aspects of a wetland nature reserve*. Publisher: Tom Wall. https://tomwall.co.uk/

Comment – see my gap year, 1979. I worked there under Tom.

Warnock, A.J. Fitter, A.H. & Usher, M.B. (1982). The influence of a springtail *Folsomia candida* on the mycorrhizal association of leek *Allium porrum* and the VAM endophyte *Glomus fasciculatus*. New Phytologist 90: 285-292.

Comment – the paper that launched my PhD

A Path of 21 Ms

PhD Studentships supervised to completion

PhD: *The Biodiversity of coffee forests in Ethiopia*. Zerihun Fole. August 2021.
PhD: *The movement ecology of a breeding seabird: An investigation using accelerometry* Phil Collins, March 2017.
PhD: *The impact of native and exotic plans on soil biodiversity and ecosystem function*. Stephanie Bird October 2015.
PhD: *Temporal and spatial patterns of dipteran and collembolan abundance in a Nigerian tropical forest canopy*. Dan Weaver, 2012.
PhD: *The effect of diffuse nitrate pollution and land use on hyporheic habitats in lowland English chalk rivers*. Octavian Pacioglu, 2012.
PhD: *Towards an understanding of hydrogeological controls on lowland hyporheic assemblages in the UK*. Mark Dunscombe 2012.
PhD: *The physical and biological factors affecting meiofauna in the Jubilee river, UK*. Barbara Hancock April 2008
PhD: *Invertebrate colonisation of the Jubilee River, a man-made river channel*. Roger Baker, Roehampton university July 2006.
PhD: *Meiofaunal communities in a recently deglaciated stream in Alaska*. Mike McDermott, Roehampton university November 2005.
PhD: *Invertebrate colonisation and succession on a grazing marsh, the wetland centre, London, UK*. Erica McAlister, University of Surrey Roehampton, June 2002.
PhD: *Amerindian ethnoecology, resource use and forest management in Southwest Guiana*. Christie Allan, University of Surrey Roehampton, June 2002.
PhD: Mairi McLeod: *The reproductive system of Samango monkeys (Cercopithecus mitis erythrarchus)*. University of Surrey Roehampton 2000.
PhD: *Evolution of Bat Life histories*. Kate Jones, Roehampton Institute London, 1998.
PhD: *The influence of acid rain and ozone on lichens*. Simon Ellin, Bradford University, May 1992.
PhD: *Nitrogen transformations in an acid forest soil*. Euen Brierley, Reading University, October 1989.

PhD vivas conducted

9 October 2018 University of Roehampton: "Links between hydrology, community ecology and ecosystem services in the hyporheic zone of streams and rivers: an interdisciplinary perspective". (Nacho Peralto)
10 January 2018 University College Dublin: "Soil microarthropod community assembly and their value as indicators of soil biodiversity". (Tara Dirilgen.)
20 March 2017 University of Roehampton: "Geological controls on hypogean assemblages." Damiano Weitowicz
2 October 2013: Royal Holloway (University of London). Quantifying the soil community of green roofs. (Heather Rumble).
22 July 2013 University of Ballarat Australia. Collembola as indicators of human impact. (Penelope Greenslade). Review conducted remotely without face-face viva, this being

because of the distance and because it was before we all became familiar with online "zoom" meetings.

4 October 2011: University of Roehampton: Masticatory adaptations of extant and extinct ursidae: an assessment using 3dimensional geomorphometrics. (Anneke van Heteren)

6 May 2010: University of Roehampton: The diet, habitat use and conservation ecology of the golden backed uakari *Cacajao ouakary* in Jau national park, Amazonian Brazil. (A. Barnett).

29-9-2004, University College Dublin: Effects of acid rain on soil arthropods (F. McCarthy)

5-12-2001, Sheffield Hallam university: Ancient woodland indicators. (A. Vickers).

M.Phil vivas conducted

13 July 2007, Dundee Abertaye University: The microarthropods of Dawyck Cryptogamic gardens (A. Garside).

Major Funding

2011: £14K Linnean Society / Systematics association. A molecular taxonomic approach to resolving species boundaries within British members of the genera Lepidocyrtus and Entomobrya (Arthropoda: Pancrustacea: Collembola).

2011: £30K from RHS Science to PhD: The Effect of Native and Exotic Plants on Soil Biodiversity and Ecosystem Function

NERC/ CASE studentship awarded (in association with EA) Towards an understanding of hydrogeologic controls on lowland hyporheic assemblages in the UK (value approx. £70,000): NE/F009518/1. Awarded 2007 – start date 2007

Other funding

£1500 Guild of St Ursula March 2013: "Kittiwakes at Puffin Island"
£1000 Guild of St Ursula March 2008 "Roehampton springtail web page".

APPENDIX 2

Acronyms used in the text

1CC: 1 Chester Close, where Louise and Alex were born, almost. 1993-1999
4BMC: 4 Barley Mow Court, my house 1986-1993
4LW: 4 Larkspur Way, our home June 1999-
5HT: Serotonin or 5 Hydroxy tryptamine, a CNS neuro transmitter.
Anova: Analysis Of Variance, a powerful statistical analysis which partitions variance in a data set into "explained" and "unexplained", and calculate their ratio (a "F value", after Ronald Fisher of Rothamsted, who invented the analysis). High signal to noise ration imply something non-random.
APL: Array Processing Language – a computer language I used at CERL. The commands took the form of special hieroglyphics needing a special keyboard – only ran on a mainframe.
BTDT: Been There Done That
BTW: By The Way
CBC: Common Bird Census
CEH: The Centre for Ecology and Hydrology
CEGB: The Central Electricity Generating Board
CERL: Central Electricity Research Laboratories
CNS: Central Nervous System
CoG: Centre of Gravity (the centre of mass of any object)
FSC: Field Studies Council (who ran Orielton field station)
GIGO: Garbage In, Garbage Out! (The aphorism behind all databases)
ICP: Inholms Clay Pit, LNR
ITE: Institute of Terrestrial Ecology (later CEH = Centre for Ecology and Hydrology)
Kyr: Kiloyear = One thousand years
LNR: Local Nature Reserve
MYBP: Million Years Before Present
MBU: Michael Usher, my PhD supervisor in York

NOAA: National Oceanic and Atmospheric Administration (A US government research body).

NCC: Nature Conservancy Council. Government owned conservation body, precursor to Natural England – they ran Rostherne.

NLP: Neuro Linguistic Programming – a posy name for a school of psychotherapy using hypnosis to direct people's thought processes. A key axiom is that everyone has a preferred mode of thought, whether visual (like me), auditory, tactile etc. You get a good idea what SORT of though mode people run by eye movements – up and L (or R from as seen by an observer) is creating a visual image, up and L (as seen by an observer) is recalling a visual image. Horizontal eye movements imply auditory access, downward ones are said to imply tactile access. I got the impression of a lot of overblown hype and not much proper data, but maybe I am denigrating a truly powerful key to accessing human thought processes.

PCA: Principal Components Analysis. A standard multivariate analysis, also known as Factor Analysis (though purists query this, since at one stage some experts used this name for a subtly different algorithm.) In PCA you plot a multivariate dataset in a high dimensional data space then examine its two-dimensional shadow, in a projection called an Ordination Diagram. This is a really good tool for visualising multivariate data, and even I wrote code to run PCA in DOS BASIC which actually got used in a student project before Roehampton installed proper stats packages!

PCR: Polymerase Chain Reaction. The near magical tool for amplifying targeted DNA sequence, arising from an LSD vision of Kary Mullis.

R: A free and wonderful computer language for statistical analyses.

RSI: Repetitive Strain Injury.

STLOT: Sod The Lot Of Them!

TINA: There Is No Alternative (hence the derivative TINFA – hazard a guess!)

TMR: Mike Roberts, section head at CERL.

TRC: Tolworth Recreation Centre (where Masaki Maehara's Tolworth Shorinji Kempo dojo was based).